Antonín J. Liehm

The POLITICS of CULTURE

Translated by Peter Kussi

Illustrations by Adolf Hoffmeister

With "The Socialism That Came in from the Cold"
by Jean-Paul Sartre

Translated by Helen R. Lane

Grove Press, Inc.,   New York

Contents

Introduction:
*The Socialism That Came in
from the Cold*
by Jean-Paul Sartre

The Socialism That Came in from the Cold

by Jean-Paul Sartre

The voices heard in this book were raised between 1966 and the first months of 1968; a timid dawn shed its light on the Slovakian Carpathians, the Moravian plain, the mountains of Bohemia. Had there been just a bit more light, we might have seen these men— men who had been hidden from our eyes by clouds ever since we turned them over to the Nazis in return for twelve months of peace—in broad daylight.

It was not dawn, no lark was singing; since then socialism has been plunged back into the long night of its Middle Ages. I remember what my Soviet friend used to tell me around 1960: "Be patient; it will take time perhaps, but you'll see. The process is irreversible." But sometimes I have the feeling that nothing has been irreversible except the continuous, implacable degradation of Soviet socialism. These Slovak and Czech voices remain, bouquets of snipped-off puffs of breath, still warm and alive, disavowed and unrefuted. One cannot hear them without feeling ill at ease; they speak of a sinister and grotesque past, they tell us that it is buried forever, and yet this resuscitated past has once again become the interminable present of Czechoslovakia; they prudently

3

gave voice to a better future that a great gust of wind soon snuffed out like a candle. One is tempted to compare these voices to the light that comes to us from dead stars, all the more so since they bore a message, before the country was once again plunged into silence, that was not addressed to us. However, we today *must* understand them; I shall try to explain here why these voices concern us.

Fourteen interviews, fifteen accounts, or if you prefer, fifteen confessions. For a confession, in the sense in which Rousseau took the word, is the exact opposite of self-criticism. Those who speak here—Nobel Prize winners, dramatists, poets, essayists, and even a philosopher—seem relaxed, eventempered, rarely harsh, and often ironic; if they burn with revolutionary rage, they scarcely show it. They affirm less than they question, less than they question themselves. Aside from this, they differ in every respect. Some of them are sons of workers, of peasants, of teachers. Jiri Mucha's father was a painter, Milan Kundera's a musician, and Vaclav Havel comes from the prewar upper middle class. Some are Czechs, others Moravians, and others Slovaks. Laco Novomesky, the eldest, was sixty-two when these interviews took place; the youngest, Havel, who was thirty-two, could well have been his son. Novomesky saw the birth, in 1918, and the collapse, in 1938, of the first Czechoslovakian Republic; he was one of the known leaders of the Slovak National Uprising;* and as a cabinet minister after the war he helped make his country what it has become, though this did not prevent him a little later from acquiring, like so many others, firsthand experience of what a prison was like.

Havel was two years old at the time of the surrender at Munich, fifteen when the trials began. The mature men's ages range between the ages of these two. They represent three generations, the first of which was the destiny of the third, and the third of which willingly made itself the judge of the two others; the second, both victim and accomplice, was attracted to both the others by undeniable affinities while, at the same time, it kept itself apart from

---

* The Slovak National Uprising—a crucial event in the nation's history—was organized by the underground Slovak National Council; it broke out in August 1944 when the collaborationist Slovak government requested German troops to put down increasing partisan activity. Although the Uprising spread rapidly throughout Slovakia, it was quelled, largely as a result of the failure of two nearby divisions of the Slovak Army to join the insurgents.—*Ed.*

them because of definite antagonisms. This is what this book is about—intellectuals take a look around them and inside them and ask themselves: "What happened?"

I fear that these last words will put more than one reader off: "Intellectuals? This mandarin caste has no right to speak in the name of the people." These witnesses have therefore been very careful not to do this; they speak as Czech citizens to their fellow citizens. Not to you. And the people to whom they are really addressing themselves seem to have been less supercilious than you are, since for several decisive years, culture, as Liehm puts it, took over the role of politics. The reason for this is that despite their divergences, their opposition, it is possible by reading between the lines to reconstruct a common discourse on twenty-five years of Czechoslovakian history from their various shades of meaning, their hesitations, and the diversity of their characters. It is this discourse—such as I understood it when I read it—that I would like to analyze with you before you read the accounts themselves.

"What happened?"

Novomesky, the first of these intellectuals to question himself, goes straight to the heart of the matter: Czechoslovakia's present misfortunes stem from its having adopted a ready-made socialism. He is in the best position to speak of the years that immediately followed the war: In 1945, nobody wanted to restore the First Republic. It had collapsed *before* the occupation, in Munich. For these angry young men capitulation was not only the fault of their allies, but first and foremost the fault of their national middle class.

The humanism of Eduard Benes* was nothing but a plaster mask, a mask that had crumbled to dust. Behind it there was no human face, not even a pitiless one—only cogs in a machine. As a proof of this: Why had the united Czech people not risen up against the German *Diktat* in 1938? Would this have been useless? Would insurrection have resulted in a bloodbath? Perhaps. But perhaps, too, an uprising would have forced the Allies to revise their policy. In any event, resistance was better than passivity. But what was the cause of this passivity? Beyond the shadow of a doubt

---

* President of Czechoslovakia, 1935–1938; 1940–1948.—*Ed.*

it stemmed from the relationship of people to production, that is to say, from bourgeois institutions. The country's high degree of industrialization developed "massifying" forces that destroyed the unity of the workers and tended to make each of them a solitary molecule; the reign of profit, which is a thing, imposed the dispersion and the inertia of things on men. When the insurgents came to power after the liberation, they swore that no more would be seen of this powerless society.

Socialism for them was first and foremost the overthrow of the golden calf, the integration of everyone in a *human* collectivity, full citizenship for everyone, full rights to participate in the economic, political, and social administration of the country; they would strike while the iron was hot and obtain this national unity that they had been unable to obtain when circumstances demanded it, putting the fate of all in the hands of all, which could be done only on one basis: the socialization of the means of production.

The reasons that a nation has for coming to socialism matter little; the essential thing is for the nation to build it with its own hands. The truth, Hegel writes, is something that has *become*. And this is also the underlying principle of psychoanalysis: It would be useless, or harmful, if one knew the secrets of the patient (which is not possible), to reveal them to him, to *give* him his truth like a hard blow on the head with a cudgel; the only proper way to do this is for him to look for it himself and change himself by the very act of searching, in such a way that he will discover it when he is prepared to bear it. What applies to the individual in this case also applies to great collective movements: The proletariat must emancipate itself on its own, forge its arms and its class consciousness in daily battle, so as to take power when it is capable of exercising it. This was not the case in the USSR, but the fact remains that one makes oneself a socialist by making socialism, as much by the efforts one forces oneself to make to set up the required structures and destroy the old ones, both outside oneself and within, as by the functioning of the institutions that have been set up. This is what Lenin said, pointing to Soviet men who were uncertain, still imbued with ideologies of the old regime, and for the most part illiterate: It was *with them* and *by them* that the new society was to be built. And this is exactly what the revolutionaries wanted in Bohemia, in Slovakia: To change themselves by changing the world, to make themselves, by the patient and stubborn

building of *their* socialism, socialists who have *become*. Today, as
you will see in this book, several of them call Yalta "another Munich." At the time, they were full of gratitude toward the USSR,
which had just freed them, and dazzled by its victory, which they
held to be the triumph of a free society over a great capitalist
power, or, more simply, the triumph of Good over Evil. All they
asked was to remain within the zone of Soviet influence, not dreaming of denying the leadership of their "big brother." What they
wanted was to benefit from its experience and its advice but do the
work themselves, taking their own problems, their own particular
situation, their own resources, their own history, and their own
culture as the point of departure. This little binational country,
Czechoslovakia, highly industrialized, a hundred times invaded
and enslaved, had no model to copy. It was necessary for it to in-
vent its own path, by way of errors surmounted, deviations corrected, distortions set to rights—as was to be the case with Cuba
fifteen years later—so as to be able one day to recognize itself in its
work.

The country was spared this trouble. The two great powers each
made a contribution: after Yalta, the Marshall Plan. We know
what followed. In 1948 the communists took power and the big
brother gave its little brother a prefabricated socialism as a gift. In
the USSR, this socialism had evolved as best it could, turning out
more on the very bad side than on the fairly good side. At least it
was an answer—during the first years—to the difficulties of a vast
country that was almost entirely agricultural and still in the process of being industrialized, without a middle class and almost without a proletariat after the civil war and its massacres, a country
which the bloc of capitalist powers forced to be autonomous—
that is to say, to sacrifice the peasant class to the production of
heavy equipment. Since there was no working class and since it
therefore could not exercise its dictatorship, the party saw itself
forced to exercise it in its place, or rather, in the place of a future
working class.

Most people are familiar with the extraordinary demographic
upheaval that was both the means and the result of socialist accumulation. In order to rebuild the secondary sector, money was
skimmed off the primary sector, as happens everywhere, but the
metamorphosis was so hasty that the party had to forge the new
working class by forcing the peasants required by industry into a

mold. These mutants had none of the traditions of the old revolutionary proletariat. Where could they have come by them? It was
necessary to proceed with an accelerated acculturation through
various manipulations: in the face of the stubborn vestiges of the
old ideologies, that "first nature" that passed itself off as spontaneity, an effort was made to create a "second nature" which
would wipe out the first by conditioning reflexes and weighing
down people's memories with a ballast of mini-Marxist maxims
that would assure that the thought of the masses would have the
required stability, weight, and inertia. Driven by the necessities of
the moment, the party, far from *expressing* the consciousness of
the workers, was forced to *produce* it. The only real force in this
immense invertebrate country, it saw itself obliged to enhance its
powers: instead of contributing to the state's withering away
through its critical independence, the party reinforced the state
by identifying itself with it, but it was thereby afflicted with administrative sclerosis; constituting a majority in all elected assemblies, this gigantic apparatus was half-paralyzed by its omnipotence: in its omnipresence and its solitude, it could not *see itself*.
At first all this was only a means to cope with problems as speedily
as possible, only a dangerous deviation (Lenin was aware of this),
a provisional means that doubtless could be corrected, until the
bureaucracy, the inevitable product of the accumulation of responsibilities, transformed it into a definite system. Soviet society
little by little built a structure around this spinal cord and in a
half-century became what it is today.

Everybody is familiar with this history; it is useless to ponder
whether things could have turned out differently. What is certain
is that the relationship of people to production was *set up* in the
USSR because of the pressure of a vital need: production at any
price. This end, at least, was *forced upon* an almost entirely agricultural country which had just socialized the means of production; electrification gobbled up the Soviets, but it was at least partially successful in that it was a necessity in that place, at that time.

Czechoslovakia, for its part, had gone beyond the phase of primitive accumulation and was very embarrassed by the sort of socialism so politely bestowed upon it. Czechoslovakia had no need of
developing its heavy industry since its resources came, before the
war, from prosperous processing industries. As for autonomy—
that horse medicine which, in the beginning, the USSR forced

down its own throat*—this little nation that lived on exchanges with the outside, exporting consumer goods and importing most of its heavy equipment, had no reason and, despite the richness of its subsoil, no means to bring this about. With firm ties to the socialist zone, all Czechoslovakia needed to do was to change customers.** The extension of its production and above all the absurd reversal of its top-priority objectives was to rapidly lead it to *produce for the sake of producing,* when it should on the contrary have reorganized its already existing industries to conform to the needs of the people and to the *just* demands of its new clientele, and when, above all, it should have sought to improve its productivity. Though the identification of the party and the state had been necessary—or had appeared to be necessary "in fateful circumstances"†—in order to control demographic trends in an agricultural country in the process of industrialization, what sense did it make for a nation of fourteen million inhabitants, a considerable portion of which was made up of an intact proletariat that during the First Republic had acquired, through its struggles, its defeats, its very powerlessness, an undeniable class conscience and strong workers' traditions? Czechoslovakia could have been the first power to pass successfully from an advanced capitalist economy to a socialist economy, thereby offering the proletariat of the West, if not a model, at least an incarnation of their revolutionary future. It lacked nothing, neither the instruments nor the men; if administration of a country by workers was possible anywhere, it was in Prague and Bratislava. To its misfortune, the string-pullers in Moscow, manipulated by their own manipulations, couldn't even grasp that brand of socialism. They imposed *the system* instead. This imported, unsuitable model, without real foundations but supported from the outside by the solicitude of "big brother," thus presented itself as an idol—that is to say, as a fixed whole made up of unconditional demands which neither could be nor were discussed, which could not be explained and which remained unexplained. The Czech workers had freed themselves of the reign of profit only to fall into that of fetishized production. One nail drives out another; the "thing in power" in the old republic was

---

* Also because the USSR had the means to live on its own resources.
** Which, moreover, it did, substituting the USSR for Germany, though under conditions that are common knowledge.
† Rosa Luxemburg.

driven out and replaced by another "thing," one alienation substituted by another alienation. As soon as the heavy machine was put in working order it dislocated the country's structures and ravaged it, slowly at first, then more and more rapidly.

One can, of course, say that this socialism bestowed on Czechoslovakia was made by the Czechs and Slovaks, or rather through them. The trouble is that it did not socialize them. Let us be clear on this point: The men of 1945 were convinced revolutionaries and most of them remained so, but the system forbade them to experience the building of socialism themselves. In order to change them, they would have had to be taken as they were; the system took them as they were not. Instead of presenting itself as an open set of problems requiring at one and the same time a rational transformation of the structures and a continual, thoroughgoing re-examination of ideas—in short a reciprocal and dialectical conditioning of *praxis* and theory—it lay claim, with incredible conceit, to being a gracious gift of providence, a socialism without tears—in other words, without a revolution and without the slightest chance of being called into question. The tasks were already defined, and needed only to be performed; knowledge was a closed area and needed only to be learned by heart.

Let us not be surprised if, under such conditions, the men of the first generation, those who militated within the Czech Communist Party before the war and resisted under the occupation, returned, as Novomesky says, to their 1920 options after 1956. Having been unable to build anything, they changed nothing; boxed in, hidden by the slogans raining down like stones, the memories of former times, the hopes of their youth were intact; all the more so in that, for many, they provided a silent refuge from the official line. It is their misfortune that this memory, however vivid it may seem to them, smells of mold. What a mad idea—to relive one's twenties when one is sixty! In the same way, and for the same reason, the old collective base was not touched.

Our fifteen witnesses insist on this point: Families, churches, local or national traditions, currents of thought, ideologies, the entire heritage that would have been superseded or modified by a socialism in the process of becoming, was either maintained or strengthened under the established order. We hear of the growing influence of Catholicism in Brno, while some of our witnesses report that the relations between Bohemia and Slovakia, which were always somewhat tense, have steadily deteriorated rather than improved, as perhaps they would have done if both peoples had been engaged in a great common undertaking. Even though the old ways have remained virulent beneath the mantle of semisecrecy, we must not conclude that human relations have not been changed by the new regime. From 1948 to 1956 they worsened day by day; a false relationship of people to a production economy was established because the economy had been doctored and power had been reified.

Let it be said, first of all, that the system deprived citizens of any real participation in this national undertaking at the very moment when it was calling upon them to work together. I shall not even try to speak here of self-management by workers, nor of control exercised by regularly elected assemblies; the system, as has been seen, is allergic to these passing fancies on the part of leftists. I am thinking of this inevitable corollary of imported socialism: the radical, dizzying depoliticalization of a country which the occupation and the resistance had profoundly politicalized. All our witnesses agree on this point. The "thing," obviously, could not function without men. It recruited men who were things, blockheads that it changed into brickheads; these then became men literally possessed by power, hierarchized bureaucrats, each of whom ruled in the name of another, his superior, this other in the name of yet another, and the man highest on the ladder in the name of the "thing," itself. The "thing" is, by its very essence, incapable of adapting itself or of progressing. (The least little shift threatens to shatter it.) It therefore has no need to renew its cadres, or rather, it need *not* renew them. If a bureaucrat disappears, he is replaced by another who resembles him like a twin and is hardly any younger than he is. The "system" keeps things in existence and keeps itself in existence; it has no other end than to persevere in its being; for this reason it has a tendency to produce a gerontocracy, for old people are generally conservative. As a consequence, the "first generation," the one that brought the system in, carefully kept the second generation out of all the key posts. "We were eternal dauphins," says a forty-year-old witness. And Kundera says: "My generation was far from uniform . . . Some emigrated, others became silent, still others adapted themselves, while others—including myself—adopted a kind of legal, constructive opposition. None of these postures was very dignified . . . The emigrants soon ceased to be involved, internal emigration suffered from isolation and impotence, the 'loyal opposition' could not help but be incon-

sistent and too prone to compromise, and those who completely
adjusted are now dead, both morally and artistically. Nobody can
really be satisfied with himself, and this bitter knowledge is the
common basis of our whole paradoxical generation. When we are
attacked by the youngsters, we no longer even have the desire to
defend ourselves."

Powerless and compromised, kept out of public affairs by their
elders, attacked by young people for having had too large a share in
them despite this—such is the "middle" generation; the members
of this generation rarely judge their elders very harshly, however;
once they've said that they were total failures and frauds, they occasionally add, with a pity that is not without tenderness: "They had
so little chance to have any effect on anything." As for the aggres-
sive young people who sometimes revile them—much less than
their elders—they are afraid both of and for these youngsters; this
generation is skeptical and cynical, they explain, because they feel
that they can do nothing about anything. Raised in ignorance,
at a time when knowledge was being degraded, they feared these
youngsters would suffer a fate worse than their own; they would
yearn for the First Republic because they would never discover
how rotten it was, then they would be progressively taken over by
the regime, and, because it would be necessary to live somehow,
would perpetuate the regime without believing in it. That at least
was what adults were predicting for their younger brothers and
sisters before the winter of 1967–1968. They were right about one
thing: This third generation rejected, with horror and disgust, that
prefabricated socialism which was supposed to be its fate. It was a
fruitless rejection because, up until 1967, this generation had no
purchase on anything. But what their elders did not understand
was that one day all it would take would be an opening, some sort
of possibility of undertaking a common action, for this impotent
cynicism to change into revolutionary demands and for these "absurdist" young people to become, in the eyes of everyone, the
generation of Jan Palach.* For this generation, in fact, the process
of turning man into a mineral had barely begun.

Kosik and Kundera give us precious information about the nature of this process, which is all the more instructive in that they

---

* On January 15, 1970, the twenty-one-year-old Jan Palach immolated himself
in St. Wenceslaus Square in Prague to protest the Soviet occupation of his
country.

consider it from different points of view. The essential point is that the "thing" thought of Man only through the intermediary of its servants and, it goes without saying, conceived of him as a thing. Not as the subject of history, but, necessarily, as its object. Blind and deaf to Man's specifically human dimensions, it reduced him to a mechanical system, not only in theory but in day-to-day practice—"a concept of Man," Kosik says, "implicit in the regime's political, economic, and moral functioning, one which was, at the same time, mass-produced by the regime because it required precisely this sort of human being."

What distinguishes *homo bureaucraticus* is a whole concatenation of negative traits. He does not laugh. "The ruling political group in Czechoslovakia considered laughter totally irreconcilable with their . . . position." This is tantamount to saying that they had unlearned how to laugh. And if someone, contrary to the nature that had been forced upon him, permitted himself a joyful outburst, he ran grave risks and compromised everybody around him as was proved by the misadventure—recounted by Liehm— of the young scatterbrains who thought that they could poke fun at [the poet Vitezslav] Nezval with impunity. This grotesque episode, I imagine, was the origin of Kundera's book *The Joke*. It is forbidden to *want* to laugh. A luminous imperative, which follows rigorously from the premise: Laughter calls things into question, so when the revolution is conservative, it is counterrevolutionary. The "official man," as Kosik says, doesn't die either "because ideology refused to acknowledge death." And for good reason: A robot isn't alive, and therefore it can't die; when it gets out of order, it is either repaired or scrapped. "In fact," Kosik adds, "he didn't even have a body." This means that the system has cogs and drive-belts, but no organs, and that those who "think" in their place and for their benefit don't have eyes to see the organisms, those antibureaucratic integers that might risk taking themselves for ends if too much attention were paid to them. The Czech philosopher adds that *homo bureaucraticus* knows neither the grotesque, nor the tragic, nor the absurd, because these existential categories have no discernible connection with production, and consequently no reality; they are merely mirages of the daydreaming bourgeoisies in the West. To conclude: "Official man had no conscience, since this category likewise did not officially exist." What in the devil would he do with one, as a matter of fact?

The paths are all laid out, the tasks ready and waiting; his reflexes will be conditioned by proven methods, including that cerebral reflex improperly referred to as thought. This marvelous object outside himself, moved by outside forces, works solely by virtue of Pavlovian mechanics; he is eminently manipulatable and infinitely liable to forced labor. "People," Kosik says, "are not born as ambitious career-seekers, blind to the needs of others, unthinking, unfeeling, prone to demoralization; rather, a certain system requires such people for its smooth functioning, and so it creates them."

The men of the system, those products of fetishized production, are suspect *by essence;* in fact, doubly suspect because they are turned into things and because they are never completely mere things. Robots can be manipulated and are, therefore, potential traitors; since those in power know how to work their controls, why couldn't foreign agents find out how to work them, too? And how does one know who is pulling the puppet's strings in that case? But to the very degree that men's mineralization is not complete—and it never is, for these mineral bipeds are men who live their mineralization in a human way—their very existence constitutes a danger to the regime. To laugh, weep, die, or even sneeze is to give proof of a lurking spontaneity that is perhaps of bourgeois origin.

To live, in short, is to question things; if not in fact, at least potentially. A live man is a man to watch. The regime benefits twice over from this double suspicion. First of all—having no other end than itself and, owing to its lack of either outside control or mediations, a victim of its own unlimited power unable to recognize itself, unable to even conceive of the possibility that it might be criticized—it lays down the principle that one must suspect men rather than institutions. It therefore suits it that the animal in these animal-machines should sometimes reappear beneath the machinery. Animality is Evil, the irreducible residue of a succession of corrupted millennia. Criticism never reveals an imperfection in the system, but rather the profound vice of the man who made it, that serf-will which impels Man as a whole to sin sooner or later, at least in spirit, against the building of socialism. But, above all, the principle of the permanent corruptibility of *homo bureaucraticus* has two undeniable advantages: it legitimizes the recourse to Machiavellian practices—buying or terrorizing, it allows the "thing" to liquidate its own ministers if need be. When the machine stalls or creaks, it eliminates a few men in charge rather than give itself over to be repaired—which, moreover, would be useless. These leaders are traitors who have sold out to the enemy; the motor itself was working quite nicely, its inexplicable "misfirings" were simply due to the fact that someone was trying to sabotage it. In short, the "thing" is forced to use men but it mistrusts them, scorns them, detests them, just as the master does his slaves or the boss his workers. Mistrust, hatred, and scorn will not cease so long as these noble sentiments essentially determine the relations of men among themselves and the relation of each man to himself.

But does it succeed in doing so? Our witnesses reply that there is no doubt that it does. At least in certain cases and up to a certain point. Who, then, allows it to? Those who have sold out, those who are cowards, those who are ambitious? On the contrary: The best men, the most sincere, the most devoted, the most scrupulous communists. Kundera tells us why. The mechanistic vision of Man is not, as Kosik seems to think, the cause of bureaucratic socialism; it is the product of it and, if you like, of the ideology.

The Revolution of 1917 brought with it immense hopes; Marxist optimism existed side by side with old dreams of 1848, with Romantic ideals, with Babeuf's egalitarianism, with Utopias of Christian origin. When "scientific socialism" took over, it did not hesitate to discard this humanist bric-a-brac; it claimed to be the heir and the realizer of these idealistic but deep-seated ambitions; it was a question of freeing the workers from their chains, of putting an end to exploitation, of replacing the dictatorship of profit, where men are the products of their products, with a free classless society where they are their own product. When the party, once bureaucratized, came to identify itself with the state, these principles, these ideals, these great objectives did not disappear for all that; on the contrary, the spokesmen for power made frequent references to them in their speeches, at a time when numerous Muscovites had acquired the habit of not going to bed until the first light of dawn, after having assured themselves that the milkman had already come by.

The bureaucratic system had, of course, given rise to its own ideology long before. But this ideology was never explicit; present everywhere in people's acts, it could be glimpsed only in the turn of a phrase, a fleeting form, in the official speeches; it was masked by the other ideology, the one proclaimed *ad usum populi,* a vaguely Marxian humanism. This is what led the young Slovaks and the young Czechs astray. In 1945, galvanized by words, they fell into the trap. Is it not striking that Vaculik, one of the most implacable critics of the system, joined the party enthusiastically —he was twenty years old—because he had read Stalin's tract "Dialectical and Historical Materialism"? It is for this reason that Kundera, without pretending to compare German society to Soviet society, declares that Hitlerism was in one respect much less dangerous than what he calls Stalinism. Where the former was concerned, one at least knew what to expect. It spoke out loud and clear; rarely has the Manichaean vision of the world been more clearly stated. But Stalinism was something altogether different; one got lost in it. There were two points of reference in it, two visions of the world, two ideologies, two kinds of reason, the one dialectical, the other mechanistic. People repeated to you Gorki's irritating slogan: "The word 'Man' has a proud ring to it," while functionaries were deciding to send *individual men,* who were weak and sinful by nature, to state detention camps.

How could one find one's bearings? The socialist idea seemed to have gone mad. It hadn't, actually, but the servants of the "thing" demanded, without the slightest cynicism (so there is every reason to believe) that the system be accepted by their fellow citizens and by themselves in the name of socialist humanism. They presented—perhaps in good faith—the man of the future as the ultimate end of a daring and sublime undertaking in the name of which his ancestor, the man of the present, was called upon to allow himself to be treated, and to treat himself, like a thing *and* like a guilty man. This was not entirely their fault; their brains were afflicted with an ailment ordinarily located in the bladder: it was suffering from stones. But for all those who tried to look at themselves with the eyes of Medusa, out of loyalty to the principles of socialism, there resulted a generalized distortion of thought. This explains the apparent paradoxes that Kundera bitterly enumerates: "In art, the official doctrine was realism. But it was forbidden to speak of the real. The cult of youth was publicly celebrated, but our enjoyment of our own youth was frustrated. In those pitiless times, all we were shown on the screen was a series of tender and bashful lovers. Official slogans were full of joy, yet we didn't dare to play even the slightest prank." He would have better accounted for this situation, perhaps, if he had written: *In the name of realism,* we were forbidden to depict reality; *in the name of the cult of youth,* we were prevented from being young; *in the name of socialist joy,* joyousness was repressed.

And the worst part of it all was that this crude ruse found willing accomplices. So long as they still believed in bureaucratic socialism—at least as the thankless and painful way that leads to true socialism—these men used their living dialectical reason to justify the reign of petrified reason, which necessarily led them to give assent to the condemnation of the former by the latter. Convinced by propaganda that, as Mirabeau put it, "The road that leads from Evil to Good is worse than Evil," first they resigned themselves to Evil because they saw in it the one way to attain Good, then, goaded by what one of them has named "the demon of consent," they saw in it Good itself, and took their own resistance to the process of petrification to be Evil. Cement poured into them through their eyes and ears, and they considered the protests of their simple good sense to be the residue of a bourgeois ideology that cut them off from the people.

All the witnesses who are in their forties recognize this to be true; they felt a need to reject every temptation to criticize in advance, for fear that it might be a sign of the resurrection of individualism in them. They tell of how they carefully buried the slightest astonishment, or any unexpected discomfort, in the darkest corner of their memory, of how they forced themselves not to see anything that might have shocked them. There was a great risk, to be sure; a single doubt would have sufficed to put the whole system in question, and then, they were certain, questioning the system would have reduced them to ignominious solitude. Born during the First Republic, they bore the ineradicable marks of a culture which they must rid themselves of, at any cost, if they wanted to find themselves in agreement with the masses. As a matter of fact, the party line of the "thing" passed itself off as the very thought of the working class, and the proof of this was plain as day since the "thing" exercised its dictatorship in the name of the proletariat and was the consciousness of that class. No one really *thought* of the declarations of the "thing," for they represented precisely the *unthinkable.* But, at the time, each individual took them to be the certified expressions of Objective Spirit and, while waiting to understand them, learned them by heart and set them up, like mysterious icons, each in his own inner shrine. Everyone—whether

worker, peasant, or intellectual—was unaware that he was the victim of an alienation and a new atomization. Each individual, accusing himself of subjectivism, wanted to break through his molecular isolation and rediscover the passionate unity of partisan and
revolutionary action, in which each person comes to each other
person not as *another* but as the *same,* and no one dared realize
that what he was asked to do to erase his suspect individual differences was to deny himself, to make himself *other than himself*
in order to join the others insofar as each of them was trying to
make himself other than himself. These serialized men communicated among themselves only by the intermediary of *that-which-is-
other-than-Man.* They thus plunged even deeper into solitude by
the very efforts they made to escape it; and each, to the very degree
that he mistrusted himself, mistrusted the other. In his introduction to this book, Liehm has vividly described the ultimate hysterical temptation, the logical consequence of the whole process: Getting down on one's knees so as to believe, and replacing the process
of reasoning by faith—*credo quia absurdum.* Which amounts to
saying that in the reign of fetishized production every real man
appears to himself, in his simple daily existence, as an obstacle to
the building of socialism and can escape the crime of living only
by doing away with himself altogether.

This obviously is an extreme consequence. For many workers
it primarily meant a growing disinterest in public affairs, darkness,
numbness. To make up for this, a title was bestowed on them;
they were all "public servants." A fairly large number of intellectuals, on the contrary, were frenetic partisans of self-destruction.
It must be noted that they were accustomed to such a role; in the
bourgeois democracies as in the popular ones, these specialists of
the universal are often encumbered by their singularity. But, as
Kundera remarks, in the West their masochism is completely
harmless; nobody notices it there, while, in the socialist countries,
they are looked down upon and the powers that be are always ready
to give them a helping hand if they want to destroy themselves. In
Czechoslovakia they hastened to plead guilty at the slightest reproach, using their reason only to work the absurd accusation over
until they had made it acceptable, and working themselves over
until they could accept it. In the party, furthermore, the best
leaders—who were not all intellectuals; far from it—also worked
themselves over out of loyalty.

It is only when they are seen in this light that the confessions during the trials of the 1950s can be understood. They did not come about without the process of self-destruction being pushed to extreme limits; no longer was it a question of tacitly working the accusations over in order to give them some semblance of truth; the "referents" had permission to stimulate the critical faculties of the accused by threats, beatings, deprivation of sleep, and other techniques in order to make them accept *those very parts of the accusation that were unacceptable.* But if the percentage of failures was practically nil, this was due to the fact that the Czech had long been trained to confess. Essentially suspect to his leaders, to his neighbors, to himself, a separatist in spite of himself merely because of his molecular existence, a potentially guilty man in the best of cases, a criminal in the worst, without being in on the secret of his crime, devoted despite everything to the party which was crushing him—to him confession, provided that it was forced upon him, seemed to promise an end to his unbearable discomfort. Even if he had the inner certainty that he had not committed the errors he was being taxed with, he would confess to them out of self-punishment. Thus certain anxiety-ridden people, tortured by some inexplicable feeling of guilt, steal in order to get caught and are at peace again once they are in prison; in condemning them for a minor crime, society has in fact punished their original sin; they have paid.

There is something else. Goldstücker here recounts how after being let out of prison he read the work of an analyst who saw in confession an "identification with the aggressor," and he adds that to judge from his own experience this interpretation is not very far from the truth. The aggressor is the party, his reason for living, which excludes him and looms up before him like a wall that cannot be scaled and that makes him answer each denial with the voice of a policeman: "There is only one truth—yours." When the truth wants to be taken for the Great Wall of China, how can a mere man oppose it with fragile subjective convictions ("I wasn't in Prague that day; I've never seen Slansky")? It is better for the poor victim to secretly join the party once again, by identifying with it and with the cops that represent it, by embracing the scorn and the hatred that they show toward him in the name of the party; if he finally manages to look at himself with the paralyzing eyes of the Gorgon in power, he will cause the dreary little incongruity that separates

him from it—his life—to disappear. Guilty! How dizzy this makes
him! He will know peace, torpor, death. As regards this subject, I
feel it my duty to add to Goldstücker's story an account whose
authenticity I guarantee. In another popular democracy, on the
occasion of another series of trials, a former woman partisan, who
had risen very far in the hierarchy, was accused of espionage and
thrown in prison. She worked for the intelligence service; during
the armed resistance, her husband had denounced her and she had
arranged to have him fall into an ambush, in which he was killed.
After several months' "treatment," she confessed everything, and
the indignant tribunal condemned her to life imprisonment. Her
friends later found out that she was no longer being tortured, that
she didn't talk much to her fellow prisoners but appeared to have
recovered her equanimity. The affair had been so crudely han-
dled that she hadn't convinced anybody; after another group of
leaders had taken over, the young woman was freed and rehabilitated. She disappeared, and it was learned that she was hiding with
her family. The first person who forced his way into her room, at
the entreaty of her parents, found her curled up on a sofa, her legs
tucked under her, absolutely silent. He spoke to her for a long time
without getting any reply, and when she finally managed to utter
a few pained words, it was to tell him in an anguished voice:
"What's the matter with all of you? *After all, I'm guilty.*" What
the condemned woman could not bear was neither the mistreat-
ment she had undergone, nor her downfall, nor her imprisonment,
but her rehabilitation.

As can be seen, mineralized thought can bring repose; one sets it
up like a gravestone in a tormented head and it stays there, heavy,
inert, bringing "security," erasing doubts, reducing the spontaneous movements of life to an unimportant swarming of insects.
Without going this far, confession is within the logic of the system;
one might even say that it is the final outcome of it. First of all, because the "thing" is possessed of neither understanding nor reason,
and therefore does not require that one actually believe what one
says, but only that one say it publicly. And secondly, because in
this imported socialism—which was meant to convince the Czech
workers of 1950 that, when all was said and done, they were nothing but Russian peasants of 1920—the truth could be defined as
institutionalized lying. Those who set up the system in good faith
or who persuaded themselves that it suited Czechoslovakia were

sooner or later to come to the point of lying desperately, without believing in their lie, so as to approximate what they took to be the truth.

The young woman I spoke of was brought out of the state she was in by electric shock treatments. This is a somewhat Stalinist way of going about things, but it is not inappropriate when it is a question of de-Stalinizing brains. Because they were not so seriously ill, a single electric shock sufficed for our sixteen witnesses: "the report [attacking Stalin] attributed to Khrushchev," as *L'Humanité* put it at the time. As a matter of fact, the report had this in common with the horse medicine that "cured" the innocent-in-spite-of-herself: It was a bolt of lightning and nothing more. Not an idea, not an analysis, not even an attempt at interpretation. A "tale told by an idiot, full of sound and fury, signifying nothing." Let us be clear on this point: Khrushchev's intelligence doesn't enter into the argument; he simply spoke in the name of the system; the machine was a good one, though its principal servant had not been; fortunately, this saboteur rid the world of his presence and the machine was going to work nicely again.

In short, the new personnel eliminated a cumbersome corpse as the old personnel had eliminated living victims. It was *true*, however, that Stalin had ordered massacres and transformed the country of socialist revolution into a police state; he was *truly* convinced that the Soviet Union would never reach communism without first passing through concentration camp socialism. But as one of the witnesses very astutely points out, when power judges it useful to tell the truth, it is because it has no better lie at hand. Immediately this truth passes through official mouthpieces and becomes a lie corroborated by the facts.

Stalin was a wicked man. So be it. But how had Soviet society perched him on the throne and kept him there for a quarter of a century? The new personnel flung these four words in the face of those who were worried: "the cult of personality." Let them be content with this bureaucratic formula, a typical example of the *unthinkable*. The Czechs and the Slovaks had the feeling that an enormous block of stone had fallen on their heads and was shattering all the idols as it broke up. It was, I imagine, a painful awakening. An awakening? The word doubtless is not the right one, for as one of them writes, this did not come as a great surprise; it seemed to them that they had always known what they were now suddenly

being told. Moreover, far from rediscovering the world where one
is awake and it is daylight, everything seemed unreal to them; those
who attended the rehabilitation trials came back openmouthed:
The dead were being acquitted with the same words, the same
speeches that had served to condemn them. It was, certainly, no
longer criminal to be alive. But this was *just a feeling,* and couldn't
be proved; the institutionalized lie still existed. Inert and intact.

The witnesses of a gigantic, distant avalanche, they smelled something rotten in the Soviet state; they learned from an authoritative
source, however, that in their own country the model imported
from the USSR had never functioned better. The machine was
running smoothly. Everything had changed, but nothing had
changed. Khrushchev gave ample witness of this when the Hungarian people made an ill-timed attempt to draw conclusions from
the Twentieth Congress. Obviously, they no longer believed in the
institutionalized lie, but they were very much afraid that they
would have nothing left to believe in. Up to that point they had
lived in what one of them called "the socialist fog"; now that this
fog was dissipating somewhat, they could survey the ruins: The
ravaged economy threatened to collapse; the factories, now many
years old, were spewing out products of mediocre quality, and no
attention was being paid to the real needs of the moment; the level
of technical and professional skills was falling day by day; "year by
year there is an irresistible decline in humanist education" (Kundera); the country had literally no idea of what it was doing, for
official lies and the faking of statistics had not only destroyed what
knowledge there had once been but also completely halted surveys
and socio-economic research on the realities of the situation. Let us,
above all, not believe that the leaders knew the truth and kept it
under wraps: the truth simply did not exist, and no one had the
means of establishing it.

Young people were, beyond the shadow of a doubt, the worst off:
"Young people's knowledge is fragmentary, atomized . . . our
schools have not yet found a method of enabling a student to form
a unified picture of anything—not even of our national history, for
example. As for world history, let us not even speak about it; there
the situation is disastrous." (Goldstücker)

Our witnesses found themselves in an unknown country, on an
unknown planet, between the secret East and the forbidden West.
They suspected that the tragi-comic speech on "Stalin's crimes"

would prove to be true if it were incorporated into a *Marxist* analysis of Soviet society. But how could they continue to trust Marxism when the "thing" in power continued to claim that its bases were Marxist? If it was the official lie, how could it at the same time be the truth? And if there were two Marxisms, one false and one true, how would they themselves—who were products of the false one—be able to recognize the true one? They realized then that they themselves were the strangest natives in this strange land. (It is said that when Joseph Le Bon, a member of the Convention, was questioned in 1795 by his judges as to the reasons for his repressive policy in the Pas-de-Calais, he replied with a sort of dazed astonishment: "I don't understand . . . it all happened so fast . . .")

Nothing went very fast in Czechoslovakia from 1948 to 1956, but —what with fatigue, force of habit, resignation, lack of imagination, and willed self-delusion—there was doubtless a dreary truthfulness in untruth, a normality in the abnormal, a daily life in the unlivable, and a fog covering the whole thing. Once the curtain of fog was torn, there were only wisps drifting over the plain and these disillusioned men also said, "I don't understand." Who were they to have lived the unlivable, tolerated the intolerable, taken the destruction of their economy for the construction of a socialist economy, abandoned reason for faith in the name of scientific socialism and, finally, admitted faults or confessed to crimes they had not committed? They were unable to remember their past lives, to measure "the weight of things done and said," to call up their most intimate memories without falling into the slightly dazed state that Freud calls "alienation." Their reactions were quite different at first. Disgust, shame, anger, scorn.

Kundera chose black humor. "I was born on the first of April. That has its metaphysical significance." And also: "In my generation . . . our egos don't live in much harmony with themselves. I, for example, don't particularly care for myself." What Kundera calls "the Stalinist distortion" drove him to absolute scepticism: "Stalinism . . . was based upon a majestic human movement . . . and was more dangerous for all its virtues and ideals, because it . . . gradually converted them into their opposite: love of humanity into cruelty, love of truth into denunciation . . . In the midst of the Stalinist era I wrote my first book, in which I tried to combat the prevailing inhumanity by appealing to universal human principles. But when this era was over, I asked myself: Why? Why should one have to love people, anyway? Today when I hear anyone mention the innocence of childhood or one's sacred duty to increase and multiply or the justice of history, I know what all this really means. I've been through the mill." This lyrical writer abandons poetry so as to recapture lost categories: laughter, the grotesque. He writes *The Joke* and by this title means to point not only to the innocent jest of the hero but to the whole system within which a trivial, childish prank inevitably causes the prankster to be imprisoned.

Vaclav Havel, for his part, discovers at one and the same time the absurdity of the world and his own absurdity. Coming from a bourgeois family, embarrassed since childhood at finding himself a rich kid among poor kids and therefore rootless and confused, Havel became, after the war, the victim of the discrimination whose target was Jews and people from a bourgeois background; numerous jobs were not open to him and he could not enter the university—with the result that, with admirable stubbornness, he kept vainly requesting permission to take courses in drama at the University of Prague and was admitted only after having proved himself as a dramatist. He was alienated, however, from the sovereign "thing." A little less than the others, perhaps. Many of them sought integration, but he knew that this was impossible for him because he wasn't wanted. The result was that he soon tended to feel absurd in an absurd world. The "revelations" of 1956 only increased his feeling of estrangement, and it is for this reason that his theater has been compared to that of the "practitioners of the absurd" in the West.*

In short, whether they felt themselves unreal in an unreal and drearily ceremonious society, the victims, witnesses, and accomplices of a monumental, nightmarish farce, or whether they floated like absurd imps in a bottle in a milieu built on a fundamental absurdity of such a sort that any attempt to adapt to it or change it was absurd from the outset, all the men who speak here suffered what psychiatrists call an "identity crisis" in the first years following the Twentieth Congress. They were not the only ones—a deaf, dumb malaise was spreading all through the masses—but doubtless they were the ones most seriously affected. What could they do? Kill themselves or try to live?

From certain allusions that the reader will find in the interviews,

---

* With this difference however: His plays have a political content that cannot escape his compatriots. In *The Memorandum,* he clearly indicated that nothing could change as long as the system remained in existence and secreted its bureaucracy.

one can guess that certain of them opted for the first of these alternatives; the others wanted to use the right to exist that had recently been officially granted them. These latter had no choice: To live was first of all to tear oneself away from a depersonalization that risked becoming an excuse, to know oneself, to recognize what one was in order to reconstruct oneself. And how could they tell themselves their own story without going to seek it out where it lay concealed, in the last fifty years of their national history?

Their individual adventures and the great adventure of the Czech people mirrored each other: in the extremely urgent situation in which they found themselves, with neither categories nor concepts for thinking about what is real, for thinking about themselves, they realized that each of these two adventures could be reconstructed only through the other. Subjectivism? No, modesty. They were forced either to find the truth or die. Not the truth of the system; they were not yet armed with the weapons to attack it; that would come later. The truth, rather, of their lives, of the lives of all Czechs and Slovaks, amid brute reality, with nothing in their hands, nothing in their pockets, holding themselves aloof from any ideological interpretation: going back to the facts, first of all, to the hidden, misrepresented facts which [former president Antonin] Novotny frankly said should not be bowed to in too servile a way.*

Slowly, stubbornly, to their great credit these men, amid all their confusion, publicly undertook this Oedipal search despite censorship and the threats of those in power. The reader will see in this book how Jaroslav Putik left journalism for literature. At one time, doubtless to avoid questioning the great synthesis of Stalinism, Putik immersed himself in facts about the outside world, as reported by radio and the press throughout the world, fruits disguised in the East by the pedantic boredom of the media, and in the West by a cagey "objectivism." "The need to write my own things, to express myself in my own way, arose only after 1956. I cannot say that the revelations of Stalinist deformations shook my whole world . . . There were many things I had already guessed long before. Nevertheless, this was the final . . . blow. It was then that I became acutely aware that I wasn't really doing what I really wanted to do." What he wanted to do was write, to know himself, and as most of the novel-

---

* An idea which in the last analysis is quite correct, and which to all appearances is opposed to *Realpolitik,* but which, coming from Novotny, meant in fact that no notice should be paid these facts when they contradicted the decisions of those in charge.

ists who speak in this book put it, to "know men," to rediscover them
in "their existential dimensions." "During the last few years," Kosik
says, "Czechoslovak culture focused its attention on existential
human problems, and the 'common denominator' was the question:
What is Man?" It was, never fear, not a question of piecing a humanism together. They had known two sorts of humanism—that of
Eduard Benes and that of Josef Stalin. Both of whom, as one of our
witnesses nicely put it, "hid men from them." Both had fallen to
pieces, and no one had any intention of putting the pieces back together again. The exciting and difficult task they were undertaking
was the only one possible, the only one necessary—that of approaching their fellow man without any sort of philanthropic prejudice.
And from this point of view, the question posed by Kundera is the
mark of a healthy radicalism: "Why should one have to love people,
anyway?" Yes, why? They would know the answer some day, or
perhaps they never would. For the moment it mattered little.
Kundera's skepticism is certainly not a soft pillow, but let us not
believe that it leads to despair. This author expressly says that he
sees in it the renaissance of thought: "Skepticism doesn't annihilate
the world; it only turns it into questions." Profiting from their
alienation, they want nothing to be taken for granted, no truth to
be established once and for all. For them as for Plato, astonishment
is the beginning of philosophy, and for the moment they do not
want to go beyond that point. Rather than affirmations of power—
those replies that precede the questions so as to prevent questions
from being raised—they prefer questions that have no answers;
thought will not rid itself of calcareous concretions, which damage
or divert it, by setting other concretions in opposition to them, but
rather by dissolving them in a problematical framework. This does
not prevent research; quite the contrary, it stimulates it, sets tasks
and temporary limits for it. In April 1968, Vaclav Havel foresaw
a social art with a profoundly realistic cast, which will show "Man
as an individual" and "the social structure in which he is placed,
his private life, marriage, children, material conditions. Soon we
may be able to write about things as they really are . . . I believe that
a new type of social realism will emerge, as well as a new psychological realism, sounding and exploring the unexplored."*

---

* As will have been noted, the art which Havel foresaw and which he hopes to
call forth has nothing in common with his previous "absurdism." This is because today he hopes that the society presently gestating will at last be able
to take in the exiles gravitating around the dying system.

Goldstücker does not say otherwise—and Marx (and Freud, too) said it before him—when, to show that the quest of these new Oedipuses is meant to be exhaustive, he declares: "Realism . . . has shown its inability to capture the essence of reality by describing its superficial manifestations."

This zeal will make more than one Western reader smile. We in the "free" world have gone beyond that! We have long been inured to reflective knowledge, metapsychology, analysis. It is true that we have another way of not knowing ourselves, that we talk more willingly of our complexes than of our material situation or of the socio-professional context we have placed ourselves in, that we would much rather ask ourselves about the homosexual component of our behavior than about the history that has made us and that we have made. We, too, are victims and accomplices of alienation, reification, mystification. We, too, collapse beneath "the weight of things done and said," of the lies we have accepted and passed on without really believing them. But we don't want to know this. We are sleepwalkers walking on a rain-gutter dreaming of our balls rather than looking at our feet. The Czechs too, of course, have to rethink these problems which the puritanism of the fifties hid from their view.* But as one of them said to Liehm: "How lucky we would be if that was all we had to think about!" The fact is that they must say *everything* or disappear. The questions that we ask ourselves lightly, abstractly, and a thousand others that we would never think of asking ourselves, they ask *passionately* and concretely; if they do not yet know themselves completely, it is because their experience is too rich; it takes time to put it in order.

This is not the only reason. I remember my conversation with a Latin American writer in 1960; he was worn out, more lucid than disillusioned, and still a militant. I knew that his life was full of battles, of victories and failures, that he had experienced exile and prison, that he had been thrown out by his comrades and then taken in again, and that in the course of this ceaseless struggle he had kept his loyalties though he had lost his illusions. "You ought to write this story—your story," I said. He shook his head—it was the only time that he let his bitterness show—and said, "We communists don't have a story." And I realized that the autobiography I had just spoken to him about, his or that of one of his comrades, had little

---

* In the interviews several of them refer explicitly to psychoanalysis as a means of access to "underlying reality."

chance of seeing the light, either there or elsewhere. No stories, no memory; none. The party has both, but they are both fake!

Anyone who writes the history of the Communist Party from the outside, from legal evidence, documents, and firsthand accounts, risks being hampered by his prejudices; in any event he lacks one irreplaceable experience. If he has left the party he chokes on his own rancor and dips his pen in bile. If he writes from the inside, in collaboration with the leaders, he becomes an official historiographer, and either lies or dodges questions according to the positions of the day. What can a militant who would like to understand his life cling to, since the organization that he has found his niche in and that has produced him and that, furthermore, discourages this sort of subjective undertaking in principle, will tend to make him bear false witness against himself even in his most secret heart of hearts? What does he have at his disposal? Reconstructed memories, dried up or canceled out by a succession of self-criticisms, or other memories that may still be vivid but are insignificant or incomprehensible. After having successfully "negotiated" so many turns in the party line, how can he remember the direction he thought he was taking in the beginning? How can he know where he is heading this very moment? And who in the party can boast that the key he uses to interpret his actions today will still be the same a year from now? Men false to the core see to it that they keep one dimension of themselves secret, like Mr. X, the Russian whose friends told me has twelve levels of sincerity, and I've only gotten as far as the fourth. This latter sort keeps his mouth shut. The others have given their lives to their party twice over; they have often risked their lives on party orders, and from day to day, out of discipline, they have let them pile up like sand behind them, in dunes where the slightest gust of wind suffices to erase their footprints.

The Czechs and the Slovaks who speak in this book are for the most part members of the Communist Party. They, too, have given their lives with enthusiasm and then lost sight of them for several years. It is they, however, who today have undertaken in these interviews, in novels, in a hundred different articles,* the task of retrieving them, which seemed impossible in 1960 and which encounters

---

* From this point of view, I know nothing as thoughtful, as tough, and as lucid as Artur London's admirable firsthand account: *Confession*.

the same difficulties today. For this reason, it was necessary to proceed step by step, to shatter their inner resistances, to scrutinize almost invisible tracks, to raise tombstones to see what was buried underneath. And above all—this was the crux of the matter—to find the right *lighting*. Fortunately, their memories are still vivid: in 1956 the "socialist fog" was only eight years old.

Khrushchev's report, however absurd it may have been, gave them the "final shock" that allowed them to speak of themselves and the party as they should. They did not attempt to fly high above this great body of which they are an integral part; it is their anchorage. If they fell under the sway of the system, they also know that they made it—even though it was prefabricated, it at least had to be installed—and that the very struggle which they all carried on to limit certain of its excesses was merely a certain way of accepting it. They therefore spoke of it *from the inside,* since that is where they still are, and with an undeniable solidarity, without ever condemning it in hatred and rage the better to proclaim their innocence, but rather taking their distance *inside,* thanks to the displacement brought on by their *alienation,* which suddenly shed light on practices that had been so much a matter of routine that they had engaged in them without even seeing them. As if they could retrieve their lives, in the very name of constants to be located, of loyalties to be recaptured, only by internal criticism of the party, and as if they could question the role of the party only by a radical questioning of themselves, while at the same time not questioning their actions and their consequences, their omissions, their failures, and their compromises. What may seem to be a vicious circle will be seen, when these interviews are read, to be in fact a dialectical movement which was to permit all their readers, as well as themselves, to find their lost truth, the concrete, continually detotalized, contradictory, problematical totalization that never doubles back on itself, that never is ended, and that nonetheless is one, a totalization that must be the starting point of any theoretical research, the point from which Marxism took off with Marx and then again after him with Lenin, with Rosa Luxemburg, with Gramsci, though it never thereafter returned to this point.

What would they use as a basis to maintain the *distancing* necessary for the pursuit of their enquiry? The answer is clear: their national culture. Is this any reason to tax them with nationalism as the old guard of mummified Stalinists did? No. Read them and you

will see. Is it their fault if the tide of pseudo-Marxism revealed, as
it ebbed, that their historical traditions remained intact because
people had not worked on them and gone beyond them on the way
to a true socialism? Is it their fault if they have perceived that the
recourse to their history, however insufficient it may be, is temporarily a more useful tool for understanding their present than
the hollow concepts they were obliged to use? They do not deny
that there must later be a return to a Marxist interpretation of these
very facts; quite the contrary. But in order to meet the most immediate needs, it is necessary to take simple, known facts as a point
of departure: The configuration of the soil, the geopolitical situation of the country, its small size, all of which have made both Bohemia and Slovakia battlefields for their powerful neighbors; the
annexation to the Austro-Hungarian Empire which in the past "re-
Catholicized" them by force as today there has been an attempt to
"re-Stalinize" them—all these factors, so many mortgages on their
future and so many explanations of their present. The two peoples
have always struggled against the occupiers of their country, whoever they might be, and against their ponderous, invincible armies
by permanently reaffirming their cultural unity. "The Czechs,"
Liehm says, "are the only people in Europe to have passed through
most of the seventeenth century and all of the eighteenth without
possessing a national aristocracy and thus were deprived of this traditional center of education, culture, and political power. As a
result of the violent Germanization and counterreformation, which
characterized these two centuries in our land, modern Czech political consciousness emerged as an attempt to revive the national language and culture . . . Thus, the connection between culture and
politics had an organic basis from the very start."

During the period of Stalinization the problems were different,
but the weapons of the Czechs remained the same: Affirming their
cultural personality in the face of the socialism that came in from
the cold. Protecting national culture, not to preserve it just as it is,
but to use it as a basis for constructing the socialism that will change
it and at the same time preserve its imprint. This is what the Czech
intellectuals discovered in the 1960s; this allowed them to place
themselves better on this planet; they were not strangers among
strangers, as they had thought. If they made this mistake it was because the reign of the "thing" had reduced them to mere atoms; in
order to dethrone it without falling into "subjectivism," it was

necessary that each of them recognize each of his neighbors as his
brother; that is to say, as the product of one and the same cultural
history. The struggle will be a hard one, and its outcome is uncertain. They know that they are "living in the century of the taking-
over of small groups by large ones." One of them even declares that
"the process of one country taking over another threatens (sooner
or later) to swallow up all the little nations." What can be done in
this case? They do not know; ever since they closed their catechism
books they wanted to be sure of nothing. All they know is that at
this precise moment the struggle of Czechoslovakia for its cultural
autonomy is part of a larger battle which many nations, large and
small, are waging against the policy of the big powers in the name
of peace.

Uncertain, already sapped by inner conflicts, those in power
thought it prudent to get rid of some ballast; for fear that the new
commitment of cultivated men might lead them to leave "socialist
realism" for "critical realism"—two concepts that are *unthinkable,*
but the servants of the "thing" do not react to the dangers that
threaten it unless they can find them already defined in the cata-
logue handed out to them—they opened the door to disengagement: If you lack the means to express your confidence in the
system, you are allowed to talk without saying anything. It was too
late. Those who express themselves in this book—and many others
whom they represent—rejected this tolerance. Goldstücker puts it
perfectly: "Concepts such as realism and nonrealism simply obscure
the real issue—namely, the issue of presenting reality as the writer
sees it, a task which calls for a personal analysis of reality which may
differ from the official picture." It was not a question for them of
calling for the return of bourgeois liberalism but, since truth is
revolutionary, of claiming the revolutionary right to tell the truth.

Those in power could not even understand this demand. For
them the truth had already been spoken, everyone knew it by heart,
and the duty of the artist was to repeat it. A dialogue of the deaf.
But it so happened that the masses suddenly caught fire; what may
have seemed, at the outset, to be the concern of a caste of privileged
professionals became the passionate demand of an entire people. It
is necessary to explain here how that which was so sorely lacking in
France a month later—the unity of the intellectuals and the working class—came to be realized in Czechoslovakia.

The economic situation in the 1960s became more and more

alarming; there was no lack of Cassandras among economists. Their cries of alarm had not yet reached the general public. Everything happened inside the party; that is to say, the struggle to repair the machine became synonymous with the struggle for power. At the top levels, the conflict between the bureaucrats of the past and those of today became even more acute. The former, whom Liehm calls "amateurs," justified their universal incompetence by the Stalinist principle of the autonomy of politics; the latter, who were younger, almost all belonged to the generation of "eternal dauphins"; without questioning the system, they spoke in favor of the primacy of economics, if only temporarily.* In short, they were reformists. The nature of power was not questioned; those in power, old men, legitimized their authority by resorting to the old slogan calling for the intensification of the class struggle; those seeking power, young men, based their demand on their abilities and on the urgent necessity of setting the economy in order. These authoritarian reformists did not see the contradiction they had fallen into when they based the unchanged principle of the autonomy of politics on the immediate demands of the economic infrastructure. They planned to abolish the fetishism of production from the top, readjusting it to the resources and the needs of the country; they planned to allow consumer demand to regulate it, to a certain extent. The conflict of these two despotisms, one of them obscurantist and the other enlightened, led both of them to turn toward the working class. It was this class that was to be the arbiter.

At the beginning, this class seemed to have sided with the old leaders. Depoliticalized by the dreary routine they had been forced into, many workers had misgivings about a change that risked threatening their job security. In order to win them over, the other clan had to allow a certain control over production by this class too and to promise the workers a "law on the socialist enterprise." In short, the reform that was envisaged involved, *ipso facto,* a certain *liberalization* of the regime: there was talk of decentralization, of self-management. There was *talk* about it, but as long as the system existed, these words had no meaning whatsoever. The Yugoslavian experience has proved that self-management remains a dead issue

---

* It is striking that the leaders in East Germany have simultaneously prevented conflicts at the top and applied the whip to the East German economy by giving technocrats a share in the exercise of power. As a consequence, their control over the masses is stricter than in the other socialist countries.

when political power remains in the hands of a privileged group based on a centralized organization. It was to the credit of the intellectuals and the Slovaks that they profited from the paralysis of power, which had been brought to a standstill by its internal contradictions, in order to incite the workers to respond to the offers of reformist liberalism by pressing their revolutionary demands for socialist democratization. In all truth, no one in either group was fully aware at first of what was happening. The intellectuals, fascinated by reformism, wanted above all to help bring the masses over to the side of the reformers by writing articles. But their writings (those that the reader will read in this book and many others as well), which were the result of the long period of reflection that had begun in 1956, had a wider and deeper effect than they themselves suspected. By seeking the truth and proclaiming it, they stripped the system bare, and by shedding light on their own experience they showed readers that in the case of the Czech people it was not a question of putting an end to the "abuses" of the regime but rather of liquidating the whole system.

The trials, the confessions, the paucity of thought, the institutionalized lie, atomization, universal mistrust—these were not abuses; they were the inescapable consequences of prefabricated socialism; no repair work, no patching could make them disappear, and regardless of what team was in power it, too, would be petrified or crushed, despite its good will, unless both Czechs and Slovaks fell upon the machine with hammers and pounded like deaf men until it fell to pieces and was ruined beyond repair. They learned firsthand the real content of their thought at the end of 1967, when their writings had the honor of attracting the lightning bolts of a power that had grown weary. Gagged—though only for a short time—they saw their ideas go down into the streets; the young students—that generation they were so afraid of—had taken possession of them and were brandishing them like battle-flags. The victory of reformism in January 1969 was no longer their victory, despite the temporary alliance of the masses and technocracy. Their real triumph came later when the working class, roused from its torpor, remembered its old maximalist demand, the only one that really came from this class: power to the workers. There were discussions wherever people worked; they learned direct democracy; in some factories the workers did not even wait for the passage of a law to force the director out and put his *elected* replacement under

the control of a workers' council. The new leaders were outdone
and had to revise their draft law in order to take account of the
pressure brought to bear by the people. But it was too late; it was
becoming clear that the process of democratization could not be
halted. In this great popular movement, the intellectuals realized
that their thought had been radicalized, and thus, radicalized themselves, they intensified their struggle against the system without
being hostile toward the new team in power.

The press and radio have never been freer than in Czechoslovakia
during the spring of 1968. But what strikes the Westerner is that the
struggle of the intellectuals for total freedom of expression and information was helped along by the workers, who quickly had come
to believe that the right to total information was part of their fundamental demands. It was on this basis that the union of workers and
cultivated men was sealed.* This underlines quite clearly how
much the problems of a popular democracy differ from ours. French
workers will not go out on strike if the government attacks the
freedom of the press, and in the present situation this is understandable on their part. Power rarely needs to muzzle the newspapers; profit can take care of that. Workers read *Le Parisien Libéré*
without believing a word of it, with the thought that the problems
of the press will find their solution with the pure and simple aboli-
tion of profit. They know, perhaps, that censorship exists in the
USSR or in Poland, but this doesn't keep them from sleeping. In
those countries, they have been told, the proletariat exercises its
dicatorship; it would be a crime to allow counterrevolutionary
gazettes, in the name of principles that are both abstract and bourgeois, to persistently poison the air with their lies.

In 1968, after twenty years of Stalinism, it was quite different for
the Czechs and Slovaks; in the beginning they, too, had had their
fill of lies, though they had never known just how fed up they were

---

* This union still existed when I went back to Prague in November 1969. The
students had occupied certain departmental offices at the university to protest
the effective re-establishment of censorship. One could still speak with a certain degree of freedom about the occupier, however, and at the request of a
student I was able to tell an audience that filled the hall that I considered the
intervention of the Five to be a war crime; they demanded freedom of information within the perspective of the maximalist demand that I spoke of
above. Without too much conviction, the government had been considering
dealing harshly with them when the personnel of important Czech factories
set a limit to its caprices by letting it be known that they would go on strike
immediately if measures were taken against the students.

and were only beginning to learn. The dictatorship of the proletariat was the dictatorship of a party that had lost all contact with the masses. As for class struggle, how could they have believed that it had intensified with the progress of socialism since they realized that socialism had done nothing but go backwards ever since it had been established? Censorship in their eyes was not just a lesser evil since it represented the censorship of truth by lies. Quite the contrary; as they became aware of their maximalist demand, the full truth, in its function both as theoretical knowledge and as practical knowledge, became indispensable to them, for the simple reason that the power of the workers cannot be exercised even on the job if they are not constantly kept informed at all levels. This demand, one suspects, concerned not only the dissemination of national and international news by the mass media from day to day.

It took on its real meaning by searching deeper: In order to orient, correct, control production, in order to situate their activities both within their own country and the world at large, and in order to remain, despite the distances involved, in permanent contact with each other, the Czech and Slovak workers demanded full participation in the scientific and cultural life of the nation. This demand, which in the "Prague springtime" had barely begun to be conscious of itself, would sooner or later have brought on a revolution in culture and teaching.

Thus, within a vast revolutionary movement, workers and intellectuals were a reciprocal and permanent factor in radicalization; the latter became convinced that they could fulfill their function— the search for truth—only in a socialist society in which power is exercised by all; the former, inflamed by the polemics that went on in the newspapers, became convinced that they would not bring about true socialism without breaking the monopoly of knowledge (it exists both in the East and the West), and without insuring the widest possible dissemination of truth, which, being indissolubly both theoretical and practical, would reach full development in the dialectical unity of these two postulates.

There is no doubt that all the agents of this process were far indeed from knowing where they were going and what they were doing. But neither can one doubt that they were trying to *bring about true socialism* by liquidating the system and establishing new relationships between people and production. The team in power, which was outstripped but clearheaded, made no mistake about this, as is evidenced by the timid plan for "revisions of the statutes

of the party" published in *Rude Pravo* [the official newspaper of the
Communist Party of Czechoslovakia] on August 10, 1968, which
forbade "holding a plurality of public offices in the Party and in the
State." It was the bureaucracy itself that was forced to administer
the first hammer-blows that were to break the machine.

We know what happened next. No sooner had this socialism been
born than it was smothered to death by counterrevolution. This is
what *Pravda* says, and I am in complete agreement with Soviet
newspapers except on the minor question of cardinal points: the
counterrevolutionary forces did not come from the West.

For once it was not Western imperialism that crushed the shift
towards democratization and re-established the reign of the "thing"
by force and violence. The leaders of the USSR, horrified to see
socialism on the march once again, sent their tanks to Prague to
stop it. They just barely managed to save the system, and another
set of leaders, rapidly installed in power, prolonged the existence
of the institutionalized lie by publicly congratulating itself on the
Soviet intervention. Nothing is changed except that the socialism
that was thrust upon them, by becoming an oppressive socialism,
has been unmasked. The party line goes on amid the silence of
fourteen million men who don't believe a word of it. Those who
repeat it at the top are as lonely as the French collaborators during
the German occupation; they know that they are lying, that the
"thing" is the enemy of Man. But the lie has gotten hold of them
and will no longer let them go; the invitation to inform on others
is within the logic of the system: In order to endure, it demands
that everyone mistrust both others and himself. But mistrusting
oneself is now a thing of the past; after the Twentieth Congress and
the act of aggression of 1968, the system will no longer get Czechs
and Slovaks to do this; it has yet to make everyone a potential in-
former and therefore a suspect in the eyes of his neighbors. Despite
a few precautions which were, moreover, quite useless, the five
invaders have taken few pains to conceal the eminently *conservative*
nature of their intervention. Our Western bourgeoisie was not
taken in: the entry of tanks into Prague *reassured* it. Why not end
the cold war and conclude a "holy alliance" with the USSR that
would maintain order all over the world? This is the point we have
arrived at. The cards are on the table and it is no longer possible
to cheat.

We are still cheating however. The left *protests*, waxes indignant, blames, or "regrets"; *Le Monde* often publishes texts inspired by a virtuous wrath, followed by a long list of signatures that always include the same names—mine, for example. But let us sign! Let us go ahead and sign! Anything is better than a silence that might be construed as acceptance. Provided that this moral stance is not made to serve as an excuse. And indeed what the Five have done is not very edifying. They should be ashamed! But if you knew how little they care! Even if they did care about the European left, the thing they would most want would be for it to stamp its foot and yell "Boo!" So long as we restrict ourselves to the field of ontology, the system can rest easy: They are guilty, but didn't they act as socialists? They thus could do what they did. They are the only ones before the bar; the regime cannot be called into question. But if we read these interviews and use them to decipher the Czech experience we will soon discover that these leaders, who have been recruited and trained by the system and who exercise power in the name of the "thing," could act no differently than they did. It is the regime that ought to be attacked, the relationships established between people and production which gave it its structure and which have been reinforced and frozen by its action.

After the month of August 1968, it is necessary to abandon the handy shelter of moralism and reformist illusions where the regime is concerned. The machine will not be repaired; the people must take it over and throw it out in the junkyard.

The revolutionary forces of the West have only one way of helping Czechoslovakia effectively in the long run: Listening to the voices that talk to us about her, gathering together the documents, reconstructing the events, and trying to analyze them in depth, beyond the present situation, insofar as they show the structures of Soviet society, those of the popular democracies, and the relations of the latter with the former, and profiting from this analysis to think, without presuppositions and without bias, second thoughts about the European left, its objectives, its tasks, its possibilities, its various types of organization, with the aim of answering today's fundamental question: How to unite, how to liquidate the old ossified structures, how to produce new ones so as to prevent the coming revolution from giving birth to *this sort of socialism*.

—*Translated by* HELEN R. LANE

Author's Foreword: On Culture, Politics, Recent History, the Generations—and also on Conversations

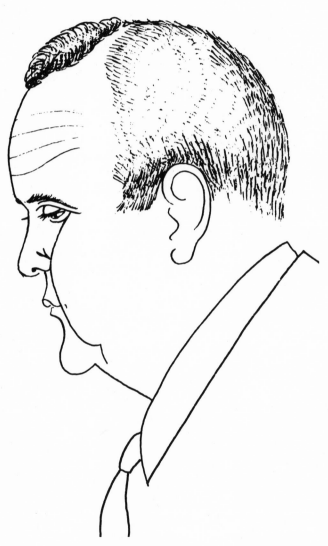

Antonín J. Liehm

On Culture, Politics, Recent History, the Generations — and also on Conversations

The Czech word for "generation" is the same in the singular and the plural, an advantage I only learned to appreciate with the passage of time.

Years ago Sartre told me that human history should be rewritten from the point of view of generations. I saw the truth of this underlined on the streets of Madrid, Milan, and, above all, in Paris in early 1968.

If someone had asked former President of Czechoslovakia Antonin Novotny what literature can do, he would have answered: "Depose me!" There is much truth in this wry anecdote published in *Le Monde*. And yet, how much more complex things really were.

Let's begin at the end. There is no question but that Czech writers and artists, Czech culture in general, played a tremendous role in the events of the 1960s. How did the intellectuals manage to affect so profoundly the development of this "socialist" country? To find the roots of this phenomenon, so incomprehensible abroad and so much taken for granted at home, we must look to history.

If I am not mistaken, the Czechs are the only people in Europe to have passed through most of the seventeenth century and all of the eighteenth without possessing a national aristocracy, and thus they were deprived of this traditional center of education, culture, and political power. As a result of the violent Germanization and counterreformation which characterized these two centuries in our land, modern Czech political consciousness emerged as an attempt to revive the national language and culture. Those who took over this task—writers, linguists, scholars—assumed the role of the aristocracy; they became the spiritual elite of a subjugated nation, and eventually transformed themselves into a political elite. Thus, modern Czech politics was born at the end of the eighteenth century as "cultural politics" and the connection between culture and politics had an organic basis from the very first. This situation persisted throughout the nineteenth century and into the twentieth. It was characteristic of the Masaryk* era, as well as the Nazi occupation and the immediate postwar period.

Only if we understand this historical background and the roots of the long-standing authority which writers enjoy among the people can we understand the tremendous power of Czechoslovak cultural publications. In the 1960s, three official cultural week-lies—*Literarni Noviny, Kulturny Zivot,* and *Kulturni Tvorba*—had a total circulation of some three hundred thousand in a country with a population of only fourteen million, and the contents of these journals was far from superficial "popular" material. Nor is it surprising in the light of history that the controversy between Czechoslovak culture and the country's ruling establishment did not remain simply an academic, intellectual revolt but had far-reaching political consequences.

Aside from the great importance of culture in political affairs, the recent crisis had broader aspects which transcend boundaries of time and space and have universal validity: whenever people are deprived of political rights, whenever a society lacks a functioning political system commensurate with its level of development, then culture takes over the role normally played by politics. And culture continues to perform political tasks until normal political processes are restored. Think of eighteenth-century France, Germany in the eighteenth and nineteenth centuries, Russia. That was and continues to be the situation in Czechoslovakia. And here lies the answer to the frequently raised question: How long

* Tomas Garrigue Masaryk, President of the Czechoslovak Republic from its founding in 1918 until his resignation in 1935.—*Ed.*

can our culture maintain itself in the forefront of the political scene?

What can literature do? "Depose me." I am not so sure about that. Nor am I convinced that this is its function, no matter how closely it is linked with life and the development of society. There is no doubt that the Czechoslovak experience during the 1960s served to confirm the validity of "engagement"—not only of authors but of their works as well. Writers like Havel, Klima, Kundera, Tatarka, Vaculik, and many others have written books that were, in effect, Molotov cocktails thrown under the tread of the tank that was slowly crushing everything worthwhile in our land. Vaculik said it quite clearly: "There's no point to literature if it doesn't lead people to revolution. . ." And yet that's not the whole story, either.

We began our criticism of Stalinism in the mid 1950s, at first rather timidly and then more firmly, first at meetings, then in the press, and finally in the broadcast media. We encountered various viewpoints in this struggle. On the whole, the opposition was rough and we met with much malice and sarcasm. Go among the workers, we were told, and you'll find out whether they're dissatisfied, whether they want risky changes, whether they prefer your black prophecies to their solid gains. Naturally, these were rhetorical questions; it was demagoguery, for as soon as we tried to reach the workers we faced a brick wall of bureaucracy. After 1956, with very few exceptions, all contact between workers and the intelligentsia was strictly forbidden.

And yet there was some reason, after all, for this malicious demagoguery. For during this period Czechoslovakia still had a much higher standard of living than other Eastern-block social-ist countries. Despite faulty economic planning and ineffective management, Czechoslovakia had a broad base as a highly developed industrial country which enabled it to serve as a showcase for socialism. Any attempt to show that the country's economic well-being was only a superficial illusion, any warning of impending danger, was summarily dismissed. I remember the momentary panic created by one high Polish official who, in the course of a series of meetings, had occasion to examine the Czechoslovak economy and current modes of thinking. "How long do you intend to live on your past?" he asked. But the Poles were considered dangerous revisionists at the time . . .

During the mid-1950s, not only was there a growing opposition to Stalinism, but perceptive people began to realize that Stalinism went far beyond the evils noted by Khrushchev—the eccentricities, concentration camps, police terror, cold war orientation, and so on. These people saw that Stalinism was, above all, a certain rigid economic and political system that had been violently and unorganically coupled to others which were quite different, such as, for example, the Czechoslovak system. But while the public grasped the more obvious errors of Stalinist thinking rather quickly, it was difficult to convince the workers that Stalinism severely disrupted the basic economic and historico-political structures of the country and thus posed a serious threat to the nation's future existence.

The cultural intelligentsia began to play a significant role only after their dark prophecies came true and the economic consequences of Stalinism gradually manifested themselves to all. Thus the Czechoslovak experience showed once again that, while the intellectual may orient himself quickly in complicated social situations and while he may be the first to sense danger and to see possible solutions, his insights are wasted unless they are accompanied by political power. As long as the intellectual is out of touch with political leadership, his role is limited to that of a Cassandra; his time comes only after the masses have become convinced of the accuracy of his prophecies. In short, when it is too late.

The voice of the Czechoslovak cultural intelligentsia thus became significant only after a considerable worsening of the country's economic situation. It was supported by a growing chorus of political spokesmen for various economic interests. Czechoslovak culture played the important role it did only because of the imminent collapse of economic structures and because of the support cultural critics received from their economist colleagues. Failure to see this mutual dependence would lead to a foolish idealization of the might and power of culture and to a distortion of the honorable role it actually played.

Furthermore, the influence of nationality must also be considered. Within this binational state—Czechs and Slovaks—political activity continually fluctuates between two poles, and both parts of the republic alternate in furthering political development. This advantage was especially striking during

the last twelve years. Around 1956 the center of gravity of the
de-Stalinization movement was unquestionably among the Czechs.
Located in Prague, its driving force came from the Czech intellectuals. The Slovaks were still paralyzed by accusations of
separatism that had been brought against them in the early 1950s;
resentment tied their hands, preventing a more radical anti-
Stalinist attitude. After the Hungarian uprising in 1956, the
pressure brought to bear on those in favor of de-Stalinization
became stronger, until it culminated in a frontal attack on the
Writers' Union and its journals, on Czechoslovak filmmakers,
on scholars, and philosophers. The novelist Josef Skvorecky, the
poet Ladislav Fikar, the film directors Jan Kadar and Elmar Klos,
the philosophers Ivan Svitak and Karel Kosik were among the
victims of the new chill that froze the first attempts at real
de-Stalinization.

Shortly thereafter, however, the same mood of anti-Stalinism
made itself felt in Slovakia, reinforced by the Slovaks' desire to
vindicate themselves of the charges leveled at them during the
political trials of the early 1950s. This movement fought to
rehabilitate individuals who were victimized by the witch hunts
of the time, as well as to clear the name of the Slovak National
Uprising, one of the most important anti-Nazi rebellions in
Europe. The Slovaks—mainly writers and other intellectuals—
thus took up the slack of the anti-Stalinist struggle at the time
when their Czech counterpart seemed to be faltering. Their
concerted effort succeeded in preserving the anti-Stalinist momentum and, in turn, gained time for the Czech intellectuals to
regroup their forces and renew the battle. The center of intellectual resistance to the ruling powers then shifted back to
Prague. In 1967, when strong repressive measures were taken
against *Literarni Noviny* [the official journal of the Czechoslovak
Writers' Union] and leading writers, many conservatives thought
that de-Stalinization could still be halted. It proved, however, to
be too late. It was at this point that Novotny made the tactical
error of raising the old accusations of disruptive nationalism
against the Slovaks; the cup of bitterness, which he had so amply
filled during his regime, finally ran over and the Slovak political
leaders gave a decisive *coup de grâce* to the Novotny era. The
Slovaks once again played their customary part of complementing
the political activity of their Czech fellow citizens.

At this point another actor who played an important role in speeding up political developments appeared on the scene: the student. During the early 1960s students appeared in the background of political events on several occasions, but they did not become significantly involved in political activity until 1967. Their emergence in October of that year and the police brutality to which they were subjected converted them into a major power in society and stimulated them to political action. As far as I know, theirs was the only student movement in the contemporary world which succeeded in fulfilling a concrete goal and helped to bring about the overthrow of a ruling establishment. The success of the student movement was made possible by the fact that it acted in harmony with the thinking of the majority of citizens and that its emergence coincided with a major crisis within the country. The deep involvement of students in political life was, I believe, one of the distinguishing characteristics of the Czechoslovak experience. It would be a tragic mistake if the students were to be pushed back once again into the position of a manipulated mass, estranged from fellow citizens and governmental leaders.

This, then, was the way that Czech and Slovak intellectual forces helped defeat Novotny's regime. The part they played in this historic process, while certainly extraordinary, was by no means decisive. Culture was only part one of the three factors contributing to the liberation struggle, along with politico-economic forces and the student movement. It is difficult to determine the power of culture more precisely, for its involvement varied in the course of time. But whatever its share in the final result, Czechoslovak culture acquitted itself most honorably in the battle for democratic socialism. It has gained the right to carry itself with pride and to consider itself once again a significant part of world intellectual life.

To rewrite history from the viewpoint of the generations . . .

Let us examine today's students as we approach the first real generational transition since World War II. A century — roughly four generations. The first generation of the twentieth century was massacred by World War I; its revolt brought about the revolutionary postwar avant-garde; it was the stimulus for mass revolutionary movements, only one of which succeeded at the time. In Czechoslovakia, it was this generation that toppled the

Hapsburg eagle after centuries of foreign rule and began to govern itself.

This generation reached the end of its road in the late 1930s. Many of its members died in Nazi concentration camps and on the battlefields of World War II. Now its sons stood on the postwar revolutionary barricades, a young generation as disgusted with bloodshed as its predecessor, as determined to prevent another war. In the mind of most young people who were twenty-five at the end of World War II, the generation of their fathers, the founders of the First Republic—along with the concepts upon which that republic was built—came to an inglorious end in Munich. What an easy and simple attitude for the young radicals! All they had to do was to reject the thinking that had led to Munich and to World War II, to make a clean sweep, an about-face turn, and with banners flying and bands playing they would march into the wide-open gates of the millennium.

Today, their sons are twenty or twenty-five. They had one great advantage: Their ranks weren't decimated on the battlefields of World War III. And that fortunate circumstance also implies a problem: There is no large revolutionary current against which to measure their unappeasable radicalism. Their father's generation has bequeathed to them either a totally manipulated, alienated consumer society, with its Vietnam, its Negro revolution and the hungry underdeveloped regions, or else a somewhat liberalized Stalinism which, though it failed to give freedom to the individual, freed large numbers of people from fear and economic uncertainty, at least on the surface. The twenty-year-olds, in their radical purity, can find no societal movement in Europe with which they can identify. And so, deprived of positive goals, the young people furiously resent a not too happy but rather solidly entrenched society, a society that threatens to engulf them and to fit them into its ranks. Will they succeed in precipitating a real crisis? Can they convince society that material well-being does not in itself solve anything? I don't know. They have won their fight in Czechoslovakia, but they weren't ready for victory. And like their fathers and grandfathers before them, they are taking up ready-made slogans and may provide easy prey for demagogues or *provocateurs*. Then again, they have the opportunity for a truly fresh start as a generation raised in relative security.

From the viewpoint of the generations. . . We ran through

those gates of paradise in 1945 and once again in 1948 [the year of the Communist takeover]; our eyes were blazing, we hardly had time to catch our breath. Most of us were spared the existential skepticism that plagued our generational peers in the West. We felt that we knew how to solve human problems. We stepped from the darkness of Nazism straight into the sunny realm of freedom, friendship, happiness—in short, socialism. We considered anyone who failed to understand this as a reactionary bourgeois; people were neatly divided into good and bad; everything was clear and simple.

But behind those opened gates of paradise sat Stalin.

What happened to us? What sort of generation are we? Where lies our fault, our excuse? Is our fate the same as that of all forty-year-olds who look mournfully at the ashes of their youthful fires—or is our story different in that we were offered certain historical possibilities which we failed to live up to? Or was it, from the beginning, an impossible task?

We have all been asking ourselves these questions for the past decade; we struggled both with them and with ourselves. It wasn't easy since loyalty, too, is an ethical principle, loyalty toward others and toward oneself. It isn't easy to accept the idea that one's life is not a unified whole, that it isn't possible to say: I stand behind everything I have ever said or written. There is probably no one alive who could make such a statement. The young generation looked at us with a steady gaze, and we had nothing to offer them but our lives—the lives of our past, the lives we are leading now. But in order to justify at least the present, we had to consider the past. It wasn't easy. There was no point in doing so privately and there were few opportunities for public discussion. Such things were not debated in the press at the time, it was neither customary nor permitted, censorship was alert and watched one's every move. But in the spring of 1964 we finally had opportunities to give the long-delayed answer to those searching youthful eyes. Opportunities, pretexts, ruses— we searched for ways of telling our story; either we thought up nonexistent anniversaries or else we were ostensibly honoring the lives of obscure figures. And so in May 1964, after they had taken away my passport and accused me of contact with enemy agents, I published the following article in *Literarni Noviny*:

ATTEMPT AT AN ANSWER

I have long intended to write to you and I have postponed it over and over again, as a person longs to procrastinate everything which is difficult and not very pleasant.

One night, two or three years ago, you asked me with all the arrogance of your twenty years: "What in the world happened to you people in those days? After all, you weren't children but adults. You should have had some sense of responsibility, you must have known what was going on." This question came at the end of a discussion about contemporary events, about present-day socialism, about our present convictions and how they were arrived at, about ways of preventing the mistakes of the past from recurring. And your question started a new dialogue, which lasts to this day and won't be finished for a long time to come.

And then you wrote me letters. You yourself, your friends, comrades, young people of your generation. Letters that were friendly, encouraging, the kind a person loves to receive even though he may not completely agree with them. But there were many accusing letters, too, in which the same question came up, and many others in a similar vein: "How could you have . . ." There was one other note, too, that began to sound in my correspondence, a note that came from members of my own generation: "What gives you the moral right to talk as you do now, when not too long ago you yourself . . . ?"

I have owed you an answer for a long time. As a matter of fact, I could put some rather uncomfortable questions to you, too, not so much about your past as about your present. I could ask you, for example, just how concretely you envision the tomorrow in whose name you are in the habit of talking. But a person of my age can ask questions only after he has honestly tried to answer yours.

Well, then: What were we like? In 1945 we were just about as old as you are now. In contrast to you, we had lived through two political systems: the bourgeois republic and the German occupation. Our knowledge of bourgeois society didn't come from short-wave radios or from books and journals, but from our own experience. And I can assure you that it didn't present a very attractive face. As a result of Munich we began to think about the political aspect of things, and the occupation definitely confirmed our belief that it wasn't enough to change the external forms but that the very core of the nation had to be reorganized.

Our first encounter with communism, with Lenin and Marx, was a revelation for us in the darkness of the occupation. It gave us a key to the door on which we had been pounding in vain, the door that led out of the old world of our fathers into the new world we wanted to create for ourselves and for you. And the abstract truths that we had discovered were fortified by concrete events—Stalingrad, liberation, May.* On the intellectual level— in terms of culture, art, feeling—our generation identified with the prewar avant-garde. This avant-garde became a kind of religion for us, though we knew little about the controversies that had once raged around it.

We launched into the new era with all the élan, enthusiasm, sincerity and sectarianism of our twenty years—and believe me that all this was very similar to your attitudes today, including the taste for debate and the distaste for silencing one's opponent in any way other than through reason. This last trait developed in us during the occupation, whereas in you it was nurtured during the era of the "cult." Stalin was a symbol for us, but we knew nothing about Stalinism; it had had no effect on us as yet. We learned our socialism from Lenin, Marx, and Bukharin. Socialism represented an answer to the experiences of our short life; it was an ideal that until then had no practical significance. We knew nothing about deformed socialism, we had no inkling of the fact that during those years this tyrannical type of socialism was the only one that had any chance of surviving in our country. You may object, in the light of present knowledge, that many people had warned us about the dangers of Stalinism. You must realize, however, that these warnings were not taken very seriously by us for several reasons. First of all, at that time there was a sharp division into black and white, enemies and friends, and we mistrusted the motives of anyone who doubted the regime. Secondly, the warnings were not borne out by our own initial experiences in the class struggle. These are merely facts, not excuses.

We considered ourselves to be intellectuals; we weren't ashamed of that term as yet. Our mission, as we saw it, was to dedicate everything we knew, everything we had learned, to the service of the emerging new class. There was a messianic streak in us, too; though we realized that the power of the working class had to be consolidated at all costs, we didn't want to liquidate our enemies but rather to convert them, to save them, to lead them into the paths of truth. And we were typical intellectuals in our resist-

---

* May 5, 1945: uprising in Prague; May 9, 1945: arrival of the Red Army in Prague.—*Ed.*

ance to certain types of discipline that were, in fact, essential in that stage of the revolutionary struggle. This lack of discipline led to our first disputes with comrades in our own ranks. But we didn't take these problems too seriously; we were convinced that within the framework of communist discipline there would be enough room for freedom and individual responsibility.

February 1948 [the date of the communist coup] . . . that was our revolution. We lived it passionately, sleeplessly, with all our hearts. We were very young, but each one of us took responsibility for his little piece of the revolution. In those few days we reached maturity. As we saw it, it was a revolution of youth; older comrades were in charge but we respected them, we trusted them, and—so we firmly believed—they trusted us.

I could go on and on. But I must explain why I have decided to try to answer your questions today rather than another time. In May it will be exactly fifteen years since "the Nezval affair," an event that marked a milestone in the cultural struggle I am trying to describe.

Vitezslav Nezval was one of the heroes of our youth, a symbol of the union of the artistic and social avant-gardes, a revolutionary in word and deed. Then we met the poet Nezval personally, with the result that our attitude to Nezval the man became more complex and ambiguous, without this in any way detracting from our admiration for his work. We waited eagerly for his new collection of poems, *The Great Clock,* hoping that it would reflect serious thought about our time and life. When it finally appeared it proved to be a disappointment, for it was much closer to Nezval as we knew him from recent personal experience than to Nezval the great poet of *Edison* or *Poems of the Night.* You must realize, too, that many of us believed that poetry should play a direct social role; we were in a hurry, and we still had a secret weakness for the agitprop type of poetry. In any case, there was bitter disappointment over Nezval's book, and many unfair reviews were published. In this atmosphere, the "affair of the pamphlet" had its origins.

Two young students, who were just beginning their career as journalists and literary critics, reacted to Nezval's collection of poems in a typical studentlike manner. They wrote a pamphlet containing a long satirical poem that rather ruthlessly and arrogantly attacked Nezval's lack of involvement in the political realities of the day. Basically, it was nothing more than a youthful indiscretion, a prank on the part of young people who laugh at all idols, who hold nothing sacred—not even those things they are willing to die for (as many of them have subsequently demonstrated). After a few days, the pamphlet about *The Great Clock* was circulated and, by and large, it was accepted in the spirit in which it was written—as a specific reaction to a specific work, as an elaborate joke.

What followed seems today like a bad dream. Many of my friends and acquaintances who are still prominent in Czech cultural life and whose allegiance to communism cannot be doubted, admitted to me how deeply they were shocked by the nightmarish course subsequent events took.

In May 1949, I had just returned from a trip to Moscow when my colleagues informed me that the staffs of several key literary publications were being investigated in connection with the distribution of a pamphlet hostile to the state and to the party. The pamphlet in question turned out to be the attack on Nezval which I have just described. At first I didn't believe my colleagues; then I assured them that there must be some mistake, which would be quickly cleared up. I admitted that the joke perpetrated by the two students was not in good taste, but added that it hardly constituted a criminal offense.

I was wrong. The satirical pamphlet was used as a pretext for a tremendous campaign, the goal of which was to prove that anyone who came in contact with the pamphlet and failed to see the mortal threat implicit in it must be infected by bourgeois intellectualism, or Trotskyism, or at the very least must be an unwitting tool of the class enemy.

In the course of an extraordinary meeting at Charles University in Prague, it was pointed out that just as Trotskyist-imperialist agents had murdered Kirov—Stalin's close associate—in 1934, so the pamphlet was a "manifestation" of similarly ominous tendencies and dangers. (Today, I realize how justified these fears were, though in an ironically different sense.)

The accusations sounded horrible and left us totally bewildered. After all, we knew practically nothing about Trotsky; we opposed imperialism body and soul, and we did our best to combat whatever bourgeois intellectualism we could find. But the alternatives gradually became clear to us: Either we should have enough courage to admit that these hostile ideas still had a hold on our mind—in which case such a confession should be carried out publicly and self-critically—or else the accusations were correct in that we had failed to see the terrible dangers confronting us. We spent weeks and months threshing about in this trap, searching for the fault within us—for surely we must have been guilty of some

grievous error; obviously we hadn't been in sufficient rapport with
the movement, hadn't shed yesterday's modes of thinking, and
must have been intellectuals in the worse sense of the word if we
were incapable of recognizing what the party recognized at once.
And how could we doubt the party? It had so much more experience in the struggle that had come to symbolize the very meaning
of our lives!

The self-criticism we indulged in was neither a pose nor a ruse.
We managed to convince ourselves that we had slipped into the
heresy of Trotskyism even though, as I said before, we knew nothing more about Trotsky's ideas than what we read in Stalin's *The
History of the Communist (Bolshevik) Party of the USSR.* In spite
of our initial resistance and distaste we finally had to accept the
idea that the intensified class struggle necessary to make socialism
secure required unceasing vigilance. Thus, "lack of vigilance" in
such matters as the pamphlet—even though the case seemed trivial and related only to cultural politics—could be seen as virtually
a crime against the party and against socialism. You may laugh, you
may shake your heads, you may ask what has happened to our brains,
you may talk about the Middle Ages. I am simply trying to show
you what happened and how we reacted. I have chosen the example of the "Nezval affair" for this purpose, since it was the first of a
number of events of this kind that helped to create a pogromlike
atmosphere of mistrust and suspicion on the cultural front.

Perhaps in the light of what I have just described you may be
less surprised by our first reactions to the subsequent wave of accusations and arrests that culminated in the notorious trials of the
early 1950s. Many of the people who were arrested and accused of
antiparty activities, as well as many of those who were summarily
dismissed from the party, happened to have played a prominent
role in creating the "Nezval affair," or in similar incidents. This
helped to confirm the feeling that our doubts about the party policy were justified and that the severe punishments meted out were
not necessary under the circumstances. We felt that after all there
had to be an enemy in our midst, who was trying to weaken the
party by attacking people devoted to socialism. It was only much
later that we began to see matters in all their complexity, and it
took many years before we fully understood.

I still haven't answered the question of how those of us who continued to publish regularly could adopt a set of opinions and attitudes in such sharp conflict with not only our former thoughts
but with viewpoints we would later return to. Several reasons for
this behavior were, so to speak, "in us": the weakness of our own

opinions, insufficient education and experience, the journalistic aspects of our Marxist beliefs. Then, too, it was easy to condemn an opponent who represented such an abstract entity, who sat anonymously somewhere, far away, separated from us by a wall of ideology. Nor can we omit the cold war, the highly charged international atmosphere in the light of which many things looked quite different than they do today.

But while all of these factors played a definite part in our behavior, I do not wish to cite them as extenuating circumstances. Nor is it excusable that in the name of a high ultimate purpose we were willing to overlook certain apparently marginal matters and to close our eyes to the methods used. I believe that most of us were motivated above all by a desire to break through the barriers of mistrust that had grown up around us, to regain clear confidence in the movement which was—and still is—our very life. You may believe it or not, but such considerations as personal gain, career, office, and honors played a very minor part in our motivation. For that matter, none of us ever achieved such advantages anyway. Our problem was much more basic: It was a conflict between our intellect and our faith in an ideal that made living and working worthwhile. And since we couldn't accept the idea that the movement was at fault, the fault had to be within us, in our "intellectuality." To regain identity with the movement we had to root this "intellectuality" out of our own minds, once and for all. After some initial hesitation we accepted Zhdanov's* dogmas with respect to art and culture. What's more—and this seems even more shameful to us today—we accepted the slanderous accusations against socialist Yugoslavia as well as false charges of zionist intrigue in the international workers' movement. Yes, all this contradicted common sense, but at the time there was serious doubt in our minds whether our common sense was a valid criterion, whether it could be set above the mind of the movement, the mind of the party which spoke so firmly and unequivocally through Stalin's mouth. It was only a short step from this doubt in our own reason to blind faith in Stalin's infallibility and indispensability.

When we finally achieved this faith—and it is paradoxical that we became most keenly conscious of having done so at the time of the death of Stalin and [Klement] Gottwald [Czechoslovak Communist Party Chairman, 1929–1953]—it came as a liberation. Finally, the differences between ourselves and the masses had been

---

* A. A. Zhdanov, a member of the Soviet Politburo notorious for his dogmatic pronouncements on art and his maltreatment of Russian writers and artists during the 1940s.—*Ed.*

swept aside; we were unified by that deep mystical faith which dissolved our "intellectual complex." This complex, incidentally, deserves special thought and study, for it explains a great deal of what happened in those days as well as much that is going on today.

Fortunately, this period of hysteria didn't last very long, although it left damage which still has not been completely repaired. The first ray of light came with the arrest of Beria. I remember staring incredulously at the Tass article in which Khrushchev condemned the dogma of intensified class warfare. I wasn't able to recover my equilibrium, I showed the article to all my friends, I called people on the telephone—Khrushchev had attacked the very crux of the system! Not even the famous Twentieth Congress surpassed the intensity of this initial shock. Ten years have elapsed since then; we are still trying to clear up these matters; and they will not be fully understood for a long time to come. But we are convinced that socialism is the only reasonable system for the modern world, for contemporary humanism, for the complete liberation and development of man. This conviction imposes on us the duty to fight for socialism with all our might; we don't have the our own actions during the early 1950s or because we fear that right to abdicate this struggle simply because we have doubts about these actions may have impaired our moral credibility.

I can only repeat that the right to fight for a better future is neither earned nor bestowed. A man simply takes this right on himself, with all the risks that this action entails; the danger that he may prove unequal to the task, that he may not achieve what he set out to do, that he may be found fickle or, simply, wrong. But this last risk, the danger of being wrong, is one of the fundamental conditions of humanity.

This doesn't in any way mean that we are the only ones who have a right to discuss the past. I am convinced, though, that we have a greater right to do so than others; in fact, I believe it is our duty. We didn't set out to create a Stalinist, deformed socialism. After all, who could have entered the movement with such a goal in mind? Thus, if we have played any part in this deformation, it is up to us to do everything in our power to bridge the gap between theory and practice that we ourselves helped to widen. I admit that those people who have "clean hands" in this regard, who recognized the negative trends earlier than we did and refused to take part in them, are in a better position to lead the way toward genuine socialism. But I refuse to be led by those who have "clean hands" only because they stayed out of the struggle for socialism altogether, or because they tried to "save socialism" by collaborating with its professed enemies.

Where do we go from here? I am terrified by comrades who consider it prudent to prove their loyalty to the party and to socialism by repeatedly proclaiming that if they had to do the same things again, they would do so gladly. I feel like asking them whether they are ready to do so even with the clear knowledge of the tragic consequences for the entire international proletarian movement, for world socialism, for the party, for the younger generation? I believe the absurdity of such a position is self-evident. Even those who readily mouth such words would be shocked to discover their true implications. Nor is it helpful to echo the attitude of a certain comrade who wrote in a letter to *Literarni Noviny:* "I prefer to have erred along with the party, rather than to have been correct against the party." After all we have learned and experienced, we realize that the question should be phrased very differently: What can be done to avoid such dilemmas in the future, to avoid discrepancy between party and truth, not only with regard to historical matters but in specific situations, in national and international problems of our day? Everything, I believe, depends on our answer to this question, for in our country no problem related to socialism can at this time be solved outside the party framework.

I know there are many young people who are doubtful even about our new and more limited goals, and who question our confidence after all that has been said about the past. They shake their heads skeptically, they regard our continuing loyalty to socialism and to the party as no more than a new version of the old, unquestioning, blind faith. Let me comment on this question, too. I have been thinking about it for a long time.

I am convinced that it is impossible to live without faith. Man cannot live without faith in human existence, in the meaning of his own life and life in general, in the meaning of thought and action. Such faith seems to underlie everything, and beyond its borders there is only metaphysics and agnosticism. That is why it is important for our faith to remain within rational borders and to avoid becoming metaphysical; this applies to faith in socialism as much as to faith in God or the hereafter. Such faith would mean abandonment of the attempt to discover truth by rational means; it would be a form of escapism. I have tried to indicate how metaphysical faith in socialism became our escape out of the situation in which socialism found itself during the Stalinist era, when we despaired of finding the truth by rational means. There is very little difference between metaphysical belief in a social system and that of a person who can find the meaning of life only in the beyond.

One of the most valuable results of our experience was the fact that it saved us from socialist metaphysics and returned us to our original starting point: rational conviction. There is, after all, a certain basicness to our new experience with socialism as well as our old experience with capitalism which we are apt to forget. What we tend to overlook is the fact that the socialism of the past was not merely a matter of certain deformations, but also a radical change in the class structure of society which served as the basis for everything that followed and without which we would hardly be in a position today to debate what kind of socialism we now wish to construct. On the other hand, capitalism is not only a matter of an impressive development of industrial capabilities, but above all a society which, subordinating human beings to the needs of manufacture and commerce, engenders the profound sense of emptiness and alienation so characteristic of the highly developed American society. I am convinced that as you gather more experience you will come to the same conclusions. Thus, our ideal, our understanding of the goal of life, hasn't changed. Our hope still rests in a society in which industry is subordinated to the needs of man, and in which the highest aim is maximum development of human personality. The only system capable of achieving this remains socialism. Without any metaphysical considerations whatever, but basing my judgment solely on rational analyses of our current conditions and our historical situation, I am convinced that it is possible to build such a socialist society *here* and *now* only in close cooperation with the party. The party's function would be to act as the center of the society's organizing power and as its cumulative intellect. If we ponder Hegel's statement concerning means and ends we must remember that it is also valid on the level we have just discussed, and that slighting the means may prove disastrous to the end.

But I wish to emphasize once again that we must proceed without metaphysics or blind faith. For we know perfectly well that nobody and nothing will ever absolve us from our own responsibility, that history will not ask us what we believed and whom we obeyed but only what we knew, what we did, what results we achieved, and how our lives measure up against our professed ideals.

Real socialism is still history's avant-garde movement. To explore unknown territory under the conditions of the contemporary world when so many things still hang in the balance is a very difficult task. But this is our lot in life, a task assigned to us by the demands of history and of our own country. In external terms, there is little difference between those who consciously wish to live this life and those who complain that they must. But let us live it to the full, knowing our task; let us live it in such a way that we must never be ashamed of the results. My own generation, and yours, too.

After finishing the article I had the feeling that now, for the first time, I should be able to look those young people straight in the eye; I felt that I had said everything that was on my mind and in my heart, publicly, and that from now on only my own life and my own acts would count. As I had occasion to learn later, this was a sad error.

When I reread that article now, there is little I would care to add. The censors took out a couple of words which I have now put back, they added one or two words which I now delete, but that's about all. There is, however, one major consideration that ought to be stressed, one which I did not consciously try to hide but simply overlooked when I wrote the article and which now, in retrospect, I consider to be extremely important: Namely, the vague but paralyzing sense of guilt which many of us felt as a result of our bourgeois background. Our notorious penchant for self-criticism and the desire to measure ourselves with the party's yardstick stemmed largely from the bourgeois intellectual's guilt complex. We were painfully aware of the fact that, unlike many of our comrades, we had never gone hungry, that our fathers had never been unemployed, that we had had every opportunity to finish our education in peace and comfort, and this knowledge created a complex which drove many intellectuals to extreme radicalism or to the acceptance of the unacceptable. This feeling of hereditary sin, this guilt about one's own origins, and the desperate longing for expiation has caused a great deal of suffering and has greatly harmed the socialist cause. Familiarity with this complex issue and ways of dealing with it are among the most valuable experiences we can transmit to the leftist movement throughout the world. No socialist or revolutionary movement can do without intellectuals. The majority of intellectuals tend to come from bourgeois backgrounds and are full of the best intentions. It isn't enough to give them a sense of confidence, although, as we have learned through sad personal experience, such confidence is extremely important. But if intellectuals are to be truly useful to the movement, if they are not to stray from the path and lead others astray as well, they must be helped to rid themselves of the "guilt complex"; they must be warned against it and it, if need be, must be pounded out of them by force. Otherwise they will prove to be useless and turn into cold-blooded radicals or enervated forty-year-olds thrashing about in the labyrinth of their own plans and acts, in the ashes of their own ideals. Neither Marx nor Engels suffered from such a complex; it didn't occur to them to apologize to the workers for their nonproletarian origins or to think that some loudmouth had to be right simply because he came from the working class. And because they were free of complexes they could devote themselves freely to their original work, much of which will remain valid for many years to come.

A bourgeois intellectual about to join the revolutionary social-ist movement faces the challenge of a double liberation. The first is liberation from the class of his origin, which is relatively easy since it really involves only a radical rejection. The second libera-tion is much more difficult, because it means freeing oneself from an inferiority complex and a sense of guilt. This twofold libera-tion requires a good deal of sacrifice. It is paid for by the necessity of giving up many pleasant things and of living through a period of suspicion and lack of confidence. But the freedom gained as a result more than makes up for the cost involved.

To come back to our story—which, in a way, is actually the his-tory of *Literarni Noviny.* From 1962 to 1967 this newspaper be-came the focal-point of Czech intellectual opposition to the No-votny brand of liberalized Stalinism, represented in the area of ideology and culture by Vladimir Koucky [in charge of culture and ideology under Novotny] and later by Jiri Hendrych [Novotny's closest associate]. I use the term "intellectual opposition" delib-erately, for it comes directly out of the vocabulary used by these two gentlemen and for years this phrase served as a kind of club wielded against anybody who tried to oppose their policy of cul-tural regimentation and rigid censorship. These men fought tooth and nail to prevent any further growth of the liberalization process tamely begun in 1956 and interrupted after having reached its first stage. This stage, reached in the early 1960s, brought Czechoslo-vakia to roughly the same level of development that Hungary and Poland had achieved some five years earlier.

The crisis of Czechoslovak socialism was continually deepening. The gulf between the political leadership and the citizens was taking on alarming proportions, and those who tried to appeal to common sense and to arouse the nation, to get it to reverse its course and save the country for real socialistic development, were stigmatized as "the opposition." The staff of *Literarni Noviny* was put in this category. Such a designation often made people the victims of public discrimination, and it placed them under the watchful eye of state security organs. Personally, I never made any secret of the fact that I belonged to "the opposition," even during my meetings with political leaders of the time. Our opposition was, of course, not directed against socialism as such, but against the way in which it had been needlessly deformed since 1956. We believed that after 1956 there was no longer any valid reason to prevent Czechoslovakia from setting out on the road of true democratic socialism and from casting off the constricting fetters of the Stalinist economic model. In short, we hoped that the country would find political and economic forms that would correspond to its basic structure and tradition. Until 1956 various errors and other acts later shown to be destructive were excused on the grounds of the prevailing international atmosphere. But it was our conviction that since the late 1950s there were no longer any extenuating circumstances to fall back on and that people had to assume full responsibility for their actions. Political leaders had to accept the blame for delaying the country's progress. We pointed out that energetic steps were needed to start the country on the road toward democratic socialism, that we had to right the wrongs of the previous decade, to restore the confidence of the people, to correct disastrous economic policies, and to prevent further errors. Unless such steps were taken, we warned, the harm threatened to become more irreparable with each passing day.

That was the general attitude of "the opposition." We also tried to show that what was needed was not merely a change in leadership, but a change in organization (we were later accused of wishing to replace socialism by an antisocialist system). We further maintained that the various embryonic manifestations of democratic socialism, which up till then had been barely tolerated, should be not only legalized but nurtured and encouraged. Such groups as the Writers' Union and other intellectual organizations, *Literarni Noviny*, the student movement, should be regarded as models for similar organizations, we believed, so that new structures would gradually emerge and provide a new democratic alternative. At first they laughed at us, then they shouted at us, finally they gagged us. The same fate befell others who fought along similar lines. When the noted economist Prof. Ota Sik declared at the Thirteenth Czechoslovak Party Congress that economic reforms could not be put into effect unless political changes took place as well, his speech was published only in drastically abbreviated form and Sik came under scathing criticism.

It is crucial to understand the concept of "the opposition." Even today, many people try to attach a pejorative meaning to this term, to use it as a red herring. We are told that the only opposition that can exist within a socialist country is antisocialist in character. I maintain that this is not so. Every socialist government needs its socialist opposition if it isn't to risk the danger of degenerating once more into a system of totalitarian dictatorship. As long as Czechoslovak socialism fails to see this and fails to create the conditions for a healthy opposition it will jeopardize its further democratic development—a development that could make it one of the models for a better human future everywhere.

But let us return to the chronology of the events. The years 1965–1967 were characterized by a determined campaign against "the opposition." The noose around *Literarni Noviny* was continually tightened, the Writers' Union became the subject of mounting economic and financial pressure, Czechoslovak filmmakers were exposed to ever greater threats, the Ministry of Culture was reorganized in order to make it a more effective watchdog over culture and was staffed by people whose names speak for themselves. On the occasion of the Fourth Congress of Czechoslovak Writers we all seemed to sense—without explicit discussion—that this might be our last opportunity for years to come to express publicly what was on our minds. This is how the famous "conspiracy" that brought so much undeserved publicity to the Novotny regime came about. Nobody familiar with the methods employed by this regime was surprised by the wild accusations regarding the Fourth Congress: There was dark talk of a carefully laid antigovernment plot, of foreign hands pulling the strings, and so on.

The fact of the matter was, as I have already indicated, that the events that took place at the congress were not organized beforehand. I am not trying to suggest that this spontaneity was necessarily a good thing; on the contrary, the failure of "the opposition" in the 1960s was precisely due to its lack of organization and unity. But in a way this impromptu method of making decisions had its advantages. Every member of "the opposition" was under more or less rigorous police surveillance, telephones were tapped, and at *Literarni Noviny* we often had the feeling that our very offices were wired. In view of these circumstances, everyone acted individually. Those occasions on which individuals decided to take action at the same time, as was the case at the Writers' Congress, testify to the basic unity of attitudes and a common understanding of historical events. I believe that this unity does the intellectual opposition of the 1960s great honor.

At the time of the congress, I was greatly interested in the question of cultural politics. I felt that cultural politics provided a most effective means of demonstrating the stupidity and narrow-mindedness of the prevailing political system, particularly in view of the tremendous success that Czechoslovak culture was enjoying abroad at the time.

In June 1967, I made a speech to the writers' congress on this subject. I believe that the things I said in that overheated, packed ballroom are still valid, and that they are relevant to the questions posed by this book. That is why I include the speech here:

Up until a few centuries ago, it was a custom in Bohemia and other European countries to call an assembly of the common people or its representatives at regular intervals to prepare a so-called book of complaints. This book was then turned over to the sovereign in the hope that the injustices or wrongs described therein might be corrected. All of us who are sitting here could probably write such a book, on our own behalf as well as on the behalf of others. As a matter of fact, most of us are continually writing such a book in one form or another, and we shall be compelled to continue to do so until we create more democratic conditions, conditions more in line with the needs of the twentieth century. However, I do not wish to read any list of complaints on this occasion; all of you would find it equally interesting. Instead, I want to take for one thing, it would take too long, and then I am not sure that advantage of this occasion to speak in a constructive manner.

I have long found myself baffled by a peculiar circumstance that accompanies the process of democratizing public life in our country. We have achieved a fairly extensive, if not very intensive, freedom to criticize. Whenever we disagree, reject, ridicule or expose, we are greatly encouraged in our efforts by the authorities—pro-

vided, of course, we know when to stop. But the situation is quite
different in the case of counterproposals, of submitting positive
alternatives. In this area there is almost total lack of freedom. This
is one of the paradoxes of our political life, and it has certain definite consequences. The critic of society is much better off in Czechoslovakia in the year 1967 than in most places in the world, and I
include myself and *Literarni Noviny* in this picture as well. The
critic is under no obligation to think his criticism through to its
ultimate conclusions. He doesn't have to suggest what should be
done or how it should be done; he doesn't have to prove that his
alternative is any more effective than any other. As a result, our
critics live in a state of happy irresponsibility; they can hardly be
blamed for this, since they really bear no responsibility for anything, nor is there the slightest danger that they ever might. And
so we all busily go about, gathering lists of slights, sarcasms, malicious complaints, as well as serious opinions and criticisms. These
lists serve no useful purpose beyond providing historical footnotes
and salving our consciences. We have no hope that our plans and
ideas will be taken seriously, that we will become involved in
building that beautifully named entity, the *res publica*. It seems to
me that many of the statements made at this congress belong
in the same category; they are like shouts that have no other
purpose than to be heard. And who can blame people, after all
they have experienced, for doing no more than shouting? We need
look no further than today's newspaper to learn how useless our
voices have become. All the same, I should like to make an attempt
at a positive analysis of a particular problem; namely, the problem
of cultural politics.

In one form or another, all societies have a particular cultural
political program. It behooves us, on the basis of past experience,
to arrive at last at a definition of what sort of cultural political program a socialist society ought to have. In other words, we ought to
decide in what way our society, which has inscribed on its shield
the motto of human liberty, intends to liberate culture from the
subservience imposed on it by previous social systems. I don't want
to digress into history, but the history of ancient cultures tells us a
great deal about the cultural politics of the states in which they
originated. Thus, Greek and Roman cultures were essentially designed for a cultural elite and the vast majority of Greeks and
Romans died without the slightest knowledge of people like Soph-
ocles or Horace. Incidentally, it is an interesting paradox of these
societies that the periods of their greatest cultural flowering failed
to coincide with those of their greatest political development.

The cultural-political attitude of medieval society had two fundamental characteristics. Extremely ideological and intolerant, it was based on the premise that culture was an expression and a servant of ideology, as well as a tool of the ruling class. If we look at the great medieval works, we see how one part represents complete identification with the predominant social and religious order, while another seems to reflect a suppressed countermovement and is drawn toward concrete social reality.

Looking at medieval culture today, through the perspective of the intervening centuries, we see that it was made up of both of these streams and that, despite its intolerance, medieval cultural-political power failed to eliminate this duality.

The Renaissance, from the viewpoint of cultural politics, was quite interesting in a different sense from the Middle Ages. In the Renaissance, culture became, to a large extent, a symbol of the support which cities or nobles accorded their artists. Popes and rulers, if they did not wish to lag behind, engaged in the same cultural policy. This mutual competition among patrons, breaking up the monolithic cultural attitude of the Church and the medieval state, was one of the major forces in the development of the European artistic Renaissance.

The period which followed was characterized by a reverse trend. After the Thirty Years' War, Europe, particularly Central Europe, was once again undergoing violent ideological unification, with all the cultural consequences which that entails. In our land, this era is often described as the "dark period," for our language and national culture reached their lowest ebb. The "dark period" once was the subject for much scholarly debate. Without wishing to reopen this debate, I want to comment briefly on one aspect of it. Even the most enthusiastic proponents of the "dark period" theory admit that the nation was not entirely lacking in culture at this time, and that the seventeenth and eighteenth centuries cannot be described as a cultural wasteland. Rather, an epoch is generally described as "dark" when culture is permitted to have but a single voice, when the only existing culture is the one officially recognized. So, in our country, too, the "dark period" can be regarded as that era when the face of our culture was distorted beyond recognition by the complete cultural uniformity created by the rigid political system and cultural policy of the time. The majority of mature countries have at least one such period in their history, a period which is later regarded with the utmost contempt and used by educated parents as a warning to their children.

The nineteenth and twentieth centuries are characterized in the more developed European nations by economic, political, and cultural liberalism. It is true that the bourgeoisie had been building its own new cultural churches and that with the help of tremendous financial resources it assumed the cultural prerogatives which formerly belonged to the aristocracy—and did so, one might add, with more ostentation and less taste. But the main difference between past ages and the present era lies in this matter of liberalism. The artist is told: Go, write, create, you are free; if you succeed in the marketplace you have won the battle; if you don't it's your own fault, people don't want you, life itself has given its verdict. And so the last century was strewn with the corpses of artists who weren't burned at the stake nor excommunicated from either the Church or society, but who were left quite free to die of hunger, disease, despair, and the indifference of a society which decades later acknowledged many of them as geniuses. We must not forget that though the consumption of art has risen sharply during this period, art was still the province of a small minority of the population. The cultural market was closed for most people. The voices of certain writers, such as Hugo or Zola, occasionally reached large popular audiences, but a Flaubert or a Dostoevski never gained a mass readership and a large part of their own people knew nothing of their existence. The consumer society of the last twenty years has altered this situation. The character of the capitalist market has changed. Culture has become an expendable commodity—low-cost mass editions of books or graphic publications have proven extremely profitable, especially in countries with large populations. And liberalism has, in its own fashion, brought about a truly impressive democratization of culture that often fills us with envy. Of course, in these societies liberalism brings about not only the wide dissemination of cultural products of unquestioned merit, but also various types of second-rate material based on scandal and new opportunism.

Now, following thousands of years of varied experience with the political aspects of culture, socialist society comes on the scene to try to define its own relationship to culture, its own cultural concepts and policy. Socialism comes, we fervently hope, to guard this precious national heritage, to liberate culture from the two tyrannies of the past—the tyrannies of power and of the marketplace. Socialism must make culture available to the broadest masses of the people, or rather create a need for culture among the masses of the people, and by so doing setting this epoch apart from all previous epochs.

It is hard to believe yet nonetheless true that in spite of all historical experience the cultural policy of socialism involves the repetition of all the errors of which past regimes have been guilty. Slowly and painfully, we are beginning to see that the basic fault lies not so much in any particular cultural policy as in the concept of cultural policy as such. The constant debacles which socialist cultural policy has suffered in the past and continues to undergo to this day have finally convinced many people that socialism is incapable of solving cultural problems and this, in turn, has resulted in an idealization of the cultural life of the West. These debacles, I repeat, have their origins in a faulty concept of cultural policy. We are forever pointing the finger at this or that work, at this or that author, accusing him of misdeeds, only to reverse ourselves a few months or a few years later. There is a continual turnover of officials responsible for cultural policy. The reasons for dismissal are always the same: they were too liberal or too intolerant, too sensitive to pressure from below or too ready to invoke administrative machinery. Yet we all know these administrators are very similar in their attitudes and opinions, and the practical results of their regimes are almost indistinguishable. But still they come and go and come back once again —not because they are good or bad, clever or stupid, hardworking or lazy, but simply because they are supposed to do a task which is, by its very nature, impossible to carry out. And as long as the cultural policy of socialism fails to define itself as a sum total of concrete social tasks that are capable of being done and that are intrinsic to socialism, so long will we continue on our present road of disaster. We will advance from one fallen head to another, we will build a barrier here and knock one down there, we will tolerate this and prohibit that, but we will continue to thrash about within a rigid framework that hasn't been renovated in decades and that consists of mutually contradictory approaches and viewpoints.

All this naturally not only fails to help culture; it discredits socialism by revealing it to be a system incapable of solving a problem as old as humanity itself.

In my opinion, the cultural policy of a socialist state has a twofold task: To liberate culture from the dictates of power, and to liberate culture from the dictates of the marketplace. It is this fundamental goal which must differentiate the cultural policy of socialism from that of any previous epoch. However, socialist cultural policy has failed to proclaim this task clearly and unequivocally. It has vacillated and compromised, now sharpening its attack in one area, now relaxing in another. The difficulties of socialist cultural leadership stem from a refusal to embark upon a program of fundamental cultural liberation. This is also the reason why socialist cultural policy has come to resemble just another worn-out experience with which mankind is already familiar, rather than the qualitatively new kind of approach which mankind is longing for.

How has the call for twofold cultural liberation been answered? The persistence of the dictatorship of power has usually been justified on the grounds that socialist society and its organs must be always alert, that this or that call for freedom really represents a call for licentiousness that cannot be allowed, and so on—we all know many examples of cultural manifestations that were labeled "off limits." And yet the very history of cultural policy over the last twenty years makes the "off limits" concept absurd. The "limits" have changed their contours so many times, the respectable and the dangerous, the praiseworthy and the destructive have traded labels so many times that it must be clear to anyone that culture can never serve simply as a tool for carrying out a particular program. In fact, culture can never become "simply" anything. Rather, culture is the total of all the manifold creative forces in a nation, it is a people's living memory, it is its painful consciousness and conscience, it is a manifestation of the diverse facets of its spiritual life. Only the eye of history is able to distinguish true values from false ones, truth from falsehood, cultural wheat from chaff. And perhaps even history cannot provide a true measure of culture. Needless to say, this does not by any means justify an unprincipled, nihilistic attitude; quite the contrary. In any epoch, every branch of national culture must grow out of a set of basic principles, for such principles serve as the life-giving soil on which culture thrives. But the socialist state must proclaim itself a champion and guarantor of culture in its variegated existence, rather than merely an arbiter in factional cultural disputes, or an organ of power that accords all the possibilities for growth to one faction and withholds them from another. Naturally, a socialist state, like other states, must defend its existential interests. But the scope of activity constituting legitimate protection of national interests must be clearly delimited by law and must not be covered by blanket proclamations or arbitrary decrees.

The experience of all social organizations, including that of socialist countries, clearly demonstrates that no cultural atmosphere or particular cultural product has ever been responsible for the destruction of a society or a state.

As a matter of fact, history unmistakably refutes the notion that cultural freedom could ever hinder or stop social progress. On the contrary, history demonstrates that the opposite is true, and socialist cultural policy cannot disregard or deny this long historical experience of mankind.

"Are you then advocating liberalism?" you may ask. Not at all.

As has already been stated, liberalism means making the market-place the arbiter in questions of art and culture. And here again, history reveals that the marketplace is no better as a cultural arbiter than the state, the church, or any other power. The dictatorship of the marketplace in questions of art and culture is again nothing but the dictatorship of obsolete taste, the dictatorship of the average, of the consumer, of ideas which society has already accepted or digested. In short, it is at best the dictatorship of that which is already established, as against that which doubts, questions, leads to uncharted depths or unknown possibilities. In essence, the dictatorship of the marketplace is thus similar to the dictatorship of power; in reality, the tendency toward mediocrity is the same, whether motivated by political power or market power, and the two forces generally manage to come to terms with each other in the end. Liberalism simply takes the burden of cultural responsibility away from the state and transfers it to vague, undefined forces hiding behind the cultural market. It is noteworthy that socialist cultural policy finds itself tempted to follow this capitalist-liberal road at the very moment when we seem to be closer to an understanding of the relationship between culture and power than ever before during the last twenty years. What would be the results of such a cultural policy, such Socialist liberalism? All the disadvantages of capitalist cultural liberalism cited earlier would manifest themselves, without either of the two major advantages that exist in capitalist countries. First of all, our cultural market is too small, too limited to make large-scale commerce in cultural products sufficiently profitable to bring about the dissemination of true mass culture. And secondly, our society is organized in such a way that there are no individuals or groups who would have the means of resisting the pressures of the marketplace and of waging a successful battle for the supremacy of their own values.

If a socialist state were to embark upon a liberalistic cultural policy, the inevitable result would thus be a deterioration of the general cultural level, a further "bourgeoisation" of taste, a further loss of engagement—in short, it would mean the decimation of all the vital forces that now elude mediocrity and guarantee the survival of our cultural life.

The first article in the new charter of the principles of socialist cultural policy must therefore contain a proclamation of complete cultural freedom, limited only by essential provisions of criminal law. The second article must contain a commitment of the socialist state to become the material guarantor of such a culture. The state must pledge to do everything in its power to ensure that culture in all its diverse manifestations would become the property of the broadest segments of the population.

What does this actually mean? That the socialist state, for the first time in human history, would pledge itself not only to eradicate the conflict between formal freedom and the dictates of the market-place, but also the conflict between culture and its consumer. Until now, the socialist state—either openly or surreptitiously—has attempted to make the current average taste the decisive criterion of culture. As an inevitable sequel of this policy, there were conflicts, collisions, misunderstandings and breakdowns, ultimately endangering the very existence of the various components of national culture. The current situation (June 1967) in Czechoslovak films is an eloquent example.

This point of view must be radically changed. For the first time in history, the state must make it a cardinal principle of its cultural policy to provide as many people as possible with the basically liberalistic right of choosing between various available cultural values. The state, in its practical daily activity, must make every effort to bring these values into ever closer contact with masses of the people, rather than limiting cultural contact to a small elite as is the case in the liberalistic approach. Such a policy would at last remove irrelevant cultural criteria and enable people to take part in cultural life on the basis of real talents and abilities. At the same time, this policy would demonstrate that socialism really signifies something fundamentally different from past epochs, a real change, that socialism is really offering culture and its potential consumers the solution to a situation which no previous society was capable of solving.

There are those who believe that the approach just outlined is only possible in the distant future, and open only to very rich societies, such as the American. I do not share this opinion. Even a poor or impoverished society, even one which has paid a disproportionately heavy price for its search to find a working model of socialism, has one important advantage over nonsocialist nations with substantially higher living standards. Namely, the advantage of measuring man and his capacity by criteria other than merely market value. It is possible, I admit, that it will be the United States as the wealthiest country in the world which will ultimately establish the kind of cultural policy we are dreaming about. All the same, I wish that a socialist country be the first with this achievement, particularly a socialist country with as rich a cultural heritage as our own. Above all, I wish that this achievement will come precisely at the moment when so many people believe that questions of the market and of consumption are the most important of all. I doubt that in the area of economics Czechoslovak socialism has anything important to teach the world, any lesson supported by concrete examples. But in the area of culture and cultural policy we do have something valuable to transmit, at once, today.

We can successfully solve the problem of cultural policy, providing that we will have the courage to examine these questions from the very roots up, and in a fundamental socialist manner. This cultural search seems to have been the deposit—by no means a negligible one—which this small socialist country has made into the fund of the world's experience. If our kind of socialism proves to be a viable and desirable model for the world to follow, the investment will have been worthwhile.

The events that followed are well known: *Literarni Noviny* was forced to stop publication, there was a wave of purges and expulsions from the party, members of the staff who were offered the questionable honor of joining the so-called *Lzi-Literarky* (Lying-*Literarni Noviny*) flatly refused to do so, and were subjected to various reprisals including blacklisting from any job connected with journalism, culture or education. There was the impressive solidarity of the Czech and Slovak intellectuals, manifested by the post-September boycott of the "new" *Literarni Noviny* (taken over by the Ministry of Culture under Karel Hofman*), a boycott conducted both by readers and by potential contributors. Nobody organized this boycott, it too was a completely spontaneous action. And again, such a response was inevitable, for reasons discussed earlier. The ideological section of the party's central committee distributed proclamations among the intelligentsia warning that if the boycott did not end immediately, security organs would be notified and the culprits brought to light. Even the people who issued these warnings realized how ridiculous they were. After *Literarni Noviny* was taken over by its new staff, circulation dropped drastically from the pre-September level of 130,000 copies. In the spring of 1968, Josef Grohman [responsible for publishing in the Ministry of Culture] stated that the entire operation of the publication was a fiasco, which had to be paid for out of public funds. It actually turned out that the *Literarni Noviny* continued to be printed in the original number of copies, but most of the run was secretly burned. The Prague newsdealers ran contests as to who could sell the fewest copies of the "new" *Literarni Noviny,* and amusing anec-

---

* Hofman, in August 1968, was one of the staunchest supporters of the Soviet occupation of Czechoslovakia.—*Ed.*

dotes describing the sales pitch between newsdealers and customers made the rounds.

Seen in perspective, the entire situation of that period now seems somewhat ridiculous, and there is no question that it really had some comic elements. But that's not the whole story. It was an open conflict, in which one side had the active support of the intelligentsia and the passive support of the majority of the people, while the other side leaned on the apparatus of the state as well as on foreign power interested in keeping the status quo.

By pushing the situation to the extreme, Czechoslovak intellectuals took a step which had loomed as an ultimate alternative from the very beginning. This step naturally involved grave risks. (We only learned of the full extent of the potential danger after the departure of Novotny and Miroslav Mamula, the party official responsible for the Ministries of Defense & Interior and the security section of the central committee.) The action taken by the Czechoslovak intellectual opposition was based on the following unformulated assumption: If the Novotny regime proved unwilling to allow true democratization, if it refused to permit alternative methods for dealing with the country's problems, then the regime must be thoroughly unmasked. Its false liberal front, put on mainly to deceive the outside world, must be ripped off, thus forcing the regime to attempt a return to Stalinist methods. In short, the goal of the intellectuals was to demonstrate that without thorough democratization there could be no de-Stalinization, and that the mere removal of Stalinist trappings must sooner or later be followed by reversion to raw force, for such was the inner logic of the system. This was the transition point at which Czechoslovakia stood in the fall of 1967.

It turned out that there were forces in the country—even inside the government apparatus itself—that were determined to avoid a regression to Stalinism, and that were powerful enough to open the door to a democratic alternative. The door has been opened, but just barely. If the champions of the post-January movement fail to act with thoroughness and energy, they will soon find themselves once again in the thrall of the old system, facing the same unpalatable alternatives as their predecessors.

The second speech on cultural policy was written in Tokyo, on a certain rainy Monday in March 1968. It was intended as the introduction to a nation-wide conference of the Union of Czechoslovak

Film and Television Artists, the first large gathering of Czechoslovak cultural and artistic leaders since January of 1968. It ties in closely with the previous statement on the subject, and it was intended to serve as a continuation of the ideas presented at the Writers' Congress nine months earlier. It is the concluding part of a general concept for a socialist cultural policy, seen primarily from the viewpoint of cinematography, but applicable to cultural life generally.

A persistent, fine rain washed the tiny Tokyo windows, while thousands of miles away, in Prague, generals committed suicide, people rushed to and fro through the city, the president abdicated, and everybody wondered where the country was going and how far it would get.

This is what I wrote:

The questions remain the same: Why does culture need socialism? Isn't culture better off without socialism? Wasn't it better off before?

It isn't enough to respond with worn clichés and stereotyped declarations. We must carefully deliberate and frankly weigh our experiences, examine the effect of socialism upon culture in our country. The problem of how culture should be directed, how it could be directed better, more wisely and more joyfully, that problem of leadership is at the moment beside the point. After all that it has gone through, our culture longs above all else to be left in peace. It doesn't want to be led, neither badly nor well. Rather, it wants to be shown by an enlightened socialist government how to make the people of this rather unusually endowed country participate to the greatest extent possible in what cultural life has to offer. Not long ago, Paul Auersperg* raised his finger high and raised his voice high, too, to rage against unbelievers who wanted to reduce cultural policy to a mere program subsidizing culture and assuring the conditions for its material survival. . . Maybe this is how it should be. But that is not all.

This September (1967), when the events we all remember so well took place, the Viennese social-democratic newspaper *Arbeiter Zeitung* published an editorial which said more or less the following: "Czechoslovak intellectuals are currently being dragged through the mud, their heads are bared to the anger of the mighty,

---

* Former secretary to the First Secretary of the Czech Communist Party under Antonin Novotny. He was restored to high party position after the Soviet invasion.

they are pursued by thunder and lightning, one of their main publishing outlets has been silenced, the nation is divided between
those who sympathize with the intellectuals and those who harshly
condemn them, the conflict has spread throughout the social structure and the outcome of the struggle is highly uncertain. And yet
we envy these embattled individuals, from the bottom of our heart.
In Austria, at present, there is no censorship, culture and intellectuals enjoy absolute freedom of the press and of personal expression, and yet with all of this freedom the intellectuals possess no
importance or authority. Nobody insults them or argues with them
or excludes them because of their words or ideas, but at the same
time nobody bothers to read them, nobody pays the least attention
to them, and the vast majority of the people couldn't care less. It is
no wonder that such conditions of complete freedom in the end lead
to the destruction of intellectuals and an absence of culture. We
envy our Czech and Slovak colleagues, we envy the fact that their
word still means something. In spite of all that is happening to
them, they are playing a role in society which their colleagues in
Western consumer-based countries have long ceased to perform."

And a few months later, after the cultural congress in Havaña
(where we were represented in a manner so bizarre that the incident
deserves further attention later), I read in the left wing West European press a series of remarkable articles and statements by leftist
intellectuals, people I highly respect and some of whom I count
among my close friends. These people declare that the only dignified response of the left wing intellectual to the state of impotence,
frustration, and meaninglessness to which he is condemned by
Western society is to take an active part in the socialist struggle
along the lines of the Cuban model and revolutionaries such as Che
Guevara. In my mind, such statements are to some extent a reflection of unrest as exemplified by the thousands of little red books in
the hands of young people in England, West Germany, France, and
other parts of Europe. For this segment of the young intelligentsia,
radicalism is more attractive the more simple and schematized it is,
and the more they themselves are aware of the marginal societal
role to which they are consigned by their own university education.

All of these voices deserve to be heard, and deserve an answer on
the basis of our own experience and concepts. Dogmatism and anti-
dogmatism, when translated into slogans, differ little from one another. Perhaps you have noticed, in reading our press during the
last few weeks, how much closer we now seem to be to the Chinese
mentality and outlook, to those resolutions of the Red Guards demanding the dismissal of officials having conservative attitudes,

hints to the effect that such and such an official has not yet pledged allegiance to progressive principles, appeals to persons to change their minds, the willingness of large numbers to comply . . . But let us be careful; too great a similarity of external form should warn us against making facile comparisons. I believe, in any case, that the campaigns conducted in this style should be ended as soon as possible, for methods that seem inevitable at a particular point and appear democratic in a certain context have a way of becoming permanently inevitable and permanently undemocratic. We should quickly enter an era in which meetings, conferences, congresses, and elections are run democratically on the basis of broadly based decisions made by well-informed people. Such an approach will gradually eliminate from public life not only the handful of compromised leaders, but all individuals with whom our society in its various stages of development has had unfortunate experiences. Such persons will be gradually replaced by those who give real promise of better achievement. But all this is only in the nature of marginal remarks.

It is certain, that the position of the intellectual as well as the position of culture is not very secure in modern society, giving rise to serious questions. It is true that socialist society, as we have known it in our country so far, emblazoned culture on its shield and posed as its champion. Nevertheless, it was the ambition of the socialist state—and to a considerable extent this is still true—to liquidate intellectuals as well as their functions through means which this kind of socialism had at its command: administrative fiat, fear, and when necessary, violence, legal persecution, and imprisonment. Unfortunately, all this was by no means limited to other countries; we have much of it ourselves.

Highly developed capitalist societies generally do not use such drastic methods against their intellectuals. Rather, they eliminate the intellectual from any socially meaningful role. By installing the principle of technocracy and the rule of consumption, capitalist countries turn the intellectual with his fragile conscience and his ethical criteria into a harmless eccentric, who can occasionally serve as an ornament, a pearl in the crown of the mighty, or a court jester whose master is so secure in his rule that he can permit impudence to go unpunished now and again. But as far as the actual determination of policy is concerned, the influence of the intellectual in capitalist countries is as minimal as it is under socialism. If this were not so, the Vietnam war would probably have ended long ago, there would have been no war in Algeria, the first Indochina conflict would have never started or at least it would have been settled far sooner, with the same result as was ultimately achieved but with thousands of lives and tons of explosives saved by both sides.

Just recall the tumult that was created by our politicians and scribblers when Ernst Fischer's* outstanding essay on the intellectual and power appeared in Czech. In this essay, one of the foremost European thinkers of our time pointed out to socialist countries the tremendous advantages that accrued to the United States during the eras of Franklin Delano Roosevelt and Kennedy, because these presidents surrounded themselves not only with braintrusts of technocrats, but with intellectuals as well. The function of these intellectuals was not only to come up with solutions to current problems, but above all to anticipate questions and theoretical complications likely to come up in the future, for which political leaders would have to find practical answers.

It was Ernst Fischer who told me recently: "Socialism has only two alternatives. Either there will be a victory of the forces pejoratively called 'socialist revisionists,' and developed Western societies will look to this form of socialism for solutions to their problems, or else the doors will be wide open to a radicalism of the Chinese kind. If real democratic socialism fails to develop in Europe, this is the perspective West European leftists will be increasingly forced to adopt."

Let's leave the word "revisionism" aside for the moment. This word belongs in the same category as "the opposition"; both of these expressions have been used with great gusto and abandon to stigmatize any dissenting viewpoint. (I have consistently refused to accept the term "opposition" as an insult, and after our recent experiences such words will soon lose their function as curses.) But to get back to Fischer's argument: Many people believe that the revolutionary role of culture and intellectuals is inevitably linked with societies which are underdeveloped, backward, with simple internal structure, undemocratic or even antidemocratic. This revolutionary role of culture presumably vanishes as soon as society becomes economically developed, industrialized, consumer-oriented, structured on the basis of legal guarantees. How true is this analysis? I am not sure. I know, like everyone else, that all previous experience, including our own, tends to support such a formulation. I know that intellectuals and culture only played an important role in our country when the conditions of backwardness and antidemocratic rule were present, and that intellectuals tended to become a mere ornament without political influence as soon as general conditions began to improve. Their voice was heard—for

---

* The Austrian Marxist philosopher.

example, during the economic crisis at the beginning of the 1930s, or at the time of Munich—but this voice was no longer capable of stirring society. I am also aware that the role of culture and of the intelligentsia must vary under different historical circumstances. The particular role that intellectuals are playing in Cuba or Latin America is quite understandable; it is defined in a way different from ours, because it involves a different type of society, a different structure, life at a different moment of national existence, and I have no intention of judging or condemning. At the same time, however, it seems to me extremely foolish, unhistorical and un-realistic when intellectuals from developed European countries look to Cuba or to Latin America for the answers to their own problems.

Our answer will lie in a different direction. What saps the soci-etal influence of the intellectual in developed Western countries? In my opinion, when intellectuals are no longer active in helping to create mass political movements of a class nature, they are de-prived of the means which in capitalist societies constitute the only criteria of weight and influence. The intellectuals are eliminated as sources of power when no social group any longer depends on them, when under the thriving conditions of modern capitalism no social class needs them to solve its immediate problems in the strug-gle against other classes. In addition, in the midst of the present sci-entific-technical revolution, when advanced countries are racing to meet the twenty-first century, the intellectual—with his char-acteristic questioning, warning, and protesting—seems to be an un-necessary hindrance. The technically educated person seems to be the only effective ally of progress.

Our society is of course different. Hopefully, it will gradually be-come less backward and more democratic. Nevertheless, it must not turn into a mere small-scale model or replica of contemporary industrial, consumer society, not even a replica with its own some-what more pronounced social features, or its own particular politi-cal orientation. Rather, our country should strike out on its own, and create for itself its own social and political structure.

For the first time in the modern era, the human spirit could be given an entirely new, independent, and socially useful role, not merely in the form of a technical brain, but in terms of conscience, consciousness, and historical continuity. This role would in effect be similar to that of religion. Our experience demonstrated that the attempt to create a centralized atheistic religion with new icons and fetishes was a disastrous failure. It failed simply because modern Man, with his knowledge of nature and of the world, and with a living standard incomparably higher than was the case during religious epochs, has no desire or need for that type of religion or pseudoreligion. Of course, there are old aunts and uncles all over the world who still enjoy lighting candles and taking part in rituals, but this represents a social type rather than a religious manifestation. No society, however, can get along without the kind of "religion" represented by culture. It is "religious" in the sense that, like religion, culture is a constant reminder of tradition, history, memory, a criterion of values, a touchstone of morality and character in the individual and in society, a keeper of the sacred flame.

Of course, this modern religion is the religion of Man on the threshold of the twenty-first century, Man independently thinking and judging, Man who has at his disposal all the modern means of information. Modern Man will turn to the artists and intellectuals—authorities who follow their own calling—to remember the past, to listen to warnings and to grasp new ideals, ideals of beauty, wisdom, morality, personal conduct, and social well-being.

If socialist society comes to understand this, to understand that this is not a Utopian dream but a concrete possibility opening up before it, then the society will also know what it has to do. It will realize that the task of its leaders is not to direct, but only to organize, to support, with ultimate ideals and perspectives clearly in mind. It will realize that the last thing it wants from its leading organs is tolerance, for neither culture nor intellectuals can ever be tolerant toward the state in return. Rather, society will organize cultural matters with the full knowledge that in our irreligious era it can only be the intolerance of culture and of intellectuals toward raw power that can assure Man of maintaining his humanity. Only the intolerance of intellectuals toward philistinism and technocracy can see to it that Man has an inner life more highly developed than that of a prehistoric monster.

This then, in my judgment, is the task of the intellectual and of culture with respect to socialist society. The creation of the right conditions that will enable culture to fulfill this task is in turn up to those who have responsibility for the practical governing of society. The evolution of cultural policy should not take place in an atmosphere of mutual admiration and sobbed pledges of righting all past wrongs, but in a context of continual struggle between culture on the one hand and political power and technocracy on the other, a continuous dialogue about the meaning of the past, the present, and the future in terms of the nation and every one of its citizens.

In certain kinds of cultural enterprise, responsibility for the proper atmosphere is to a large extent an individual matter, and culture can fulfill its mission even though society as a whole does not create the proper conditions. There are other types of cultural activity, however, which cannot exist without societal help. Films and television belong in this category. I would like to call attention to one aspect, for it is one of the most remarkable traits of history that it likes to repeat itself and, contrary to the opinion of classicists, this repetition need not invariably take the form of farce. Due to the fact that cinematic art requires large sums of money, film in capitalist countries becomes a by-product in the manufacture of mass-culture, or else it cannot exist at all. Strangely enough, the situation is remarkably similar in socialist society, though the underlying reasons are different.

Of course, unusual conditions may arise, such as the stalemate we experienced recently: Culture and political power were balanced to such an extent that for a time neither side had the strength to liquidate the other. It was under precisely such conditions that the Czechoslovak film "miracle" took place; contrary to the opinion of some, our cultural policy can take no credit whatever for this miracle.

The means necessary for making films and broadcasting television programs require centralized power. And such power is rarely given to intellectuals, though an intellectual may occasionally sneak in, or the powers running the show may decide to co-exist for a time with these odd, disturbing, never-satisfied characters, and even ask their opinion from time to time.

Centralized power (needless to say, the less centralized the better, both for the rulers and the ruled), the power that rules over agriculture and railroads, foreign policy and prostitution, seldom lives by art and culture. Nowhere, never. It is a pity, and the loss is mainly its own. But it may also be a loss for those who not only live by culture, but have a share in creating it.

Consider the situation in our country. Our leaders didn't read books, didn't visit theaters or exhibits or concert halls, didn't go among the people or travel abroad, and yet they sat down once a week and examined films. And because the people who made these films read books, visited theaters and concert halls, traveled in the world—their experiences were remarkably evident in their films, especially in the better ones—misunderstandings naturally arose. I do not understand, shouted the centralized omnipotent power, and this of course meant that the film was the work of Satan. Now I understand, shouted the centralized power, I understand only too well, I recognize that this is the work of Satan.

And there you have it. We all know what the consequences were. And because the vast majority of people do not read books, do not visit theaters or concerts, and go abroad only to certain countries and with certain prejudices, the centralized power is convinced that its opinion is the opinion of the people, and vice versa.

With television, the matter is even more complicated. The ruling power has no time to check it all, there are too many programs to examine. Now there is even the "danger" of a second network; there is simply too much to keep an eye on. But the supreme "state-nik," "district-nik," or "county-nik" has underlings on whom he can depend. First of all, there is his own family—his wife, then there is a son, sometimes even a daughter, then a brother, sister, in case of the younger potentates possibly a father, uncles, and cousins, and these in turn are not without relatives of their own, not to mention friends and acquaintances. The effect of all this family surveillance on television can be imagined. To use a popular expression—it doesn't stand a chance!

What is the answer? Once upon a time, in a certain socialist country, there was a wise, all-powerful king. The courtiers showed him a film to find out what they were supposed to think about it. According to legend, the king scratched his head—at that time only slightly bald—and said: "I don't like it at all, in fact, it is positively harmful. If I had the power, I would forbid it." These were wise words indeed. They resounded all over the land and far over the hills into other socialist countries, and everywhere they caused much joy. But before long, the king realized that he actually *did* have the power to forbid everything. And from that day on, for the next ten years, weeds grew in the once beautiful film pastures.

Fairy tales are fairy tales, but every king, every centralized power, every film or television czar sooner or later finds that he has the power to do as he pleases. One day he may get up on the wrong side of the bed, or find out that his shoe pinches, or learn that his treasury is empty, or get a thrashing from a neighboring king—and the jig is up.

Unfortunately, it is difficult to arrange to have every representative of centralized power read at least some of the books which have been read by a filmmaker, see some of the same exhibits and foreign countries, live among the same people, before being allowed to enter the projection room or television studio. It would be equally difficult to ask such a ruler to stop looking at films altogether. But one thing can certainly be done: He can be deprived of his omnipotence! He can be stripped of absolute power, the power to decide what to produce and what to kill, which television program to broadcast and which to cancel.

But you may object: "How can we deprive the state of its power when we ourselves want cinema to be a national enterprise subsidized by the state? We don't want to force film to earn its own way, that would be its downfall." This is a valid objection. Nevertheless, I believe that there are ways of overcoming the dilemma, there are ways of limiting absolute power over film and television. At the moment, I have two approaches in mind. The first is a legal one. Socialist society was the first to guarantee people the right to work. And no matter how difficult it may be at certain times, we must insist that this right be respected.

How does the right to work apply in the case of a film artist? Does it amount to nothing more than giving a man the right to be employed, to collect his pay, to shoot films—if not his own, then someone else's, if not his own way, then some other way? I don't think this is the point. I think that in the case of any artist, the right to work means the right to create the work that is inside his mind, the right to submit this work to the judgment of the public for whom it was intended. In the special case of the film artist, this also implies that in addition to his own means the artist would have ample societal support at his disposal. Though the means needed are often very substantial, I believe that a socialist society should pledge itself to provide them, for film and television have a special significance in any country's artistic structure.

The legal approach to the problem of support for the artist is consistent with the dignity of socialism and constitutes one of the answers to the question we posed earlier: Why does culture need socialism? This approach would be based on the legally enacted duty of the socialist state to guarantee the realization of an artistic project and to provide necessary support for it, whenever an organization responsible for evaluating its merits makes a positive recommendation. Of course, the organization called upon to pass judgment would have to be totally independent of state control; in the case of film, it could be the National Artists' Union. Similar provisions would apply to various aspects of the film's distribution, such as export arrangements. In my view, this is the only truly socialistic solution to the problem of creative freedom of the film artist and his right to work.

The second approach, which of course can go hand in hand with the first and which does not apply exclusively to socialism, involves a reorganization in the structure and scope of the present national film monopoly. I know that there are a number of different opinions regarding this question. If socialist society declares as its fundamental position an interest in the dissemination of culture, not as a luxury but as a basic necessity, and if the question of cultural values and cultural education is approached in the same spirit, then we probably need not fear a further decentralization in the structure of our film industry. We need not fear the possibility of financing film production by means other than state support; naturally, cultural and artistic criteria rather than commercial ones would still have to be dominant. Finally, we need not fear the freedom of any film artist to undertake work for foreign clients. I believe that one favorable result of such free competition with foreign filmmakers would be the challenge posed to our own studios to create the best possible working conditions for our artists. At the same time, there could be culturally advantageous coproductions with foreign companies, with resultant assurance of foreign distribution. Such activity would be fully consistent with the best interests of our society.

It seems to me that the socialist solution to the problem of guaranteeing the material existence of filmmakers should not consist in turning such artists into government employees. In my opinion, our film workers should not be employees of the Czechoslovak film industry, nor of particular film studios. Rather, this part of the total payroll should be transferred through an appropriate organizational mechanism into a Film Fund, which would then pay film artists a basic salary in the form of a continuing stipend. The stipend would include provisions for social security and other benefits, just like any salary from the state, but it would give the film artist a certain independence vis-à-vis the studios and would place him on the same level as artists in other cultural areas.

In conclusion, I want to touch on a question which has occupied filmmakers for a number of years. It has to do with culture, and at the same time with the new economic model. FITES (Film Artists Guild), as a matter of principle, rejected the idea that the film industry should become completely self-sufficient economically and that films should be marketed in order to make profits, as is the case in capitalist countries. The arguments are well known, the position of FITES was published in the press, and I need not repeat it. The basic question remains, however: Czechoslovakia cannot afford to remain a backward country, lagging behind the rest of the industrialized world, a country with limited production and limited consumption. Our country must do everything possible to return to the road from which it has strayed, the highway leading to the twenty-first century on which the developed countries are racing ahead at full speed. If we look carefully at these consumer societies of the West, we see that in proportion to the general growth of consumption there is also a corresponding growth in the consumption of culture, namely the so-called mass-culture market. This leads to the question whether a similar pattern would emerge in Czechoslovakia; almost all of the debates about culture linked to the new economic model seem to veer in this direction. We know, of course, that mass culture—though it undoubtedly has a rightful place in modern society—is a phenomenon which can be described as cultural only in the broadest sense of the term. This question of terminology should interest us very much. Mass culture has certain external manifestations which it shares with culture, but it differs from true culture in a fundamental way: In relation to a work of mass culture, the consumer is never anything but a consumer. In the case of a true work of culture, on the other hand, the consumer becomes an active participant in a process which begins with a particular work, and continues after the consumer has experienced it. Mass culture does not pose questions, but gives simple, dangerously positive answers; it doesn't disturb, but confirms; it doesn't doubt, but creates a certain quite primitive ideal; it doesn't struggle with Man, but offers itself to him; it doesn't make demands, but exists in a region of that which has already been achieved, on the level of the general average, or even below the general average. It is simply one of the many modest ways of filling the spare time which accrues as a result of economic development, something like bowling. Sometimes I find bowling preferable to the consumption of mass culture, for in bowling there is at least some activity involved. The conversion of cultural forms and materials into commodities for mass consumption is a basic manifestation of a consumer society. But, may I ask, *only* of a consumer society? Or can this happen under socialism as well? This, too, will have to be answered as part of the broad question about the usefulness of socialism to cultural life, the question whether culture may not be just as well off without socialism, or perhaps even better off.

Let us return to the beginning. For a long time, capitalist society proceeded on the assumption that culture was a luxury, an unessential adornment, at least as far as the masses were concerned. At the moment when capitalist society reached the opposite conclusion it gave rise to a double culture, one for the elite and another one for the masses. It was only at this point that capitalist nations became aware of the full consequences of this separation, and tried to find ways of correcting it.

The specter of two cultures, one for the elite and one for the masses, has until recently haunted our defenders of socialist ideological and cultural integrity, and gave rise to various remarkable texts on this subject. But this is where we made our mistake. Without being fully aware of it, the staunch fighters against cultural elitism longed to imitate capitalist society; the ideological content which they would have given to mass culture would have been surprisingly similar to the capitalist counterpart. But the true way of socialism does not lead to mass culture, but to making true culture available to all who are interested, accompanied by strenuous efforts to make such interested people more and more numerous. In this sense, a socialist state—at least the Czechoslovak state—must come to regard culture neither as a necessity nor as a luxury, but as a necessary luxury, as one of those imposing, inspiring projects which are extremely costly but which are nevertheless necessary for national grandeur and historical survival, much the same way that de Gaulle's France regarded development of its own atomic bomb or England the need for a powerful independent navy. We will never fly to the moon in our own rockets launched from our own launching pads, nor will we have occasion to borrow a foreign desert for the detonation of our bombs.

If our small socialist country ever produces anything impressive, it will have to be something cultural. Czechoslovak films demonstrated that this contribution could be sizeable, it penetrated into areas our culture was unable to reach before, but as a result of a shamefully inadequate cultural policy at home the majority of our own people could not see the films that made such an impact abroad. Such discrepancies must be corrected as soon as possible. This must be our starting point: The declaration that culture constitutes our country's richest source of pride and prestige, a force that will help determine our place in the contemporary world. We must further proclaim that the creation of proper conditions for the growth of this culture is a task of the highest priority, which no one can measure by yardsticks of the marketplace. We must proclaim that the search for the means whereby our people could play the widest possible role in our own cultural life as well as in the cultural life of the world is a crucially important aim of our educational and social policy. A worker who gets up at five o'clock in the morning and spends three to four hours every day traveling in desperately obsolete conveyances will never become a consumer of culture, no matter how easily available and inexpensive it may be. And a state that fails to solve such problems will never be a truly socialist state. To turn to mass culture is an evasion of the problem, a facile, unsocialist answer. Capitalism has already traced this route to the very bottom.

Fine, fine, but this is much too idealistic, you say to yourself, or
you whisper to your neighbor. Yes, idealism, perhaps quite different from the sober realism which we are so often called upon to
support, especially on the part of economists and technical experts.
The modest, sober attitude we are asked to display is reminiscent
of the cynical era we have just left behind, the era of so-called
"political realism." But the very concepts and ideas which give a
nation strength and courage on its march through history are dismissed as "too idealistic." It is precisely by realizing such "idealistic" concepts, or at least by attempting to do so, that nations remain vital. The history of the Czechoslovak nation is an excellent
example. We are too small to be able to live only on stark political
realities. We would probably never survive the loss of our ideals
and the capability for idealistic thought. On the contrary, it is
idealism alone that gives us the right to an independent existence
in Europe, and the hope of making a contribution to the growth
of mankind.

They applauded, and then the discussions over the next two days
veered to other topics. Among other things, there was much debate
about specific people who shared the responsibility for all the lost
opportunities between 1948 and 1968. And once again, as in the
first days of de-Stalinization, I heard the same question: What gives
you the right to talk? How can *you* judge others, when you yourself—in the 1950s you wrote such and such, said so and so. But this
time the questions were not posed deceitfully, by men in power, in
an attempt to discredit an opponent. The questions came from
persons who were on our side, people in whose name and for whose
sake we have fought so hard over the last decade. And there was no
doubt that we were vulnerable to accusations of guilt, of youthful
complicity. We never had any share in actual power, it is true, but
for a variety of reasons—good and bad—we enlisted our pens in
the service of the rulers' opinions and postulates. (The high and
the mighty of the 1960s, smirking and contemptuous, came to call
us "the kids with the conscience-complex.")

Now, the questions came from individuals who had a perfect
right to pose them, though I must admit that they took me by surprise. This moment was harder to bear than the worst moments of
the preceding years. A man is capable of fighting a bloody battle
against a powerful antagonist, against the very incarnation of
power, knowing that the battle is all but hopeless. But he is de-

fenseless against blows such as the ones we now received, blows that were at the same time justified and terribly wrong. There was no defense against them; that's why they could be so final, in a sense so mortal.

I didn't answer. I couldn't. I admit that the world began to spin in my head. Suddenly I saw everything through *their* eyes, I was again a young . . . but no, we were no longer children, after all, youth and foolishness are no justification for anything, men and history are only interested in definite acts, in clearly written lines. Only weeks later did I come to understand—and perhaps this was the last step in the process of liberation—that I was making a mistake, the same mistake with which I had reproached my friends: What I had found shattering and incomprehensible from an ethical viewpoint I left incomplete and badly thought out from a political viewpoint. That's why so many of us wanted to commit socio-political suicide at the moment of our embittered victory, to flee as far as possible, to work only for ourselves. But nobody of my generation—the young standard-bearers and scrappers of 1948—had the right to go away, to disappear, to merely vegetate. Not as long as he knew that the battle was far from won, not as long as he was able to carry this realization to its logical conclusion. Too much is now at stake, and we are too deeply involved in the historical process to turn our back on it now, regardless of who was shouting what. After all, such heckling and shouting is nothing new, and will always be with us.

Here, then, is the delayed answer which I owed my questioners: By what right did I speak? By none. I spoke out of a sense of duty toward this country, toward the people of this country. I have nothing to give them except my life, and the experience of that life, which was neither easy nor clear cut, and which is filled with errors. I have always lived my life publicly, before the eyes of our people. Let them weigh it and let them say whether they accept it or not, whether they trust it or not. They have the opportunity to do so. And while we are talking about rights, about the right to speak, I insist on repeating what I stated and wrote four years ago: This kind of right is not requested, it is not bestowed, it is simply taken. It is supported only by one's own life, one's own conscience. And the case is far from closed. Not as long as we breathe. The same is true of our whole puzzling, contradictory, and—in the end— ridiculed generation.

The Czech word *"generace"** means both the singular and plural ["generation" and "generations."]

It took me some time before I fully realized the advantages of this grammatical feature. My original plan was to collect the statements of a certain number of members of one generation. Namely, the generation of people who were twenty years old, or older, in 1945–1968, and who were, therefore, in their forties and fifties in 1962–1968. These were people who more or less actively accepted the 1950s as an era of progress, and who were called upon ten years later to liquidate that era's consequences.

The persons I was about to interview would supposedly reminisce about themselves, the period which they had lived through, its conflicts and historical necessities. Each interview would of course represent a somewhat different viewpoint, depending upon the person involved. But there was to be one common theme in all of the conversations: By presenting intellectual biographies of creative people, I hoped to show the readers—particularly the younger ones—how that fascinating phenomenon known as human being/writer or human being/artist is born. To show that this is not the product of chance, that there is a certain underlying logic, a certain law, the understanding of which would perhaps also help in grasping the essence of what literature or art is all about. And in the background there was one additional idea: To prove that decent people in this small Central-European country—thoughtful, talented people who sooner or later made a mark in cultural life—necessarily had to come into conflict with themselves and with their society, and that in order to avoid self-mutilation they had to see this conflict resolutely through to the end. Finally, as a practical working journalist I was also thinking of the needs of the newspaper in planning this series of interviews, and I was hoping that I could deal with matters that would otherwise have been difficult to handle at that time. Here I was influenced by earlier experience, particularly my first little book called *"Rozhovor"* (*"Conversations"*). These conversations with a large number of left-wing European intellectuals became a means of smuggling fresh new thinking into the pages of our press. I believe that all of those who took part in this undertaking could rightfully be called The International Brigade, volunteers who helped Czechoslovak culture get back on its own feet during the early 1960s.

---

* *"Generace"* was the original Czech title of this book.—*Ed.*

The project was barely under way before the singular/plural ambiguity of the word *"generace"* assumed a special symbolic relevance. First of all, it became clear that during moments of historic breaks and transitions, when the tectonic layers of society begin to crumble, only a few years are needed to change the generational feeling. Sometimes only two or three years suffice to divide people who are roughly contemporaries into two quite different generations. But there is more to it than that. As a particular generation begins to split into separate horizontal layers, it becomes more and more difficult to draw a clear demarcation between this generation and the one that precedes and the one that follows. Precise contours are erased, the generations overlap, the picture becomes plastic, three-dimensional. The ambiguity of *"generace"* thus seemed highly appropriate and we kept it in the title, even though the book turned out to be not only about the generations, but about other matters as well.

After January 1968, we have been asked more and more frequently: What kind of society, what kind of democracy? How do you envision a future Czechoslovakia, what do you understand by the concept "democratic socialism"? And it was then that we began to realize quite clearly what we had vaguely sensed for a long time: That the greatest crime committed by the Novotny regime consisted in making the development of any new concept, any political alternative, impossible. This system of eternal suspicion, jealousy, terror of anything new, this epitome of Czech narrow-mindedness, provincialism, cowardice, and vulgarity finally forced everyone capable of preparing an alternative to concentrate instead on the immediate problem of removing the regime from power at all costs. And when this struggle was at last successfully concluded we realized that no alternative had been prepared, that the country was desperately searching, groping, confused. And it will continue to search and to grope for a long time to come.

Czechoslovaks who had practical experience with liberal, bourgeois democracy after having reached the age of their own political maturity are now in their sixties. After all, this era ended in 1938. The years 1945–1948 were hardly a school for democracy; they couldn't be, everything was still overly influenced by the wartime atmosphere, the struggle for power, the international aftermath of the war years including the incipient cold war. There didn't even exist a basic political chart of the country, various political forces often operated under strange banners; in brief, every-

thing was confused. And now, after thirty years, this country is to
embark upon democracy? In the spring of 1968 everyone could
see for himself that such a change could not take place overnight,
that democracy was something all of us would have to start learning all over again, that everybody's conception of democracy was
different, and that the segment of the population most crucial to
democracy's success—the working class—looked upon democracy
with the greatest suspicion. It will be a long and difficult learning
period, and we can only hope that our country will have enough
time. Enough time before a smooth-talking man once again makes
his appearance, a man with a big smile, decisive hand, broad shoulders (though perhaps leaning against a neighbor's wall for support), a man handing out ready-made prescriptions for the proper
conduct of life, happiness, democracy, freedom—and in no time at
all this country will be sewn up in a bag.

We will, therefore, learn democracy. Long and hard. And while
we are learning, we will try to define just what this democracy
should really be like. There are some things we already know. We
know, for example, that there are no ready-made models for democracy. Neither in the East, whose traditions, history and spiritual atmosphere are so different from ours, nor in the West, with
whose economic system we have parted. We know, too, that we
must liquidate the monopoly of political power, but we have no
idea how a plurality of organized political forces can function in
an arena of socialist economics, or how such pluralism can be rec-
onciled with the necessary ties between economics and politics.
All solutions, all decisions which we must make are ahead of us;
we cannot return for solutions to the past, nor is there anything
ready-made lying at our feet. But how are we to find answers in a
country which has learned so little about itself, which really
doesn't know itself at all?

To chart a country's political contours with any degree of accuracy is a difficult, almost impossible task. This is true even in
countries where the exchange of information has been going on
continuously for many decades, or even—as in the case of America
and Great Britain—for centuries. Concrete problems concerning
the size and nature of political and social groups, the problems of
tracing precise socio-political boundaries during periods of rapid
change, often lead even experts to desperation. Again, this is true
even in countries where public opinion is well developed, where

the press, radio, and television—among their useful and useless functions—also act as sources of information, where any interested citizen can gain access to a wealth of available data, and where people charged with the task of keeping abreast of developments have at their command a wealth of information—not *about* citizens, but *from* citizens.

But now imagine the situation in a country such as ours. Just try to answer any concrete question about political changes or developments in a country where for the past three decades there has been no dissemination of information, where for more than a quarter of a century there was no such thing as public opinion, where the press, radio, and television for all practical purposes have spent the last thirty years in disseminating propaganda and concealing reality, where not even the government itself had any reliable data on the state of the country and where information about the people was most unsatisfactory, for police records are notoriously misleading. That's why I don't believe anybody who says he knows what the country is thinking, what it is like, what it wants, and how its political structure should be arranged. Everything in our country looks different on the surface from what it really is. The only political dividing line seen from a distance, that between communists and noncommunists, is meaningless, for numerous other divisions and categories run across this boundary. Young Vietnamese tore down an American flag, and our students returned the flag to the American embassy. The meaning that this gesture had in our country is different from what it probably would have been almost anywhere else in the world. And yet, what did it really mean? Countless similar examples could be cited.

It will take a long time before Czechoslovakia of the last third of this century begins to know itself again; that is, of course, if it is given time before new upheavals come about. In the meantime, we are gathering crumbs of information about ourselves and our nation, bit by bit, and we wonder how to proceed. There isn't a single individual in our land who could sit down at his desk, surround himself with "material" and prepare a rough political chart, an approximate political analysis. For such "material" does not exist. During the last ten years I found out that the safest method of obtaining at least a little bit of truth is to illuminate a problem from many angles by many kinds of human experience. That's why I believe in conversation, in a method of analysis through dialogue, repeated many times, but with a single underlying theme: a single country, a single historical period. And a unifying hand. That was the last part of the plan for this project. Perhaps the undertaking gave rise only to a document about a country, its culture, and its thought during a particular moment of history. Perhaps more was accomplished; perhaps those fourteen people, so different from each other and yet so united, made a collective statement about something which we hadn't known before. That's what should have happened. If it didn't succeed this time, perhaps it will the next time.

An anecdote is connected with each one of these fifteen interviews. We began in the fall of 1966 with Ester Krumbachova. You should have heard the storm of protest that was created by Czech literary ladies when *Literarni Noviny* had the effrontery to devote so much space to "that woman," a woman who hadn't published a single book and wasn't even a member of the Writers' Union. The interview with Milan Kundera which took place shortly thereafter was not allowed to be published until the spring of 1968. It seems that Kundera's comments on Stalinism incensed the enlightened mind of a certain former Latin professor named Havlicek, who was chosen by Novotny and Hendrych as their chief ideologue. On the other hand, the conversation with Josef Skvorecky was greatly praised by the anonymous censor in the spring of 1967, because he "said a mouthful about that nuthouse." As far as the conversation with Ludvik Vaculik is concerned, we were afraid to put it into the newspaper for many months, and when we finally tried it—shortly before the Writers' Congress—the censor congratulated us on an excellent article. And yet soon after publication, security organs began to take great interest in the article and its authors. The attitudes of the censors were altogether unfathomable. The conversation with Jiri Mucha, far from flattering to the regime, came out in the magazine *Orientace* in the fall of 1967 without a single red mark, while the interview with Jaroslav Putik was literally massacred by the censors (the passages about Munich, the uprising, the generations, the 1950s). The only way that Tatarka was finally able to convince the party secretariat to permit publication of his interview in the Slovak Writers' Union's weekly *Kulturny Zivot* was by threatening to turn in his party card. That interview was also interesting in the sense that it was conducted in Switzerland shortly after the Writers' Congress, when both of us knew what was coming up and both of us tried to keep our inside knowledge from creeping into the conversation. The same thing was true when we chatted with Eduard Goldstücker for two days in August of 1967 on a North Bohemian mountain; we chose our words carefully, and yet we were both convinced that the material we were putting together would only have significance as a document for the future. The three last interviews—with Karvas, Klima, and Havel—were completed in 1968. And, in my opinion, this revealed something significant: There is no difference between these three interviews and the preceding ones; every one talked with equal freedom whether it was during a period when it wasn't at all certain that a single word would ever be printed or whether the interview took place when the battle seemed won, at least for the moment.

This confirmed once again that Man's freedom is within him and not around him. And if Man doesn't find freedom within himself, he will find it nowhere, and he will receive it from nobody. And this is doubly true of intellectuals, for they can help mankind only through their own freedom.

Now, if you turn the page, you will meet Laco Novomesky, you will encounter the words which he told me in 1965 and which closed the first volume of interviews, those conducted abroad. The words of Novomesky were supposed to stress the connection with home. That's why this interview belongs at the beginning. That, as well as the fact that the new generation cannot define itself without a confrontation with his. Similarly, no new generation can complete its own portrait without looking into the mirror provided by the generation of Vaclav Havel, the generation that's fifteen years behind us but seems so close on our heels.

The conversations are naturally arranged in the chronological sequence in which they arose.

I want to add one more thought. I keep thinking that all of these conversations will only gain their full meaning if I or someone else will be able to repeat them in some fifteen or twenty years. With the same people, those that survive. And to confront them in the future with the ideas they hold now . . .   May 1968

NOTE FOR THE ENGLISH-LANGUAGE EDITION: The original manuscript was completed at the end of May 1968. Nothing has been added to reflect what has occurred since that time other than Josef

Skvorecky's response to Jean-Paul Sartre's introduction. Both the Sartre essay and Skvorecky's response appeared earlier in *Evergreen Review*.

As of this writing, all but two of the Czech writers interviewed in these pages live in Czechoslovakia. The two who have left are Josef Skvorecky, who is now in Canada, and Eduard Goldstücker, who now lives in England. Of those who remained behind, all have lost their original jobs and, with the exception of L. Novomesky, all have been expelled from the Party as well as the Writers' Union if they had been members before. Also, they are barred from publishing in Czechoslovakia.

AJL
January 1972

Laco Novomeský

Born in 1904 in Budapest. Between the wars he was active in the Communist Party, mainly as an editor of journals and magazines (including *Pravda Chudoby* and *DAV*). Member of a group of proletarian poets oriented toward avant-garde art. In his books of poetry published between 1927 and 1939 he combined a lyrical note with social themes. During World War II he took part in underground party work in Slovakia and in 1944 was one of the leading political figures of the Slovak National Uprising. After the war, he held a number of party and governmental posts, from which he was removed in 1950. In 1951 he was expelled from the party, was tried and sentenced to long imprisonment for alleged "bourgeois nationalism." In 1956 he was released from prison and in 1963 rehabilitated. Since then he has published two collections of poems, *Villa Tereza* (1963) and *From That Place* (1964), as well as a long narrative poem, "Thirty Minutes to Town" (1963), which are mainly reminiscences of the period between the wars. In the political conflicts between the Novotny regime and liberal writers in 1967, Novomesky joined the latter. However, more concerned with Slovak national aspirations, he later opposed, in the Slovak Writers' Union, some of his more liberal-minded colleagues. Shortly after the Soviet invasion he became a member of the Slovak Communist Party Presidium and in this position he has been, at least, a passive participant in the suppression of all liberal communist ideas in Czechoslovakia. He resigned from all party and state functions in 1971.

Laco Novomeský

The town of Bratislava somehow couldn't decide between spring and winter. The paneled, two-year-old apartment house already looked as if it had been through a war. From the warm hall, smoky fumes curled upward against the windows. All around there was a sea of mud. And yet all this was not surprising, for he had always lived the life of ordinary people and among ordinary people. And when he hadn't, things had been even worse, much worse. Better to forget. Indeed, he didn't say a word about the darker side of his life. In the presence of this ash-gray head, those sunken eyes looking over at me from behind the table, our own little catastrophes, tragedies, and struggles seemed like child's play. For half a day we had been chatting about various things . . .

. . . Yes, we must learn everything, learn to master all kinds of techniques, travel, look around, but then start talking about ourselves, our people, our country. At times we have a tendency toward exaggerated self-sufficiency, which is rather foolish, though understandable under the circumstances. We can only overcome it through continued local progress. But we must never confuse national pride with national arrogance; I think the Tiso* era has

---

* Jozef Tiso, President of the Slovak state under the German Protectorate, was executed after the war for collaborating with the Nazis.—*Ed.*

taught all of us the dangerous consequences of such confusion. But to reiterate: These tendencies can be overcome only by improving the Slovak environment.

Now we've landed squarely in the midst of the old controversy.

This continual debate—or controversy, if you wish—has long been a characteristic of our cultural life. As a matter of fact, I'd say that this friction is precisely what justifies the coexistence of two national cultures side by side: they rub against each other; everything is seen from two aspects, with two pairs of eyes; there is a constant dialogue. This is no great discovery; this was already known by [Ludovit] Stur [nineteenth-century Slovak poet, scholar, and patriot] and also by [F. X.] Salda [author and founder of modern Czech literary criticism]. Salda claimed that he didn't understand Slovak problems, that he knew nothing about them, though actually few people ever understood them more profoundly. And it was he who demonstrated how essential it is that Czech and Slovak creativity—literary and otherwise—remain in constant touch, growing ever stronger through mutual struggle.

This mirror, this viewpoint of a neighboring people is particularly important for us Czechs, for we suffer from the tendency to believe only in our own traits as we dreamed them to be in the last century. And who are better qualified than the Slovaks to constantly remind us of what we are really like?

On the other hand, though, we Slovaks could use a bit more national modesty. Before chastising our neighbor, we must make sure that we have swept all the dirt away from our own doorstep, that we have put our own house in order. Putting one's house in order means, among other things, learning the difference between well-meant advice and useless grumbling.

Of course, the same thing works the other way around, too. The Czech has a habit of patronizing the Slovak as if he were a younger and somewhat retarded brother. I have lived in a Czech environment, among people who took broad-mindedness for granted, and it never occurred to them that I was a Slovak and they were Czechs. I have always been more interested in Czech poetry, in analyzing its specific character, than in arguments and chauvinistic debates about nationality.

Nowadays we've become saddled with a certain kind of nationalist mathematics: two Czechs here, one Slovak there. I think that this is a fundamentally unhealthy approach, a poor substitute for what should be—but isn't—self-evident: that we ought to work together on a common task, breathe a common atmosphere, without any offense taken on one side or sense of injustice on the other. The rigid mathematical approach is simply an institutionalized substitute for the immediacy of human contact. All this should be replaced by a totally different approach, based upon quality. After all, [Ludovit] Fulla [a Slovak painter] is as important for Czechs as [Josef] Sima [a Czech painter] is for us.

[*On the wall hangs a beautiful Sima nude, strangely white against a red quilt and surrounded by a gray-blue space, and in the next room another one, a print or a drawing, and a Fulla, too— and all this in that unremarkable, ordinary apartment so unlike the museumlike quarters of many artists I know.*]

When it comes to art, nationalist motives are absurd. The absurdity of the mathematical type of thinking is just as great. A case in point is the fact that we allow artists such as Fulla [the important Slovak avant-garde painter of the 1930s], Stefan Bazovsky [the Slovak painter] or [Ctibor] Filcik [the actor] to stew in their own local juices instead of trying with all our might to make them truly all-Czechoslovak figures, if not all-European. In the end, they may unfortunately be remembered thanks only to some "proportional" justice, rather than because of their unquestionable, intrinsic merit.

Don't you think there was a time when Czech and Slovak artists somehow managed to live in closer contact than is the case today?

Yes and no. First of all, in those days we stood in sharp and unmistakable opposition to the regime, and this actually served as a very strong element, much stronger than any family ties. Sometimes it may have been just two people who frequented the same coffeehouse; around this nucleus things crystalized in all directions. These two may have brought with them a couple of Czech writers— a [Vitezslav] Nezval or a [Karel]Teige*; they may have dragged them off to look at a Slovak castle or some other local place of interest. In this way, our mutual cultural life was replenished and refreshed.

Something happened, though, during the war and in the postwar

---

* Nezval, one of the founders of the Czech surrealist movement, was the greatest poet of the 1930s. Teige was the most important Marxist theoretician on art.—*Ed.*

years. The two societies developed along different lines. On the Czech side there was a great deal of irritation and even thirst for revenge for the events of 1939.* There was sympathy for the Slovak National Uprising, but at the same time it was regarded as only an act of atonement for past sins. But this wasn't what the uprising was all about. The Slovaks needed it to put their house in order, and to some extent it also liberated us from the errors of Czech bourgeois politics. How can we erase the bitter legacy of those years? In my opinion there is no other way except by demonstrating that "the blame" should not be imputed only to the Slovaks, but that quite a few Czechs must bear responsibility for past mistakes, too. Furthermore, the voice denouncing past and present Czech errors must be a Czech voice, not a Slovak one. All other means of wiping the slate clean would be futile.

As a matter of fact, the most progressive tendencies in a culture never become official state ideology, neither here nor anywhere else in the world. We have simply written everything down in the appropriate column and added it up; the letter has killed the spirit. We'll understand this cultural dilemma better if we look at it at the governmental level. In the fall of 1944 I was in London; I negotiated with Benes and demanded certain guarantees for Slovakia. Later we discussed this with Comrade [Klement] Gottwald, and I told him: "We Slovaks must finally free ourselves from a situation in which we are all gathered at our own end of the soccer field furiously defending our goal. Once equality becomes a self-evident fact, we'll come of our own accord and shout 'away with a bipartite state.' " The fear that Slovak interests are not taken sufficiently seriously still persists. It is compounded by Czech indifference to the whole problem.

In jail I often asked myself why I had been singled out as a nationalist, when actually I held the antinationalist opinions I have just described. My brand of Slovak awareness was simply based on realizing the need for protecting our vital interests while at the same time wishing that such protection was no longer necessary. Furthermore, Slovak nationalism is unthinkable without Czech

---

* In March 1939, having worked up anti-Czech sentiment among the Slovaks to a proper pitch, the Nazis used it as a pretext for annexing those remnants of their nation still left to the Czechs after the Munich Conference. The newly seized territories were officially designated as the Protectorate of Bohemia and Moravia. Slovakia became "independent."—*Ed.*

chauvinism, paternalism, and indifference. Without these it would wither away. Slovak nationalism and Czech chauvinism is like a U-shaped glass—if you fill one side, the level in the other is bound to rise. Of course, communism introduced a new factor into the situation, since for many people communism simply covered over the faults and failings of all parties and all tendencies, so that everything ended up under one hat, so to speak. Before we understand all this and sort it out, we shall all have to put up with more nonsense. Let us always keep in mind that if we communists who rule this land are unable to solve certain basic problems, or if the population feels that we are unable to solve them, then it is only a small step to the conviction that they'd be better off under some other system. On the other hand, if we—Czechs and Slovaks—could ever manage to get together, we would be in a much better position to take action against those who create discord and are only interested in feathering their own nests.

Why do I dwell so much on this subject? We are on the eve of the Congress of the Czechoslovak Writers' Union; this, too, is a national organization and it, too, faces these problems. At the Third Congress we were, of course, up to our ears in other questions. At that time the main task was to reject socialist realism as the only god and to rehabilitate those persons who needed rehabilitation. For Czechs and Slovaks alike, the great struggle was to defend everything great in literature. Slovaks realized perfectly well that the rehabilitation of Czech writers like [Jaroslav] Seifert, [Vladimir] Holan, and [Frantisek] Halas was a victory for Slovak literature, too. There was no question of nationalism. And it would be desirable to continue to progress this way, in our own country and elsewhere, so that the meaningful separation is made between what is progressive and what is regressive, rather than between things Czech and Slovak. To split along nationalist lines is stupid, and it is stupider still to place one group of people in a reactionary category simply on the basis of nationality.

Much has changed, of course, since the Third Congress. Seifert has been named a national artist, Holan's poetry was finally published and critically analyzed. What has happened is simply an acceptance of reality. A tremendously broad field for progressive creativity has been opened up, and this field must be jealously guarded against all trickery designed to narrow it down—even when the attack appears in the guise of attacking errors or poor quality.

All the same, these great improvements still exist only in relation to what was, and not in relation to what should be. Here and there, I am told: "Things are pretty good; just compare our situation with what's going on elsewhere!" But what sort of yardstick is that? What should be will only come into being when everybody who so desires will have the right to state—to paraphrase Brecht—that Minsk (or Prague, or Bratislava) is boring as hell. Somebody told me recently that he didn't know of a single banned book or manuscript still lying around unpublished in an office. But it isn't only a question of material already written, of negative restraints. There are authors who should be writing and who aren't, because they believe that their work wouldn't be published anyway or because they don't want to jeopardize their hard-won freedom.

Thus, the next task of writers—though of course not their task alone—will be to ensure absolute freedom of expression to the most far-reaching extent possible. I am aware of the fact that there are areas, such as modern painting, which are not too well understood by the public, and that people ask how the workers' money can be "wasted" in this way and so on. Such know-nothing voices can, of course, help bring about a Philistine or conformist tendency, or even, in the name of progress, push things back again. This represents a great threat to cultural growth and expansion. Let me formulate the problem this way: When and under what circumstances can a writer be openly critical, even about matters which are "holy" or "untouchable"? That's how the problem appears to us communists who have always raised the banner of freedom. To put it more concretely, I want to make sure that any potential Dostoevski in our midst is encouraged to develop fully, so that even in a socialist society he'll be able to speak about crises of human values. After all, we have learned that no social order is perfect. That is the tragedy of Soviet literature. You cannot solve the problem of conformity simply by citing Lenin instead of Stalin.

I remarked at this point that I often heard people say that too much freedom of expression, even in the artistic area, might subtly prepare the way for the reform of capitalism.

No. That's not where the road to capitalism begins. One of the reasons people accepted socialism was that they hoped it would open the way to a far greater freedom of thought and expression than had been possible under capitalism. I mentioned Dostoevski not because of his opinions but because of his conception of freedom, not because of his orthodoxy but because of his contributions to mankind. I'd go even further. I demand free expression even for those people who are not geniuses but who nonetheless contribute to establishing a new and healthier atmosphere. Socialism differs from capitalism—and this was one of its basic promises—in that it lifts barriers which capitalism cannot lift. Naturally I realize that any society needs discipline, but discipline must be exerted within a structure built on freedom of expression and not on its limitation. To limit, to gag—that's no solution. I am not idealizing capitalism; those who make use of the possibilities it still offers are in no way the "official" spokesmen for capitalist society; this is as true of Rolf Hochhuth or Heinrich Böll in Western Germany as it is of Peter Weiss in Sweden. But a nation's culture is seldom the product of "official" writers. In our country, too, those writers who really matter will be the ones who go forward, knock down barriers, clear the way.

How should culture be directed, then?

That's a question of cultural politics. I believe government should have one goal: to be in harmony with the strivings of avant-garde writers and artists. This raises a whole complex of questions connected with the autonomy of culture, the sort of questions frequently discussed in the West, especially in Italy. But we must be careful in understanding and following those foreign debates. Let's not forget that Italian or French communists are an opposition party and that they are talking about cultural autonomy within this revolutionary opposition which coexists with a much larger cultural domain based on quite different conceptions and ideas. Here, in our country, we don't want communist ideology to become diluted in a boundless sea of opinion; it must develop within a certain framework and its integrity must be preserved. But our situation differs from the situation of communists in capitalist countries, since we as the ruling power must be at the same time guardians of differing opinions, even opinions diametrically opposed to ours. As soon as we ignore this, we ignore a basic tenet of socialism. Where, then, are the real limits? I would say that the limit is the private ownership of the means of production and exploitation of man by man. This is the dividing line. But behind this line there is ample room for all sorts of concepts, ideas, and opinions.

Anyway, in art one must never become too dogmatic; one must

start with the work itself. Recently, in preparing an encyclopedia, we came across a certain Slovak writer who lived abroad. From a dogmatic viewpoint, this writer belonged to the émigré category, but looking at his actual work, we saw that he didn't fit this category at all, that he was quite close to our own authors. In this respect, we are in complete agreement with Lenin. Or take the Church. Popes John XXIII and Paul VI, in initiating reforms, were naturally concerned above all with the interests of the Church; nevertheless, these reforms had an important bearing on us, too. A way has now been found whereby a Catholic can live productively in a socialist country without coming into conflict with his conscience, and Catholics are extremely important for the building of socialism, nobody would deny that. The socialist world-view gains strength only in struggle, in conflict; it must continually rise above opposing ideologies, and if it ever fails to do so it will succumb. But if that were to happen, the defeat would result not from permitting conflict but from insufficient ideological vitality. After all, we shouldn't emulate the stance typical of the Church: Accept my faith and I will enable you to exist. It is essential to respect the opinions of others. Marx would never have become what he was if he had lacked that fundamental stimulus of conflict and strife which drove his thought forward.

I now had the feeling that something had still been left unsaid about the problems of the two national cultures and their common life within the republic.

Questions of Czech and Slovak literature are common questions; nothing is only Czech or only Slovak. When one half of the house is burning, sooner or later the other half will catch fire, too. I have already said that the problem of progress versus reaction cannot be fruitfully examined from the viewpoint of nationality. And it would be good if this same attitude were applied to everything. It would be good if everyone represented the entire Czechoslovak culture, if equality reigned and, except for administrative details, there was no division into Czech and Slovak. The worst thing of all is indifference, indifference to each other and to our mutual problems.

Both literature and cultures must enter into each other, must interweave. Take Talich,* for example. The Czechs say that we are

---

* Vaclav Talich, an outstanding Czech conductor accused of collaborating with the Nazis, found artistic asylum in Bratislava after the war.—*Ed.*

to be thanked for saving him. That's nice to hear, but there is another side to the matter which interests me, too: we have profited enormously from Talich. He played a great part in the creation and development of Slovak symphonic music. We mustn't be isolationists. Whenever we are tempted to go our separate ways and to loosen the common bonds of literature, we always come back to Salda. His warnings about the errors and the dangers of separatism are certainly clear enough.

There is something I have long wanted to ask you: When you look back at the literary battles of the 1920s and 1930s, when Salda was writing, how would you judge that era today? What passed the test of time and entered into the stream of literature? What perished with its own time?

I am not a theoretician and what I say will probably reveal more about myself than about literature. Well, then, at the beginning of this period—as is true at the beginning of any new movement—there was much overreaction and excess in all directions, and there was also tremendous devotion and enthusiasm. Perhaps today's younger generation has many of the same qualities and perhaps we don't see them quite clearly enough. I don't want to adopt the attitude of "when we were young, things were different."

The 1920s followed on the heels of World War I and the Russian Revolution, and similarly the years 1945 through 1950 followed a world war and we were virtually surrounded by revolution. And yet there was a difference between the two periods; the recent one was somehow less clearly defined. I explained this to myself by virtue of the fact that the recent societal changes, the whole revolution, came to us more or less ready-made. It didn't develop as a response to demands but somehow came to us out of the blue. Perhaps it has something to do with dogmatism, the cult of personality, or God knows what else, but the fact is that in the events of the 1940s we acted merely as executive organs carrying out a predetermined program, whereas in the twenties we were creators, we were hammering out a new concept. This creative phase may perhaps be compared to what happened after 1956, after the Twentieth Congress of the Communist Party of the USSR with its denunciation of the "cult."

What remains from the 1920s? As far as literature is concerned, I believe this era brought about a certain "civilizing," humanizing influence; it brought literature down to earth from its ivory tower. Of course this didn't happen all at once; authors like [Frana] Sramek and [S. K.] Neumann* provided the original impulse as if they sensed the winds of change. And this impulse became the subconscious heritage of young people and was transmitted over subsequent decades. Today, the revolution of that time is taken completely for granted, and the revolutionaries of those days are the honored national artists of today.

Again, what remains? First of all, it gave all of us a tremendous desire for liberty, freedom of thought and action. This attitude created difficult tensions and conflicts during the complex years of the 1940s. The same thing happened to many Czech poets and other artists of our generation. They simply weren't able to bear the burdens that society demanded of literature. This helps to explain why in periods of liberalization, when the situation that gave rise to conflicts is eased, people do not move forward but rather return to positions they held long before. In other words, the sense of liberation did not produce new artistic trends but rather brought us back to the principles of the 1920s. This is our curse and our blessing, and we can't help being what we are. Our cultural situation is unique; it has its unique place in the context of world socialism; it has its own specific past, its own tradition, its own specific youth.

To return to literature . . . Every current of that time made its contribution; one cannot say of any trend that it left no mark whatsoever. I don't like any one-sided exclusion or deification, and that's why I don't like statements such as the assertion that the only basis of the literary revolution of the 1920s was surrealism. Such absolute statements are misleading, and surrealism doesn't need them. Personally, I adhere to the philosophy that poetry should remain poetry and not become transmuted into other genres, but all sorts of means and methods can serve poetry; only the final result counts. I have never been a surrealist and I don't share the surrealist view of the world, but I greatly respect many of the movement's contributions. I'd say that this has an analogy in the case of the Bible. Take the Song of Songs, for example—it's great poetry, and no matter how a particular period feels about religion, it remains a source of poetic attraction and inspiration.

---

* Frana Sramek was an impressionist poet and writer who had a great influence on pre-World War I youth. S. K. Neumann was the principal poet of communism until his death in 1945. His grandson, a distinguished Stalinist poet, committed suicide in 1970 as a protest against the Soviet occupation of Czechoslovakia.—*Ed.*

What has changed? I like to read the manifestos of all literary schools, but I don't swear by any of them. After World War I there came a period when free verse became sacrosanct as the only expression of modernism; it became mandatory to break up the old forms. Teige attacked Nezval for writing poetry such as *Edison;* he accused him of denying his own self. But was this really so? In my judgment Nezval not only continued to be a great poet, but *Edison* actually represented further growth. Or consider Seifert. He, too, developed a virtually classical form, and if we were to compare some of his earlier pieces with *The TSF Waves,* we might accuse him, too, of "denying his own self." All the same, his achievement has marks of greatness; he developed the various trends and currents of the modern era, and at the same time he reached a Neruda-like transparency. Seifert's example will be discussed for a long time to come. You know, literary schools mix, intertwine, adopt, influence each other, and this is the basis of artistic progress.

Of course, the question of generations must be taken into account, too. One cannot expect different generations to have the same experiences, the same feelings Things that for us were holy are seen by the new generation with a different logic; the young have a new hierarchy of values and perceive their lives in new ways. It is a great error to suppose—in life or in literature—that one generation hands its heritage on to the next like a torch which will be carried farther and farther. On the contrary, every new generation brings along new problems and attitudes, which from the viewpoint of its elders seem as strange as if they had come from another galaxy. They will scoff at us, they will damn us, but we should be wise enough not to damn them. It is the banal truth that in the end they will find out quite a bit for themselves, and it is equally true that they will love their grandfathers more than their fathers. But above all, we must respect their differing sensibilities.

Your generation and mine have certain experiences in common: a world war—whether Wilhelm's or Hitler's—and a postwar atmosphere, and that's why we feel so many things in a similar way, even though we might look at them from a somewhat different angle. But what about today's generation? Does it think about war or not? I am impressed by its fearless attitude. I have advocated such fearlessness, and I certainly don't want to be an alarmist, yet on the other hand I wouldn't want young people to take current world problems too lightly. The threat of global conflict persists, and warnings to that effect mustn't be taken by the young simply as the mumblings of old fogies.

But to get away from the role of mentor . . . this whole business of the generations is quite complicated. Take mine, for example. The people in their sixties or fifties are divided by their life-experiences, their attitudes, the things they've lived through and endured. Some members of my generation prize their convictions above all else. Others still haven't reached this point yet, and according to their strength and skills still struggle to realize the ideals of their youth. Finally, the third group sits around, twiddles its thumbs, and observes with surprise that its accomplishments are greeted with so little enthusiasm by younger people. In every generation there are those who are satisfied and those who still seek. One group no longer strives, the other still does. I'd like to belong to the latter, but where is the strength, the strength? . . .

And the future?

I am not able to get up in the morning and say, "Look how beautiful the present is! Hurry for the future!" I am incapable of singing praises. I often feel that we had more faith than ability, that we promised more than was in us to give. And yet I am convinced that we were right, and that we're on the right road still, no matter how muddy the present stretch may be and no matter how many beautiful asphalt roads we see all around us. And I don't mean to say that as a socialist country we must be automatically in the right. Rather, I believe that we are justified by many other circumstances that are rooted in the past as well as in the present, in Czech and Slovak reality as well as in the world around us. I don't know why many things went wrong, but I think we must hold on to the basics and patiently go on repairing, remodeling, solving. We cannot hold on to something at all costs simply because it served a purpose in the past! Still, in all my experience with the world I have found no better method of solving its problems than socialism. The challenge is to find the road that leads to the true realization of true socialism. Of course, this is not easy. It never was and never will be. You know the commandment: In the sweat of thy face . . .

Two years later I went to see him at the sanatorium, to allow him to conclude his story. By that time I had already realized that there was no better way to begin this mosaic of the generations than to start with this man who belongs to the old and to the young equally, not only because of his life and work but also because of the tremendous confidence with which people of all ages turn to him, whether they agree with his opinions or not. He wasn't sick, just tired. I came to see him for an hour, and our visit turned out to last half a day, as usual. I asked him to talk about himself. Snow was falling, the atmosphere was full of hope, and we weren't sure whether we dared to hope again. It was January 1968.

As you know, I was born in Budapest. My parents come from Senica in southern Slovakia, but like all good Slovak artisans of the time my father learned his trade in Budapest and then stayed on there.

In those days, a person living in Hungary simply wasn't socially acceptable unless he spoke Hungarian. For that reason, my mother thought it important to send me to a Hungarian school. However, she also wanted me to stay in touch with my Slovak heritage, and so my sister and I used to spend our summers in Senica. Compared to Budapest, this was paradise. You jumped over the fence, ran across a couple of backyards, and you were free—out in the fields with the shepherds and cowherds. In 1919 my mother went to Senica for her brother's funeral, then was unable to return because of the outbreak of fighting between Hungary and Czechoslovakia.* I set out after her, right through the battle zone; I was caught by the soldiers but, seeing that I was only a boy of fourteen, they decided to help me get to my mother. This was the first time I passed through Leopoldov under armed guard. My real acquaintance with Leopoldov came only much later, after a prison for political offenders had been established there.

I did very poorly in school in Budapest. I don't want to blame this on nationality, but there was definitely a class factor involved. The war was going on, the school was full of the future Hungarian intelligentsia, and there was a prevalent opinion that the son of an artisan—unless he was really exceptional—should not aim too high. My mother was told: "I hope you are not under the delusion that your son will become a cabinet minister." In 1919 my mother enrolled me in the teachers' college at Modra [in Western Slovakia]. The students were for the most part sons of neighboring farmers,

---

* From the summer of 1919 until the signing of the Treaty of Trianon on June 20, 1920, the two nations clashed over newly drawn borders.—*Ed.*

among whom I had a good chance to excel. I had graduated from Budapest schools, I had a metropolitan outlook, I had read a great deal, and even though my Slovak was not too good, I was outstanding in everything else. The professors were for the most part Czechs; they were impressed by my knowledge of literature and by the fact that I had picked it up on my own. They praised me, and praise can work miracles.

In those days I wrote my first poetry and it was printed in a couple of small reviews. As an "expert" on literature I was, of course, primarily interested in the moderns, especially the avant-garde Devetsil group headed by Karel Teige. I began to read Salda's early poems, and on a school trip to Prague I picked up Neumann's *Red Songs*. I liked those poems very much, they were so beautifully provocative; and so for the first time the word "proletarian" made its appearance in my school notebooks. There was a bit of adolescent bravura in it, too, a kind of raising of dark spirits to see what would happen. In the end I passed my examination and came to Bratislava.

At that time Bratislava had a wonderful book store, Misak's, where one could browse freely—an ideal place for people who like to approach things in an irregular, disorganized, piecemeal fashion. During this period I met the poet Jiri Wolker and became acquainted with his *Difficult Hour,* as well as with other literary works that weren't widely known, especially in Slovakia. Soon I met a whole group of leftists and with their help I began to contribute to communist publications. In those days Gottwald maintained the wise position that we were extremely useful to the party and that the future depended on the building up of party intelligentsia in Slovakia. And so I came to *DAV* [the most influential left wing magazine in Slovakia during the 1930s] and to [Vladimir] Clementis.*

I'd be doing an injustice to my own past if I didn't also mention [the Slovak poet] Jan Smrek, who even at that time already had a significant reputation as a poet. It would be hard for me to say today who had a greater influence on my development—Teige, Nezval, or he. Nezval fascinated me, partly because he was a poet of the left but, above all, because he was a great poet. I was greatly impressed by this combination of poet and politically engaged

* A founder of *DAV* and the Slovak avant-garde. Clementis served as Foreign Minister of Czechoslovakia and was sentenced and hanged as a result of the Slansky trials.—*Ed.*

man. The local Slovak developments interested me far less than
the activities of Seifert, Nezval, the Devetsil group. Gottwald once
asked me to do some work for him in the editorial offices of *Pravda
Chudoby* [the weekly newspaper of the Slovak Communist Party,
1921–1925]. I had always had an exalted picture of a literary editor,
surrounded by an imposing desk and a battery of telephones, but
when I saw what a real editorial office was like I lost much of my
enthusiasm. It was too late to back out, however. So I used to sit on
a pile of newspapers, since there wasn't even an extra chair in the
room, and help out as best I could.

Practical politics and poetry—how do they mix?

I don't know. I can't say whether I have managed to combine the
two successfully, and I am really a political amateur. But it is hard
for me to imagine a life without politics, not in the sense of a profession but as a citizen's legitimate concern. I can't imagine any
subject on which I as a citizen should not speak out. And surely
this kind of concern is compatible with poetry. Certainly, it ties
the poet's hands to some extent, but it is a tradition in our country
that literary men play a double role—that of *homo politicus* and
that of poet. It's the only state of affairs I have ever known. That's
why I have always been repelled by the opinion that a poet should
write his verses and stay out of politics, even when this opinion was
expressed by my own friends. As far as practical politics are concerned I am an ignoramus, but take someone like Teige—he was a
skillful politician besides being a poet. Of course, he was not a high
party functionary.

*What happens when a poet becomes a government official dealing
with cultural matters?*

I have no idea whether I have acquitted myself badly or well. I
simply did what I considered right, both as a poet and as a human
being. These two things can never be separated, not even in the
kind of position we're talking about. And this implies a certain relationship to people. In 1950, when my activities or lack of them
were being closely reviewed, I asked one of the comrades who was
criticizing me what he would have done in my place, how he would
have behaved as head of the Department of Culture and Education.
"You should have done the same thing as our German comrades,"
he said; namely, fire the entire teacher corps and then, from the

ranks of those who had been let go, select capable people to form
new cadres. I must admit that such an idea had never even occurred
to me. On the contrary, I felt myself duty-bound to follow Lenin's
dictum that in cultural revolutions, as in all revolutions generally,
it is best to make do with available people, just as they are. I was
later confronted with many errors of this kind. For example, I
understood the principle of "democratization" in higher education
to mean, primarily, getting rid of "eternal students" and outspoken
enemies of the social system. I regarded the wholesale dismissal of
students as practiced after February as an expression of lack of faith
in our schools and in their educational capabilities. I am sorry that
my successors were faced with the thankless task of completing this
process, which marred the attitude of an entire generation of young
people toward our socialist state. This—truly and sincerely—is
my greatest regret.

You reminded me about Talich. I suppose I understood his significance for national culture better than a true political professional would have. I was also attacked for providing a haven in
Bratislava to Prof. [Bohumil] Nemec.* But for me he was not a
right wing opponent of Benes, but an extremely progressive botanist
who had at one time allowed himself to be politically exploited. Or
[Karel] Jernek [the stage director]. Here again, the significant question was not his politics, but his great skill as a stage director. After
the war a certain party line opposed teaching German and performing the music of Beethoven and Wagner. Slovaks who didn't
follow this rule were suspected of Nazi sympathies. Today all this
seems ridiculous, but in those days perhaps it took a poet to judge
how important such trends and currents really were.

Even in the light of subsequent events I still maintained my basic
position, that as a political figure I was given certain opportunities
which it was my duty to grasp. I'm not sure exactly when the conflict
between my two roles—of communist official and of poet—first
broke out. Who won? I personally lost the battle, yet I am still convinced that these two roles cannot be combined. I say this despite
the fact that my dossier was adorned with numerous accusations
of the kind I have just described.

In any case, even when a poet isn't called upon to practice politics
professionally, it is still his duty to interest himself in everything

* The world-famous Czech biologist who was a right-wing candidate for the
Presidency of the Republic against Benes in 1935.—*Ed.*

that concerns the nation and the world. He can express this interest in his poems, if he likes. Which doesn't mean, of course, that he must write something like Neumann's *Red Songs.*

There was one other role, too: of poet-soldier.

You exaggerate somewhat, if you are thinking of my part in the Uprising. It was primarily a matter of those who carried arms, namely the soldiers and partisans. But I was neither a soldier nor a partisan, though naturally this didn't free me from the duty of serving the goals of the Uprising. These were, in brief, the desire to return Slovakia to the fold of democratic and freedom-loving people and to gain for Slovakia a more honorable place than it had had heretofore.

We felt that the best way to achieve our goals would be by overcoming Slovak separatism and by close cooperation between the Slovak and Czech people within a new Czechoslovak republic. This republic was to be based on new principles, not those of the pre-Munich era. These are still our goals and principles; in fact, today we believe in them more than ever before.

We were never opposed to a Slovak state as an autonomous home of the Slovak people. On the contrary, we engaged in conflict—occasionally armed conflict—precisely because it was not autonomous but, from the very beginning, only a product of Nazi machinations and, to the very end, tied to its fascist origins. In other words, we opposed the Slovak state *as it existed,* not *because it existed.* We stood for the re-establishment of Czechoslovakia not because we felt that the Slovak people had any need to play second fiddle along the lines of the pre-Munich model. Rather, we had faith that the aspirations of the Slovak people, after its wartime agonies, would find their best expression in a new Czechoslovakia and in close harmony with the Czechs. I did as much as I could in this direction.

You yourself mentioned your dossier. I never asked you about this . . .

At first I didn't understand the accusations made against me, and I succumbed to the impression—as did the whole party—that the fault must lie within me, and that the so-called "criminal activity" must be the consequence of my failings, my political errors. So I accepted the accusations and constantly tried to convince myself that I must bear the consequence of my errors. Of course, in jail I began to realize that this was all nonsense, and that the whole thing was based on *a priori* lack of confidence in people. Later I realized, too, that this was no personal duel between the state prosecutor and Laco Novomesky, but that I was condemned by a small clique of people who felt they had the right to dictate ways of behaving, thinking, and living, and who judged not on the basis of one's actions or contributions, but on the style of one's mind, one's way of thinking.

There is something else which belongs here more than might seem at first glance. I always had a very special feeling about Masaryk. He always struck me as being a decent and clear-headed man and I believed that his humanistic democracy was a step in the direction of Marxism. Even the Communist Party at one time saw Masaryk in this light, in spite of areas of conflict. I was therefore greatly surprised that, after 1948, we tried to sever ourselves completely from him, even to take down statues erected in his honor. And now I know that this was a mistake. In the final analysis, we owe our existence to the fact that he preceded us and prepared the ground.

After you were released, you wrote so many poems . . .

Poetry always supported me and never deserted me. Even in the worst times I expressed my truth in unwritten poems. My spoken dialogues with Gottwald took the form of poems, too. After my release there was no possibility of political activity; they didn't want me to return to Slovakia or to be in touch with my friends, so I sat in Prague and wrote a great deal. Perhaps you can see from these poems how much I longed to see socialism in our country turned into something better. I was greatly depressed by my years in prison; I was ashamed that I was a walking example of the horrors of a system that also calls itself socialism. I was free, Clementis was dead, and I decided it would be better not to make things any worse. In my collection *From That Other Place* there is a poem which says that bad as things are I have no right to be bitter about myself or my past. Socialism can take other forms, too, and perhaps the kind of experiences I have undergone will eventually give rise to a genuine socialism.

It was January 1968. And I was ashamed to think about the way in which the little man sitting high in Hradcany Castle had dealt with the letters that this great man had written him after returning from darkness and horror—letters written in the foolish hope which we all shared at times: that voices trembling with care about our socialist future would be listened to by our leaders, or at least be heard by them.

January 1965–January 1968

Ester Krumbachová

Studied at the Arts and Crafts School in Prague. Because of political persecution, she had to work in a factory for a time in the 1950s and later got a job as a stage hand. She started designing scenery and costumes, first for the theater, then for films. Later, she published a book of short stories and wrote the screenplays of films directed by Jan Nemec (*The Party and the Guests, The Martyrs of Love*) and Vera Chytilova (*Daisies, A Tree in Paradise*).

Ester Krumbachová

It wasn't long ago that her name began to appear on theater pro-grams, and theater audiences learned to look for the wonderfully expressive costumes which she designed. Her creations had an unmistakable, personal quality, an inventiveness that had been sadly lacking in our productions for a long time. Her occasional stories, which first came out in Literarni Noviny, *may one day be collected in a book. But it has been only within the last few years that the extraordinary and multifaceted talents of this petite woman came to full fruition in a medium which could do full justice to her literary and philosophic vision: the film. She wrote the script for two major "New Wave" films by Jan Nemec—*The Martyrs of Love *and* The Party and the Guests—*as well as for a recent film by Vera Chytilova,* Daisies, *and worked on quite a few others.*

Her apartment is full of plants, books, and paintings. An oleander stands in the hall. Apparently there was no room for it among the Becketts on the bookshelves, or between the Mirós and Hieronymus Bosches on the walls. There are more plants, pictures, and books until you reach the glass doors and go out on the balcony, which isn't really a balcony at all but a miniature Garden of Semiramis.

You know, no carpenter ever set foot in this house. I did every-thing myself.

I had been preparing for this interview for a long time. I knew what I wanted to ask, but I had hardly gotten out my pencil and pad when the little blonde with those extraordinarily intense eyes bubbled over . . .

Before we begin, I must really tell you something. Even as a young girl, right after the war, I belonged to all the youth brigades; I ate plain bread and drank plain water, and though I never joined the party I was full of enthusiasm for its cause. In those days we learned to regard the rest of the world very skeptically, especially America and American prosperity. The trouble is that when you learn to look skeptically at anything, at other people, you inevitably learn to be skeptical about yourself as well.

What does it mean to think correctly, anyway? When do you stop thinking? Where is the barrier? Whenever I look at a painting, I always ask myself how the painter knew when the picture was finished. I suppose that when you paint or write or think, you try to go as far as you can, and just stop when you can't go any further.

I'll show you what I mean. It's winter. You're feeding the birds. You have a nice, warm, sentimental feeling because you just gave some tasty crumbs to a sparrow. You watch him hop away—and at the streetcorner a cat pounces on him and gobbles him up. If you're a moralist, you may get very angry at the cat. But if you give up your moralistic attitude, you may find out that the poor cat hadn't eaten in four days, while the sparrow was caught only because he was so fat he could hardly move. But of course you shouldn't stop here either; you should go on. There's a gentleman sitting by a window, munching a chicken leg; he's watched the whole tragedy. He picks up a shotgun and blows the cat to smithereens. Morally, he was obviously in the right. But you go over and ask him why he shot the cat, and you may find out that he'd just bought a new gun and was itching to try it out. Or perhaps he was simply a sadist. You see, this is the sort of theme that interests me.

And now let me go back to the beginning: when you are in the midst of creating something or thinking about something, you can't stop until you reach the limit, the immovable wall.

Superficial people, burdened by all kinds of ideologies, always regard the results of honest thinking as dangerous, as a plot of some sort. You encounter that type of mentality all the time. But you cannot exist only within carefully prescribed bounds nor can you say anything about the cat until you've learned the whole story. Otherwise your ideas become fuzzy. After all, a person doesn't think *against* anybody else, nor *for* anybody else, but simply against himself, against the darkness within himself.

I wanted to explore other strata of her mind. Also, I wanted to learn about her youth.

I'm not sure my life is worth recounting. For a time, at the end of the war, I wasn't even sure whether life was worth living. I resolved this question only when I was about thirty. That's how deeply I was marked by the wartime experience. I longed for justice with an almost Puritan passion. For a while I studied in Brno; I majored in a field called "artistic trades," but I had all sorts of problems and I left. I think that my basic feeling was my inability to recognize any authority over me. But the Brno school had one great advantage: It taught me how to work with my hands, and now I can make just about anything, even scenery.

As I said, I had a lot of trouble with authority. For instance, I would return the official party greeting with some casual reply like "Ahoy there!" Or I'd ignore instructions on the size of the red flag in one of my posters. For such transgressions I'd often find myself out of work for long periods. And then they said that I was too smart, too bright for my own good. That was intended as an insult. But in reality I am not at all conceited, and I don't try to use intelligence for any ulterior purposes. I suppose that's characteristic of the female mentality; women don't like to puff themselves up too much. I am much more interested in men, anyway, though they are far more dangerous. Even in the erotic sense. Their aggressiveness has little to do with love; it's actually closer to war . . .

The conversation turned to her wartime adventures.

Toward the end of the war, after my return to Brno, I used to take occasional trips to a nearby estate to sketch farm animals. Prisoners of war of various nationalities worked on the estate as farm hands. I got into the habit of bringing them little presents of food, and I'd take their letters back to be mailed. One day, a Czech prisoner with whom I had become acquainted asked me to smuggle a roll of paper back to town for him. I was quite frightened, but I told him I would do it. The next day he brought the roll and just as he was handing it to me one of the German SS guards appeared in the doorway of the barn. I will never forget his face; he had a kind of small mustache like villains in French films. I smiled at him, quickly covered up the illicit package with my sketch pad, and proceeded to draw a cow. He stood behind me, watched me for about fifteen minutes without saying a word, then left. I grabbed the roll and, shaking with fear, carried it to the address given to me by the prisoner. In my excitement I'd forgotten the house number, so it took me quite a while to find the right apartment. An elderly lady came to the door and I turned the package over to her. She laughed, unwrapped the roll, spread it out on the floor—and it turned out to contain awful cartoons of German guards in all sorts of grotesque situations, sitting on the latrine, using chamber pots, and so on. In short, the ugliest drawings I've ever seen. The old woman laughed and said: "That's nothing, the boys want to have some fun; just tell him it's safe right here under the sofa."

This silly episode depressed me for a long time. You try to be as honorable and useful as you can, and then you learn that you've risked your life for nothing at all, for a piece of childish nonsense. You have no idea how ashamed I was at the time . . .

To come back to your present work—how do you reconcile your work in the theater with your activities in film?

If I were a director, there probably would be no conflict. But in the case of a writer or designer the situation is quite different.

And yet directing for the stage is not quite the same as directing films . . .

A stage is not simply space in which imagination is free to roam. It is space which must be analyzed, understood, delineated. And in that space human beings and objects have their lives. I wish that I had one more life to live, then I'd devote more time to the theater. In school, theater was reduced to specialized categories in the curriculum—costume, stage design, and so on. In this way, one could approach the work in a fresh, unburdened way; that is to say, in a dilettante way. I'd like to be able to approach film in the same innocent manner. But it isn't easy. Just imagine standing on an empty stage, without any esthetic preconceptions or ideas. I think that only artists like Miró or Klee are able to create in this way, without myths. Of course, you must know a great deal before you can attempt to realize your freedom. But nobody, neither your predecessors nor your contemporaries, can teach you anything except precisely this freedom. Klee cannot give you his little squares, but only the freedom of his conception as represented in his work.

Where is your studio?

Everywhere you look—the floor, the walls, the table. Whenever I am involved in a project I start drawing like mad. Right now I am making designs for several films, including films for which someone else wrote the scripts—and I have just gone through some 300 drawings. Just look at my calluses! They come from the special pen I use. I try to study people, to observe them and to catch their special flavor, their individuality. Characters in films must be whole, complete persons; everything must fit them down to the last detail. This perfectionism can be turned upside down, too: I am intrigued with the idea of experimenting with a master pattern in which all characters would be molded, and which would transcend their individual idiosyncrasies. It might be an interesting experiment in costume design.

You mentioned Klee. What is your attitude to Western art in general?

I am interested in many types of arts; one has to know as much as one can learn . . . but let me try to answer your question somewhat differently. Recently I was visited by some French cultural officials. They were very enthusiastic about my work and told me that I must leave at once . . . for Paris, London, and God knows where else. I tried to explain to them that even though their advice was well-meant, it was based on a fundamental misunderstanding. Some people believe that even though we ourselves have chosen this rather uncomfortable way of life we really live in this country by some sort of mistake and are always longing to be elsewhere. But my roots are here, and they go very deep; and the roots of my work are here, too. I could easily have gone abroad; that wasn't the problem. I may live on the dirtiest street in Prague, but that too is part of my life and my work, and it probably couldn't be otherwise.

Since you asked about foreign art, I should mention the tremendous impact that classic Chinese opera had on me. I felt enormous poetic power emanate from the Chinese stage, and when the lovers slowly pointed at each other without their fingers ever touching, I felt shivers running down my back. I am convinced that an artist should have an especially strong feeling for those two fingers that never touch.

Lately I have thought about a great many things other than art ... about bread and wine and the right to having your own personal tastes ...

And so we're back home again.

I believe that what's going on in our cultural life has its deep roots in the people. An excavation process is taking place; many layers that have covered reality are being shoveled aside, illusions of all kinds are being discarded, and something very valuable is beginning to appear: conscience. I am convinced that this country has a strong sense of conscience, which has taken the form of a desire to know the root causes of events and to grasp their interconnections. Unfortunately, however, there are still too many people among us who are narrowly orthodox, who measure everything against some dogma.

It is widely assumed nowadays that the ferment in Czech culture is a response to the events of the 1950s and to certain specific political events. I believe that the current cultural activity goes much deeper, and that it is an attempt to resolve problems that have been present in our cultural life for the past century and a half.

Recently, a German director who was here on a visit confided in me that he had never encountered so many ardent, intellectually excited people before. Certainly the atmosphere of round-the-clock discussion and argument that has come to characterize our country indicates that something basic and important is taking place.

(*I recalled an incident that was quite typical in this connection. In the summer of 1965, a group of us were visiting a film festival in Italy, and after a merry-go-round whirl of activities Milos Forman* [*director of* Loves of a Blonde *and other films*] *took us for a brief rest to a particularly beautiful spot which was serenely free of tourists. Late that night, driving back from Rimini, someone remarked with a laugh: "Do you think anybody in Prague would believe us if we told them we spent this whole gorgeous day discussing nothing but the situation back home?" This kind of involvement is rather unusual in the world today, and it explains a great deal.*)

I have often been accused of being a cynic, simply because I refused to believe everything I was told. I think that Hitler showed quite clearly what happens when humanism is replaced by grandiose goals and projects. Concentration camps, the occupation—those were fantastic realities which showed people as they really are. That's why it is no longer possible to get down on your knees and offer up thanks to God. Gods have vanished, and so have myths and illusions about the goodness of man. But some people remain children; they are incapable of abstraction and confuse symbols with realities. But that's another story . . .

Life can be broken up into small segments: first you learn what is going on, then you learn what is happening to you, and finally you learn who you are. Only then can you begin to find out what you can do, and you learn that it really doesn't amount to very much. This is true even of the giants, like Bach or Vivaldi. They spent their entire lives developing a certain circumscribed area, and their possibilities were limited. No real artist can be expected to perform all sorts of somersaults. Only a person with no real moral sense can jump from one thing to another. A moral man develops his own area of usefulness as best he can. And he has only a limited repertory of choices.

Many of us like to lean on an intellectual doctrine which conceals our own contributions. We must get rid of idols. It is difficult enough for us to understand one another; there is so much coldness, such a terrible winter between us. No use denying it. We must remove all superficial layers and sediments, carefully and honestly, until we feel the truth between our fingers. And when you get to the bottom, when you uncover the foundations and find that they are not very pretty, you will also find that the most fundamental truths of our time are revealed by people who are unhappy, alienated, desperate.

Why are you so attracted by the cinema?

I am fascinated by the harmonious interplay of the huge number of components that make up a film. In other ways, too, a film resembles a Gothic cathedral. The painter paints, the sculptor contributes his talents, the large army of people who contribute to a film remains more or less anonymous. It seems to me that anonymity is one of the truths of the twentieth century (think of the army, politics, freedom fighters, the resistance movement). Anonymity suits me quite well, except of course for anonymous letters. Our century simply has its own characteristic art form, and that is the cinema. It is still quite new, practically *terra incognita.* And it is characteristic of the twentieth century that this art form is simultaneously an industrial product, and this duality is a source of a host of problems.

We live in an age of film. We are no longer informed about events by a town crier or drummer, but by television and all kinds of visual media. And it seems to me that the cinema is a more accessible medium than an art gallery. Not because there are more movie houses than galleries, but because films stimulate a different kind of participation. People of our time love the wonders of technology, and film is one of them. It is one opiate that really works. Of course, it is essential to understand the fundamental basis of every art form. Toward the end of his life, Klee painted a big colored canvas onto a big white canvas in order to stress the nature of color and the nature of canvas and the relationship between the two. After completing the film *The Martyrs of Love,* I realized that the story of the three people could not be told in any other medium or art form. Their fate required a motion picture for its expression. And this is the essence of the cinema: nothing limits you, neither space nor time.

But surely there are analogous aspects in literature, in theater . . .

Yes, I suppose so. I overstated the case because people look down on film; they don't believe that filmmakers can ever reach the same level of expression as artists in other areas, a Klee or a Faulkner.

And yet film involves many unique means of expression, many elements in addition to speech. When an author states in a book that a host had a vase of artificial flowers on the table, this tells you very little, whereas in a film such a vase could function as an important and organic part of the story. And where but in film can you show beauty in the foreground, beauty in the background, while in between the two levels appears an ordinary, vulgar face!

You are referring to The Party and the Guests?

Yes. It took a lot of long, hard work before the script was written and the film was finally shot. You have to say everything you know about your subject, and you can stop only when your theme has been completely exhausted. I am afraid I keep repeating myself. Faulkner's statement is absolutely correct, too: every work leaves the author with a sense of shipwreck . . .

I was very interested in the audience reaction. When the film was shown in a Prague theater, the response was terrific, people laughed and applauded; they were as amused by our attack on stupidity as if they had been witnessing a classical comedy. And I was told by the director, Jan Nemec, that the showing was followed by a serious and highly intelligent discussion. There was similar audience participation when the film was shown in one of the school theaters. All this is terribly important—the desire of people to understand and to discuss.

How did this film come about? I am sure you know people who are the embodiment of apathy, who manage to survive everything, adapt to anything. That's how the theme originated, as an attack on indifference. I don't mind the most ordinary person, as long as he wants something, no matter how stupid it may be. But I cannot forgive indifference.

Daisies actually deals with a similar theme. The heroines of the film are two naive young girls intimately portrayed. There is always the risk of blackmail in such films by easily gaining the viewer's sympathy, by winning his affection. But the main point of the film was concerned with apathy: the heroines would remain untouched and unmoved even if dead bodies were falling around them.

In *The Party and the Guests,* the main creative element was distorted dialogue. I tried to create conversation in which the characters said nothing meaningful about themselves. The audience heard only isolated fragments of sentences, as if they had walked suddenly into the midst of a sophisticated party and had no idea what the conversation was about. Some critics claimed to have found hidden meanings in the fragments, but it was my intention to demonstrate that people generally talk only in terms of disconnected ideas, even when it appears that they are communicating with one another. I tried not to mimic real speech but to suggest its pattern, to find a language for the sort of phenomenon that Ionesco discovered in drama.

Not a single word in the film was intended as a secret code; the dialogues were not intended to conceal anything but to reveal the nonsense we hear around us every day. In the past, heroes used words to express tragic situations. Now, tragedy is revealed by pictures, and our words have no relationship to what we see. Newspapers and television are full of the killed and wounded, and people sit around with legs crossed and sip coffee. I know that all this is connected with the development of communication media, but all the same it is hard to accept.

Ionesco consciously looks for absurdity, not only in language but in the real world as well. He conceives of the world as absurdity. I do not share this view. I tried to use paradoxes and absurdities to characterize people who fail to utter a single reasonable word and whose opinions are ridiculous—yet the ultimate result is tragic.

The Party and the Guests thus developed from a fairly clear initial concept. *Daisies* was improvised to a much greater degree. There was a lot of last-minute writing and thinking, and this is what makes film so interesting. The heroines are a pair of silly young girls, but they could just as well have been two generals. They talk a lot of nonsense, mix everything up, and the inevitable catastrophe follows.

Do you believe there is such a thing as a feminine approach to reality, to creativity?

The feminine temperament is, of course, quite different from the masculine. We live and function in a man's world. We live in the twentieth century, yet in many respects it is still hard for a woman to get along without a man. Particularly in the social sense. We are still living as guests in a man's world. Naturally this also implies a certain advantage for women, since we can laugh at the world made by men. Generally a woman isn't a fan of this or that soccer team, and so she can laugh at the antics of men who get so worked up about a silly game that they start fighting with each other. It's hard to define the woman's outlook precisely, but I think there's no question but that women are more spontaneous. They don't filter everything through reason. And yet they have brains. You know what I mean. When a woman is in love, she'll run over sharp stones or through the mud; she's capable of a demonic force quite different from male abandon. And men and women take different things seriously. It would be good if all these traits could be more mixed up.

Basically, of course, all this isn't very important. True respect is earned only by thought—a man's or a woman's—real, honest thought, which can't be squeezed into any stereotype.

We stopped, not because there was nothing more to say, but because even the dynamic Ester Krumbachova can get tired. In the course of the interview, which lasted several hours, she managed to prepare a meal that would put a first-class restaurant to shame, answered a dozen telephone calls, and spoke to me about numerous fascinating matters which for one reason or another could not be included here. Czech culture was always fortunate in its women. Whether they have received all they deserve in return remains a moot question.

Autumn 1966

Milan Kundera

Born 1929 in Brno. Wrote poetry, studied film directing and script writing at the Prague Film School (FAMU), where he later became a teacher. His book of poems, *The Last May* (1955), was a portrayal of Julius Fucik, a hero of the communist anti-Nazi resistance in Czechoslovakia, in Nazi prison. His other book of poems, *Monologues* (1957), a series of confessions of lovelorn and frustrated women, was considered too brutal, pessimistic, and erotic and in spite of enormous reader interest the book was not allowed to be reprinted until some years later. In 1960 he published an essay on the work of one of the greatest modern Czech novelists Vladislav Vancura, *The Art of the Novel*. This was followed in 1962 by a successful play, *Owners of the Keys* (Majitele klicu). Stories originally published in magazines were later collected in two books, *Ridiculous Loves* and *More Ridiculous Loves*. His novel *The Joke* (1967), one of the most penetrating indictments of the futile cruelty of the Stalinist period in Czechoslovakia, was filmed by Jaromil Jires. At the Fourth Writers' Congress in 1967 Kundera delivered a keynote speech, dealing with the position and role of the Czech nation and its culture in the European context. It could be published in full only after the suspension of censorship in 1968. In 1968–1969 he published the third book of *Ridiculous Loves* and a play, *Two Ears, Two Marriages*. His second novel, *Life Is Somewhere Else,* will be published in France in 1972.

Milan Kundera

My first contact with the manuscript of The Joke was in the spring of 1966. I held it in my hands for a long time, so long that my arms were burned by the strong spring sun and hurt for two days. So did my heart. And then the pain went away and all that remained was admiration. Admiration for literature, for Kundera's courage, his laughter, his ability to see everything—including his own life— in a comic perspective. We are too grave about our lives; we moan and wring our hands and curse and explain and beg for understanding, and yet most likely what we need, above all, is the courage to laugh at our existence and through laughter to clear the way for understanding. And in this way we earn the right to laugh at cowards, at those who refuse to understand. We desperately need laughter—evil, ironic, malicious, heartless, mocking laughter. All of us as individuals and all of us together. Perhaps then at last we'll be able to come to our senses, to stand up and walk erect. Yes, it is a difficult road, but it's the only road from Bohemia to Europe, the only road into the world in the second half of the twentieth century. Naturally, there is a human being behind the laughing face, a human life—mine, yours, his . . .

He entered the world of art through the portals of music. He studied piano with his father, a former rector of JAMU [Janacek Academy of Music, in Brno], a pupil of [the composer Leos] Janacek

and one of the first interpreters of his piano compositions. And as a
young boy he began studying composition under Paul Haas . . .

Paul was the brother of the actor Hugo Haas, and was one of the most remarkable composers that we produced between the two wars. Yet he was relatively unknown, another victim of the handicap of growing up in Brno. I was ten or eleven at the time, and it was actually more like a game than serious study, but Haas belongs in my personal pantheon. Even my first published poem, a peculiarly morbid piece, was entitled "To the Memory of Paul Haas." During the occupation, he was forced to move from one apartment to another, and I followed him with my notebook to the very end, when he shared a single room with several other Jews. At last they dragged him off to the Terezin camp, where he died.

My next teacher was Vaclav Kapral, and I studied with him until his death. He was my father's closest friend, a sensitive and humorous man, and it was from him that I learned to love various kinds of mysticism. His musical world was rather narrow, yet within his limits he was a master.

Perhaps my lifelong weakness for artists *minorum gentium* had its origins in my love for Haas and Kapral. The history of art is cruel and forgetful. It comes down to a few remarkable geniuses by which an epoch can be grasped and explained; all the rest are simply cast aside. [Bohuslav] Martinu is certainly a greater composer than Kapral—though in the long run even Martinu will be classed as a minor artist—and yet Kapral wrote two or three compositions which are unique and irreplaceable. His wonderfully pure *Lullabyes* would be famous if only they bore the signature of someone like Martinu. As it is, they are forgotten and even if they were ever recorded it is unlikely that such a record would find many buyers. People orient themselves in the garden of culture according to public signs; they all push their way along the same crowded paths. Few strike out on their own, to find their own values. It is a pity. The works most valuable for a person are those which he discovers on his own and which become part of his life's adventure. I am always moved by certain compositions of Zoltan Kodaly, for example, even though Kodaly has been all but lost behind the huge silhouette of Bela Bartok. And I will never forget my first experience with the music of [the French composer Charles] Koechlin, a composer almost unknown here. In the same way, the

Lithuanian poet O. W. de Lubicz Milosz (also known as Milasios) whom I had translated from the French has a greater significance for me than someone like Guillaume Apollinaire, simply because Apollinaire stood on the main road whereas Milosz was my own discovery, found along an untrammeled path.

You referred before to the "Brno handicap." Do you know Vaclav Havel? He expressed it in a drawing: a sheet of paper, completely blank except for the word "Prague" in tiny print.

For many years now I have been living mainly in Prague, but I know Brno quite well. It is an odd town. Neither completely metropolitan nor provincial. It has all the prerequisites for becoming a cultural center, a metropolis: it has its own specific hinterland, Moravia; it has a university, art schools, its own cultural traditions. In a word, Brno has in a relatively smaller degree everything that Prague has—yet the prerequisites never turn into reality. Brno may give birth to noted literary historians, painters, composers, violinists, they may spend their whole active lives in that city, yet no matter how good their work may be they will never reach national awareness, because the brain of this national consciousness is Prague.

We have mentioned Haas and Kapral. Both of them had their works performed in Brno innumerable times. Kapral was even performed in Barcelona and Paris, yet he is rarely heard in Prague. And so the Czech cultural brain hardly took notice of these composers. Brno is an example of a place eternally on the verge of becoming a cultural center, of putting forth quite justified claims in this regard, and yet somehow never quite making it.

And Janacek?

Jenufa was performed in Brno as early as 1904, but until the opera was produced in Prague, in 1916, the Czech cultural brain failed to take much notice, even though Janacek was highly respected in Brno and had strong and vocal supporters there. Now he is finally honored on a national scale, but I believe that he's still regarded as a somewhat mysterious phenomenon, as if he had slipped into Czech culture from the "outside." Because whatever happens outside of Prague is considered somehow foreign. It seems significant to me that one of the people who did most to gain acceptance for Janacek—Max Brod—was a German Jew and thus a person who was also an outsider from the viewpoint of Czech culture. Besides, I think that the characteristic anxiety in Janacek's music, that basic semantic element in Janacek's work from the early years of this century, is closely related to this Brno sense of being left out, to this lonely and isolated life outside the mainstream. But even if unfavorable conditions in Brno paradoxically helped Janacek find himself, this was an exception; these conditions are as a rule destructive.

And your father?

After the First World War, he was offered a position as professor at the conservatory in Prague. If he had accepted, he probably could have enjoyed a successful concert career. But after four years of war and two more of his wanderings as a legionnaire, my father wanted to spend some time at home with his parents, and he wanted to be near Janacek. Besides, he liked Brno. He probably had no idea what a tremendous difference there is between the life of a pianist in Prague and in Brno. But even if he had understood this, it probably wouldn't have altered his decision, because he is a man whose lack of ambition and gentle timidity are almost incredible. I remember a trip he once took with other JAMU professors to Znojmo. They were treated with outstanding hospitality, and my father drank more than was his custom, probably out of politeness. The next day there was a festive gathering; they were founding some sort of society which bore a long and impressive name. As a rector, my father had to play a leading role and he behaved as always: he smiled shyly, held himself back, said little, shook hands with academicians and members of the government, founded the society and returned home. And nobody guessed that all this time he was suffering from a tremendous hangover and hardly knew what was going on. He even blocked out all memory of having been present at the ceremony. I cite this as proof that nothing could sway my father from his habitual gentleness and kindness.

Did he have a big influence on you?

Yes. I was fascinated by his grasp of a composition, by the manner in which he played so that in his rendition each note was given a meaning, every *crescendo* and *ritardando* became justified and significant. To this day I enjoy listening secretly, on the other side of the door, to my father lecturing or explaining some measure to his students, who are mostly concert pianists. I have come to understand the essence of the interpreter's art, and I know that the concert public does not appreciate it properly. The public looks for bravura, glitter or at best a certain suggestiveness of performance. The average listener is unaware of the innermost task of the interpreter, which is one of understanding—how to understand a particular musical phrase, what meaning to give this or that note. Every concert is a great misunderstanding between performer and public. Just imagine, my father was all but disqualified as a pianist—he stopped concertizing twenty years ago—only because his memory was poor and he had to have his music in front of him! Those fools, those snobs! You know, I am very fond of music but I have always disliked the musical environment, even in my early youth. Musicians are generally not particularly witty. Musicians are often rather limited, and I saw that my father suffered among them. The thought that I might spend my whole life only among musicians gave me goose pimples.

And so you turned to literature . . .

When I was fourteen or fifteen, I began to write poems. My cousin Ludvik, nine years older than I, belonged to the Prague-Brno group of late wartime surrealists, including artists and sculptors such as Zikmund, Lacina, Tikal, Istler, and the poet Lorenc. Of course, I didn't know these people; I was probably prevented from meeting them by my congenital shyness, and so for a long time cousin Ludvik personified for me the literary world. With his help, one of my poems was published and, as a result, Jan Grossmann informed me that he would like to meet me. So I took the train to Prague. I was in my teens, and during the entire train ride I tried to think up interesting ideas to use in my conversation with a man whom I worshipped like Socrates. Grossmann, who at that time held a minor post with the National Theater, received me with his customary graciousness, treated me as an equal, and even invited me to have dinner with him. We were joined by [the writer-psychiatrist] Josef Nesvadba, who at that time sported a huge head of hair which, for a long time, was what I remembered most vividly about him.

I think that my earliest poems were actually much better than many I published later; they had a strong surrealist cast in the style of the poetry written by Group 42—Ivan Blatny, Josef Kainar,* Jiri Kolar. I was extremely fond of those three poets.

From your earliest youth, your orientation in music and literature was exclusively toward the modern. You joined the Communist Party as a very young boy. This may seem like a silly question in view of present circumstances, but how did you reconcile your own modernist outlook with the cultural principles of the party?

First of all, in those days the party was not nearly so opposed to ·modern art as was later the case. At that time, various concepts of art were sanctioned alongside Zhdanovian socialist realism.** Besides, don't forget that all three of the poets I just mentioned leaned toward communism, even though after February [1948] they took quite different paths; Blatny emigrated and Kolar was jailed. But I don't wish to dismiss your question by pointing out that the conflict of which you speak had not become explicit before February. There is no doubt that the intimation of such conflicts had been in the air for a long time. Human memory is unreliable and reconstruction of psychological states of the past is difficult. But recently, while thinking about this period, I recalled that sometime during my last year in the gymnasium, in the course of a political debate, I remarked that even though socialism might bring about a period of cultural darkness I would continue to support it since it represented a necessary phase in the liberation of the people. Coming from the mouth of a politician, such a pronouncement would sound like utter cynicism. Coming from a student totally devoted to culture, however, such words have a different inner meaning. They signify self-denial. And one cannot understand the psychology of intellectuals during revolutionary times without this key.

An intellectual is a doubter. Above all, he doubts himself, with great persistence and brilliance. Crisis, alienation, impotence, isolation—these supposed characteristics of intellectuals were actually

---

* Josef Kainar was installed as President of the Czech Writers' Union by the post-Dubcek regime. Before the new Union could hold its constituent meeting, he died of a heart attack at the age of 55.
** "Zhdanovian socialist realism" was a later codification of the 1934 Gorki-Bukharin theory of art in a socialist society. Art was required to be realistic in method, romantic in spirit, optimistic, and always a reflection of party attitude.—*Ed.*

invented by the intellectuals themselves and turned into the great literary theme of the twentieth century. Intellectuals constitute the only segment of society capable of unmasking and analyzing itself. Thus, there exists a certain masochism among intellectuals. They are only too eager to agree with the very people who deprive them of their liberty. To understand truths unfavorable to oneself requires great mental effort, and such an effort flatters the intellectual. Recently, while speaking with some Western intellectuals who expressed remarkable understanding and sympathy for the anticultural work of the Chinese Red Guards, I knew I was witnessing that vice of passionate self-denial which has proven so destructive in my own life. Lately, I read in a left wing French magazine that Voltaire's advice in *Candide* to "cultivate your own garden" was stupid. I don't wish to talk about the article; it only served to remind me that I would no longer be capable of making such an attack myself. I have discovered through sad experience what it is like to live among gardens that have been destroyed, neglected, ravaged, gardens both real and symbolic. The Western intellectual finds it easy to deny his own values and to mock centuries-old gardens. For him, it is only play-acting. But the intellectual in our half of Europe lives in a quite different situation: he has already been suppressed many times, not only by himself but by circumstances; he has been rejected theoretically, practically, even economically. And thus he was finally forced into a situation that left him no alternative but to begin to understand his own importance, his own lot, to start defending his own liberty and the cultivation of the gardens of the mind.

In 1948, after graduation, you abandoned literature and started studying filmmaking. Is this related to what you have just been saying?

Yes. I went to FAMU [the Prague film school, which virtually all members of the Czech "New Wave" attended] and I remember the reflections which guided me at the time: I'll give up music and poetry, I thought, precisely because these are too close to my heart, and I will make films because cinema doesn't have any special attraction for me. In this way I will get rid of personal considerations and I will take part in the only art which is just, the "art which serves the people." Once again, a paradox, a self-denial. First I studied film directing and then scenario writing at FAMU under

M. V. Kratochvil, who taught me a great deal but nevertheless couldn't prevent my becoming a rather second-rate script writer.

That sounds like an ideal qualification for party enthusiasm.

Not really. First of all, enthusiasm is not one of my best talents. Besides, quite early in my film experience I was given a few good kicks in the behind, and shortly after February I was expelled from the party. [The novelist] Jan Trefulka was kicked out at the same time, and apparently his only crime was not having warned the party of my hostile thoughts. We had gone to public school together in Brno, and in Prague we lived together in a dormitory for a time. We were such close friends that people often mistook one of us for the other. This confusion proved to be Trefulka's undoing. On the other hand, when my case came up for review later on, I was given credit for activities which Trefulka had performed in the Council for Czechoslovak-Soviet Friendship, and these helped to turn the situation in my favor.

You are associated with the joke as a literary theme. What about humor and joking as your life-principle?

I was born on the first of April. That has its metaphysical significance.

In 1953, your first book of verse came out, Man, the Vast Garden.

It was an attempt to polemicize with the contemporary inhuman model of man and with the esthetics of the time. If you read the book now, removed from its contemporary context, the poetry seems quite weak; it doesn't transcend the possibilities and limitations of its time. And yet, in the atmosphere of those days, even that much couldn't be tolerated. The book was attacked while it was still in manuscript; it just barely succeeded in being published, and then a whole army of critics jumped on it for being too individualistic, hostile to the party, and God knows what else.

I imagine that everything you wrote during this period had a polemical character. Verse, essays . . .

Yes. I was opposed to the socialist realism being imported from Russia. I had quite a different conception of socialist art and I tried to further it. But you yourself know all too well what a tiresome and thankless task that was! What self-evident truths we had to fight for! That poetry has a right to be sad, that lines don't have to rhyme, that modern art is not the product of fascism as claimed by Soviet ideologues, and so on, *ad nauseam*. By what tiny steps we advanced! When a teacher spends his whole life teaching first graders, he is bound to become somewhat childish himself. We were forced to polemicize with so-called dogmaticians and these debates had to be carried out on their own soccer field, so to speak, since no other arena was available, and we had to use their language, since no other terminology was published. No wonder that we began to talk like idiots ourselves as a result.

All the same, those polemics were necessary.

Certainly. The relatively free creative atmosphere which we now enjoy didn't come to us as a gift from heaven; we had to struggle and fight for it. It was an honorable battle, and yet this activity was intellectually on a low level, as is necessarily the case in every debate with an idiot.

Your book of poems Monologues *created quite a furor, too.*

It was published in 1957, and the second edition, which was supposed to come out right after the first, was held up for eight years. The fate of this book of poems was similar to that of Skvorecky's *The Cowards,* which came out a year later. I like *The Cowards* very much; as a matter of fact I prefer it to my own *Monologues*. But certain analytic poems of mine that lay bare various extreme situations concerned with love still seem valid to me. It was these love poems, which formed the bulk of the book, that stirred up most of the antagonism; they were condemned as improperly cynical. The book also contained some romanticized verse, tending toward broad emotional gestures, and these later became repugnant to me. I removed them from later editions.

I have the impression that you have soured on poetry altogether.

In general, I have come to dislike my poems; also, I have lost the touch of writing poetry. To tell the truth, when people referred to me by that somewhat ridiculous title of Poet, I never felt quite right about it. When I'd get together with some friends for a night out or for a few rounds of boxing in the ring, I pretended that Poet

Kundera was somebody else. And the moment I realized that I no longer had it in me to write poetry, the thought that this phase of my life was behind me came as a relief.

And so you turned to theory.

I lectured on literature in the cinema faculty and, because my lectures were addressed to future writers, devoted a lot of time to the practical, technical aspect of the craft of writing prose. That's how my book about Vladislav Vancura,* *The Art of the Novel,* came into being. But to be perfectly frank, one reason for my devoting so much time to theory during that period was that I was having difficulty with the practice. I wrote the play *Owners of Keys* filled with anxiety whether I'd still be able to write anything at all.

Which brings us to the present: the unfinished cycle Ridiculous Loves *and the novel* The Joke. *It seems to me that your adherence to prose also means a greater emphasis on the spirit of analysis and irony. And perhaps a reflection on the generations, too.*

We were told in school that the generations change every thirty years. But this is no longer true. The pace of history has accelerated tremendously, and the interval between generations has proportionately shortened. It makes a big difference whether a person became engaged in his first conflicts with society under the occupation, or during the heady years of 1945 and 1946, or during the peak of the Stalinist era, or after it. The difference of a few years is felt as a generational gap because various historical segments gave rise to totally different generational stances, different generational tactics and character, different generational philosophies. I have the impression that we are living through a period full of treacherous intergenerational gullies and that there is more misunderstanding among the various age-groups than ever before.

My generation grew to adulthood during the Stalinist period. I am distressed when people equate Stalinism with fascism. This comparison is false not only from a political viewpoint, but it also fails to distinguish between the totally different human situations under the two systems. Fascism was based on a frank antihumanism,

---

* Vancura—novelist and playwright, one of Czechoslovakia's greatest stylists and innovators—was among those killed by the Nazis in the mass executions carried out in reprisal for the assassination of *Reichsprotektor* Reinhard Heydrich in 1942.—*Ed.*

and it created a moral situation which was perfectly clear and simple, black and white. Stalinism, on the other hand, was based upon a majestic humanist movement, and even in the midst of the Stalinist distortion this movement retained a great many of its original attitudes, ideas, slogans, and dreams. It was a tremendously confusing situation. Moral orientation became extremely difficult, sometimes impossible. Fascism left humanist principles and virtues untouched, because it emerged as its antithesis. Stalinism was more dangerous for all its virtues and ideals, because it began as the advocate and gradually converted it into the opposite: love of humanity into cruelty, love of truth into denunciation, and so on. When one sees how a great humanist movement can be subverted into something entirely different and how all human qualities are destroyed in the process, one begins to realize the fragility and uncertainty of human values altogether. This leads to complete skepticism, in which all assertions are turned into questions and it is necessary to re-examine everything, down to the most basic question of all: What is man?

This paradox obviously influenced your style, which tends more and more toward a systematic irony that holds nothing sacred.

The period we are discussing had no sense of humor, but unwittingly it produced some marvelous paradoxes. In art, the official doctrine was realism. But it was forbidden to speak of the real. The cult of youth was publicly celebrated, but our enjoyment of our own youth was frustrated. In those pitiless times, all we were shown on the screen was a series of tender and bashful lovers. Official slogans were full of joy, yet we didn't dare to play even the slightest prank. We went through the school of paradox. Today, when I hear anyone mention the innocence of childhood or one's sacred duty to increase and multiply or the justice of history I know what all this really means. I've been through the mill.

In the midst of the Stalinist era I wrote my first book, in which I tried to combat the prevailing inhumanity by appealing to universal human principles. Against "gloomy priests" who "locked themselves up in Marxism as in a chilly castle," I proclaimed that only those individuals should become communists who have a love for people. But when this era was over, I asked myself: Why? Why should one have to love people, anyway?

But not only love for others, love for oneself was shattered, too.

Recently, I was reading Montherlant's *Carnets,* in which this writer who knew how to treat everything outside of himself with consummate irony proudly declares that he would never wish to be anyone else except Montherlant, so satisfied was he with himself. I told myself that nobody in my generation could possibly feel this way about himself. Our egos don't live in much harmony with themselves. I, for example, don't particularly care for myself.

Of course, my generation was far from uniform, and this is often forgotten nowadays. Some emigrated, others became silent; still others adapted themselves, while others—including myself—adopted a kind of legal, constructive opposition. None of these postures was very dignified, and none was really satisfactory. The emigrants soon ceased to be involved, internal emigrants suffered from isolation and impotence, the "loyal opposition" could not help but be inconsistent and too prone to compromise, and those who completely adjusted are now dead, both morally and artistically. Nobody can really be satisfied with himself, and this bitter knowledge is the common basis of our whole paradoxical generation. When we are attacked by the youngsters, we no longer even have the desire to defend ourselves.

A thoroughgoing skepticism?

Of course. Even a skeptic must "go to the bottom." Skepticism doesn't annihilate the world; it only turns it into questions. That's why skepticism is the most fruitful attitude I know of. It is precisely this kind of constructive skepticism which can change our unfavorable situation into an advantage.

Isn't this also connected with your dislike of lyricism, which has already been mentioned?

You remember that in *The Joke* I frequently use the term "lyrical age." That is the period of youth when a person is a mystery to himself and therefore exhausts himself in endless self-contemplation. Other people are merely mirrors in which he searches for his own significance and worth.

Lyricism is a form of self-expression; it contains the narcissistic principle. A person becomes mature when he leaves his "lyrical age" behind. I get frightened by people who remain lyricists and nothing but lyricists all their lives. I have met wonderful lyric-poets who remained oddly untouched by education and never quite knew what it was all about. Yet they produced metaphors that left me breathless with admiration. It is as if all your life you exercised only one arm; you would develop a monstrous muscle capable of lifting a bookcase. And when all your life you do nothing but think up poetic images, you will develop a similarly fantastic prowess; but it seems to me like an anomaly, a defect, a tumor. I have the classicist prejudice that great literature calls for a broadly developed and mature personality.

Take our own literature. It is predominantly lyrical. The greatest figures in our literature have been our poets. This is typical in the majority of young cultures. But when a national culture reaches maturity, its lyrical dependence becomes a form of prolonged childhood, a childishness. Look: Czech literary theory is oriented primarily toward poetry; Czech structuralism, though lacking a theory of prose, has numerous theories of poetry. The predominant element in our drama and novel is lyricism. We don't have a single literary journal which doesn't regularly publish poetry. Even *Rude Pravo* [the official party newspaper] prints a daily poetry column. I believe that this may be unique in the world. Recently I thumbed through a handbook of gall bladder diseases, and even that contained several poems. In the abortion clinic, where women wait for interviews with the dreaded commission, they used to display a poem in which the unborn child begs its mother not to permit it to be scraped away.

This shameless bit of propaganda, serving a repulsive national population policy, was full of strong and beautiful imagery, and it was written by Karel Kapoun—a born poet fully conscious of his art. Brrr! Or take translations. I'd bet that nowhere in the world is there so much poetry being translated—and so well—as in our country. There is scarcely a single poet of any significance who hasn't been translated, and some quite insignificant poets have been translated, too. Baudelaire, Rimbaud, Mayakovski have been translated to the last letter. Now compare this with the amount of translation done in prose or drama and you will be amazed by the tremendous gaps. As for the holes left in philosophy! . . . Our culture, which has hardly let a single couplet escape its clutches, has failed to translate a single sentence of Husserl, a single essay of Camus, and even Hegel has been rendered into Czech only in recent years. The situation in such fields as historiography is even more appalling. This one-sided emphasis on poetry helps to create a public mentality that is not very rational, not very clever or witty, but rather hysterical, sentimental, and partial to kitsch.

This mentality is indeed characteristic of our cultural environment, but can it be blamed on, say, Nezval or Rimbaud?

Lyrical poets in themselves certainly can't be blamed. But one-sided concentration of interest on lyricism creates a tendency to perceive the lyrical as decoration and to turn everything into perfumed, rosy clouds. My least favorite author, in case you're interested, is Frana Sramek. There the transition from pure lyricism to trite lyricization takes place right in front of your eyes, especially when Sramek tries to use lyricism to "uplift" his prose or dramas. I don't think it will especially surprise you to learn that I don't like the Club of the Friends of Poetry, in which the mentality I have been describing has become institutionalized. They have almost 50,000 members and now they even have a special lapel-pin!

Yet you have prepared two collections of poems for them.

Yes, gladly. The books the club brings out seem to be unique in the world, in terms of the quality of their format and type, as well as in the size of their editions. When I tell Frenchmen that we have published some 50,000 copies of Apollinaire they are amazed and mistakenly take it as a sign of our general education and cultural level. This interest in poetry would be beautiful, if it weren't the only wildly blooming branch on the bare stump of general national cultural backwardness.

You will be accused of exaggerating.

I am afraid I am not exaggerating. I am generally present at the university entrance examinations and I can see how year by year there is an irresistible decline in humanist education.

And yet our nation has some truly outstanding poets.

Without doubt. And poetry has given Czech literature some of its most meaningful evolutionary impulses. The most recent of these was the avant-garde of the period between the wars. Our writers continually revert to it, because it was the last great creative wave of more or less national origin. However, the avant-garde saw literary problems primarily from the viewpoint of poetry. As a literary practitioner, I am not too interested in this return to the prewar avant-garde, because Czech literary evolution is thereby once again tied to lyricism. On the other hand, world literature has been under much more imposing influences during this period, based either on the novel or on philosophy. These influences have had practically no effect on our writers.

Still, aren't you somewhat unfair to lyricism, after all?

I suppose I am. I have often been accused of being a rational type. I only wish it were true. During the occupation, they stuffed us with German lessons day after day for six years, and yet after several months I succeeded in forgetting all the German I ever knew. From sheer aversion. I began to study Russian during the war with great enthusiasm and soon learned it extremely well. Today I cannot bring myself to pronounce a single Russian sentence. As if the language of Pushkin were to blame for the people who organized our political witch hunts! And it's the same thing with lyricism. My own youth, my own "lyrical age" and poetic activity coincide with the worst period of the Stalinist era. And this of course has done much to prejudice me against youth and lyricism. I got a close look at poets who adorned things that weren't worth it, and I am still able to remember vividly this state of passionate lyrical enthusiasm which, getting drunk on its frenzy, is unable to see the real world through its own grandiose haze. Yes, I am prejudiced, but this doesn't mean that there isn't a rational basis for my bias. Have you ever noticed a strange phenomenon? From the novels, romances, and dramas of the 1950s nothing at all survives, except for those few works that went completely against the prevailing current. But the lyrical works of the time fared much better. Nezval, Biebl, Mikulasek,* Kainar, even when they wrote conformist poetry, produced beautiful works and remained true poets. In a sense this speaks well of them, but at the same time it seems to mitigate against lyricism as such. It is an indictment of its existential innocence, because past years have placed a burden of guilt upon innocence. On the other side of the wall behind which people were jailed and tormented, Gullibility, Ignorance, Childishness, and Enthusiasm blithely promenaded in the sun. And so in periods of angry bias it seems to me that among the accused standing before

---

* Biebl was one of the leading pre-World War II avant-garde poets. He was closely linked to communism yet he committed suicide following the Stalinist takeover in 1948. Mikulasek was a leading Czech poet of the 1960s.—*Ed.*

the court—somewhere between Enthusiasm and Guillibility—I recognize the face of Seduced Lyricism. But please, enough of that.

I will turn to a question which has interested me for a long time. You are close to Sartre. Young writers, especially in France, still honor Sartre, yet at the same time they regard him as part of the past. The same attitude seems to be taken by structuralists in the theoretical realm.

Here again, my personal prejudices will confuse the issues. Sartre evokes my last great literary experience before February 1948. I remember a performance of *No Exit* in 1947 in Brno. I had shivers running down my back. No theatrical piece since then has wrenched me to such an extent. Throughout the period of the socialist-realist quarantine, Sartre represented my last great memory of the "rejected world." You can't imagine how moved I was when several years ago I suddenly came upon Sartre face to face.

Is he passé? I have heard it said in France. People here heard this rumor, too, and immediately began to accept it as fact. I cannot judge whether Sartre represents the past or the present for France, but let me ask you this: Are today's Czech and French literatures really contemporary? Are they living in the same historical time? Of course, they are united by a single European *Zeitgeist*. But Czech history and French history of the past twenty years are totally different. Our history is in a state of flux, we are living in an epoch of great adventure. Sartre's outlook was shaped primarily by the war and he was influenced by the immediate postwar atmosphere, and therefore Sartre was also fascinated by the story of man in historic flux. For this reason, Sartre seems more contemporary to me than current writers such as Robbe-Grillet.

This characterization probably wouldn't apply to all of Sartre, to works such as Nausea.

Nausea isn't really a novel in the true sense of the word. Sartre himself referred to it as a "novel-essay." He became a dramatist and novelist only after having become a somewhat different person.

Lyricism, the epic, the drama are not simply artistic genres from which an author is free to choose as he pleases; they are also existential categories. Sartre became a dramatist only at the moment when the question of action and the choice of action became for him the fundamental question of life. He became a novelist at the moment when he became concerned with the question of man and history, and when he himself began to live fully in history.

We have come to the novel. A while ago you expressed doubts about lyric poetry. But these days one hears much more outspoken doubt expressed about the novel and its survival.

The great flowering of the novel is related to the historical conception of the world as formulated early in the nineteenth century. If man has no unchanging essence but is, instead—to use Hegel's terminology—the product of his own actions inside history, then the literary genre best able to represent him is the novel. A stabilized society, continually reproducing the same problems and situations, a society through which historical change moves all but imperceptibly—such a society brings the survival of the novel into doubt.

In other words, you see the novel as a literary form of history?

Not at all. When, in my novel *The Joke,* I returned momentarily to the 1950s, I wasn't interested in some sort of sensational revelation of new facts, nor in painting a so-called portrait of the times. Rather, I was drawn to the 1950s because, during that period, history was making all sorts of experiments with Man; the unique historical circumstances showed Man from unusual angles and thus enriched my knowledge and my doubts about human nature and human fate.

Then you don't believe that the novel is dead.

No. I believe in its new transformations. Not transformations which disturb its epic essence, but which on the contrary will develop it further. I like Hermann Broch, who combined the epic quality of the novel with an essayistic element, and I like the continually youthful Aragon, who merged a novelistic story with the thousand-year-old history of European man. Picasso did the same thing in his canvases, and in their radical novelty he preserved all the accumulated heritage of the human vision.

I am trying to read your novel in the context of the whole current Czechoslovak cultural explosion . . .

Perhaps you can call it an explosion. Our country has a very old cultural tradition and at the same time an intensive tradition of modernism, and so a great deal of dammed up energy has accumulated during the last thirty years. The question now is whether we will simply catch up with the rest of the world, which we are doing quite brilliantly, or whether we will reach our own discoveries, develop our own language. It seems to me that up till now we have made our most striking and original statements in those areas of art which tend toward the objective and the descriptive, and which use historical experience as their basic subject matter.

The events we have lived through in the last thirty years were no milk and honey, but they gave us a tremendous working capital for artistic exploitation. Our experience with democracy, fascism, Stalinism and socialism contains everything essential that makes the twentieth century what it is. Our experience may thus enable us to ask more basic questions and to create more meaningful myths than those who have not lived through this whole political anabasis.

It's quite a fascinating situation: in addition to the events you mentioned, today's seventy-year-old has lived through the disintegration of a semifeudal monarchy, the creation, destruction, and rebirth of the national state; he has seen the liberal republic, its fascist caricature, two world wars . . . I know of no other country where so much historical experience has accumulated in such a short period of time. And you said yourself that art has that special gift of transmuting catastrophes and failures into valuable capital.

It seems to me that theater, literature, and cinema are now quickly becoming aware of the possibilities you outlined. The growth made within our film industry, for example, is simply fantastic. It is unbelievable that suddenly we have ten, fifteen, perhaps twenty filmmakers, most of them very young, who can compare favorably with any in the world. It is a bit of a biological miracle, though a great deal of credit must be given to the school—FAMU—that has given these people an atmosphere of quiet concentration in which they could develop their own potential. Our nationalized cinema industry has freed film from the bonds of commercialization and profit, which hamper the film art all over the world. If our socialism is at all capable of becoming conscious of itself, it is bound to encourage this growth and to guard the freedom won by the young filmmakers, because this freedom is a source of honor and of pride.

The opportunity that Czech art has today is perhaps unique in our entire history. Czech culture is old, and yet it still hasn't quite found its niche among European cultures. All its starts and flower-ings were always prematurely disturbed. The great epoch culminating in the work of Comenius* was interrupted for two centuries. At the beginning of the twentieth century, Czech art again began to stir and it produced works of European stature. Then the thread was broken once more and there was no certainty that it would ever be picked up again.

In the nineteenth century, when the Czechs began to re-emerge as a national entity, [the historian and humanist] G. H. Schauer asked a scandalous and indecent question that almost caused him to be expelled from the national fold. Was it really worth it, Schauer asked, to have spent so much energy in the rebirth of the Czech consciousness and of the almost vanished Czech language? Will the cultural works produced by this language ever be of such value as to justify the present labor of resuscitation? Wouldn't it be better, more advantageous for mankind, to devote all this energy toward the perfection of German culture, which is on a much higher plane than its barely germinating Czech counterpart?

All of Czech culture rose up against this provocative challenge, but the definitive answer has yet to be given. The questions live on, and the Czech people still haven't completely justified their new national existence. It can finally justify it only with the excellence of its cultural achievement, its own contributions to European and world civilization.

Beer from Plzen is world-famous, but only under its German name, *Pilsner Urquell*. And Pilsner beer certainly will not justify the right of Czechs to their own language and their own national existence.

But I believe that in the twentieth century Schauer's question has an even more pressing aspect. The twentieth century is an era of integration of small units into larger ones. Recently I talked to a Flemish-speaking Belgian who complained about the dangers his language faces. He noted that Flemish culture is becoming bilingual, and in certain areas—such as science—preference is being given to English because it facilitates more direct contact on the international level. All small nations are threatened by this integrationist trend, and they can defend themselves only by means of the intensity of their own culture, its individuality, the uniqueness of

---

* Comenius (Jan Amos Komensky, 1592–1670) was famous throughout Europe as an educational reformer and as a theologian of ecumenical scope.—*Ed.*

its contributions, and by nothing else. The defense against the non-violent integrationist pressure of the twentieth and twenty-first centuries will become much more difficult than the victorious battle against Germanization in the past.

Under these circumstances, very serious matters are at stake. It is a question of whether Czech will continue to be a European language or become only a dialect, whether our culture will be a European culture or only European folklore. In the final analysis, what is at stake is our very existence as a nation.

And now, suddenly, almost overnight, Czech culture has been given the opportunity to end its sublease in the European house and to become a rightful inhabitant. I am certain that we have something valuable to say and that we will succeed in saying it, providing certain so-called subjective conditions are present: a culturally favorable political atmosphere, sufficiently magnanimous and freedom-minded, a proper level of national education, and—this is vital —a proper amount of national investment in cultural life. Under these circumstances, ideological snoopers or political bigots who try to prevent our current cultural expansion jeopardize our very future as a European nation. Anyone guilty in this way will have to answer to history.

What if the idea of a national state is an anachronism in the twentieth century? What if world evolution really demands the gradual dissolution of small nations?

A writer is too closely bound to the national language to be able to identify with such a development. In the end, he has but one choice: If the trend you are describing is indeed inevitable, then the artist must create works of such worth as to make the evolution as described as unjustifiable as possible.

February 1967

Josef Škvorecký

Born 1924 in Nachod, northeastern Bohemia. He graduated from Charles University, Prague, and worked as editor in a publishing house, in charge of translations of English and American fiction. He established his reputation as one of the finest Czech translators with his editions of Faulkner and Hemingway. In 1958 he published his first novel, *The Cowards,* which was banned shortly after publication and became the cause of a major political and literary scandal and served as a pretext for the suppression of any liberal and independent development in Czech literature and the arts for the next few years. As a result of this scandal, Skvorecky also lost his job as an editor of the bimonthly review *Svetova Literatura (World Literature).* His second book, *The Legend Emöke,* could not be published until five years later, followed in 1964 by a collection of short stories, *The Seven-Branched Candelabra.* Since then, he has devoted his full time to writing and has published a number of books, some of which were filmed. His most recent novels are *The Lion Cub* and *The Tank Brigade.* He is also a great jazz-fan, writes detective stories, and has written and co-edited some books on these subjects.

Josef Škvorecký

By interview time, I had not yet read either Skvorecky's Bass Saxophone *or his* End of the Nylon Era. *But the night before I had spent many hours over his commentaries on Hotchner's reminiscences of Hemingway. I had the feeling that Hemingway's merciless comments about literary criticism, as reported by Hotchner, found a sympathetic echo in Skvorecky. This antagonistic attitude toward the critic's role has been expressed throughout history by the greatest writers and artists. Similarly, the connection between this attitude and a great writer's tragic end, as described by Hotchner, can be observed in dozens of cases, old and new. The writer is a highly sensitive and vulnerable person, and it is commonplace in literary history and psychology that such sensitivity is often disguised by a powerful physique or apparently extraordinary self-confidence. I have always been surprised, however, by the mental agility of certain people who are able to decimate a writer they dislike, yet, the very next minute, get highly indignant over the rude treatment given by critics to some other writer whom they happen to admire. As a critic, and therefore belonging to this most horrible and contemptible category of people, I began my interview from this tangent . . .*

Criticism is essential, there's no getting around it. It is needed for a variety of reasons but it should always be aware of its dangerous potential. Even with the best of intentions, it may do harm. Every artist must overcome tremendous problems with himself; he generally knows his own weaknesses only too well, they torment him and make him hypersensitive. Hemingway stylized himself into the likeness of a tough boxer, but in reality he was a bundle of tender emotions. The impact of criticism on such a person may be so violent as to destroy him as an artist. Of course, there are other destructive forces as well. Hemingway was not a spontaneous writer, and he spent a tremendous amount of thought on how he should write. He didn't worry much about what to write, but how. I recall statements made there about culture a few years ago to the effect that one sign of greatness in an artist is that he is mainly concerned not with the *how,* but the *what.* In my opinion, the truth is just the opposite. The literary giants know perfectly well what they want to say; they practically overflow with their subject, it's in them and can't be held back; but they desperately struggle with the *how,* the form, how to tell it, how to organize it. After prolonged and persistent thinking Hemingway finally evolved a style which influenced everything in subsequent Anglo-American literature. Some people think that I exaggerate, but in my opinion Hemingway's significance to literature is equal to that of Picasso's to painting. And yet this very man struggled with fantastic problems in his work. He continually crossed out and rewrote—he rewrote a single chapter thirty-eight times—and he never gave up. He kept wrestling with the material, with what he had seen, experienced, and carried in his head; and when they suddenly began to tell him that his writing had gone bad, this had its effect and took its toll.

When I as a writer say these things, it may seem like a defense of my own work, a kind of confession. But I don't mean it in that sense. I have lived through a great deal of criticism. I have walked around Prague trying to look as if I were really a night club saxophone player rather than a writer, but it shook me up and hurt me all the same. By and large, though, it caused no major damage. Hemingway is simply my kind of author. He is terribly close to me. We have much in common in our feelings and attitudes ...

It is extremely important for a writer to believe in himself. Take that famous author of detective stories, Raymond Chandler. He wrote some beautiful letters about literature—a pity they haven't been published here yet—which convinced me that the only reason he hadn't written so-called "serious" novels was that he didn't believe in himself. He wrote only detective stories, though actually in this way he produced more literature than many a "serious" author whose books often can't even touch a good detective story. Chandler, too, inveighed against the critics. In the West, critics have a notorious influence on a writer's commercial success. You know, he used to say that critics understand a work of art, too, but with a totally different kind of understanding from the authors. Perhaps it's like a soccer game. The spectators and referees know the game, but their understanding is quite unlike that of the players on the field.

Yet criticism plays an immensely constructive role, too, especially in societies and situations where art is endangered not only by its own internal problems and stresses but by external ones as well: commercialization or misunderstanding. Under such circumstances the creative artists reap all the glory in the end, but the critics deserve boundless credit. They had to create the proper atmosphere, to prepare the ground; artists can't do this all on their own.

Then again, the critical profession is often seduced into a kind of exhibitionism, a temptation to attract attention. It is easy to trample on a failure. But the question of what to do in a constructive way about a truly bad work is not easy to answer. And in our country, especially in Prague, the problem becomes compounded by the fact that everybody knows everybody else. In any case, as soon as a writer or other artist attains a certain level, no subsequent work is likely to be really bad through and through. For that matter, even the classics contain all sorts of defects, if you want to look at them with a merciless eye. Only time can decide what will survive, what has real merit.

I want to come back to Chandler for a minute. He once wrote a very fine article: "The Simple Art of Murder." It was a sharp attack on the contemporary English detective story, on its lack of realism. And then he wrote a letter saying that the article shouldn't be taken too literally, because he could equally well have written another piece defending the English detective story and showing how American realism had ruined the genre, how the old form was actually superior.

So that actually . . .

Art is art because nobody has yet quite grasped the art of doing it. To achieve complete certainty in this area is impossible. And I am not defending the golden mean, either. There must be extremes, there must be avant-garde writers who act like voracious pikes in a pond, and they are needed even if they don't always speak the truth. Their job is to provoke—arrogantly, even using lies when necessary. They're needed to chase the lazy carps that wallow at the bottom and grow fat.

I myself have never belonged to any group. It's not my nature, even though I am extremely attracted to certain movements, such as surrealism. I like to cite the American journalist Joseph Barry, who wrote on the occasion of Henry Miller's obscenity trial in California: The artist must go too far, so that others can go far enough. —Extremist manifestations in life such as, for instance, the beatniks have tremendous importance; they serve a vital function because they destroy conventions that threaten to retard or stifle life. Those artists who have done the same iconoclastic job may not all have been the greatest creators, but they have played an extremely important role.

So, you see, I am by no means advocating the idyllic, the golden mean, the careful avoidance of insulting somebody or other. That is unrealistic; it doesn't do justice to life. But there is always a kind of mainstream, even in jazz, and people who are concerned with theory must realize that, in matters of art, a certain continuing relativity obtains. It is therefore good to have both types: opinions which are purely theoretical and extreme, along with exponents of sober wisdom—the wisdom of those who merely observe the passions and try to form objective judgments about them insofar as it is possible to do so within the limits of art . . .

Don't you think that criticism also plays the role of maintaining "mental hygiene"?

That is related to what I said about the pressure of commercialization or organized power. Wherever criticism comes across a dishonesty that tries to seduce the taste of some segment of society, it must act with great vigor. It must be able to distinguish that which is offered honestly from that which merely panders; it must recognize fraud and expose attempts at superficial effect. I believe that style is a reliable hallmark, style behind which one feels the author's personality. To paraphrase Chandler again: Style is the greatest thing an artist can bequeath to his era. Style is the projection of personality. But, of course, this presupposes a genuine personality to begin with. There are quite a few authors who succeed in everything they do, readers like their work, yet personality is missing.

On the other hand, take someone like [the "New Wave" film director] Vera Chytilova. She herself boasts that each of her films is entirely different, yet the trademark of her personality is unmistakable. And even though I intensely dislike certain things she does, I find her work as a whole quite fascinating; one senses that behind it there is a human being with urgent things to say. That's personality.

In literature one encounters authors who actually wrote quite badly—Dreiser, for example—but who nevertheless had true personality, and therefore their work survives. Of course, we have been talking about the great figures, because by and large we are not familiar with the smaller ones. But the critic must deal with average work, too. Only occasionally does he come across something truly outstanding. To recognize genuine personality is not an easy task. Those authors who only wish to please, to please their era or their readers, must be attacked mercilessly by the critic. Actually, such writers generally aren't very sensitive, anyway.

One often hears people talk about the beneficial effects that external pressures and obstacles have on creative work. Oddly enough, even artists themselves often express this opinion. You are a person who knows a lot about this subject, and not just from theory, but from experience . . .

I believe that this idea is just a myth. Of course, people vary. There are some who need a punch in the nose to wake up, and there are others who would be knocked out cold.

Let's examine the great authors. Look at Shakespeare, for example. We know—in spite of what occasional articles may say to the contrary—more about Shakespeare than we do about a great many other great writers. Shakespeare, then: he was successful, lived well, wrote fairly good plays, made money, and died. In Elizabethan England there was little cultural pressure put upon the artist; this particular writer, though he never got into any real trouble, produced worthwhile work. On the other hand, consider Edgar Allan Poe. Life gave him a terrible beating. He lived in wretched poverty, he was sick, his beloved died, he was an unhappy man through and through. And he himself says that the circumstances of his life were such that he couldn't accomplish in literature what he would have liked. I suspect, though, that even under better conditions he would have written just about the same things. An explosive talent and yet a true builder, too. For he invented the detective story, and after him nobody has discovered anything really new to add to this genre. That's Dorothy Sayers' opinion, and she ought to know. The ones who came after Poe made all the money, of course. God only knows what Poe would have written if he had made all that money himself.

There are, no doubt, some writers who need pressure in order to develop. But it is also a matter of degree.

In the early 1950s I knew some young people who wrote quite decent stories. But they simply had no chance to publish. In those days even getting published in second-rate periodicals was difficult. So these young men stopped writing, got married, had children, got divorced, but their literary careers were over. It is said that talent always breaks through in the end. Perhaps. Obviously, none of these "Sunday writers" was a great genius. But quite a few might well have developed into good professional writers, and they, too, are needed. Or perhaps some of them might have written only one or two valuable pieces, but then many great authors have written only one extraordinary work, even though they may have followed it with fifty mediocre ones.

I respect good work, because I know what it costs. Sometimes I come across a manuscript which is quite ordinary and yet contains some brilliant pages, better than anything I could do myself. I cannot recommend the book as a whole, it is returned to the author —and yet, that one chapter . . . Such decisions can be heartbreaking. For that reason I don't like to pass judgment on manuscripts by new writers. That's also why I like to review only those books I greatly admire.

How did you come to be a writer?

Literature had long been the most important thing in life for me. Right after the war came a great revelation: Freud's *Introduction to Psychoanalysis.* (This is why I found it intolerable when, years later, a fool's cap was put on Freud's head. Even if his theories were to be eventually abandoned, his one great truth will always remain—namely, the decisive power which subterranean forces play in human life. Of course, he was right about many other things, too.) When I read Freud's analysis of how a person becomes a writer, I had the feeling that I was reading about myself. I had been a rather sickly child, I had several bouts of pneumonia—in those days there was no penicillin and pneumonia was a serious illness— I was out of school for nearly a year and I had to give up sports which was a big blow because I was an avid soccer player and skier. As a result, I became much more introverted than is normal at that age, and I began to write things down for myself, dreamlike stories. I enjoyed going to movies; Hollywood was a magic realm for me, and I started to write ten different novels about Hollywood. I couldn't live a normal life like my friends, so I sat in my cozy home and compensated for my isolation by putting the world on paper.

When I was fourteen or so, in my fourth year at the gymnasium, a new wave in jazz culminated in swing music, and I succumbed to its magic. There was a sudden craze for swing, just like youngsters nowadays are attracted to rock. I played the saxophone and dreamed about becoming a professional musician. Only I didn't have the talent. When I realized that, I turned to writing in earnest. Faulkner has one sentence that fits my case like a glove: Those who can, do—those who can't, write.

When *The Cowards* was published I went to see a friend of mine, a priest. He told me: "I read those 'cowards' of yours"—and I was afraid of what he might say next; after all, he was a priest, and this wasn't exactly a supermoral story. But he came out with the most perceptive judgment of all who wrote or spoke about the book. "You know," he said, "it's something like the sacred rite of confession. In the confessional, too, a person tells everything about himself and makes peace with the good Lord. And in this book, you've talked yourself out very nicely."

True enough. Most literature, before it is a statement about the world, is first of all a testament about the author. Sometimes I wonder whether this aspect isn't neglected in literary scholarship. In other words, the question of just what can be expected of a particular writer and what can't. A psychological study of the phenomenon called "the writer." One should start talking about matters formerly taboo. Diaries, of course, have now become accepted as rich sources for study, and this type of approach is extremely interesting and will lead to great discoveries for literary criticism.

For a long time, I thought Bozena Nemcova's *The Grandmother* —required reading in school—was a rather boring book. But when I later discovered some of her letters and found that Nemcova [one of the founders of modern Czech literature] was far from being the virtuous, puritan lady described in the textbooks, I felt very much closer to this nineteenth-century writer. I realized that she was actually just the kind of person a real woman ought to be, and I began to reread her and to understand what a great writer and human being she was.

These days things are better, but there was a time when demands were made on writers that they had no way of meeting. I was always irritated by the Marxist maxim that "freedom is comprehended necessity." That is correct in principle, but how is it to be applied? After all, it's a question of freedom in a biological sense. Just ask a great poet like Jaroslav Seifert, for example, to write a novel. It probably wouldn't work out too well; he wouldn't be free—his necessity leads him to comprehend that he is a poet rather than a novelist. And he knew perfectly well what he was. Formerly, the maxim was interpreted as the comprehension of the necessities of social demands. But this goes as far back as Epictetus, who insisted that even a slave can be free once he understands which aspects of life can be changed and which can not. For example, since a slave cannot change his status, he should not expend his energies to achieve freedom in this sense, since such efforts would only enslave him still further. But he can influence his thoughts and inner life, he can dream, and in this he is free. For Epictetus too, then, freedom is understanding necessity. But with Engels it is a question of necessity seen scientifically. And that is a significant point in terms of the demands made on a writer and his capability for meeting them.

I wrote a novel [*The Cowards*] about which there were two divergent opinions: It was considered either epoch-making or scandalous. But I never set out to create art at all; I simply tried to write a book. Only on rare occasions, when something ripens and a number of circumstances seem to coincide in the right way, only then can I think of my work as art with a capital A. Basically, I consider myself a craftsman, which is why I like to write such things as detective stories for my own pleasure and for the amusement of a few readers, perhaps. I am often taken to task for not writing more books like *The Cowards*. Certainly, I would love to write nothing else; such works go deeper, catch more, last longer. Perhaps I will be able to complete another such book. I keep on trying, but meanwhile I don't think that writing detective stories is any sin. They have their value, too. When I was ill I found that out. I simply don't know how to act like the great author who withdraws into himself and refuses to put pencil to paper until seized by an inspiration of genius. I like to amuse myself, to watch comedies, and one of my ambitions is to write the script for a film comedy. In other words, I'd like to divide my work, like Graham Greene, into novels (serious work) and entertainments (written for amusement). Greene is one of my favorite authors. Many people in England turn up their noses at him; they say he's *passé, passé*. I hate that kind of attitude.

I prefer to read books as if they contained news from a dear friend. This is different from a pure author-reader relationship. And on one level or another I always manage to find the author as a human being. After all, what can any single person really accomplish in this world? The idea of permanent revolution is nonsense. New ideas every day . . . who in the world can do that? Let's be grateful for small blessings.

You do a lot of translating. Many writers throughout the world translate, even though they are under no financial necessity to do so. Why is it that there are no such writer-translators in our country?

There are some. I know at least one, Jan Zabrana. A fanatic. He falls in love with an author and then turns the world upside down to make sure he gets published. Some time ago he did that with Isaac Babel. He read some Babel in the 1950s and didn't rest until he had translated all of his work. Later, he translated Allen Ginsberg and Lawrence Ferlinghetti. I honor such devotion. When you love a certain author, it is a delight to translate him. I feel that way about Hemingway and Chandler. Translating poses a great danger to a writer, though. When you translate something, you feel somewhat like a co-author. And that is a psychological illusion. But the effect is to turn an author into a translator. As a matter of fact, this may be one of the reasons why our art of translation is among the best in the world. And there is another reason why translation is attractive to a writer: The best way to read a book is to translate it. Then, too, you may learn to like even those aspects of a book you couldn't appreciate at first. For me, Faulkner's *A Fable* is a case in point. At first I thought the book rather drawn out, full of mysticism, and to this day I have the feeling that I may be the only person who has truly read it. And yet how powerfully Faulkner's personality begins to emerge! How much that man knows! I worked on it for four years. I lost a lot of money on the project, had to have the whole manuscript retyped four times, and yet the work was a great pleasure and in the end it even proved to be useful.

In our country we do more translating than elsewhere; we publish more translations than original literature. That's why a whole translating profession has established itself here. In the West there are relatively few translations. With us, translation is regarded as a distinct activity, and some of our translators are masters of the art. Perhaps only poets do both original work and translation. Another important aspect: In spite of its great importance and extraordinary quality, our translation work is incredibly poorly paid. Anybody who can write anything original—it doesn't even have to be particularly good—is much better off. We hardly have any writers wealthy enough to afford the luxury of translating. Then, too, a good writer does not necessarily make a good translator. Translation is not only an art but a craft; a translator must know the language he is working from to perfection; he must be able to respond to the most delicate nuances. To this day, we don't have a manual for translators in our country; for years I've been urging publishers to bring one out. But no—people simply learn by doing, like making a pair of shoes. Somebody gives them hell and they learn . . .

To come back to something we talked about earlier: Even excellent writers may be poor stylists. Literature is not simply a matter of beautiful language. Dreiser again. Or even Dostoevski. Some may indulge in boundless stylistic arbitrariness, like [Vladimir] Paral.* And yet he is quite a writer.

It is said, even by some writers, that contemporary literature is boring.

Obviously, literature must never be boring. But that is no argument against certain new forms, such as the novel. If it seems boring to me personally—well, that's my affair, but there are others who may find it interesting. Boredom is an objective phenomenon but its sources are subjective. It is nonsense to use the argument that this or that work does not take the reader into account. It always

---

* A chemical engineer by profession, Paral has written several novels exploring the empty lives of the "affluent" classes under socialism. His novel *Private Hurricane* was made into a film.—*Ed.*

turns out in the end that authors of such works actually addressed themselves to a rather broad public.

Sometimes I think that the old method of publishing had a good feature; every author found a publisher. It never occurred to anyone to take Kafka to task for being dull. After all, society is made up of minorities. And a publishing monopoly has a tendency to discriminate against certain types. No matter how cultured the men at the top of such a monopoly may be, they cannot possibly be so liberal as to erase their own prejudices and tastes and accept everything. Read the autobiographies of writers. How many times did Erskine Caldwell have to make the rounds of publishers with *God's Little Acre?* Think of the trouble Faulkner had before he found a publisher! Even Hemingway practically had to publish some of his stories himself.

A concept such as boredom actually has no place in a public discussion of literature. There are people who are bored by detective stories. I find some of them pretty dull myself. Boredom is a question of quality, not of genre.

We once discussed the question of universality . . .

I think about this problem quite often, because I'm fairly well acquainted with Anglo-American literature and it is read all over the world. And I ask myself how many of these writers would have a world-wide reputation if they wrote in Czech, and how many of our own writers would be known abroad if they wrote in English. I know that this smacks of sour grapes or of a kind of Czech chauvinism of which I want no part. And yet we sometimes encounter this situation as an objective fact. For example, Karel Polacek* is in my opinion a writer who deserves an international audience, yet he will never become recognized as such because he was never translated and probably never will be. Who in the world translates Czech, anyway? Let us not delude ourselves with rare exceptions. These translators aren't as well qualified as our own. Just imagine what would happen if our country gave birth not to just one writer of international merit, but to a whole literature of world significance! There would still remain the very prosaic problem: How would these authors become known to an international public; who would

---

* Polacek—a writer and journalist whose books are widely read in Czechoslovakia today—died in a Nazi concentration camp.

translate them and publish them? It is true that Czechoslovak films have achieved a world-wide reputation, yes, but film people have the great advantage that they are not so closely bound to language. Literature is worse off in this respect, even though lately there have been some fortunate successes. Paradoxically, this was predominantly due to German interest.

You come from a small Czech town. What role did this play in your development?

I don't know. I haven't really thought about it. The small town atmosphere is, of course, closely connected with my youth, and I live above all from my childhood experiences. My youth still has a magic power over me. What is *The Cowards,* anyway? The story of a small town, its jazz, its student life, the end of the war . . . And then I came to the university and found out that in the United States there is a mode of writing called "magic realism." I knew nothing about it, but whenever I wrote anything I tried with all my might to relive my memories, and at the same time I wanted my writing to have the magic, to be truer than truth, as Hemingway put it. I think I know what he meant. While we are living it, an experience means little, but when it is recalled it becomes beautiful. I wrote that the war years were the most beautiful years of our lives. And I was severely criticized for this statement. But we were young in those days, everything was surrounded by a halo, we promenaded in the square surrounded by pretty girls. In a small town, people know each other; countless tales and legends float through the atmosphere and a kind of unexpressed enchantment fills the air. I hope that one day I'll be able to write a book about the war, about forced labor, about the huge underground hall, about how people tried to goldbrick, about the beautiful girls, and the days when we sat for hours in the men's room debating about politics and art. These experiences are still extremely vital for me. I tried to capture some of this magic in *Bass Saxophone.* But before writing a novel about it, I'll probably try to do it as a musical. Actually, the theme lends itself better to a musical.

Your relation to jazz is, of course, a very special one.

It's like this: sometimes I feel lonely, suddenly I hear jazz and it affects me like a shot of some powerful stimulant. It isn't only a matter of esthetics. Jazz goes deeper; it is a psychological force, a beautiful force which gives me joy and pervades my whole emotional life. That's why I have devoted one of my works to it. It is a source of never-ending pleasure, one of the things in my life which time has not spoiled for me. I am not a collector, I don't sit in a corner and listen to records. I probably couldn't give the right answer to a single question on a jazz quiz, but I love that anonymous music. Recently I realized that I haven't written a single book in which jazz doesn't play some sort of role. Jazz, and everything it symbolizes, represents for me a key to all human striving. There are other currents that enter into my attitude to jazz, too—certain wartime associations, the role that jazz played for us during the bleak war years, the fact that it was semiforbidden music, but all this is relatively unimportant. Jazz is, above all, a kind of fraternity.

But you want biographical data. First the gymnasium, then forced labor, then medicine—because I was an idealist and took it into my head that the world needed people capable of helping others. The trouble was that I was an absolute moron as far as mathematics and physics were concerned, and I couldn't stand being an intern. Even autopsies were better than having to watch people dying and not being able to do anything about it, not being able to help even though many were still quite young. I'm no good at putting on an act, at solacing people, and so I became terribly depressed. Occasionally I tried escaping to a movie, but no sooner had I sat down in the theater than the question began to gnaw away at me: Do I really have any right to amuse myself while others are dying? So I switched to philosophy. And to this day I am convinced that a certain amount of callousness is necessary to survive in this world. In one of my pieces I wrote that indifference is our salvation, our mother as well as our nemesis. Just imagine—if we didn't have a bit of indifference in us, how could we face the idea that in this century in which, though life has reached pinnacles of civilization, there are still millions who are hungry and naked . . . Without a bit of callousness, we would be continually screaming and revolting, and this would probably not help much but would only lead to chaos.

From my university days I especially remember the lectures of Prof. Vladislav Vancura on American literature. He had a habit of talking with a kind of dry English objectivity and wit, and yet it was obvious that he loved his subject very deeply. Except for the lectures of Vaclav Cerny [professor of comparative literature at

Charles University], these were the only ones I attended with any regularity. In 1949 an order was issued to the effect that everyone who had passed the state exam should serve for a period of time in the border regions. I was the sort of person who thought that laws meant what they said, so off I went. Of course, many of my colleagues realized that laws were made to be broken and stayed in Prague. But I have no regrets. I had graduated with a major in English and a minor in philosophy, but both subjects had disappeared from school curricula around that time, so I ended up teaching social studies in a provincial girls' school. There were, of course, no textbooks, no curricula, nobody knew exactly what social studies meant, but the school was supposed to be "socially oriented" and so social studies became the main subject. They assigned it to me, and I taught it, four hours a week. I don't remember how we passed the time in class; we probably just chatted a lot. But suddenly an order came stating that compulsory certification exams would include my subject, and I was to prepare seventy questions at once. Somehow I managed to lay my hands on a few pages from an old textbook which mentioned that hospitals were founded as early as the Middle Ages and that medieval monks used unscientific methods of treatment. From this single source I sweated out seventy different-sounding questions, and I believe that this test belongs among my most inspired literary accomplishments.

During the oral exam, each student was given a different question, but they all gave pretty much the same answers because all their learning came from the same few pages of the same book. By the time the fifth student started out on her by now familiar recitation, things started to look rather embarrassing, even though the chairman of the examining board didn't seem to be aware of what was going on. Fortunately, these girls were resourceful. The school was no bourgeois finishing school; it was run on a more practical basis, and the girls also learned how to sew and cook. The cooking instructor was fabulous, a real artist who had written several books on the subject. Naturally, during the exams the kitchen was going full blast and every two hours relays of girls in white aprons trooped into the examination room, bringing trays of luscious delicacies the examiners never dreamed existed. And so the exam became one long banquet and social studies were completely forgotten.

There was a sculpture school in town, too, and ours was full of pretty girls between the ages of seventeen and twenty-two; I myself was twenty-seven and I was supposed to chaperone them when they went dancing. So, you see, here it is again: the early 1950s, the second beautiful period in my life. I used the material from this time as a theme for one of my books.

But I didn't feel like making teaching my career; I longed to do something connected with literature. I was a docile student, though, and I thought that I must first complete my doctorate before I could consider doing anything else. So after I received my degree and served my hitch in the army, [the author and translator] Zdenek Urbanek helped me get a job in the State Publishing House.

But hadn't you started writing much earlier?

I had written *The Cowards* while I was still at the university. At the "social school" I retyped the manuscript and showed it to one of my colleagues, a woman, who was so disgusted by it that I never showed the book to anyone again until finally I gave it to Zdenek Urbanek, who restored my courage.

When I was at the university, I met [the poet] Frantisek Halas. It happened like this. A union publication sponsored a contest. I sent them an enormous poem entitled *Don't Despair,* and though I didn't win a prize they wrote me that Halas admired the poem and would like to meet me. It was a beautiful meeting. "I didn't recommend your poem," said Halas. And I answered: "Of course not. I didn't really want to have it published anyway." And he said: "Keep working; sooner or later you'll have to lose your virginity." And then he explained that even though he was impressed by my poem he hadn't recommended it for the award because he was afraid everyone, from the Catholics to the Communists, would be after my neck. He had a prophetic nose for political winds. Anyway, it looks now as if the whole thing may be published at long last. We'll see then whether it still has any merit; most probably it will be interesting only as a document.

Subsequently, I submitted a piece to a university-sponsored contest. It was called *New Canterbury Tales* and was about a gang of boys. One of them mentions that it's Chaucer's birthday—though of course nobody really knows when Chaucer was born—and then they start recounting tales about their wartime experiences. I won the contest, under the pen name Fred Errol. This name has its roots in my subconscious. When I was ten years old I fell madly in love with Freddie Bartholomew, and he played the part of Cedric Errol, the little Lord Fauntleroy. You see, quite infantile.

Anyway, the results of the contest were announced three days be-

fore the political upheaval of February 1948, and first prize was to
be a two-month trip abroad. But because of the political events, the
entire contest was called off. Halas tried to send me over to the
magazine *Kytice* to see Seifert, but by the time I got there Seifert was
gone and so was the magazine. From all this work I was able to
salvage only *Rebecca's Story,* which eventually came out in the
collection *The Seven-Branched Candelabra.*

I had participated in a contest even earlier, in 1945, sponsored
by the Czech Academy. A man from Nachod, my home town, had
won the contest the year before—a good omen. I sent them a kind
of surrealistic novel with the significant title *Inferiority Complex.*
I won honorable mention and then a group called the Society of
Czech Writers nominated me for membership in their organization. It was an odd group. Only one of the members had actually
published anything, and he wore spats. Another member, a lady
named Carmen, collected stories about the Prague Uprising which
she cut out of popular magazines. It was my first experience with
literary groups.

After Halas died [in 1949], Jindrich Chalupecky found some remarks about me in Halas's diaries; and he invited me to come to
see him and introduced me to Urbanek and to Jiri Kolar, Jan Rychlik, and Bohumil Hrabal.* We sat around together and debated
about art. Kolar acted as a kind of intellectual center and source of
continuity. I remember Hrabal reading his first stories to us, which
the bibliophile Kolar was the first to publish, though few people
nowadays know this. (Kolar played the same role of patron and
publicist that Pound played for Hemingway.)

Here I developed respect for the avant-garde, although I myself did not share their viewpoint, and I learned to admire people
who love art so much that they are willing to sacrifice everything
for its sake. To live it day after day, to remain steadfast to certain
ideals, that's a rare and precious thing. Too many people aren't
loyal to anything, not even to their favorite authors. And it was this
loyalty which, more than anything else, fascinated me about the
surrealists. Once I heard a semi-secret lecture on surrealism given
by [the art critic and historian] Vratislav Effenberger. It was held
in the psychiatric faculty, but the hall was crowded with all sorts of

---

* Chalupecky: philosopher, critic, and art historian; Kolar: poet and artist;
Rychlik: author and composer; Hrabal: poet, artist, and author of *Closely
Watched Trains.*—*Ed.*

gentlemen who looked more like policemen than poets, and that was the end of that. It is beautiful to see people who are capable of total sacrifice. One surrealist even worked as a driver for a brewery . . .

I myself am not much of a theoretician, my mind is more drawn to the spontaneous and the intuitive. Not that I don't think about literature, you understand, but when I succeed in writing something it's like a successful jazz improvisation. Inspiration is a phenomenon that used to be explained in all kinds of mystical ways. But I believe in it; I think it is real and exists widely. Not universally, of course. There are rational kinds of writers, too, and perhaps they are the more valuable ones.

Unfortunately, I belong to those who must write thousands of pages before hitting on the one thing that seems to have some inspiration in it, that on rereading makes me doubt that I was actually capable of writing it. This is my method, or perhaps I should say "my disease." Some things are simply the result of inspiration, while others are created from elements that one inherits and that one develops somehow or other later on. As I said, I would be much happier if I could write in a more rational way. But I think of writing as a pathological manifestation; anyway, it certainly isn't part of normal life. There ought to be more information in this area. What would happen if everything were done on a rational basis? What would be left for me in the world?

In 1946 I wrote *The Age of Nylon* (the first chapter is included in my new book, *A Babylonian Story*), and in 1948–1949 I was writing *The Cowards,* and then, in 1950, *The End of the Nylon Age.* This book was supposed to be published in 1956, but they decided to bring out *The Cowards* instead, because they thought it would create less of a scandal.

And then the real writer's life began?

In 1956 I began to edit the magazine *Svetova Literatura* [*World Literature,* a review devoted to publishing translations and reviews of contemporary writing]. I loved doing it, it was a wonderful job. During this time, I asked Ladislav Fikar* to read some of my manu-

---

* Fikar was an important Czech poet and translator of Russian poetry who was the director of the Czechoslovak Writers Union Publishing House. In this capacity, he was responsible for the publication of books by Skvorecky, Hrabal, and others. In 1959 he was removed from his position and then became one of the most important guiding forces of the Czech "film wave" of the 1960s.—*Ed.*

scripts. How great he was, both as a person and as a publisher! How that man could spark enthusiasm! People in the field know all about him, but I am not sure whether the general public is sufficiently aware of all he's done—for literature, for films. He should write his memoirs.

The Cowards came out quite smoothly, without any problems. In fact, on the very day the book was being distributed, I heard—just by chance—that the cultural ideologists had read my novel and, by God, they said, that was some book. I expected to be attacked for excessive naturalism, slang, some of the erotic scenes, and I was ready to defend myself on literary grounds. But I never would have dreamed that I might become the target of attacks for having sullied things which are holy and glorious—no, this was the last sort of thing I expected, I assure you. I wrote the book shortly after the February [1948] events, filled with a kind of socialist enthusiasm (although I must admit that I was never a political thinker). I recall that the book had some sort of idealistic blurb on the jacket and once I was standing in a book store next to a gentleman who had just read the blurb and with a grimace of disgust he put *The Cowards* back on the shelf.

For a long time after publication, nothing much happened. *Literarni Noviny* gave it a fairly favorable review; Jiri Lederer, writing in the Prague newspaper *Vecerni Praha,* noted that the book showed talent. And then somebody came up to me and said, "Have you seen this?" waving an article from *Prace* [the trade unions' daily] which contained Vaclav Behounek's review entitled "A Slap at the Living and the Dead." Right after that came Josef Rybak's piece, "Rotten Fruit," and soon each day brought a new attack.

First of all, of course, there was the notorious "mangy kitten" statement by Karel Novy.* Personally, I am convinced that he had no intention of stirring up the "aparatchiks" against me, but that was the result all the same. Neither Fikar nor Vitezslav Kocourek—though one was the managing director and the other editor-in-chief of the Writers' Union Publishing House at that time—was able to explain the reason for the storm; they themselves didn't know what was going on. Just then, when verbal bombs were falling all around and many people refused to see me altogether, I got an in-

---

* Novy, in his review, referred to Skvorecky as "a mangy kitten." A novelist himself and nearly seventy when *The Cowards* appeared, Novy had little sympathy for young writers.—*Ed.*

vitation from Alfred Radok [film and stage director, one of the founders of *Laterna Magica*] whom I hadn't known at all until then, and this gave me a big lift. In the end, though, except for having been forced to leave *Svetova Literatura,* no real harm came to me. Jan Rezac took me right back into the editorial offices of the State Publishing House. I was supposed to get a reprimand from the Writers' Union, but when they met nobody really spoke up against me. Professor Burianek [literary critic and professor of Czech literature at Charles University] came to my defense, and of course Fikar and Kocourek did, too.

As I now reconstruct the whole affair, I believe this is what happened: a number of reviews of *The Cowards* were scheduled to appear, and as far as I know many had already been written—including those of Antonin Jelinek and Josef Vohryzek [whose reviews probably were favorable]—but they never came out. In this way, an artificial and distorted critical atmosphere was created. Lederer's review caused quite a scandal all on its own. On Thursday his favorable review of *The Cowards* came out in *Vecerni Praha;* on Saturday an article appeared in the same newspaper denouncing "this politically unreliable person," and Lederer got the axe. Step by step, the same thing happened not only to Fikar and Kocourek but also to Jan Grossmann, Josef Hirsal, and finally even to Kamil Bednar [the last three, like Fikar and Kocourek, were on the staff of the Writers' Union Publishing House] whose only sin was to praise the book at the office. Ironically enough, the axe job was done by the same people who only a short time before had been praising *The Cowards* to me to the sky. This climate didn't affect only people; literary works fell victim to it, too. Hrabal's *Pearl at the Bottom,* Lubomir Doruzka's book about jazz—all such works were set aside and had to wait a number of years before they could return to grace. A conference on criticism was called, at which Ladislav Stoll [an ultra-orthodox party ideologist and critic] delivered his famous denunciation of my book, and so on. In short, it was a victory for the conservative elements who felt that things had gone too far. But now comes the paradox. A year after this purge which was supposed to result in the production of healthy and constructive literature, everybody began to write and to publish books that actually went much further than *The Cowards.* A similar thing happened in film. After the conference at Banska Bystrica [a conference called to make films conform more closely with the party line] the entire leadership of Czechoslovak films was changed, with the tragi-comic result that under the new leaders our film industry produced works which the previous regime would have found totally unacceptable. I had already had similar experiences in 1945 in Nachod. I used to edit a publication there. I put out three issues, and you wouldn't believe how fast I got fired. Then a friend of mine took over, and he got away with all sorts of things that I never would have dreamed of trying. That's always the way it goes, I suppose. Still, I'm surprised that people still go along with this farce.

Why do you think it was The Cowards *rather than some other book that caused the roof to fall in?*

The Cowards was, in its time, a real innovation—a fact which was due less to my genius than to luck. I had been studying English, and so at a time when others were struggling through typical Stalinist-era works such as *Knight of the Golden Star,* I was able to read literature of a higher order. I was surrounded by fine examples of writing, and this includes Marx and Engels as well. These classics were not required reading at the time, but I saw that these men knew how to write, that they knew how to create a system, present an idea. I have not read any political writings since. I found no difficulty in reconciling Marxist ideology with the literature of sincere, truthful exposition as practiced in England and America. But even this was somehow an unusual idea at the time.

It often happens in art that something totally new—or, as in the case of *The Cowards,* relatively new—makes its appearance in the midst of scandal. A scandal attracts people, and the bigger the furor the more people it lures and seduces. All prohibitions are in vain once the devil has appeared; as is well known, only God can prevail against the devil. That's why, in such cases, theoretical victories are usually promptly followed by crushing practical defeats. All the initial excitement about *The Cowards* was stirred up by an edition of approximately 10,000 copies. Since then, 120,000 copies of the book have been printed, and the world still hasn't come to an end.

All art is a manifestation of a more or less critical attitude toward society. Artists usually have a strong moral consciousness and dislike producing "on demand." And when their works are wronged, though they cannot fight back and struggle in the same way as other people, their opposition hardens all the same. That's just a normal dialectical process. Those who hate repression—and they are in the majority—don't react to it with the thought "we will obey," but on the contrary, "we will disobey." That's because they realize that otherwise they would lose their identities. A decent person never criticizes those who are defenseless...

To come back to foreign writers: You are probably our best authority on Hemingway and Faulkner. You have a very special relationship to these two Americans...

That is a complicated and rather personal matter. At one time I struggled with the problem of writing dialogue. Then I read *A Farewell to Arms* and learned that dialogue can be absolutely bare. This profoundly affected my sensibilities, and the magic of the text reached me. I kept reading more of Hemingway; I thought about him and studied works written about him. I think I was so fascinated by him because he managed to merge literature and life, because literature became his fate, his destiny. He felt that if he stopped writing, even for a while, his life would stop too. And then, in the early 1950s, I was struck by his absolute sincerity: "The writer's job is to tell the truth." That is as simple as a commandment, and it is a commandment that is difficult to evade.

For me, there is no basic difference between Hemingway and Faulkner. In Faulkner I found once again the magic, luminous text. And once again I got a peek into the author's life, and a number of details drew me even closer to him. For example, his love for detective stories. Until 1946 he spent several months each year in Hollywood writing movie scripts. For rather commercial films, too, I believe. He used to say that if he were ever to write himself out, to lose his inspiration, he would write detective stories and get by on pure skill and craftsmanship. I am impressed by his broad taste, his refusal to turn up his nose at anything. His brother, John Faulkner, tells how William once entered the local drugstore and saw a stack of detective stories on the counter. They had been picked out by a prominent Oxford citizen, but when this gentleman saw Faulkner enter the store, he felt ashamed of his plebeian reading habits and pretended to be busily examining some serious books. "These yours?" asked Faulkner, pointing at the detective stories. "Certainly not," answered the gentleman. Whereupon Faulkner started to rummage avidly through the stack and bought a handful on the spot.

There is still another reason why I am so fond of Hemingway,

Faulkner, and Greene. Who was it that said he'd give his life for a good aphorism? In their books you will always find, at a crucial point, some key words, some truth that would make the book precious even if it contained nothing else. For example, in *A Farewell to Arms* there are two such moments that make the book unforgettable for me. The first is the idea that the world breaks almost everyone, and those it cannot break it kills. This is not a philosophical discovery. Writers aren't philosophers, they simply formulate in a better way what starlings twitter to each other across rooftops. The second great comment comes in the scene in which the military police are shooting deserters: The interrogators, writes Hemingway, were distinguished by that beautiful objectivity and devotion to strict justice which is typical of people who deal with death but stand in no immediate danger of death themselves. How succinctly this expresses the boastfulness of people whose mouths are full of phrases such as "I'd rather be dead than . . ." but who at the same time build deep atomic shelters in their backyards.

Faulkner, in *A Fable,* presents sensitive and extremely convincing arguments against war. Not simply a vague statement like "peace is good," but resistance against everything that supports war, no matter in what holy or seductive guise it is presented. By the way, I am well aware of the practical difficulties connected with pacifism, and yet to me it is the only rationally consistent position there is.

And Graham Greene! In *The Heart of the Matter,* when Scobie kills himself after committing a long series of sins, his wife is convinced that he will be denied salvation. And yet in answer to the priest's question, she replies that she herself no longer feels any bitterness toward her late husband. "And do you think God's likely to be more bitter than a woman?" asks the priest. I love an author for such lines, and I am willing to forgive a great deal for their sake alone.

What do you think about present American culture, and what role do you think it will play in the future?

At one time America was a province, a small town on the cultural map of the world. Of course, cultures have frequently gathered fresh strength from provincial influences. At one time I occupied myself with the question of Russain influence on American writers. Modern American writers were extremely fond of the Russians and of their ideals. And the currents stirred by this admiration had a great influence on Hemingway. Now this cultural migration has been reversed and Hemingway is a god in Russia.

Today's American society is quite different from the European. It is wealthy and has gone through a phase of total commercialization; this may be related to the rapid growth of general education, too; but suddenly Americans feel the need to concern themselves with art. I have the feeling that America is now on the verge of establishing itself as a cultural "great power." At the same time, Americans have the advantage of a strong tradition of individualism, so that they are not as susceptible to currents and influences. Hemingway, for example, had very close contacts with the avantgarde; he knew how to use it for his purposes, but never attached himself to any one group. European thought is much more theoretical. A new type of novel would probably never originate in America, because nobody there would bother with its theoretical basis. Americans are, of course, extremely gifted when it comes to films. I am thinking not only of the pinnacles of the art, but of people such as Hitchcock—an Americanized Englishman. Here is a man who knows his métier thoroughly.

In conclusion, the usual question about the generations . . .

Whatever I say will no doubt seem like generational self-praise. Once I said to Josef Hirsal that a generation is related by choice rather than by age, that it is a collection of people who have undergone the same experiences and arrived at the same set of beliefs. I feel in no way a generational colleague of such people as, say, Stanislav* Neumann. That's why I get irritated by statements such as "your generation did this" or "your generation is responsible for that." These are meaningless generalizations.

But those people who, according to my definition, really form part of my generation are still by and large at the start of their lives' work. Dorothy Sayers wrote that a person cannot really produce a novel until he has something concrete to say about life. It is a fact that every artistic work, no matter how abstract or theoretical it may be, is built upon some strong experience in real life. Otherwise nothing comes into being. In my view, the only true art is realistic,

---

* Grandson of the great Czech communist poet S. K. Neumann. The most Stalinist poet of his generation, Stanislav Neumann committed suicide in the fall of 1970 in protest against Russian occupation of Czechoslovakia and its consequences.—*Ed.*

in the sense that realism is neither a trend nor a direction but a level of quality. When art attains a certain quality it is real. I believe that our generation has undergone unique experiences and is now in a position to express itself. It has experience to draw on and is still far from senile.

At one time, a lot was said and written in our country about the qualities of the "New Man." God knows what was actually meant by this expression, but I believe that we are still talking about the same eternal human qualities such as love, honesty, and so forth, qualities which have always existed but which circumstances have rarely allowed to blossom. If this generation, which has lived through all sorts of unbelievable somersaults and clashes of ideologies and pseudo-ideologies, can be said to point toward any truth at all, it is the truth that good men have survived all of this and continue to live. This generation is learning to value tolerance— human tolerance—perhaps just because of the realization that there are certain situations that must be solved in a radical and intolerant way. Nevertheless, these are always extremely dangerous situations, with a frightening potential for enslaving good men no matter how much they initially appear to expand human horizons. This is why intolerance must be limited only to very brief periods and to situations in which it is truly unavoidable. As soon as this limit is transgressed, evil reigns.

My generation, which by and large has accepted socialism as a solution to the problem of organizing society, is painfully aware of the degree to which socialism remains only a word. And we know that the word has yet to become flesh. And that this incarnation will not be realized until human capabilities are given a much greater area of freedom than has been the case so far.

I believe that society will have to think in these terms before it can progress. And because our generation has gone through so many antithetical experiences, it appears to the dogmatists as too liberal and to the young as too formless. At least that's my impression. Young people are, of course, always intolerant, which is a healthy reaction against conventions. Sometimes I am almost repelled by their cruelty, but it is difficult to blame them, given the current atmosphere and circumstances. In any case, I am convinced that if we respond to the intolerance of youth with the intolerance of age, the young won't become any wiser and the old will stupefy.

December 1966

I hardly can add anything to Jean-Paul Sartre's penetrating analysis of the political agonies of my native country, and I certainly cannot make any corrections.* Sartre is a brilliant philosopher; I—in spite of my Ph.D. (my thesis was on Tom Paine, who, fine man that he was, certainly was a much simpler thinker than Sartre)—I am a storyteller. So let me just add one story, if I may.

Much space is devoted in Sartre's essay to the feelings of "guilt" experienced by men who lived in the period immediately following the revolution, *i.e.,* in the case of Czechoslovakia, following the political takeover by the Communist Party. Probably nobody else experienced this with greater intensity than writers. I did, too; although I never was a communist. But I was serious, as most intellectuals are, about a social justice. I was living in a country swept, to a certain degree, by enthusiasm,** and so I—to a certain degree—got the communist guilt complex. In 1951 I was drafted into the army. There I could not help but see the discrepancy between what was being said about life and about the working class, and what life and the working class in G.I. outfits proved to be. The experience resulted in a novel, *The Tank Corps,* which I wrote after my dismissal from the army in 1954–1955. I did not offer it for publication then. In the first place, I knew it would be silly; those were the times of arrogant socialist realism, and I had always been a realist in estimating the publishing possibilities of satirical novels under socialist realism. But also, in the second place, as Sartre says: *Laughter calls things in question.* Readers of *The Tank Corps*—members of the Prague literary underground who read the novel in typescript—certainly did laugh. And, absurd as it may appear now (even to myself), I was afraid that the *wrong* things could be called in question: the *good* things that even this imported dictatorial socialism had done. Free medical care and the absence of unemployment, for instance, because I still remembered the Great Depression, and my

---

* In February 1971, Josef Skvorecky responded to Jean-Paul Sartre's "The Socialism That Came in from the Cold." His rejoinder first appeared in *Evergreen Review* No. 87.—*Ed.*

** But let us get this straight: the party enthusiasts had come to see things in their real perspective only after the Twentieth Congress of the Communist Party of the USSR; that does not mean, however, that there had not been people in Czechoslovakia, and lots of them, who from the very beginning had grave doubts about what was going on; by no means were those men less honest, less humane, less intelligent, or less socialist.

old schoolfriends, in their patched-up pants, begging for a piece of my bread-and-butter in the breaks between classes. For me, this was a traumatic experience, and has remained so to this very day. So I just circulated my manuscript among friends, and worried whether I had done the right thing.

In a way I had not. The typescript fell into the wrong hands. A girl who was after me, and whom I tried to avoid, got hold of it. What happened is described in Milan Kundera's last play *Ptako-vina (Two Ears, Two Marriages).** I suffered terribly for some time, until an army friend—one of the heroes of *The Tank Corps*—helped me, using a method which would probably be described as "breaking and entering." He then read the novel himself and liked it, particularly those parts where I had described him as a foul-mouthed whorer. Strangely enough, this, for some reason, gave me assurance that the novel would, after all, not be harmful to socialism. Perhaps it was due to the fact that my friend was a blacksmith by profession.

Then, when the ice melted a little, I started offering parts of the novel for publication in magazines. Some were confiscated, others published. A very dear friend of mine, the wife of one of the executed defendants in the Slansky trial, told me about an interesting experience of hers. She was sitting in a street-car, watching a man who was reading a magazine. The man was oblivious of the world around him, and from time to time burst into fits of uncontrollable laughter. Eager to get a glimpse of what was making him so merry, she leaned over his shoulder. It was the excerpt from *The Tank Corps*. When she told me—maybe it just flattered my ego—I was also more and more convinced that I could not have harmed socialism.

Then they took my father to the hospital. He was one of the last men killed by World War I. Wounded in 1917 in Poland, he never completely recovered. His wound never healed, and on Christmas 1967 he died after an attempt to operate on the infected shin-bone. While he lay in the hospital, I used to supply him with detective novels but these, somehow, failed to take his mind off his approach-

---

* *Ptak* means a *cock* in slang. A rather horrible woman in this play by Milan Kundera secretly tapes a damaging conversation of the hero. Threatening to expose him to the authorities, she forces him to visit her regularly for the purpose of copulation.

ing death. Then the magazine with the excerpt from my novel appeared, and, for the last time, I saw my father in a good mood. He laughed so heartily that his leg slipped out of the noose which held it in mid-air, and only then did he stop laughing. The magazine circulated then among the patients, and later was stolen by a visitor who had tried in vain to buy it at newsstands.

By then I had almost totally overcome my guilt feelings. Having been meeting, for some time, with young people, particularly the students of Charles University, I observed another strange thing: *they* had no guilt feelings at all. *They* saw no reason why a swinery should be called a "distortion of socialism," and a rascal an "untypical exception," or a man "suffering from remnants of bourgeois manners." They were free of any masochistic self-torturings, for to them socialism was the *status quo;* not something that had to be fought for, that people had died for (which is one of the chief sources of guilt-feelings). They liked my satire. The idea that this could harm socialism never entered their heads. "Why?" asked a young man, a brilliant student of logic whose father, another victim of the Stalinist terror, had died in the camps. "Stupidity should not be an integral part of socialism, and it is stupidity you make fun of in your novel, isn't it?"

So I somehow began to trust this new generation, and I felt grateful to them, too, for they helped me to cure myself of my implanted complexes. But the definitive cure had yet to come.

When the tanks arrived, one of the first military objects they occupied was the building of the Publishing House of the Czechoslovak Writers' Union. After about three weeks they evacuated it again; the editors moved in, and found nothing missing, with the exception of some fountain-pens and—the original of an illustration for *The Tank Corps!* (The book, finally, had been accepted for publication in the summer of 1968, and then again "indefinitely postponed" in the fall of 1969.) The drawing was a *frontispiece:* it showed a group of army officers' faces in magnificently cheeky caricature, somewhat in the manner of George Grosz. Gosh! I thought. They have confiscated it, and will use it at my trial!

But then one of the editors discovered the drawing. It was stuck among some old proofs, and the man who had put it there obviously got scared of what he had done to it. Under the most repulsive-looking, potato-shaped officer's head there was an inscription in careful *azbuka: Eto galava praklyatoy svini lejtenanta Gleb Grigoryevitcha*

Belochvostov!—"This is the head of that fucking swine, Lieutenant Gleb Grigoryevitch Belochvostov!"

And so my cure was complete. That anonymous soldier of the Sòviet forces certainly did not have any guilt feelings about insulting an integral part of a socialist army, which Lieutenant Belochvostov undoubtedly was. Or was he?

February 1971

Ludvík Vaculík

Born 1926 in Brumov, Moravia. After a succession of jobs, he joined, in the mid-1960s, the staff of *Literarni Noviny*. While his first novel, *A Noisy House*, based on his experience as a boarding-school tutor, did not arouse much attention, he became one of the best known Czech writers in 1967, when he published his second novel, *The Axe*, and delivered a historic speech at the Fourth Writers' Congress. In it he accused the regime of not having solved a single relevant problem of the country in the past twenty years. Speaking from the position of an idealistic and disillusioned party member, Vaculik expressed the feelings of a great part of the nation. His speech circulated for months in clandestine copies all over the country, as it was not allowed to be published. In the fall of 1967 he was expelled from the party together with two other editors of *Literarni Noviny*, Klima and Liehm, but this decree was nullified after the demotion of Novotny. In 1968 he wrote, at the request of a group of well-known persons, the *2,000-Word Manifesto*, urging the speed-up of reforms and expressing support for the reformist leadership, by whom, however, it was rejected as too far-reaching and dangerous. Vaculik's role in the Czech liberal and reform movement could be compared to that of Thomas Paine in American history. In his writings, which included a number of excellent reportage articles, he evaded all the usual clichés and phraseology developed by the politicians to cover up the real state of things. In a simple, earthy style with a touch of his native Moravian dialect, he appealed to the common sense of the average citizen. In 1971, his third novel, *The Guinea Pigs*, was published in Switzerland.

Ludvík Vaculík

We have been brushing against each other in the editorial offices for quite a few years now; we have competed for space in the pages of the next issue; we have discussed our likes and dislikes and sometimes we have completely disagreed. And every time a new issue of Literarni Noviny *comes out I have come to repeat a question that he made famous: "Anything there for my buddy?" "My buddy" has become for us the symbol of the nonintellectual reader; every newspaper that prides itself on the fact that it is aimed at the intellectual nevertheless also has the ambition to attract "my buddy." Though we have also met on various other occasions, we didn't really know each other. From my end, this situation drastically changed shortly before Christmas. He gave me his second book,* The Axe—*it now occurs to me that we never discussed his first book at all. I read it through in two evenings and since those two pre-Christmas evenings I have been breathing more easily in this world. Here was an author who had found a name for the incredible collapse of all structures—that collapse we all felt happening around us but could not define except on the level of political slogans. At the same time, this author demonstrated that life-giving impulses persist, that within the chaos there are still feelings that give meaning to life. These values, these certainties have their roots deep in the earth, in the depths of time, and in oneself. If you yourself can't find*

*them, if you can't find ways of bringing them to life, there is nobody
else who can help you.*

*Vaculik's strange optimism is expressed in his confession: "I have
deliberately scattered all sorts of traps behind me so that I would
never be able to go back. I am weak, yes; I am afraid, yes; but my
fears are equally strong in all directions. No direction offers me a
better way out, and, after all, there is great freedom in this—to be
able to go in all directions with equal danger. Now at least I can go
forward of my own free will; that is my reward for all-embracing
fear." So we locked and bolted the door and sat down facing each
other in this apartment house which had no telephones, because we
were living in a reasonably civilized country in the middle of Europe
in the year 1967. The advantage was that we were assured of some
privacy. We took off our muddy shoes; he pulled a bottle of Moravian wine out of his briefcase; I started heating up some sausages,
shredding a horse-radish, and I sliced—or rather split—the hard
fruitcake left over from Christmas. For the first time in years, we
really had things to say to each other. The interview started off with
a bang . . .*

Interviews? I know what they are and I can't stand them. I pity
anybody who has to indulge in that sort of thing, no matter which
side of the table he happens to be on. It's like lighting up stars on a
cardboard heaven. When I was in radio I always felt ashamed when
I tagged after some poor chap with my microphone like a pawn-
broker or a ragpicker: "Don't you have a little idea for sale, or
maybe a tiny experience, or could you possibly favor us with a small
impression or two?" And I'm not very smart. I haven't read anything, I don't know anything, I am not the right person with whom
to have dazzling discussions about politics or the situation in communist parties at home or abroad, or about film. I simply never go
to the movies, or hardly ever. And I know nothing about literature.
I read something and the next minute it's completely forgotten. I
don't understand how authors manage to converse at receptions;
I suppose they talk about whatever they read last. So there we are—
we have now clarified all cultural problems. But I know you can't
leave things like this, and so you're writing everything down and at
least you'll try to make an interesting character out of me. By the
way, that wall over there with the footprints on it interests me no
end. If I wasn't looking at it with my own two eyes, I wouldn't be-

lieve it. It is the indelible mark of our kind of workmanship. Say, do you know that I find a book much more amusing if it's illustrated?

I tried to provide a theoretical justification for interviews, at least certain kinds. After all, it is my profession. We grappled for a while, and finally, like two wrestlers locked in the same grip, we rolled over to the subject of literature ...

My opinions on literature are probably terribly dogmatic. I can't help thinking that there's no point to literature if it doesn't lead people to revolution. Or to some externally visible movement. Take *Werther,* for example: people read Goethe's book and committed suicide in droves—that's what I call a literary success!

I am not sure that any literature has ever directly led to revolution. Perhaps it would be better if we talked about an orientation ...

If literature were left free, it would lead to revolutions, all right. Not all literature and not always, but at least certain works. After all, literature is directed outwardly, toward the people; this is its ambition. Its aim is not to crawl back into itself.

Literature as an impulse to action?

I am not as simple-minded as all that. Let's look at literature more as a means, a way of bringing a man into a certain state in which he succeeds in doing what he had long intended to do. It will confirm —or fail to confirm—that he's right in the way he evaluates the world and his own life. It may demonstrate to him that his indecision is only cowardice, and so on. From that point on, of course, everything depends on the reader himself. If literature, or art in general, is supposed to liberate people, that means it leads them to act. And action is essential for health. In the political and social spheres. What's wrong with action? Everyone agrees that art and literature purify Man, free him of prejudices, and lead him to a better moral state. This is accepted as far as intimate, personal morality is concerned. Why shouldn't the same apply in a much broader sphere?

For example in the political area?

Yes. I am always concerned about the application of moral criteria to the broadest area possible, the socio-political area. Today anyone who'd ask a person working professionally in politics or propaganda what his personal ideals are would be considered naïve. Politics and personal creativity are considered two separate entities. You don't think that this is a literary subject? Relations directed toward the outside world are just as human as those which take place entirely within a single human mind. I understand the vehemence of the reaction to the prose of "reawakening" that has been produced here since 1956. I recently read a review that said this sort of prose was unpopular because it tried to solve other people's political problems. But for me this sort of prose still has its validity. It is by no means a matter that's been talked to death. My desire to write in a literary way about political problems wouldn't compromise me, as far as I can see.

What is literature, anyway?

My God, why don't you ask me about photography? I almost prefer taking pictures to writing, and I'd be just as pleased if people were interested in my pictures. Unfortunately I don't have enough time for photography. I kept wanting to start in on something else, to try something different. Life is a continually sharpening definition of that which we will never become. I call myself a writer, and yet . . . no, I won't. But I *will* call myself an author; that makes more sense. I had a lot of trouble with *The Axe;* it's too closely connected with myself and my family. Usually these things are disguised in a book; you change the profession, the surroundings, the number of brothers and sisters. But if you have the courage to ignore such amenities, you can concentrate all your energy on what you really want to say. It was only after I had completed the book that I realized that a person actually spends his whole psychic life within certain narrow bounds: childhood and early adulthood. But this type of writing creates problems. Relatives and neighbors always read in a stupid way. To this day, people in Valasske Klobouky abuse Mnacko [Ladislav Mnacko's novel *Death Is Called Engelchen* is set in and around this Slovakian town.]; nobody wrote so beautifully about them as he, but they are angry because things were different from the way he described it—a certain girl had a green blouse and not a red one.

If I were you, I wouldn't lose sleep over the question of whether you are a writer or not. If you look long enough you'll always find plenty of people who'll tell you that you aren't. I have a different

*question. How much does a writer learn from literature, from the
books he read in his childhood, for instance? (I asked this question
for a particular reason, and it was unfair of me not to mention it.
In Vaculík's* The Axe *I was fascinated by the style, which seemed to
me a synthesis of the essence of Czech traditional literary style and
modern European prose.)*

In my childhood I mainly read Wild West stories, pulp novels, as
well as Verne, Dumas, and Sienkiewicz. I probably read the Czech
classics, too, although they left no conscious impression.

In my fourth year of public school I decided to make a confrontation between Nemcova's *The Grandmother* and the pulp novels.
My thesis was that any fifteen-year-old who claimed he really liked
Grandmother was a liar. He enjoys pulp novels, and at best puts up
with a classic like that. I never gave *Grandmother* the opportunity
to have any greater influence on me. In fact, I never allowed myself
to become so enraptured with literature as to become interested in
it as an academic subject. Only once. I wrote an essay about Vladislav Vancura's *Marketa Lazarova* entitled "The Principle of Revenge." What I liked best about the book was the robber's motto:
"Away to the woods and the highways!" Yes, that was really something! Since then I've occasionally been accused of plagiarizing
Vancura, but I've only read that one book of his, plus *Jan Marhoul
the Baker*. I read *Three Rivers* so long ago that I've forgotten what
it's all about.

The first story I ever wrote was influenced by Jean Richard
Bloch's* novel . . . . . *and Co.* My interest in Bloch was stimulated by
"my teacher." "My teacher" plays an important role in my life.
When I was thirteen, she became a kind of third parent to me. She
took care of me both physically and mentally, and guided my reading in new directions. She had a real library, though I realize now
that it wasn't a very extensive one. The library contained only
books she was fond of at any given moment. You know the kind of
provincial educated person she was. She subscribed to the usual
women's magazines; she took part in various civic activities, visited
museums, belonged to Sokol and the Red Cross, organized theatricals, literary evenings, get-togethers. With the destruction of this
type of person, Czech country life deteriorated. I deliberately said
destruction rather than disappearance, because a definite attempt

---

* A French communist writer popular in Europe in the 1930s.—*Ed.*

was made to replace these provincial intellectuals with people who
were either too frightened or too lazy to do anything they didn't
have to do. To come back to "my teacher"—she directed my reading
toward Rolland, Nexø, and Melville, although I found *Moby Dick*
so fat that I never did get through it. I also remember reading some
Selma Lagerlöf.

The Axe is largely autobiographical. As the book suggests, my
father was really in Persia. I lived in southeastern Moravia until I
was fifteen, then I had to go out and make a living. It might have
been possible for me to study; my family might have been able to
manage somehow, but I heard about Zlin [headquarters of the Bata
shoe industry]. I wanted to go out into the world, as far away as
possible, even to Asia, and Bata was a way of going there. You could
go through a commercial training school at the firm's expense. My
ambition was to get to Bata, graduate from a training school, and
then go abroad, perhaps as a purchasing agent for raw rubber in
Borneo. It all came true—except for Borneo! There you have the
ever-narrowing definition of our limitations. But even getting to
Zlin was no simple matter. First I had to fill out a complicated ques-
tionnaire, which seemed highly deceptive to me. For example:
Where do you prefer living—in the country or in the city? I
thought: If I say "in the country," they'll get the idea that I won't
be able to adapt to life in Zlin. If I answer "in the city" they'll think,
here's a hick who wants to act like a city slicker. Or: Were you ever
the leader of a childhood gang? Well, I'd been an Indian chief in
my time, but again, I thought, if I admit it they'll think I don't
know how to take orders. On the other hand, it might have helped
if they thought I was some sort of born leader of men. I didn't know
what to do; I was dying to be accepted. I had a cousin who was at
Bata and she had married a fellow Bata employee whose single-
mindedness astounded me. His advice was: persistence, stubbornness, and, if necessary, arrogance. Never admit you don't know how
to do something; you know everything, even if you have to learn it
overnight. Then they asked me to undergo a psychological test. It
was all very peculiar: they made people feel as if they were being
picked for top executive positions, and then they were sent to do the
most menial chores; nobody said an intelligent word to them and
they were treated with great rudeness. These were people who had
come to Bata with all sorts of grandiose ideas, and now they were doing the very opposite of what they had expected to be doing. And

here is where people were separated into psychological types: some knuckled under, caved in, let themselves be pushed from one machine to the next; others realized what was happening and tried to find ways and means of beating the system. Only the toughest and most capable succeeded. It's an interesting thing: I am sure that some sort of favoritism must have existed there—when I think back now I'm convinced of it—yet at the time we didn't let such excuses weaken our resolution. We believed that hard work, and still more hard work, would get us ahead. It's an age-old complaint of the incompetent and the lazy that good jobs depend on good connections. But sitting on the hard dormitory beds at night, the boys would swap stories about their progress from one machine to the next, always to the more and more complicated ones, always to the more difficult and better-paid jobs. I remember one of them boasting about how, when a certain cutter fell ill, he took over his work so successfully that the foreman was probably going to let him stay on at the machine.

The basic principle at Bata was that a person had to show a willingness and capability for better, more demanding work even before he was assigned to it. Today the situation is the reverse: people sit in a certain spot and collect pay even though they're still learning their jobs. The young people stare at you in disbelief when you ask them to perform some new task. The stenographer simply can't get it into her head that if she wants to be a secretary she'll have to know secretarial skills a good six months before anybody will think of promoting her. But to get back to Bata: when I listened to those fellows talking, I began to realize with quiet horror that I wasn't the least bit interested in becoming a cutter, or a foreman, or a section chief, or a director, or even Bata himself. I was greatly interested in the operation as a unit; I was fascinated by the structure, the atmosphere, the system. I approved of the idea of the survival of the fittest, but my own ambition wasn't aimed in that direction. It was an excellent industrial system and I still have tremendous respect for it. What it needed was a bit of kindness, less shouting at people, more courtesy, humanization of the working conditions. These are the changes I foolishly expected socialism to bring about. I believe that the original system was sufficiently productive to have earned itself the means to provide a humaner atmosphere and better conditions. Instead, a deterioration set in; the system was doomed without a decent trial. The hard labor re-

mained but instead of resulting in well-paid workers we ended up
with poorly paid workers. Technical progress was forbidden for a
decade; the entire industry was condemned to planned obsolescence.

I left Zlin of my own free will to study in Prague. My colleagues
at Bata regarded my departure a bit contemptuously, and to some
of them I seemed ridiculous. When I left I felt almost like a deserter.

While still at Zlin I had joined the Communist Party. I believed
that it was the only party that had a definite plan for the future. It
was supported by literature, by theory, and it presented an extensive
program, whereas the other parties defined themselves only in a
negative sense. I admired Stalin's tract *On Dialectical and Historical Materialism*. Everything was very clear and concise. Yet I was
already becoming uneasy about certain aspects of partisanship. For
instance, we were supposed to go out and tear down posters put up
by the National Socialists [a socially progressive Czech political
party, the party of Eduard Benes]. I didn't go. I had imagined that
we were about to begin the struggle for decency and nobility, that
we would hold philosophical discussions like Stalin and party intellectuals, when in reality here we were dealing with mundane
matters, and not very justly at that. I was in a great hurry to join the
party; I wanted to become a member before the 1946 elections because I considered it extremely important to reach a decision before
the mass of the people did.

At the university in Prague, life was totally different. Everything
was free and easy, attendance at lectures wasn't compulsory, but
the lack of any strict routine made me nervous. I wanted to do
something definite, and so while I continued my studies I took on
the job of tutor in a boarding school in Benesov. I liked tutoring
very much. Education is more than a job; it's a whole style of life.
Few people have that. My wife did. All by herself she taught one
hundred girls; nowadays they'd hire a big staff for the job. One
quality that's needed above all to be a good teacher is modesty. Of
course, I was full of grandiose plans. I saw myself as the political
awakener of youth. Such tasks as issuing bedsheets I regarded as
senseless delays. This was a mistake on my part, and my attitude
caused me much unpleasantness.

In 1949 I had to leave. They told me that I had the choice of
handing in my resignation and getting a good recommendation, or
of being kicked out. Naturally I resigned. Nobody really appre-
ciated my work, and this was my first lesson in the tactics of living

in a socialist state. As I recall, they came up with thirteen different reasons for getting rid of me. For example: the students had been seen marching to work in disorder, blocking traffic and causing motorists to complain . . . Christ, they had all kinds of things against me! We had a terrific fight. I want to write about it some day; I have a feeling it will help people understand China. After all, in our country, too, the young people called the tune. The kids were the real teachers. An apprentice barber from the school did the barbering, and the regular barber was sent off to a factory. And I kept going to the same place and got my shaves from the apprentice. Why? My God, why did I let that kid shave me? A crucial question actually.

When they fired me they threw out my wife, too, and so we moved to Prague. All this was between 1949 and 1951. The only reason I wasn't fired from my next job was that the office where I worked had been eliminated. Next, I was called into the army. A novel about the army? I've been tempted. But in those days, through the optics of the time, the army was seen in an idealistic way, and I respected it. At party meetings you could criticize your own commander, and no matter how naïve a particular opinion might be it was always taken seriously. I met many idealists there— some really great people. Of course, time eventually sifted and sorted them out. Either they couldn't take it and dropped out or they trudged on, knuckled under. Naturally, any army is basically a lot of nonsense and stupid playacting. Even so, the soldier still has the choice of acting like a human being or like a beast. In the army you face the same questions as anywhere else, except that there the questions are put much more bluntly, more brutally. There's the question of sex, the question of alcoholism. I'd like to know how certain noble, pacifist-minded souls would approach the problem of discipline, command, insubordination . . . A very interesting human situation, no doubt about it.

When I got out of the army, my wife took a hand in my fate. You'll give up teaching, she told me; it's too dangerous a profession. So she found a quiet, cultural occupation for me: editor. It made sense. First I worked in the *Rude Pravo* [official daily paper of the Czechoslovak Communist Party] publishing offices where we put out brochures and a magazine for country families, and then I got into broadcasting. In 1959. Those brochures were a terrible bore, but I learned a lot about printing.

Broadcasting is beautiful work, and in those days the youth department was staffed by an outstanding group that had an excellent and stubborn party organization. In this connection I should mention Dr. Ferdinand Smrcka, an extremely serious, educated and noble person; he represents the finest kind of executive our society is capable of producing; the sort of man who knows how to lead, yet manages to preserve his own character.

(Another example of the intertwining of people's lives. This same Dr. Smrcka had been, some twenty years earlier, my professor in the lower gymnasium. I thus came in contact with him at a crucial character-forming age, and he left the same impression on me as on Vaculik. I especially valued the way he communicated his own love and respect for history, both our own history and that of other countries.)

And Smrcka managed to maintain his equilibrium. His thinking remained quite pure; he was aware of the arrogance that surrounded him—including my own—but the decisive thing for him, the only thing that really mattered, was the work. How many such people like that do we have, people who have managed to maintain the ability to turn their ideas and plans into reality?

The crash came during an annual conference that was held in, of all places, the main railroad station. For a time it looked as if I was going to get sacked. And then something odd happened and I was given a national award "for outstanding work." That same day they broadcast the program for which I and one of my colleagues had been severely censured two months before. As you can see, our life was like a ride on a swing; success prevented debacle and vice versa. The funny thing was that, though I plugged ahead the same as always, I was praised to the skies one moment and sharply reprimanded the next.

Then I got a job with *Literarni Noviny.* Once again I spoke my mind . . . Mind you, I don't see any special bad luck or black magic in all this. Certain professions simply involve certain risks. Under the old system, a manufacturer either sold his wares or went under. A journalist or writer in those days also produced the best goods he could, and his product was either bought or rejected. The same process goes on today, only it has been given a different label.

Whenever I encounter an outstanding journalist who switches over to the literary metier, I remember what Egon Kisch told me

just before his death, some twenty years ago: "Watch yourself.
Every first-rate journalist has just one ambition—to become a
second-rate author."

Many people aspire to be writers, many others to be journalists.
There are many ways to get one's name into print. It used to be
possible to be a postal employee or a teacher and at the same time
to get one's work published. Now it's more difficult. In order to
get published now an unknown author either has to write something sensational or have the means to publish his work on his own.
For this reason, so many people concentrate on journalism. As for
me, I probably always longed to be a writer, even when I imagined
I wanted to be a businessman. But I didn't dare admit it to myself, so meanwhile I patiently accepted my lot. While I was working in broadcasting, I didn't really think of myself as a reporter.
People can't understand why I am so happy not to be running
around with a microphone any longer, since I was apparently
fairly good at it. But I did it mainly to get even with society. This,
incidentally, is my definition of a writer: someone who wants to
square his debts with the world. Though, to be frank, I'm not sure
how I really felt about being a writer or a journalist. I think we try
to categorize too much. Actually, I wouldn't mind being the
director of a school, if I could write at the same time—which is
probably impossible. Seriously, if I could choose the kind of
teachers I wanted, and if I could pay them according to the
importance I attach to teaching, I'd love to make education my
second profession.

You called me an outstanding journalist. A really good journalist
never has an opportunity to write a book. He is continually occupied with current problems; he feels a pressing desire and need to
speak about them, and thus never has time for anything else.

Then, too, there's the question of the sheer craft of writing. Take
my first book, *A Noisy House.* When I wrote it I had no idea where
the documentary ended and the novel began. It seemed to me that
I ought to write about industrial discipline, about idiotic foremen
and pampered apprentices. In short, I made a list of problems that
I wanted to deal with. This novel didn't turn out well; today it's
just a curiosity that I wouldn't recommend to anybody. I feel sorry
for the book, I treat it like an abandoned child, but I have become
completely detached from it . . .

*To come back to education. You said you wouldn't mind being
the director of a school, if . . .*

Come to think of it, that's an interesting question. Well, first of
all, if I had the courage of my convictions I'd kick out everybody
who was too docile. I'd go over the whole staff and I'd keep only
those whose looks and way of talking I liked. I'd hire only people
with some special skill or knowledge; they'd have to be personally
interesting in some way.

The trouble is that teachers are, for the most part, people who
couldn't make it in other fields, or else they're students who consider teaching just a temporary phase while they're finishing their
studies. And now I'll say something else I probably shouldn't:
Every educator, in his own way, should try to establish his own
pedagogical school, his own direction. That would mean the rejection of today's pseudo-democracy.

*You said that you'd like to write about children, about their
games.*

Yes, but I don't want to dismiss the subject with an indulgent
smile nor do I want to write children's books. I'm sure you've had
the experience of meeting somebody you'd known as a boy and who,
even after all these years, looked exactly the same, except maybe his
face has shriveled up a bit.

Look around for yourself. The unreliable kid, the one who
promised to bring a frog but didn't, is just the same now. You still
can't count on him to bring the frog, except that maybe now he's
a cabinet minister. Maybe for that very same reason. The kids call
a meeting of their gang, and you can be sure that in spite of solemn
vows two of them won't show up. Or they'll start something with
great enthusiasm and give up halfway. Or their game will suddenly
seem silly to them. I remember one time we read that Indians could
lie stock-still on the ground for three hours! We all found this
terribly exciting and as chief of our tribe I did it first, but after me
nobody else tried. In a word, children are just like adults: they take
nothing seriously; there isn't a single agreement or promise they
won't break.

Furthermore, neither children nor grownups permit an idea to
be tested sufficiently to demonstrate its possibilities or shortcomings.
It's also interesting to observe the lack of a sense of style, which

often begins with children. I always used to get terribly annoyed when we played at Indians and some kid would come wearing a helmet, for no other reason than that he had one lying around at home. Have you ever noticed how many adults still put on helmets even though they're playing cowboys-and-Indians? Look around. You'll see.

And look how children play nowadays. Have you noticed? They've lost all sense of the gentlemanly, the magnanimous. For instance, they no longer play at releasing or exchanging prisoners. . . . These are some of the viewpoints from which I like to look at childhood. Not just as a return, an era of innocence that's nice to read about. Childhood may well be the only period in which a person is given the chance to develop freely.

A while ago, you made a distinction between fiction and non-fiction. Would you care to elaborate?

A documentary exposition tries to win the reader over through rational arguments. Fiction seeks understanding through the emotions. It makes possible an ordering of otherwise unrelated entities, an ordering which other means are unable to bring about. It gives the writer the opportunity to shake up large masses of people, to alarm them. The writer can create a new human type. But, above all, fiction enables a writer to make statements and assert values without giving proofs. He can base his judgments on nothing but his own personal experience, and yet be absolutely right. I am speaking quite generally now; I myself haven't yet had enough experience to be worth talking about.

As I told you, what most impressed me in The Axe *was your description of the collapse of all structures.*

I was angry about a great many things, especially about the violence being used to bring about reform, and I told myself: it was probably always like this. I am referring to primitivism, dullness, narrow-mindedness. The feudal epoch went under in the same sort of morass, so why not others? But I was really concerned about something a little different: What power—what group—finds it eternally necessary to make people as characterless and submissive as possible? Why must people's support be won only at the price of their moral devastation? After all, such moral destruction carries with it the danger that people in the future will be unable to resist a potential enemy. And the most crucial consideration of all: Why must this moral destruction be carried on by a system supposedly invented precisely for the purpose of freeing people from such an evil?

Is it your impression that a new structure is already beginning to grow out of the ruins of the old?

I would rather say that we're living in a magmatic or still fluid stage. The structure has not yet been decided, because questions of values must be decided first. And in this respect people are still living under anesthesia. I'm glad that readers didn't accept my book as expressing any longing for the good old days. This wasn't my intention at all. But it is time to realize that there are certain values in life which are eternally valid and which should be made inviolable to all regimes and all epochs. Why are we sitting here in this idiotic modern apartment house with its footprint-smeared walls when everybody has been pointing out for years and years how foolish this kind of "modernization" really is? I won't weep over the demise of the Moravian countryside—the population is increasing and urbanization must go on—but at least there should be some rhyme and reason behind it. Capable people have practically disappeared from the administration of villages and small towns. In the eastern Moravian village of Brumov there used to be a mayor who was a hero in my eyes. There were two bare, ugly hills near the town. He took some money out of the public treasury and planted the hills with beautiful cherry trees. As you might expect, there was a big hue and cry about wasting money, and the mayor was told that he ought just tend to his own affairs instead of sticking his nose into things that didn't concern him. The fact is, however, that this one man left a bigger and more lasting imprint on that countryside than the whole agricultural cooperative put together. In short, we are short of people who conceive of progress as a continual addition of new values to the old. We're just beginning to realize the need for defending certain true, established values, and defending them stubbornly, ruthlessly, though in a rational manner.

In the cities the situation is a bit better, and certain values do tend to crystallize around cultural and spiritual centers. But what about the country? What can the "televisioned" village masses find as centers for crystallization? The villager needs someone to give him a good dose of disquiet, to make him realize that he isn't living his own life but an alien one.

Another thing: how is it that power invariably ends up in the hands of relatively characterless and second-rate people? In political life, one dull-faced dolt always wins out over a dozen noble-minded and intelligent people. Once I saw, in an Italian magazine, a column of pictures showing Lavrenti Beria and other leading Stalinist figures, while another column consisted of photographs of their victims. Without even looking at the captions, just by studying the faces, one could tell who was destined to kill whom.

A few years ago I had some business with the Ministry of Education. I opened one door after another and only rarely did I see a face that seemed interesting or that expressed an experienced, educated, sensitive person. No, again and again, one and the same physiognomy: well-nourished types with the lower half of the face prominent, good solid jaws, modest foreheads. One could almost say that, beside the class conflict and the conflict of the generations, history knows the conflict between two distinct physiognomies.

Your novel has something which has been rather rare in our literature recently: a positive hero. A father. A communist.

Yes, positive in the sense that the purpose of his activity transcended his personal interests. I am certain that there also existed positive heroes during this period who weren't communists. As a matter of fact I suspect that novels about them are lying in drawers, already written. But the fact that he was a communist and remained one until his complete destruction, this sounds a tragic note and constitutes the paradox of his situation. The positive hero is characterized by the fact that he comes in conflict with a powerful force. And my hero is struggling not against the village, but against the irreconcilable conflict between his duties and himself. This hero's fate also provides proof of how distorted forms and structures may become as a result of realizing an ideal.

What would you say is the most characteristic experience of our generation?

I don't believe it's all that different from the experience of other generations. Every generation enters life with certain illusions, and when its turn comes it lives through its disillusionment. I am not quite sure whether our turn has come yet or not.

Basically, our main experience is the fact that we haven't succeeded in building the socialism of our ideals. Naturally, we have learned a great deal about socialism and the concept has become much more carefully defined, but it is really a negative definition: we now know, more clearly than ever before, what socialism *isn't*. We have also—along with the rest of mankind—gained one other experience: namely, how *not* to attain a happy future.

I am aware that there used to be another more "positive" kind of generational thinking, but I believe that this was not genuine, that such thinking was essentially foreign to us. We have simply been thrown back on Czech realism.

Do you really believe that the experience of this generation is in no way unique?

I don't think it's unique, no. The theme may vary, but basically it's still a form of the usual generational disillusionment. Perhaps, though, it is new in one respect: we can no longer simply dismount and return to our castle; we can't escape to Gniezdno (like Comenius), Göteborg (like Smetana) and Paris. The disillusionment is thus made more definite.

This doesn't mean, however, that nothing good can come of it. If everyone were to become aware of this disillusionment, this in itself would have tremendous significance. Without a lot of discussing and organizing, people could begin a kind of angry silence. At the moment, I can't see beyond this point, though I don't doubt that there is a beyond.

A positive alternative?

Though I don't like to admit it, that brings us to the next generation, to the assumptions of this rather spoiled younger generation. They are able to criticize—yes, in that sense our liberalization has gone far enough—but that's about all. They have no opportunity to formulate or present their ideas nor any chance to try to put them into practice. I'll tell you what I mean by this. These young people are not getting any experience, either political or economic. They won't be able to test the soundness and fruitfulness of their plans; they won't be able to mature. By the time they reach forty they'll be in more or less important positions. They will have lost all their enthusiasm, and they will have gotten as far as they have only on one condition: that they remain basically conservative throughout the course of their careers.

Besides, this coming generation is rather lazy, and the workers among them don't even know their own trade very well; I am talking about an honest knowledge of the job. I'll tell you a story which is quite typical. In a certain automobile repair shop a young mechanic was working on his own car after hours. The foreman came around, looked at him, and said: "Good God, don't do it that way; you'll ruin the car." "But that's how I always do it." "Sure, that's all right for a customer, but you don't want to mess up your own car, do you? Didn't they teach you how to do it properly?" "No."

You see, they're not even acquainted with the original, unfaked way of going about their job; they didn't learn it and they're incapable of performing it on their own. If I want to get a rise out of my boy, I tell him he's been tricked by his teachers. "You're a loafer," I tell him. "You're sloppy. You write poorly and you're always looking for the easiest way out. That's just what your teachers want. Pretty soon you'll be exactly the same as the people you're always ranting against."

The young think that they are carrying on a revolt. But they have long been enslaved by their own slipshod work. They don't try to get to the bottom of things, they don't seek confrontations. They readily accept many of the evils and degenerate attitudes of our era: don't feel too much, don't become too fond of anything, don't care too much about people, work, nature. In the end, they'll be worse off than we are. Their libraries will probably contain no books more than a few decades old. They'll be missing a whole chunk of human thought, a piece of brain!

And the generation preceding us?

It still plays a large—disproportionately large—role, but as a generation it's completely caved in.

In the end, that's the fate of every generation, isn't it?

Yes and no. People are differentiated not only by age but also by their ways of looking at things; everyone goes at things in a different way. But this older generation is completely finished because, inasmuch as they represented no clear-cut point of view, they simply remained completely outside of life. In other periods, a generation like theirs either won or lost their chosen battle, but they didn't just sidestep life. That was their specific fate.

Do you have any special favorites as far as literature is concerned?

That's hard to answer. A lot depends on chance. I only recently made the tremendous discovery that it isn't necessary to read everything through to the end. I also recently lost the taste for detective stories. One of my problems is that I suffer from a kind of "disease of momentum." If I finish reading a Russian book I want to read another Russian book immediately, and when I finish a German one I reach for another German one. Why? I don't know. Anyway, I tend to forget books—I told you that before—and so I can't really answer that question . . . You know, as I look at this dirty wall, it occurs to me that I probably let that young fellow shave me because I felt sorry for him. Nobody else seemed to have trusted him. That sounds like a good explanation, and it speaks well for my kind heart, doesn't it?

In your writing we kept coming back to the theme of literature and society . . .

It's a pity, but it seems to me that literature is becoming more and more the concern of literature; it's becoming a closed circle. Literature would like to play a role in shaping society, even that branch of it that says it doesn't. All the same, reading is becoming the concern of a steadily diminishing circle of people, while literature for experts is growing. Does the common garden-variety Czech reader still exist? A person needs more and more education just to be able to read a book and enjoy it.

That depends. Undoubtedly, the overall number of readers is greater today than fifty years ago. As far as the esoteric quality is concerned—that's true of art in general: painting, music, drama.

But does our technical, scientific intelligentsia really read? Do our engineers read? For me, the success of literature is measured by the breadth of its impact. When a political leader must resign under the accusing gaze of an entire district—that's literary success. Naturally, I don't mean to press this too far and to imply that literature should take over the role of journalism. Besides, the political leader I am talking about might just as well be the governor of Mississippi. People would look at him and he couldn't stand it. That would be a real literary triumph: that those a book was aimed at would read the book and die. The trouble is that these characters don't read...

Night had fallen. We didn't conclude our conversation; we just stopped.

Spring 1967

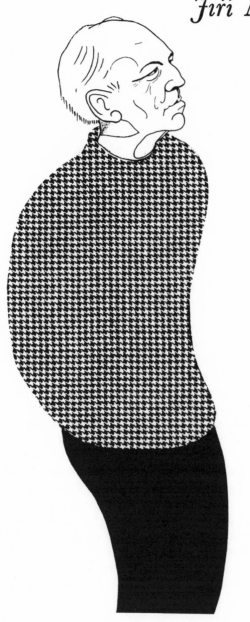

Jiří Mucha

Born 1915 in Prague. Son of the famous Czech *art nouveau* painter Alphonse Mucha. After a cosmopolitan childhood and youth, he became Paris correspondent of *Lidove Noviny*. During World War II he was a war reporter in England and Africa. Mucha started writing and publishing fiction after his return to Czechoslovakia, but was arrested in the early 1950s and spent three years in prison. After his release from jail, he translated several English and American novels and plays, until he could publish his own work again. His recent work includes a book of essays about a visit to the United States, the novel *A Probable Face* and a remarkable book of recollections from Stalinist camps, published in several countries, *Living and Partly Living*. Mucha is one of the most experienced and erudite Czech writers, prevented perhaps only by circumstances from becoming a major writer of world renown. He does not suffer from the provincial kind of thinking which often characterizes the intellectuals of small nations and his approach to many political problems discussed during the reform period of 1968 was markedly sober-minded and in this respect unequaled by most of his colleagues.

Jiří Mucha

We used to know each other only by sight. We became better acquainted after he came back and wrote that profound, bloody, mercilessly wise book Living and Partly Living, *the most penetrating portrayal of life in a prison camp in Czech literature, a book that after it was written had to wait another ten years before it was published. And then suddenly we began to understand one another. Perhaps it had something to do with the scenario for* A Probable Face, *which he had written for Jan Nemec; perhaps what brought us closer was his sad history of the Czechoslovak airmen in exile. Or maybe Aragon had a hand in our friendship, as he did in so many things. It is strange how long it sometimes takes for people to reach one another.*

I have always been fascinated by his decision to stay in his homeland. He is one of the few Czech writers who could easily live and work anywhere he chose. He wouldn't have to burn his bridges behind him; he could return anytime he wished. Yet here he remains, in spite of the fact that this country has been most unkind to him, offered him little that he couldn't get anywhere else, rewarded him for the five years he spent fighting for it in all corners of the globe by sending him to forced labor in the mines. But Jiri Mucha continues to sit in his house on Hradcany or in his country

cabin in the hills and to put in his honest day's work of writing.
Now and then he takes a trip abroad, into a world he knows far
better than most of us. But I know that sooner or later he'll be back
in that fantastic house-museum-villa or in his cabin on the green
hill. I like that feeling of continuity, just as I enjoy running into
him unexpectedly on a London street or in a small French hotel. I
am in the habit of calling him up once in a while, sometimes only
to recapture this cosmopolitan feeling. But, until now, I had never
posed the following question to him: "Why do you live in Czecho-
slovakia?"

Hm, hm.

(His characteristic quiet laugh before he starts talking.)

There are two experiences involved here, a personal one and an
inherited one. You know as well as I do what a damned delicate
business writing is. It's not like painting or music, where one can
make abstract generalizations. In writing, each word is a concrete
manifesto. The five years I spent in exile during the war have
convinced me of the extent to which a foreign sojourn can deform
a person, insofar as such a sojourn is involuntary. The causes of this
deformation needn't necessarily be political, they may just as well
be economic. The mere fact that a writer has shifted his fulcrum to
another land is enough to distort his viewpoint. Besides, even the
most welcome of guests remains a guest; after a while, the hosts
start to wonder whether he intends to continue in this passive role
of taking and accepting, or whether he plans to merge with his
environment and begin to pay back his obligations. After the great
migrations brought about by the Hitler era, the fund of good will
has became exhausted and nobody greets new settlers with much
enthusiasm. The prevalent attitude nowadays can be summed up
like this: Either accept your new nationality and pull your weight,
or else don't stay too long and don't ask for too much. There are
several countries where I'd enjoy living. France, for example. But
France is especially touchy in this respect. An artist who is willing
to become a Frenchman is enthusiastically taken into the fold. He
is treated like a king. But as long as he remains aloof, as long as he
refuses to join the French establishment, he is ejected from the
French organism like a foreign body. French xenophobia is intense
and relentless.

Are you thinking of someone in particular?

I was thinking of my own father.* He refused to become a French-man, so they omitted him from the history of French art and are only now beginning to forgive him for his "sins." He didn't ask for French citizenship; this was the main reason that, after World War I, they removed his name from art textbooks. As a result, his world reputation suffered greatly.

But the biggest problem lies in the distortion of viewpoints brought about by life abroad. As soon as you are in a foreign coun-try for any length of time, you begin to resent certain things— things that are different from the way they are at home. Even when they are much better abroad than at home. When you have nothing to reproach your friends with, you begin to resent the fact that they don't possess your own qualities. That's a familiar phenomenon, proven in practice. And so you live in a state of continual irritation, which makes orderly thinking impossible.

Exile distorts even the perception of one's own homeland. It becomes idealized; one tends to turn toward a naive nationalism. I noticed this distortion in my father, who lived abroad since the age of seventeen, coming back only for brief visits. He developed all sorts of exaggerated national sentiments that made it hard for him to realistically evaluate the actual conditions here at home, and when he eventually returned for good he quickly became dis-illusioned and bitter.

Then, too, there is the political aspect. If someone leaves an Eastern-block country these days in order to escape certain pressures or to preserve his self-respect by refusing to become a mere tool, he soon finds that in order to exist in the West he is likely to become another kind of tool and to be exposed to another kind of pressure. The outward forms may differ, but anybody with open eyes can see that this sort of choice simply involves exchanging the green for the blue. Emigration always involves antithesis. A neglected scientist seeks a well-equipped laboratory, a shrewd businessman is swal-lowed up by a huge firm, a politician joins the enemy camp, and a writer is expected to produce propaganda tracts. Nobody is inter-ested in fine shadings. Serve or stay out. A person can be completely

---

* Alphonse Mucha (1860–1939)—a leading *art nouveau* painter and illus-trator, and one of Czechoslovakia's most famous artists—lived in France for many years before returning to his homeland.—*Ed.*

honest with himself only at home; only at home can he stand firmly behind his opinions, because there he is part of a whole from which he takes and to which he contributes. There he has the right to rear up on his hind legs; in fact, it's his duty to. Whereas abroad he doesn't have the right to speak out; it would be, at the very least, a mark of bad manners on his part.

There are yet other reasons. Because I've spent a great part of my youth abroad, and have in effect gone through several different childhoods, I know how crucially important it is for a writer to be in touch with his underground roots: the place where he went to school, where he skinned his knee, got a good thrashing, ogled a girl. Childhood and the manner in which it was lived is much more important to a writer than all kinds of universities. This is where literature has its roots. Once a person leaves school and puberty behind, once he begins to analyze and to comprehend, he ceases to perceive the world as a poetical phenomenon. That which excites and stimulates us throughout life, that personal poetical treasure, that is deposited only in childhood. Later we deposit our experiences in a totally different account, a rational one. I am not referring to the polarity of poetry as opposed to prose, but of feeling as opposed to reason. The poetical values of words are also determined during this early period of life. So, too, are the separate figures that make up the individual. Everyone is made up of layers of figures, one layer on top of another, and the writer is a person who knows how to peel off these layers like the skin of an onion, and to breathe life into each one of these figures that exist within him like rudimentary homunculi. We can no longer write about people from the vantage point of a detached observer. Even if you write about a character very different from yourself or your own experience, his figure must be in you, otherwise the character won't come to life and nobody will find him interesting. For the same reason, realistic painting is no longer valid today. That function has been taken over by photography. In any case, if a character doesn't have his roots deep in the writer, he will be two-dimensional, made of paper; that's why attempts to create fictional foreigners generally end in failure. A writer must keep exclusively to what he knows, to what's inside him. Uprooting, transplanting, both generally end in disaster.

The experience of my multiple childhoods supports this point. It was in France and America that I grew up, bloodied my knees and dreamed for the first time about a fellow student. These foreign periods represent secondary rootlets for me, smaller and different from the taproot. They have produced their own layers and leaves, their own memories of school benches and solitary childhood hours, but because they were allowed only a brief term to develop in they have remained stunted. Of course, if a person gave such a stunted rootlet the right opportunity, he could cultivate it into the main bulb and the others would shrivel in their turn. Even so, I doubt that anything can match uninterrupted development.

This is related to the question of language, too. You cannot write about people in a language other than their own. Thus, if you write about foreigners you must know their tongue. But a foreign tongue can be mastered completely only as far as ordinary usage is concerned. You never develop your own style, or only to a limited degree. Usually you simply imitate examples. Your skill in a foreign tongue ends where a true writer begins—with complete mastery of his instrument. There are exceptions that prove this rule, such as Joseph Conrad. He succeeded in changing tongues perfectly. I greatly admire his work, but I know that he's completely sure of himself only in situations where the question of home doesn't come in, where there is no home—on the ocean, for instance. As soon as he finds himself on dry land, his figures become somewhat bloodless. Conrad spent his childhood in Poland, and that's why his land-locked Englishmen have no geographic dimension. Each of them is only a sort of unfinished homunculus.

Or take Nabokov. But then the Russians are in a category by themselves. They are a little bigger than the world, everything fits inside them. At least that's my impression. Even when they're Americanized a thousand times over, or Anglicized, or Gallicized or what have you, they always remain Russians. They'll never give up their soft *nya* or get rid of their Russian brain. I greatly respect Nabokov as an author—that whole fuss about *Lolita* was based on the book's advertising campaign and has nothing to do with literature—yet Nabokov, too, is homeless. In our century we can no longer talk of the eternal Jew, but an eternal Russian, wandering from country to country.

Someone may say: And what about the Rumanian colony in Paris? Educated Rumanians have always seemed to me indistinguishable from Frenchmen. Rumanian artistic and intellectual society is so close to French culture that as soon as a Rumanian settles in Paris he not only easily adopts the French mentality and style, but enriches them with his characteristically Rumanian feeling for the absurd. The French don't have much of a sense of the absurd, unlike the English. That's why French absurdity generally stems from Rumania. Or from Ireland, though the Irish are gloomy madmen in contrast to the cheerfully mad English. Neither Beckett nor Joyce is exactly hilarious.

It is true, of course, that the Rumanians easily gave up the past. Their prewar past wasn't much to give up, anyway. Ionesco once described to me how he left prewar Rumania, full of fascists. As soon as he crossed the border, he spat with relief only to find himself in Horthy's Hungary, so he spat a second time when he left that fascist nation. Now he's angry at the French, but he is a true Frenchman. Even Tristan Tzara was a Frenchman of Rumanian origin. Dadaism must be some sort of national Rumanian trait.

These, then, are the literary reasons why it is better to stay at home. The writer simply has the need to identify with a certain group of people; he may speak for or against them, but in either case he must feel that he has the birthright to do so, that he isn't mixing in the private affairs of strangers. At least that's how I see it. Of course, for the sake of calming one's nerves it is good to spend a few months abroad now and then. In such a short time, one doesn't get irritated over anything—nor inspired. I feel that if I were to live for a prolonged period of time even in the most beautiful of foreign places, such as Provence, my perspective would gradually become distorted and soon I probably would have nothing to write about. In other words, to sum it up, I don't want to lose my identity and I do not want to become an instrument of political intrigue.

Besides—and this is somewhat selfish—people nowadays are most curious about those subjects they know least about and they like to listen to experts. They are not eager to learn about themselves from some outsider. Only an authentic voice is interesting. If you want to be heard in the world, it is better to talk from far away, from your own home. That's why I consider the emigration of artists a very dubious enterprise. If some Korean came here and started writing Czech novels, I doubt that his work would arouse much interest.

You certainly can't complain of not being read at home; your book of wartime reportage sold out immediately. The same was

true of your reportage from America, A Probable Face. Living and
Partly Living *will no doubt enjoy the same success when it comes
out in both London and New York . . . Do you expect a new edition?*

You ask as if you didn't know the situation. As you well know, in
our country a publishing house that has just brought out a book
feels like a man with a bad heart who has just managed to climb a
high hill, tries to catch his breath, and wonders how he ever made it.

*You have always believed in "engaged" literature, and you have
not disdained journalism since it involves a constant engagement
with the issues of the day. How do you relate this to what you've
just been telling me?*

Since my youth I have always been drawn to places where something was happening. During the war, for example, I was strongly
attracted to the front. I am an "engaged" person, I guess, and I don't
like to watch the action from an armchair. I'd rather be where the
punches are being thrown. And right now this country is the place
for that, just as the front was the place for the bullets.

At the present time the writer is in a very unpleasant situation:
whatever happens, it happens too fast. It is hard enough just to keep
up with current events; but to analyze them and make sage judgments about them is either presumptuous or stupid, or both. One
can manage to deal with the changing times as a wartime reporter,
but not as a detached writer of epics that will once and for all lay
bare the fate of society. How many years had to elapse after the
Napoleonic war before *War and Peace* could be written, and even
at that the war itself plays only a relatively small part in the book.
Reading Stendhal, who lived right in the midst of that era, you're
hardly aware that Napoleon even existed. Stendhal realized very
clearly that historical epics are fraught with danger for a writer.
The basic question of every historical era remains the same—
namely, man's relationship to his world; and it is this problem that
attracts the writer. He is attracted to the center of activity, where
the ground is hot and where he can learn something. The writer
tells what is happening to him at a moment when things are happening all around him. And because this is my conception of a
writer, I could hardly sit on Capri and play the part of the know-it-
all.

Of course, getting it right is difficult in any case, because there are
so many distractions and pressures, and it takes great powers of con-

centration to keep from reacting to trivia and to focus on what's important. But if a writer fails to keep his eye on fundamentals, he may find that he had been tilting at targets that no longer exist by the time the book is published. Enemy fortresses have a disconcerting way of vanishing only to reappear a little further off. It is often hard to decide whether an evil has been finally eradicated or whether it is about to come back in slightly altered form. Evil is protean, and it is perhaps better to analyze its causes than to describe its superficial manifestations. By and large one comes to the conclusion that literature is less concerned with outer arrangements or with socio-economic questions than it is with the old human problems, with the age-old human attempt to build a sensible life. Obstacles and hostile forces undergo constant metamorphosis, just as government takes on ever new forms. In place of kings come presidents, in place of usurpers come elected representatives, but society is always made up of the same percentage of capable people and weaklings, of exploiters and those who carry progress on their backs, or at least try to make things just a little better. This awareness makes one a little more patient with specific current problems, because one realizes that they are temporary; yet this knowledge also makes one more pessimistic, because one knows that similar problems have always existed and will continue to exist. Hemlock is continually being prepared for a new Socrates. On a trip to Athens I once examined the hole where Socrates had been imprisoned and where he died, and I thought of the Parthenon and of Athens and everything that had crumbled away with time, except for this hole which had survived the ages and which now remains as the only living reality. It is true that ancient slavery and ancient superstition have vanished, but the principle behind Socrates' persecution hasn't changed. His speech before the court might have taken place in any century. Man is forever standing between a bowl of hemlock and the Areopagus; this is the reason why I want to be in the midst of the tumult. That's where the fate of the world has always been decided.

This is what's called "thinking aloud." You put one stone on top of another, you build slowly, each stone touching the next until at last you come to the topmost stone. And then comes the moment when you can begin to reminisce.

It was pure coincidence that I was born in this country; my parents' life was such that I could just as easily have been born abroad.

And, what's more important, it was abroad that I spent the first few years of my life. I was still a child when they took me to America and then to Paris, and so I spent the most impressionable part of my life on the sea and beyond it. When I come across the phrase "childhood landscape" all sorts of strange creatures come to my mind— animals and birds quite unknown in this part of Europe, from hummingbirds to various marine monsters like the dugong. Once I took a walk on the beach and saw a huge monstrosity, which the grownups said was a dugong that had been beheaded by a ship's propeller. These animals are rather rare, terribly ugly; they look something like a walrus without tusks. And then this exotic background suddenly merges with a purely Czech one, because I attended the first year of a provincial Czech public school. After a while they moved me again, this time to Paris. A child, when it can't understand its surroundings, thinks up all sorts of bizarre explanations. I remember that I was once taken for a drive in an ancient motorcar through the Bois de Boulogne, and they took me to the zoo where I saw my first giraffe. The animal was in a high, enclosed cage, so that its body was hidden and only the head was visible, way up in the air. I couldn't understand this phenomenon, and somehow the idea of an animal that stands on the ground and has a head on the first floor merged in my mind with the idea of Paris. Of course, the experience of a Parisian child is quite different from childhood in Prague or in America. In me all of these childhoods exist separately, though the Czech was the longest one, most of my early schooling having been Czech.

After graduating from the gymnasium I entered medical school. Why? I didn't really have any clear idea of what I wanted to study, but at that time it was considered essential to have a higher education and, since I wanted to be a writer, I thought medicine would be the best thing for me because it encompassed so much. I thought that through medicine I would eventually learn about everything, including man himself. While I was in medical school I got involved with several other things, too, such as art history and oriental studies. But once during an art history lecture I contemplated a Gothic Christ and suddenly he began to appear to me like a dissected cadaver, like an anatomic specimen.

This experience frightened me, and I set about to make sure that I saw no further visions. The human brain is quite facile; it only takes a little pebble to create waves on the surface and to distort the image. It was a peculiar experience. Later, I continued my medical studies in Paris, until I was caught up in the events of the fall of 1939. Medicine was only a kind of investment for me anyway, it wasn't my real calling, and so I dropped everything and devoted myself to a more exacting educational experience: war.

You never doubted that you would become a writer?

This certainty—or rather, this desire—arose when I was about six years old, when I first learned to write. My house is full of notebooks from that time, in which I continually wrote down my experiences. I wasn't interested in composing plots. Rather, I noted down details from reality; it was a kind of instinct to record experience, to report on reality, on various atmospheres. That same instinct still persists in me. When you come to my house, remind me to show you crates of notes. I have always regarded periods of nonwriting as periods of loafing. I have always felt that whenever I was not busy catching something on paper I was wasting time. This often involved a good deal of self-denial. I'd be in the midst of playing with the gang when suddenly I'd run home to note down something I had seen or felt. From my childhood on I had a very professional attitude toward writing: I wrote whether it amused me or not, simply out of a sense of duty.

And yet I was far from being a lonely or neglected child. On the contrary, I believe that as far as parents are concerned, I got a pretty good deal. My parents spent more time with me than was the case with most children. My father had his studio at home, so he left the house far less often than other fathers, and I enjoyed his company. The same was true of my mother. At the same time, my parents left enough distance between us and didn't sit on top of me all the time, so that—to use the current jargon—I developed no complexes, neither of dependence nor of detachment. A child is sensitive, ashamed of all sorts of things, and generally any violent attempt to influence him results in the opposite of what was intended. In other words, the golden mean.

My father was actually quite old, nearly seventy, when I began to truly understand and appreciate him. By then he had become a sort of unearthly being for me, beyond the weaknesses of this world, something like the image children generally have of their grandfathers or great-grandfathers. My mother was much younger, extremely well educated; she spoke four languages fluently and since childhood I had studied languages and taken multilingual abilities for granted. The fact that my father was considerably older meant that my mother had to devote more care to him than is generally the case. This brought about, in turn, a rather healthy and clearly defined relationship between her and myself. I have never slept in the same room with my parents; such an idea is incomprehensible to me, and I shudder to think of the unhealthy atmosphere that must surely exist when families are forced to live in tiny apartments of one or two rooms. I consider privacy essential for a child; more important than a good diet or other considerations. Dietary lacks can be remedied. But the consequences of a child's lack of privacy, of years of being forced to grow up like a naked being among grownups, these create neurotic patterns that are hard to change. In this sense I was quite fortunate; everything worked out well automatically, without any effort on my part.

When I was fourteen, or perhaps even twelve, I began to write seriously, and to submit my writing for publication. My first book was published during the war in England, in 1944. My father always insisted that there was plenty of time to have things published, that a person should not publish until his work was truly ready. I wrote prolifically throughout my youth. I wrote three novels during my teens; I sent one of them to an international competition and was amazed that I didn't get a prize. The competition was won by a Hungarian émigré living in Paris, Jolan Földes, with her novel *The Street of the Fishing Cat.*

To keep in practice I wrote cultural articles for various publications and I acted as Paris correspondent for the *Lidove Noviny* [an outstanding independent daily which, in 1952, was transformed into the weekly *Literarni Noviny* and was to be re-established in 1968]. I also did it partly for financial reasons. My parents didn't try to keep me from going abroad, but they didn't help me either. Their attitude was that I should earn my own keep, and they didn't try to influence my life one way or the other.

What was your most significant wartime experience?

The whole war was a priceless experience for me. Because I was eager to be in the center of the action all the time, I had to run all over the world to keep up. Such a huge and global conflict breaks out now in one place, now in another; you have to seek it out. If it comes to you, it is only as an uninvited guest. I didn't look at the war from far away, and I didn't see it as a horrible spectacle, but rather I was in close and intimate contact with it, and it brought out some of man's best qualities. I know that this sounds like a paradox. But that war was actually rather simple and straightforward from a moral point of view; that kind of black-and-white conflict will probably never occur again. Everything was either good or bad, and in this respect it differed from the majority of wars. It was one of the few wars in which our enemy was, at the same time, the enemy of all mankind, and so whoever opposed that enemy automatically assumed a positive moral position. When I say that this war gave men a chance to demonstrate their best qualities, I am of course thinking only of our own side. A fighter on our side had the moral basis and other prerequisites to express his virtue: bravery and readiness for self-sacrifice. As in every war, disappointments were bound to occur, but these manifested themselves only much later. The people who did the actual fighting were honorable. It was those who hadn't fought who made the mess. Usually the dirt surfaced right at the start of a war. This time it surfaced at the end of and after the war and made up for lost time.

On the philosophical side, I was confirmed in the conviction that man always has at least two choices open to him and that it is entirely up to him which choice he makes. Naturally, chance does exist, and there are few periods more likely to demonstrate the absurd effects of chance in human affairs than wartime. All the same, there is a tremendous area within which man is left to his own will and where there is no excuse for refusing to make a choice. The only excuse is death, the fact that a man crossed the path of a bullet. Of course this is not a specific wartime problem; the role of the bullet can be played by a speeding car, an angry bull.

Another thing I've learned: you can never straighten out a dog's tail. A person is basically determined by what he's born with, and his entire development is really a matter of encouraging one set of characteristics to develop and suppressing others. If he's left to develop in normal circumstances, the chances are he'll turn out all right. But a radical change in circumstances can cause a fading of good traits; the bad ones begin to dominate and a person who originally seemed to have no such tendencies can turn into a criminal. Strange things can be drawn out of a man by his environment. I saw how wartime pressures turned goodhearted people into vicious ones, honest citizens into traitors. Instinct for survival undermined their susceptible good qualities. War is tremendously instructive.

You learn to be extremely grateful for everything good that can be found in people. That's why I say that basically it had a good influence. The combination of a just goal and great pressure brought the positive qualities into the forefront. On the other side, the same pressure combined with questionable goals brought out all the evil qualities that the Germans possessed. Of course, if this combination of circumstances had been different, the result could have been quite the opposite. I do not believe in propensities to evil or good based on nationality.

The war also left me with a deeply ingrained awareness of the incompetence of people in high positions of authority. The exceptions were extremely few. People who were called upon to decide the fate of others, to make far-reaching choices in critical moments, were generally quite ordinary people who knew little more about the situation than the man in the street. This confirmed the old historical assumption that the world is by and large in the hands of ordinary people who are influenced by their personal weaknesses to a far greater degree than it would superficially seem.

And after the war?

After the war I felt the time had come for me to start producing. I had formed a sufficiently firm foundation to enable me to speak with some authority. But I had hardly opened my mouth when I had to close it again in a hurry. Perhaps in this way I saved myself from a lot of nonsense; a person usually loses little by keeping his mouth shut. I am a bit of an optimist, as you can see. In any case I escaped the danger of becoming a fossil, an institution. In the first year or two after the war they might have been tempted to put me into the position of a writer with a capital W, and this would have had unfortunate results. Who knows? As it is, I managed to remain in the thick of the fight. When a person is dragged into the bureaucracy, he loses his élan. Of course, I probably would have found some sort of solution for this, but I am glad that the problem simply never came up.

Do you believe, then, that a box on the ear is a necessary stimulus to talent?

Good Lord, no, certainly not; at least not a public box on the ear. Some people are destroyed by a blow, others wake up. It's a matter of temperament; some work better under tension, others in peace and quiet. Many people produced marvelous things only because they were left in absolute peace; otherwise they would have gone under. Conflicts and crises arise all the time, and some people are incapable of dealing with the internal ones if they must cope with external problems at the same time. Virginia Woolf worked under almost ideally peaceful conditions, and she wasn't able to surmount her inner tensions. On the other hand, Stendhal must have had numerous external problems, yet his books give no indication of this. It is simply an individual matter.

I interrupted you; you were talking about the postwar period.

Well then, the immediate postwar beginning was very promising. I published my first books, and then suddenly I was automatically eliminated. It was ridiculous. There was really no concrete reason for removing my books from libraries and bookstores. On the contrary, from my childhood on I had always belonged to what was called "leftist youth," and so I couldn't understand why my books were regarded as being in conflict with the movement of history. Nor was I the son of a capitalist. Thus neither my origin (which is nowadays so inhumanly used as a weapon) nor my own activity involved anything harmful to the state. But whatever the reasons for the automatic reaction of the authorities, the fact is that it had numerous unfortunate results. A person is not a savings bank; he cannot save up his potentialities and withdraw them later. What isn't written, created at a particular time, will never be created later, because a man changes and his opinions constantly evolve along new lines. But who knows, perhaps I might have written things that I would be ashamed of now.

During this extremely unpleasant era the most important thing was to avoid succumbing to the seductions of conforming. That is a very complex matter, because a person naturally doubts himself and his own opinions. Stalinism was a very complicated ideologic position, and many people who opposed it had secret doubts about their own attitudes. The second problem was to defend oneself against bitterness, an "internal emigration," the temptation to play the role of a martyr. And to resist pressure, at all costs. Even when people said: "You're a fool to pretend that you're living under normal conditions, these aren't normal conditions; they'll lock you up." And I used to answer: "I'd rather learn how to live in jail than learn how to live in fear." When I returned from my wartime exile,

I was horrified to see the effects of the schooling of fear which our people had undergone during the war. I saw what had happened to the nation as a result of years of passivity, years in which the nation had simply taken the line of least resistance, waiting for someone to pull it out of the morass. The great mass of the people was simply concerned with survival—an understandable attitude but one which eventually had results far more disastrous than the bloodiest of battles. The fear of authority, learned during the war, made people react in exactly the same unfortunate way in postwar situations as they had done earlier. I must say that I was never tempted to conform; my main problem was in trying to justify myself and to explain to people why I behaved as I did. I found out later that they had had all sorts of fantastic notions about me, yet actually the whole thing was quite simple. The fact that I wasn't afraid of certain things that they considered dangerous created misunderstandings, questions about what kind of person I really was. I didn't fit into a pre-existing framework. I was supposed to either run away or be afraid. But I neither fled nor grew frightened, not because I was a hero but because I had just recently undergone situations in which the danger was far more real and concrete. To be afraid simply means to admit the possibility that something is capable of doing tremendous damage to you or of destroying you. If you refuse to occupy yourself with this possibility for any reason whatever— perhaps only because you are too busy to think about it—this doesn't necessarily mean that you are not aware of the reality of the danger. For example, during the war I never thought of the possibility of getting killed, but only because it would have been pointless. Only a chance event can kill you, an accident. It is different in a city under bombardment; there you become aware of a kind of moral powerlessness, you start to imagine all sorts of things; it is a bad situation. But at the front you face quite different problems, and somehow you are on the same level as the dangers to which you are exposed.

But wasn't the difficult period here similar to life in a bombed town?

No. Aside from everything else, the dangers weren't quite as real. If a bomb fell on you, you'd had it, and that was that. Whereas here people were certainly aware that no matter how bad the situation got it was bound to change sometime. And the tribulations which the majority of people underwent were unpleasant rather than mortally perilous.

And what happened when the consequences you were warned about finally came to pass?

It is difficult to explain my feelings in the matter. Perhaps it has something to do with my knowledge of history, and somehow this kind of behavior isn't compatible with our history; it doesn't fit. It's a different matter in Russia. But when the same way of dealing with people spread to a region like ours, which wasn't used to it . . . I suppose there is something in human nature which prevents us from believing that something evil can persist forever. Otherwise we'd all hang ourselves. Besides, history demonstrates that no evil endures forever.

But even if the dark era were to go on and on, I still believed that it was important not to give in to fear, that resistance to fear was preferable to other alternatives. And I soon encountered several cases which confirmed my belief that my attitude was not merely subjective, that it wasn't determined by the fact that I had lived abroad during the war. I even had a long, confidential discussion with Vaclav Rezac [author and director of the Writers' Union Publishing House] who confessed that he found that unnatural situation as difficult to bear as I did. I sensed that in the long run the situation was more likely to develop in my favor rather than against me.

Perhaps we misunderstood each other. What I meant to say was that in the end reality confirmed the opinion of those pessimists who had been warning you.

Perhaps. But I never agreed with those people. I knew, naturally, that such a possibility existed, but if you persist in a certain way of acting, in full awareness of its possible risks, then you have no right to weep and complain afterwards. Actually, prison is an important experience, too, just like war. It is simply a writer's post-graduate education. And though it isn't exactly the kind of experience I'd care to repeat, I know that I would be a poorer person without it. I don't mean this in a banal way, in the sense that suffering leads to a better life, or anything of the kind. On the contrary, I am convinced that suffering helps nobody. Rather, prison freed me from many illusions I had about people, and it also enabled me to come into closer contact with the worker, with his lot in life, his work and his soul. That, too, belongs—at least in part—to the category of lost illusions. Prison and war had another thing in common: both showed how man reveals himself under pressure. After such an experience, you are grateful for the handful of people whom you like and respect. And then, too, you have the same sense of satisfaction that you have at the front: you feel that you are not an arm-chair observer but someone in the midst of the fray. That is close to an obsession with me. If someone came along and asked me to join the Viet Cong for six months, I would probably do it. I can be trapped into going anywhere where there is something going on, and I never think about the consequences.

Coming out after three years in prison, the first thing I did was to work up my diary. This took me two months; then I let it lie in my desk for ten years. And then I wrote *A Probable Face*. And made some films . . .

I think I understand what he meant by the "writer's profession-alism" when he spoke about his early writing experiences. . . You've spent half of your life abroad; that, too, is a rather unique experience for a writer. I am curious to know how we look from outside, how we appear through the eyes of others.

The idea that the Czech people are firmly established in the mind of Europe is a myth. The awareness of our existence extends only a few miles beyond our borders. People have to learn to stop making conclusions based on the opinion of friends of Czechoslovakia. Just as there are friends of Finland, Hungary, or Honduras, so there are friends of Czechoslovakia, both official and unofficial. I know people who know and love Paraguay. But if you come across a person who doesn't have this special kind of relationship to Czechoslo-vakia, you'll soon find out that the country simply has no reality as far as he is concerned. Of course, there is an image of a romantic, pastoral Bohemia, which has an existence somewhat like Ruritania. And then, of course, we exist for the businessmen, for those who are directly or indirectly in commercial contact with us. But in terms of the broader consciousness of the West, especially the cul-tural public, we have just begun to exist, thanks to film. People who up to now didn't have an iota of interest in or knowledge of us are suddenly paying attention. Up to now no other cultural or indus-trial endeavor has achieved so much in so short a time. At most we used to be famous as international arms dealers. For the life of me I can't imagine what gave rise to the notion that we are well known in the world, or even loved. When a Czechoslovak traveling abroad meets somebody who has heard of the name Masaryk, he takes it as a great honor to the entire nation. Yet this means no more than my going up to some Abyssinian and saying *Abebe* to him, just to make him feel good. This is what I mean: Every European child learns the nations of the continent in geography class, and so he comes across the word Czechoslovakia. But that's usually where the matter ends. Naturally, people no longer think of us as gypsies or Tatars, but unless a person is a hockey fan or a follower of gymnastics or ice-skating, Czechoslovakia remains a vague concept for him. Our people can't understand this; they are, I think, misled by too much contact with friends of Czechoslovakia. Didn't Munich teach us anything? Apparently people suffer from a constant need to delude themselves. A rather obscure French historian, just because he happened to write a book about us, was given a monument in Prague and had a railroad station named after him—honors which were not accorded to either Dvorak or Smetana, though their music is played throughout the Western world. In short, people have not paid too much attention to the truth. Foreigners who have shown any interest in us whatever have always been presented to our nation as great men, and in general the nation believed the lie. In reality, such interest in us was generally nothing more than a hobby, mostly a hobby of second-rate persons. The idea that the greatest minds of Europe have been tremendously interested in Czechoslovakia is a tragic mistake.

Once I sat with some friends in a restaurant in London's Soho. I noticed that a party at the next table—they seemed to be Scandinavian—was trying to guess what language we were speaking. At last, one of them came over to us and asked. When we told him, his face suddenly fell; he became quite sad and said, "You poor fellow!" And I must say that, with the exception of this past year, I have never met anyone who became interested or excited upon being told my nationality. In the eyes of the world, we are a nonentity, except that recently we have become a cinematic power.

Don't be misled by the fact that *The Good Soldier Schweik* was translated into a number of languages. People aren't interested in the fact that the author was a Czech. Kafka brought laurels to Prague, but even this has no direct connection with Czechoslovakia.

This is analogous to the way people talk with great enthusiasm about Rembrandt without connecting this enthusiasm with Holland. Rembrandt represents a certain image; he is respected and honored but this does not necessarily carry over to Dutch culture ... Or Schiller—it would not occur to anybody to use his name in order to whitewash concentration camps. It doesn't even occur to most people that he was a German.

And yet there is no question but that the Czechs could become as interesting today as they were during the Reformation, the period of humanism. So far this hasn't happened, however, and the vast majority of people aren't aware of the difference between us and a country such as Yugoslavia. I don't want to be unnecessarily pessimistic, but we must face reality. We are on the map of Europe, we are involved in various scandals that reach the front pages of newspapers, but as far as European cultural awareness is concerned—no. Not even our beer has made much of a dent. People generally don't care too much where a particular brand of beer comes from. I don't think we are sufficiently aware of how many factors and values are involved before a particular export item becomes generally identified with a country. Loans are only for the rich. Nobody is interested in the fact that certain items—no matter how good they may be—come from Czechoslovakia. In order for this kind of awareness to come into being, all of Czechoslovakia would have to serve as a guarantee of quality. Or our nation would have to exist on such a lofty cultural plane that our exports would benefit from its reflected glitter. Otherwise, nobody bothers about origin. Film as a vehicle of quality—we encounter this phenomenon for the first time.

All of this means that we are not exactly in an enviable situation. On the contrary, we are suffering from great handicaps and it is up to all of us to try to change this state of affairs. In the political area, for example, we have gained the reputation of being Stalinists. And even though this is no longer true, it will take us a long time to erase this image of ourselves. It is hardly an image that we can be proud of. Everybody should examine his own conscience and see how much he has contributed to this Stalinist reputation. It was film— and I know that this has become commonplace—it was our cinema that helped to show that this business of Stalinism may have been a bit exaggerated. But one swallow doesn't make a spring. Such things cannot be forced.

I don't like to be critical, it isn't pleasant, but I am abroad more often than most people and I am more aware of our reputation than someone who spends an occasional vacation in Yugoslavia. And so I frequently have to defend our country, because criticism directed at the country hits me, too. So I defend us even when I know in my heart that the criticism is partially justified.

And here is something that makes me angry: the bad reputation we have abroad has often been caused by certain Czechoslovaks themselves who throw mud at their own country in the belief that this will make them appear sophisticated and interesting. Some have done this out of masochism; others have behaved like beggars who hope that by displaying their sores and scars they will gain sympathy from the rich. Many people believe that describing shameful conditions at home is the best way to gain sympathy abroad. They expect in this way to purify themselves and to separate themselves from these conditions. They would be very surprised to learn what is said about *them* as soon as they're out of earshot. Would you relish inviting a chatterbox to your home who immediately proceeds to regale you with all the family dirt? I wouldn't. But perhaps many of these blunders are simply due to finding oneself in an unfamiliar situation. People get so excited when they finally manage to set off on a trip abroad that they tend to lose their heads. It is sad, but these unnecessary calumnies hurt all of us for many, many years.

And what do you think about us?

I am well aware of this country's existence and I know a good deal about it, so at least that problem is settled. Otherwise, though, I fear that the general opinion that foreigners have of us is not far from the truth. If we're talking about our people as such, I believe that they cannot be blamed for being what they are, in view of what they have undergone on their journey through history. At the point most significant for a nation's development, at the point when the majority of people began to emancipate themselves and masses of anonymous subjects began to change into literate, educated persons, to pattern themselves on certain models—at this very point our nation lost practically its entire aristocracy. In all other nations, aristocracy was the bearer of cultural traditions and served as a model for various impractical virtues: sense of honor, pride, truthfulness, and so on. The aristocracy held these principles, and even though it may not have practiced them it had to justify its favored position on the basis of a higher level of morality. The awareness that a high moral level seemed somehow related to a higher standard of living lent support to the belief that moral values and a higher social order went hand in hand. When the people eventually began to free themselves from the bonds of poverty and the farmer at last began to enjoy some of the fruits of his labor, he had before his eyes a concept of how his life might ideally look, not only from a material but from a cultural and moral point of view. (For Heaven's sake, don't think for a moment that I am denying the necessity and logic of the French revolution; that is an entirely different matter. I am now simply talking about an individuals' own concept of what things would be like if he were richer and more cultured.)

In our land, during this vital period, our aristocracy was completely decimated and a foreign nobility was introduced, which represented a double form of repression: ethnic and religious. As a result, the emerging Czech, who stood in great need of a model to emulate, totally rejected the foreign aristocracy and began to pride himself on his own plebeianism. Mind you, this has nothing to do with democracy; these are not the deep roots of democracy as I have heard the phenomenon described! This is nothing but a plebeian distaste for the aristocratic principle in its original Greek sense; namely, everything which is higher and better. It is a distaste originally motivated by the historical connection of aristocracy with a threat to the nation and to its religion. But this is no virtue, it is simply bad luck.

In the course of his further development the Czech who wanted to better himself in the world had only two alternatives: either he gave up his nationality and submitted to Germanization and the Counter Reformation, or else he wore a loyal mask and secretly kicked his master's furniture, as servants will. And this unfortunate mentality—which the nation can hardly be blamed for since it was brought about by virtually irresistible historical forces—still continued to plague us after we achieved freedom and statehood in 1918.

In this new nation it wasn't the educated upper-middle-classes that ruled, but the petty bourgeoisie. The young prewar generation was just beginning to leave this unhappy legacy behind and there was some hope that the nation would at last regain its health, but then came World War II and the occupation, which swept all these gains away, and the old unfortunate characteristics which our people had relied on for centuries once again emerged. The consequences are still with us today. I am not looking at our situation from an idealistic point of view, as if some particular person or group were responsible for our plight. The nation simply does the best it can under the circumstances and there's no use complaining. I place tremendous, perhaps even exaggerated hopes in the younger generation because the young have already demonstrated that they are the only ones who are capable of leadership. Unfortunately, the young generation of prewar days was decimated by the war. Not physically, but morally.

What about our national culture?

I have already said so much that is unpleasant that now I would like to defend our culture against unreasonable demands. First of all, the flowering of a national culture is always a rather anarchic business; it cannot be planned, everything depends on a confluence of numerous chance circumstances. Sometimes a single man through his influence and power can bring about a free and mighty flowering of culture. Rome would hardly have made such an impact on the world during the Renaissance without its popes. Then again, would Raphael have achieved what he did if the Duke of Urbino had never existed? There were far more powerful families at the time, the Sforzas and Viscontis in Milan, and yet they had much less influence on art than little Urbino. Sometimes, too, through sheer coincidence, a few outstanding artists are born in a particular place at a particular time, and they pull lesser men behind them.

Thus one cannot dismiss a nation with a wave of the hand on the grounds that it doesn't have a great cultural tradition. Spain had one and lost it, and there are many highly respected nations in the world that have made only negligible contributions to world culture. From this point of view, our cultural achievement over the last century is quite respectable. And it was all done with the left hand, so to speak, because nobody in our country did anything for the sake of culture. Every people has a tendency to express itself in a particular way; some tend toward concreteness, others toward lyricism or sentimentality. Our poetry has helped to develop a whole modern movement, whereas our graphic arts are not very original. Nobody can have everything. It is a pity that poetry is so difficult to translate. If our prose had reached the level of our poetry, Czech literature would have a brilliant reputation. Kundera's attitude toward the lyrical is very interesting and he's probably right; our emphasis on lyrical genres does reflect a cultural immaturity. Still, I believe things might have been much worse.

Our failure in the genre of the novel probably has many causes, but it is obviously connected with the lack of development of our society. In my work I have encountered a very troubling fact. When a Frenchman or an Englishman or a German writes a novel, he simply picks out certain social types, gives them a name and a social background, then lets them interact, and nobody questions their verisimilitude. Take *Buddenbrooks*, for example. The reader takes it for granted that such figures existed, and their names are used as representative types. They're accepted because there were thousands of Buddenbrooks, as there were thousands of Rastignacs, in the world. They are simply essences boiled down from countless examples, and thus they become types. With us, if you want to write a novel concerned with people articulately expressing intelligent ideas, you will find it impossible to create such types. There simply is nothing in our society to generalize from. And if, in spite of the difficulties, you succeed in creating a lifelike character, readers will either regard him as a disguised living person or else subconsciously resent the character, feeling that if someone like that really existed they would surely know about him. Naturally, I am talking about characters of a certain type. We do have an extensive middle-class literature. Kondelik [hero of a novel by Ignat Herrmann; the name became a symbol for bourgeois mediocrity] is the embodiment of a thousand Kondeliks. The same is true of characters created by Hrabal or Skvorecky. Or of Schweik. In this respect we are quite self-sufficient. But these figures represent a particular type of intellect and can express only certain limited ideas within the range of their personalities. For example, a Kondelik could hardly be expected to reflect on alienation or on other problems beyond his limited understanding.

As soon as an author wants to use his figures to debate questions outside the scope of the middle-class mind, he comes up against a dearth of material from which such figures could be molded. Our intellectual layer of society isn't deep enough or broad enough to enable us to create a type. And so we turn to Jews or to professionals, experts, philosophers, poets, writers. The subconscious of our readers accepts a certain kind of internal monologue from a

Jew or a professional, but it balks at the same thing coming from a figure with a common name or mundane occupation. The reader simply feels that such a character is foreign to him. And even when the exceptional reader accepts the particular character, he takes him as a *personnage a clef*, convinced that the author has such and such a person in mind. The character either seems unreal or else the reader finds him real but cannot identify with him. A Czech author once wrote a story about a young daughter of an English lord, whose mother was of Czech descent. After spending some time in exotic lands, the daughter returns to her London mansion and declares how happy she is to be back to enjoy mamma's cooking again. This is the reverse of the situation I have been talking about, the author simply transposed the Czech mentality into a foreign surrounding and apparently wasn't aware of the absurd results.

As I say, we don't have a social layer capable of giving rise to highly intelligent literary types. Of course, here again the overall immaturity of our people exacts its toll. It is the result of centuries in which the tips of our society were continually snipped off. And we lack a developed nineteenth-century novel, which might have codified such types. Our contemporary authors seem to feel the need for excusing themselves every time a character who is not a Jew or a professional thinks about serious matters. I cannot suck such characters out of my thumb, so I try to solve the problem through a ruse, by leaving the chief protagonist anonymous. But then I run into a different problem, namely that the reader tends to identify this character with the author, and is convinced that he is dealing with an autobiographical work. But this method of working is only an evasion of the problem. Like Kafka, who created Josef K.

Don't forget that our authors have difficulties even with the mere names of characters. If you look through a telephone book to find a likely name for your hero, you'll find it difficult to come across one that doesn't suggest a simple "man of the people." Usually, to escape this dilemma, the author picks a name with a faintly Germanic ring. Today all of this is becoming less important as the novel becomes increasingly subjective, but fifteen years ago these were extremely difficult problems. A figure in a novel simply must have his or her natural background. Incidentally—to avoid any misunderstanding—I hope it's quite clear that I am not saying there are no highly intellectual people among us. The problem is rather that there is not a sufficient number of them and that they are not sufficiently visible to the public to become accepted as a type. Our plebeian attitudes have something to do with this too; the Czech subconsciously resents such a type.

How do you feel about the matter of the generations?

I don't profess to belong to any generation, and no generation even cared to claim me either. As far as definitions go, a generation is a society of people growing up in the same period, under the same conditions, and thus having more or less the same common denominator. I never had any such unified experience, and therefore I don't count myself a member of any generation. Anyway, generations always seemed to me like clubs made up of people who either mutually prop each other up or detest each other.

Nevertheless, I am very much interested in young people who are just growing up and who are still free of the faults that crippled earlier generations. Of course, a youngster is still a *tabula rasa* and there is no guarantee that by the time he reaches thirty or forty he won't prove as disappointing as his forerunner. To a considerable degree, the fate of the young people will depend on the extent to which they will be able to realize their concepts of life, to get to know the world, and to get rid of their "concierge syndrome"—that cringing and envious respect for authority that has proven so destructive to us. So far, thank God, they don't seem to suffer from this disease; respect for authority is quite foreign to them. Of course, disrespect for authority does not necessarily prevent narrow-mindedness, as soon as a person becomes old enough to head a family of his own. With today's average income, average housing, and a tendency for people to stew forever in the small pot of their native land, too much individuality cannot be expected. People living this way have but one alternative: philistinism.

The majority of our youngsters are, of course, still very much a part of the poorer ghettos, suffering from all the deprivations and complexes of children who grew up in poverty. If they cannot rise above their early years, they will end up concentrating their whole life-energy on small cars, television sets, and two-room apartments in huge housing developments. The economic question, the problem of life-environment plays a tremendous role. There is a catch, though: prosperity in itself guarantees absolutely nothing. The young generation in England, France, or West Germany is growing up under utterly different conditions, yet it still remains to be seen whether these conditions will create individuality. I might even be tempted to say that in certain ways our situation provides a better environment for the growth of personality. There must be some sort of tension between dream and reality. Our youth has that "advantage"; the contrast between dream and reality is so great that for the time being there is no danger of disillusionment. The disillusionment that follows the realization of a dream is a very bad state; it lasts long and is hard to conquer.

The difference between the two situations—the situation of our young man who still believes that cars, apartments, and sailboats are enough to ensure a good life, and the foreign young man who already knows that all this hasn't brought him a single step closer to his goal—this contrast provides a very interesting basis for literature. This is the "teeming soil" for a contemporary novel. You see the brother of our young man, who lives in France? He looks enviously toward China; he thinks *that* is the solution. We have come full circle.

Well . . . I suppose now you've got me where you want me.

No. After all, an interview is like a session with a psychoanalyst; you get everything out of your system . . .

Which reminds me of a joke. A young lady goes to her analyst. He tells her to take off her clothes and lie down, then he jumps on top of her. When it's all over, he says, "Well now, that was my problem. What's yours?"

Spring 1967

Jaroslav Putík

Born 1923 in Most, northern Bohemia. During World War II he was incarcerated in a Nazi concentration camp. After the war he worked as journalist and editor on the staff of various publications, including *Literarni Noviny*. He gave up journalism in favor of fiction and in his first short novel, *The Wall,* described the hallucinatory experience of a prisoner returning from a concentration camp. The stories in his collection *Summons to Court* show in many ways a strong Kafka influence. In 1967 he published his first full-length novel, *Passion Sunday,* about the problems of personal integrity people faced under the Nazi occupation. His book on the J. Robert Oppenheimer case became a best-seller symbolizing for the Czech reader the confrontation between an intellectual's responsibility and the power of the state.

Jaroslav Putík

Jaroslav Putik played a large role in my life, a role of which I suspect he himself is not aware. All of us have somebody who at certain periods serves as a yardstick of our own activity. Putik had become my yardstick of the possible. It wasn't a question of measuring the possible degree of ideological divergence (we'll discuss that a bit later), nor of the extent to which contrary opinions could be expressed. Rather, in the 1950s, the yardstick served to measure journalistic culture, the degree to which journalistic standards could be maintained in putting out a newspaper.

We had never discussed this matter before. Perhaps he guessed what was on my mind, perhaps not; in any case, so many other affinities developed between us that this one seemed to lose its importance. Putik eventually lost his faith, not so much in the importance and possibilities of journalism as in his own activity as a newspaperman. I couldn't really follow his reasoning in this regard; I didn't understand him. And I must admit that I was looking forward to having this aspect clarified by the present interview. Actually, though, I began the interview from a different angle. I started off from his last book, Passion Sunday, which is also the first fruit of his new profession as a novelist. It is a book in which a member of the generation born in the 1920s tells about the war, not in a historical way, but in a personal way. It is a book about the war within us, about its role in our life, and my first question was along these lines.

I wouldn't say that the war is the central theme of *Passion Sunday*. It is true that two of the major heroes of the book are people in their forties, and therefore both of them were marked by the war, just as I was. The psychic effects of the war are certainly there, but I was concerned with something else. Stendhal once wrote that all that really interested him was analyzing the human heart. This statement comes very close to my own attitude and expresses rather accurately what I tried to accomplish in my novel. The main character in the book is a woman; the feminine psyche is very attractive to a writer, from the viewpoint of his craft and thought, but of course it also poses an extremely difficult challenge. A woman is closer to nature, closer to life. Josef Jedlicka [a contemporary author whose works were long suppressed] in his *Notebooks* blames the modern woman for no longer provoking man's absurd heroism as savior, but I think that this is a dubious charge. The trouble is not that the world has grown too feminine, but rather that it isn't manly enough; it isn't a world of men without qualities, but qualities without men, as some wit once remarked. I don't want to generalize too much, but I do think that the female half of the world contains the more interesting and lively figures.

You said you are interested in the war within us ...

War is a classical, model situation for a writer, and in a certain sense Hemingway was quite right when he said that only those who had been in a war were entitled to write. The war and the behavior of people under extreme conditions interests me, of course, but I am no longer interested in the journalistic approach to this period. Good Czechs, bad Germans and that sort of thing are fallow ground for a writer. In the conversation with you, Jiri Mucha describes the situation as it looked from abroad. Everybody had a choice, Mucha said, either to join the battle or to sit back with the slackers. He looks at our situation here somewhat haughtily, and it is true that our people vegetated and tried to eke out a living in mortal fear for their existence. Yes, certainly, there still was some room for choice, but very limited room indeed! And then consider Lidice* or the fate of the Jews—confronted with the gas chambers, what choice did they have? By that time it was too late for choices.

---

* In retaliation for the killing of Reinhard Heydrich in May 1942, the Nazis executed the entire male population of the Bohemian mining village of Lidice; the women were sent to concentration camps, the children were sent to live with German families. The village was razed.—*Ed.*

Perhaps this is precisely the writer's task: to keep people from falling asleep, so that their eyes are open before they find themselves lined up in front of the cremation ovens.

Was World War II and the Nazi occupation a totally specific experience of our century—from your generation's point of view?

It is always important to know what motives people have for acting the way they do. Why did I, for example, get involved in the resistance movement, which had practically no effect and from the viewpoint of the war as a whole was completely unimportant? I think that the strongest motive was the feeling that one couldn't come to terms with the lie, the transparent sham of the Protectorate, a system in which lying and cowardice had become guiding principles. The fact that I ended up in a communist resistance unit was a coincidence, though it had important consequences for my later career; at the time I was simply looking for any group that was fighting the fascists. I might just as easily have ended up in any other organization; a young man is incapable of drawing clear distinctions. After my own experience, I understand all young people who go through similar experiences. In their desire to penetrate beneath the surface, to expose lies, young people butt their heads against the wall. But the best among them will continue to do so anyway, even with the knowledge that they'll break their heads and the wall will remain intact. Although by and large I don't share the opinions of our so-called literary rebels, in this matter I agree with them and I admire their zeal. Even if they don't win they cannot lose, because they have done the most important thing of all: they have acted. A person must not be in conflict with himself or he loses his center of gravity.

You mentioned the situation under the occupation; what do you think was our people's predominant experience during this time?

My opinion is certainly more optimistic than Mucha's. During the war I passed through sixteen jails and one concentration camp; I was in a good position to watch various national groups and to make comparisons, and it seems to me that the Czechs didn't come off too badly. First of all, a very high proportion were jailed for deliberate anti-German political activity; whether their sympathies lay with Moscow or with London is beside the point.

Perhaps this demonstrated the educational effects of twenty years of Masaryk's republic, an education for democracy and national pride. Naturally, there were also many spineless little climbers who, even in jail, tried not only to do their duties but to excel; but this is perhaps the worst that can be said of us. It was the nation's misfortune that in 1938 it could not give battle. I have thought about this many times. Sober reflection tells us that the fight would have been lost from the start, yet there are losing battles which must be fought nevertheless. Even a disastrous war would have meant a certain moral gain for the nation. I have no doubt that our nation would have acquitted itself as well as the Poles did, or the Yugoslavs. But in 1938 we ended up in a blind alley. Nobody who hasn't lived through this period can understand or feel what was involved. Yes, the bourgeoisie lost the game at Munich, but nobody can explain to me why we let it do so. Why didn't we wrest the power away from them? Is this another example of a world of qualities without men?

For the generation which had reached adulthood these years presented the decisive test. And for me these still remain the decisive criteria: What did you do during the war? Did you keep your mouth shut? Did you collaborate? Did you serve the enemy? Or did you resist in any way at all? After the war, these questions gave rise to tremendous confusion; people began to be judged solely by their political affiliations. There were all sorts of campaigns against people who had fought in Spain or campaigns against our airmen in exile or against people involved in the Slovak uprising or against former partisans or against God knows who—and yet the targets of these unremitting attacks were people who had a perfect right to walk with their heads held high with pride. Instead of attacking them we should have sought them out in gratitude. Everything that's being done now in restitution is only a token payment. And people who remember this era go away, die off, and soon all the important witnesses will be gone. We have done nothing about it for the twentieth anniversary of our new republic; let's hope we will make it for the twenty-fifth . . .

But to return to the question of why writers are interested in war. For me, war gives proof that even in a tragic and hopeless situation something positive can always be done and that someone can always be found who is willing to help. War—with the exception, of course, of an atomic war—doesn't take away all hope. At the end of the war, when I was gravely ill in the camp, a Slovak came to me and

brought me a bag of garlic. I know that this saved my life. I have no
idea by what miracle he was able to lay hands on the garlic, nor do
I know the man's name. Naturally, one could also come across men
who would be ready to kill you for a slice of bread. Yet somehow the
positive side of human nature seemed to prevail. This feeling is
hard to express; it is simply the certainty that if a similar situation
were to recur, surprising human qualities would again come to the
fore. I suspect that most people who have gone through such experiences would agree.

*Why is it then that today's young people, especially the literary
ones, think otherwise?*

I don't know. Sometimes I think it's simply a revolt against the
rather optimistic mentality of their elders. Then, too, much of it's
only a literary pose. It is interesting and sometimes quite amusing
to see how the optics of perception change. There are people who
have turned from a naive rural optimism to the blackest "Becket-
tism" and if they live long enough they may once again embrace the
good old Czech earth. The tendency to see things in terms of abstract schemata or *a priori* judgments is limited neither by age nor
by general philosophical orientation.

*Our own "optics," our own perceptions were corrected by shock
therapy. Do you think that our young people will go through the
same process?*

I doubt it. More likely, they will be affected by changing life-
experience. There are certain things that everybody must live
through on his own. It is called maturing, but I don't necessarily
mean by this a development away from nonconformity. The present
generation is fortunate to be growing up in a somewhat more
normal period than we grew up in. Note the kinds of authors they
like, writers who were either neglected or wronged—[Jan] Zahrad-
nicek, [Jakub] Deml, [Richard] Weiner, [Jaroslav] Klima [four
writers and poets whose works were banned by party ideologists in
the 1950s and 1960s]. And where do we go from here? Will they follow like epigoni in their footsteps? I marvel at all the things these
young people know, all the things they have read. Mainly, of course,
they're attracted by forbidden fruit. It isn't their fault that their perspective has become somewhat distorted. Life is sure to correct their

navigational errors, anyway. This applies not only to the younger generation, but to all of us.

The idea of differing life-experience came up. Doesn't this really play a larger role than we have been prone to admit? It's not a question of one set of experiences being better than another, but simply different.

Have you read Pecka?* He was jailed, not by the Germans but later. He underwent a rather drastic schooling in prison and emerged with pretty much the same basic experiences as I did. The crucial thing is the personality of the artist, his psychological configuration, his emotional world, intellect, character, even his health and temperament. These things are always overlooked; we place too much emphasis on ideology, philosophy, historical or generational experiences. Blinded by our illusions, we have succeeded in glossing over a great deal. We believe that just because our young people went through socialist schools they are automatically socialists. This isn't true at all. The old ties, habits, family life, superstitions, religious beliefs—all these continue to live and will not be eradicated by any socialist decree. And this cultural substratum has a tremendous, perhaps decisive, influence on a young artist. I often feel like laughing when I see learned tracts trying to explain a particular work on the basis of the influence of Heidegger or Kierkegaard, when I know the author in question and know perfectly well that he was a young man born at the wrong time: his father's tavern was nationalized, he didn't have a chance to go to college, he suffered from indigestion, he had trouble with girls.

The vital thing is to find one's own voice, but it must be one's own and not the voice of fashion or of the Church or of anything else. Still, it's hard to be sure. Sometimes you think you are expressing your deepest convictions when actually you are simply repeating the promptings of convention or echoing the common cry of the times. It was the fate of our generation that we faithfully listened to such voices in the belief that no other attitude was possible. That's why our generation was so threatened by sterility. This rigidity affected all of us, those who become engaged in the struggle as well as those who sought safety.

---

* Karel Pecka's book of short stories as well as a novel, dealing with his experiences in prisons and labor camps in the 1950s, had appeared shortly before this interview.—*Ed.*

I noted in my introduction how surprised I was when you completely abandoned journalism. It's taken some time to get around to this question.

It is often said, even by famous authors, that journalism and literary writing are complementary occupations and that it is an ideal experience for a writer to have spent his green years on a newspaper. I am now convinced that this is an error. It isn't so easy to switch. The apparent closeness of the two fields is deceptive and jumping from one to the other can lead to a nasty accident. Nor is it true that a journalist really gets to know the world.

Of course, he can penetrate all sorts of environments and talk to all sorts of people, but at the same time his job prevents him from going too deep. A newspaperman is simply part of one of society's institutions; he belongs to the power apparatus, and yet everybody knows that he doesn't have the last word or for that matter that he doesn't have much to say at all, so people tend to stay on their guard and keep back a good deal. Or else the journalist deliberately flatters his subjects, and then waits for praise and popularity in return. A writer's position is much more advantageous, especially when he succeeds in gaining someone's confidence. Ludvik Askenazy is one writer whom I've seen do this. We were together in a tavern once. A young woman was sitting at a nearby table; she was scowling and looked as forbidding as the Himalayas. Yet hardly half an hour later she was telling us the sort of things people don't tell their spouses even after ten years of marriage. I could see that she herself was quite surprised at the turn events had taken.

But there is a factual literary genre, too, such as your book on J. Robert Oppenheimer and various documentary pieces you have published.

Jaroslav Hasek's [author of *The Good Soldier Schweik*] favorite reading was the encyclopedia. I share this passion for facts. Yet even facts can prove seductive, like narcotics. For many years I wrote on international affairs. That meant that every day I had to wade through a pile of journals in all kinds of languages, to read bulletins, listen to broadcasts, follow television. A flood of facts. I began to drown in this flood; I had to get out of that line of work. It left a deep mark on me, though perhaps it doesn't really matter. After all, a prose writer cannot cook up masterworks with nothing but water and sentiments.

So you don't regret the years spent on the newspaper?

One shouldn't regret anything, but I do feel that I stayed too long with international politics. I lost many years that way. Some time ago I went through my clippings and I have no illusions about them. For the most part they were articles which served the needs of the day, and they died when their function was fulfilled. I can't help smiling ironically now at my former self-confidence, at the tremendous assurance with which I tried to solve world problems. We managed to learn the fundamentals of Marxism and this, we thought, gave us a monopoly on reason. Perhaps I needed that kind of education, but it lasted too long.

The need to write my own thing, to express myself in my own way, arose only after 1956. That is another milestone marking the end of an epoch. Together with the war, it represented a further basic experience and also a major existential shock. I cannot say that the revelation of Stalinist deformations shook my whole world to its foundations; there were many things I had already guessed long before. Nevertheless, this was the final and decisive blow. It was then that I became acutely aware that I wasn't really doing what I wanted to do, and that if I kept on in the same rut I would never say what I ought to say. This is when my novella *The Wall,* based on the theme of the occupation, came into being. Somehow I felt the need to purge myself of this subject, to shake it off, though of course it was the story of the occupation as seen through the backward glance of a person who had lived through the 1950s. At that time I was struck by another aspect of the difficulty of changing from journalism to literature. Several critics advised me, either good-naturedly or ironically, to go back to journalism. That's why I am especially grateful to critics like [Jiri] Opelik, [Jaroslav] Janu and [Ruzena] Grebenickova who paid more attention to my work than to my background. But to answer your question: My conclusion would be that it is not a good idea for a writer to start as a journalist; by bypassing journalism he can save himself a lot of bad blood and many unnecessary detours. At least that was my experience.

How about your early life?

I was born in Most, but spent much of my boyhood in Neratovice, which was at the time a fairly large village and has since grown into a respectable town. But I still cannot get used to the idea that all those wonderful pools along the Elbe have vanished forever. Now they are filled with slag; chemical plants have spread all over, and the land, water, and air smell of rotten eggs for miles around. I envy anybody who is able to return to his childhood home and find it pretty much as it was when he left it. I no longer have such a home to return to. Recently, when I went back to the place where I spent my earliest childhood, where I used to play marbles and raise guinea pigs, I found a tremendous, gaping abyss with bulldozers crawling along the bottom. Nothing whatever was left.

My family was rather proletarian. On neither side of the family could we boast intellectual ancestry. I had not counted on becoming an intellectual either, although from my early childhood on I had struggled with the question of whether it is better to live an adventurous life or to write about it. I used to be a voracious reader. In fact, I think that my passion for reading bordered on abnormality; I eagerly devoured every printed scrap of paper that came into my hands.

I finished four years of public school, then went to Prague to learn cabinetmaking. It is a noble, difficult, and, in a sense, really intellectual craft. Everything I did later seemed like a game in comparison. I became apprenticed to a Mr. Hellebrandt, who was a prince of his craft but unfortunately rather old and nervous, and we soon came to hate each other. Even so, I probably would have gotten my journeyman's papers if, in March 1942, I hadn't been arrested by the Gestapo. I was sentenced to prison for having committed high treason, and after I had served my sentence there they sent me to Dachau. I returned in 1945 in very bad health and the doctors assured my mother that I would die. This brutal experience gave rise to my optimism. I regard my life since 1945 as a gift of grace.

As soon as I had regained my health I left for the provinces. I ended up in a border region as secretary of the Youth Corps. It is hard for me to imagine anyone less suited to this job than I was. I remember a very old inspector who had come from Prague to check my accounts; the poor man almost wept. I gave up this position in time and journeyed to Prague to enroll in the School of Political and Social Studies. At that time, that was the only institution of higher education that didn't require a gymnasium diploma. I graduated from the faculty of journalism and got a job on *Lidove Noviny*. Then followed two years of military service. After my re-

turn I found that *Lidove Noviny* had been eliminated, so I switched
to *Literarni Noviny*. And there, in 1956, my heretofore unsullied
curriculum vitae was marred by its first major blemish. On the LN
there was a lot of discussion about philosophy and ideology, and
philosophers such as Ivan Svitak and Karel Kosik often joined our
discussions. By today's standards, the things that were said seem
rather tame, but at the time they were rank heresies. Eventually,
there was a big hullabaloo. Karel Kosik left for some practical work
in a factory, and I had to leave the newspaper. All of us were
branded as revisionists. It was instructive to observe the cowardly
behavior of certain people at a time when the political realities had
already become clear and ignorance was no longer an acceptable
excuse. After all, it was already 1959.

But I want to come back once more to 1956, to the Twentieth
Congress and the exposure of the "personality cult." I was shocked
by the disclosures, not because they were so unexpected but because
they confirmed a great deal that I had long suspected but had dismissed from my mind as being too absurd. My first jolt had come in
the fall of 1951 when I was in the Soviet Union with a delegation of
newspapermen. I was struck by all sorts of small details, such as the
waiting room sign in the delapidated airport in Voronezh: For Generals and Delegates Only. And then the museum of gifts to Stalin in
Moscow. The Dadaesque collection of portraits made out of poppy
seeds, whole wagonloads of devotional gifts, and those touching
letters written by people about to be executed ending with a greeting to Stalin! I remarked on these matters a little too openly and
this ripened into quite a scandal; fortunately, I escaped the consequences by entering military service. The years 1951–1953 turned
out to be the most trying ones for our nation, and I was lucky to
have been in the army at that time and thus to have escaped direct
involvement in the trials and other shocks to which people in the
press and in broadcasting were particularly exposed.

But I saw almost all of the trials; they took us to see them as part
of our military-political indoctrination. I should have listened to
my own inner voice, which told me: this is all nonsense, those
people are testifying like robots; it can't be the truth, it's only a
show, a game. But the mind resisted and was frightened at the
thought of being carried away by the consequences of such a revelation. And then came even greater shocks. Because I had seen everything up till then, I decided to observe the rehabilitation trials car-

ried on many years later. They were conducted in the same building on Pankrac Square [in Prague], and I had the same strong sense of unreality and theatricality. These are experiences with which I shall have to come to terms some day.

I consider it very important to re-emphasize that the revelations that came after Stalin's death didn't fall out of a clear blue sky. It is tempting to believe that nobody was guilty, that it was always somebody else, somebody higher up, and then even higher until finally you come to Stalin the Great himself. In reality, the basic facts had long been known, but people had simply refused to believe them— for all sorts of reasons, some base and some honorable. Nobody, however, can plead ignorance as an excuse.

For you the year 1956 also meant the beginning of a literary career.

The first books of mine to be published were halfway between literature and journalism: the reportage in *Under the Egyptian Crescent,* which appeared in 1957, and also in *Conscience (The Oppenheimer Case),* which came out in 1959, though the genre of the latter is hard to pin down. In *Conscience* there are echoes of practically all the problems we have discussed: the individual and society, the problem of responsibility for one's own actions and decisions, the problem of truth, freedom. It may be of interest to note that it was this book which the Moscow students translated and distributed in the form of handwritten manuscripts. This confirms my belief that the book had a meaning which transcended the life story of an American atomic scientist.

The next stage begins with the novella *The Wall,* 1962. Then came *Indicia,* 1963, the stories *Invitation to Judgment,* 1964, and finally the novel *Passion Sunday,* which enabled me to devote myself entirely to literature, at least for some time. Of course, I picked the wrong time to become a professional writer; all sorts of economic pressures are now becoming evident and even experienced sailors are leaving the open sea in search of quiet harbors.

With Milan Kundera we discussed the survival of national entities in the modern epoch ...

I am not sure that I quite agree with Milan Kundera. Like Schauer in the previous century, he considers a nation's existence justified only when it produces something new and unique, at least as far as European values are concerned. I believe that nations that have excelled in nothing in particular still have a perfect right to their national existence. Besides, history is not yet finished. The whole world is subjected to processes of unification, leveling, and standardization, and it is wrong to believe that such processes always imply progress. The existence of even the smallest of nations plays a part in countering this all-embracing tendency to integration. Small nations are islands that resist the stream. There is general agreement that national self-determination is a good thing, yet nationhood is regarded in a somewhat condescending way, like a necessary anachronism. Then, too, some people still accept the old Stalinist idea of a gradual formation of regional supernational languages, the vision of some sort of giant synthesis. As if this automatically implied progress!

In our country we have a small-scale replica of the problem in terms of the Czech and Slovak populations; the exceptional closeness of the two languages and cultures creates a strong temptation toward hasty union. Why put up with all these complications, the bureaucrat says to himself, when it would be so much simpler to have a single centralized government, a single language . . . In reality the constant tension and vibration between these two cultures makes Czechoslovakia an extraordinarily interesting country. But it isn't only a question of Czechs and Slovaks; it is just as important to support regional distinctiveness, to support everything that has its own face, taste, and manner. Thus, we must cease seeing our smallness as a handicap and convert it into an advantage; here Kundera and I are in complete agreement.

How do these considerations affect literature?

The art of the novel also includes the art of detachment, the narrator's detachment from the book's characters, the detachment of the hero from his own actions and thoughts. To find the proper degree of detachment requires time, maturity, and a certain inner confidence. And in our country, for various reasons, there never was enough time to reach this point. Goethe made no secret of his desire to write not only for his own time but for future generations, and he deliberately wrote with an eye on the judgment of history. We lack this outlook today, not only here but throughout the world. Modern man has a sense of uncertainty; permanence seems to him an illusory concept. Tomorrow or the day after everything may go up in flames without a moment's warning, so why worry about form and why be concerned about future generations? Yet we have no alternative but to strive for permanence.

The attitudes of the public and the critics toward works of art create a further complication. Here, too, the necessary detachment and long-range perspective is lacking. Many things have changed as far as criticism is concerned; there is no longer the same pressure upon the artist to produce works of immediate usefulness, yet among the general public and among certain bureaucratic groups the old attitudes still crop up. And sometimes with the same impudence as the historic proclamation on art made by the Prague butchers: "After all, we are paying for all this!"

Time—time to let things ripen, to leave the budding plant alone! Take films, for example. Films cannot be evaluated every year like the annual production of coal; you need a few years' distance. You cannot damn a work the first time you see it. And in literature, it's just the same. Time to ripen—which of us can say that he had enough? Hasek drank himself to death, Capek was hounded to death, Vancura was executed, and these are our greatest writers! But quite aside from such tragic cases as these, we are a small nation and it is difficult for a literary man to make a living. Think of all the stuff that a Nezval had to write to earn a living. Which of us can bring out a book every five years and then live off the proceeds? And so we are forced into a kind of violent and artificial fruitfulness; an author writes book after book, year after year. This tendency was greatly strengthened by the new tax law. With certain authorized exceptions, everybody's income will be added up each year and taxed. The year has become the official measure of our horizons.

You mentioned the revolt of youth against the lie . . .

A lie, particularly a social and institutional lie, always involves catastrophic consequences for the national psyche. Every writer comes up against this. Lies sanctioned and protected by the state embitter and outrage writers in all societies. Such lies are a goad to resistance and open conflict, of course. Incidentally, I don't understand why some people are so surprised to find that lies exist. Writers especially should not be surprised, for lies form a part of the life of any individual or society. What is awful is not the lie or the far more usual halftruth, but rather a situation in which a lie cannot be branded as such and combated. It is at this point that the trauma begins, when people begin to lose faith even in the truth. Finally they don't even believe in art.

Under such conditions art becomes politicized against its will. It is forced to assume a number of roles that actually belong to journalism, propaganda, and sociology. Art always has a greater degree of freedom than other forms of communication, and its "filter" is porous enough to permit the passage of truths that are still considered taboo. I have a strong feeling that this is the reason why many people who are basically journalists or polemicists have turned to literature. This is neither a normal nor a desirable state of affairs.

To come back to the national psyche. We mustn't assume that this is some simple or unified entity. A great deal depends on specific backgrounds, organizations, traditions. Nor are the interests of the intellectuals and other groups, such as the workers, always identical. For that matter, even among the intellectuals a variety of quite antithetical interests and viewpoints manifest themselves. It is fashionable to speak of the deformation of national character. I don't think that things are quite that bad; I don't think that people have lost the ability to distinguish truth from falsehood. Certainly, during the worst period of Stalinism, or under the influence of wartime pressures, there was the danger that this ability might be lost, but even then a healthy questioning spirit survived. The changes that have taken place in the last few years have once again confirmed our old Czech sobriety. With the exception of a few idiots, you can talk to anybody you like and you'll find that people have a remarkably accurate idea of what's going on. I think that sometimes we take this healthy critical attitude too much for granted; we forget how essential it is if art is to survive. Without it we would be trying to talk to the deaf.

There is one area we bit into but didn't explore further: the individual, the intellectual, and society.

The precarious position of the modern intellectual is best exemplified by the fate of the scientists. Modern science is actually a giant branch of industry, a tremendous public enterprise. A writer needs only pencil and paper, a painter needs canvas and paint, but what about a physicist such as Oppenheimer? Modern science has also, of course, become a part of the military establishment; after all, everything can be used for war and for the destruction of people. What can an individual accomplish in such a situation? Even rebellion is futile, since everybody is replaceable just as Oppenheimer was. Filmmakers or television people are in a similar predicament; they cannot create their work on their own but depend on an outside power which provides the means, and to which they are held accountable. Everybody must account to someone, that's only normal, but the problem is to make the wielders of power accountable and to ensure that they are sufficiently qualified, wise, and even generous. These battles should be fought out in the open, in public rather than in secret, so that the individual is given some chance of success.

This is where the significance of the various contemporary intellectual movements comes in. The intellectual is usually aware of the inner connections of events sooner and more deeply than others, and thus he is destined to play a bigger role in political struggles. The intellectual may wish to remain aloof, but whether he wants to or not he becomes a political force. It seems that this aspect of modern development is the same throughout the world. I am thinking of Sartre's initiative, Russell's tribunal, the Pugwash conferences, Negro students, and so on.

Everything which keeps things in motion and prevents rigidity is good, everything which refuses to accept the idea that nothing can be done and which goes counter to the prevailing current. [The Russian novelist Alexander] Solzhenitsyn is a good example. The act of a single man can puncture the puffed up pretensions of a whole proud assemblage. That is the wonderful thing about life, that an individual can always be found to perform an apparently senseless, yet profoundly necessary act. A single person often saves the greatness and honor of literature and of culture as a whole.

In your novel Passion Sunday, *psychology plays a large role, as it does in modern art generally.*

I said at the outset that I am greatly interested in analyzing man, in analyzing the human heart. That is the most fundamental concern of every writer and I cannot imagine how a writer could fail to be interested in those scientific disciplines which deal with human behavior. Freud, Jung, Fromm, and others. One must know these things. Someone might object and point out that Dostoevski or Tolstoy read no psychology and yet were masters of the human soul. But I believe that such an objection is false, since Tolstoy, Dostoevski, as well as the other giants of the nineteenth century, kept up with contemporary scientific findings concerning the human mind. And they'd be just as fascinated by Freud and other modern psychologists.

Interest in psychology is of course also connected with the simple fact that mental illness has become vastly more prevalent in our time. Modern man is prey to all possible kinds and degrees of neurosis and psychosis; mental illness is as much a part of our existence as modern technology and the hectic tempo of our lives. Interest in how to deal with these sicknesses is not limited to psychologists and psychiatrists.

I have read a good deal of literature on this subject and have gathered information on various ways of treating these afflictions which are, perhaps, the most widespread of our time. In this connection, I came across Zen Buddhist texts, which have been recommended by one school of psychiatry as a useful basis for therapy. Zen texts—actually, they are more in the nature of anecdotes or absurd proverbs—are diametrically opposed to European thought, which is based on logic. They exhibit a mode of thought quite close to the artistic mentality—a paradoxical mode which seeks to attain a direct comprehension of the world, without ideology and without the mediation of abstract thought or conventions. Thus, Zen is a kind of antidote to our logical, systematized, and ordered era. It has served as a starting point for American poets, also for the organizers of happenings. It is a pity that these texts have not yet been made accessible to us, except for small samples in the major world languages. The sinologist Oldrich Kral is preparing translations of ancient Chinese Taoist writings, which are quite close to Zen. I look forward eagerly to reading them.

What are your literary loves?

They are endless. From the ancient Chinese to the Russians and the latest Americans. Also Sartre, Camus, Hemingway, and, among our own writers, Vancura and, of course, Hasek . . .

Why do you think there is so much interest in our country in Camus? It seems we have almost developed an addiction to him.

The theme of Camus' work is the relationship of the individual to society. What can the individual accomplish with his pitifully

weak power? Doctor Rieux, who struggles with the plague in a
beleaguered city, knows his exertions are futile, but is convinced
that in one way or another a man must keep on fighting, that he
must not kneel in submission. Camus asks us what we can do when
we believe neither in God nor in reason. Camus is impressive, too,
in the personal consistency of his viewpoints. For a long time we
have been given his thought only in a caricatured form; now his
books are reaching us after a ten-year delay, yet his influence is
unique and will, I believe, continue to grow. I am especially attracted by his paradoxical optimism, which is very close to my own
temperament. All those things said about his pessimism were nonsense. *The Myth of Sisyphus* is a superb statement of the intellectual's situation in the twentieth century. And I am often reminded
of Camus' fine thought: "What counts in literature is not so much
intellect as the ability to say yes and to say no." He certainly had
this ability.

*What is your attitude toward the generations—your own and the
younger one?*

As far as creative development is concerned, our generation is
marred by debuts that were either premature or belated. Some
published their *Sturm und Drang* verse before they reached twenty,
others waited until they'd turned forty. In other words, I think our
generation was rather confused. Yet, given the right conditions, all
this can still be turned to advantage. I don't really dare to judge the
work of my contemporaries and friends; I am too close to them and
this always creates a dangerous distortion. But I do believe this generation could accomplish a great deal.

Just take its life-experience. It had the peculiar fortune—or misfortune—to live through the end of the First Republic. It grew up
during the occupation and reached its maturity, in 1948, as a generation of victors. It is interesting that this generation never came to
power, as it did in Yugoslavia and other countries. It is a generation
of eternal dauphins. The decisive test came in 1956. That was the
time when it acquitted itself honorably and it deserves credit for
having led the intellectual attack on Stalinism. Of course, this is
a broad generalization and therefore not quite accurate. It is part of
the irony of fate that it was precisely the generation of the young
Stalinists that became the de-Stalinizing vanguard.

What about the older ones?

On the whole, I don't think too much of them. After all the excuses and explanations, they are still stuck with Stalinism, and with Munich, too. Still, perhaps one can't really blame a generation for such things.

You said before that the real heroes of our time are its heroines— the women.

I think that we must never abandon the dream of a great, free, and universal humanity. In reality, however, the tendencies toward estrangement and alienation are becoming ever stronger; logic, mathematics, and abstraction penetrate into every facet of life. Soon even the most subtle mental processes will be planned and manipulated; perhaps this will happen even to love. I am not opposed to science, but it is essential to recognize its limits. Humor, wit, and irony can serve as antidotes. But what's needed, above all, is a non-stereotyped, authentic expression of life. Perhaps it is an illusion, but it seems to me that women are more successfully safeguarding their natural ability in this regard than men. Even the wonderful feminine ability to act illogically is part of it. I am sure you have noticed, though, that even we sensible men are capable of behaving like fools on occasion.

In conclusion: What quality do you most value in a writer?

Probably sincerity. The kind of sincerity described by the young Dumas. When asked why his father never wrote a single boring line, he replied: "Because it would have bored him."

Spring 1967

Dominik Tatarka

Born 1913. He studied in Prague and Paris and published two books during World War II, which he spent in his native Slovakia. He gained wide popularity only with his third book, *The Parson Republic* (1948), which described life in the puppet Slovak state in the years 1939–1945. This was followed by three novels dealing with the revolutionary post-war years and the building of socialism in Slovakia. At the Second Writers' Congress in 1956 he made an allegoric speech (about violets that do not smell at all, although people are being told that they do) which implied a critical attitude to some aspects of the regime. After that, he turned to reflective prose and in 1963 published a novella based on reminiscences of his stay in Paris, *The Wicker Chairs*. Another novella, published a year later, *The Demon of Consent,* was an allegoric satire on the Stalinist system. Although he took part in some of the discussions of the reform period, he did not play a major role in political life. Being a highly original and complex personality, he appeals more to intellectuals than to a mass public.

Dominik Tatarka

The interview took place* in the summer, in the middle of that terribly hot July; a storm had just passed and another was gathering, as always . . . But it had all started much earlier, this mutual desire to get together and talk; it happened after Sartre's speech in the jammed hall in Bratislava; it was then that we first realized how much we shared in common, how well we understood each other. The actual interview was postponed many times; we only saw each other briefly now and then to exchange a few words. After his [Slovak] *novels* The Demon of Consent *and* The Wicker Chairs *came out in Czech, I was eager to buy my airplane ticket for Bratislava— only to face more delays and postponements. In short, the interview finally took place in July. (A few days before I left, I met* [author and psychiatrist] *Josef Nesvadba on the street. We wished each other a pleasant vacation and he produced one of the great aphorisms of the time: "They put the rope around their neck and went off on vacation.")*

I had arrived at the lake at noon; Dominik Tatarka came in the evening. We had ten days ahead of us. As it turned out, it was to rain half of that time, the only spot in Europe with consistently bad

---

* It was shortly after the Fourth Congress of the Czechoslovak Writers' Union, but just before the Writers' Union paper was shut down and the most outspoken writers expelled from the Communist Party.—*Eds.*

weather that month. All the same, the magnolias blossomed, drops of rain glistened on the palm leaves, we had ten days, and we talked: in the hotel room, in a small lakeside café, on the park lawn, on the fantastic white boulders along the riverbed reminiscent of a sculpture by Henry Moore, at the far end of the valley where they served young red wine and cheese ... We talked until the very last minute of the last day, for we knew that we might never have the same opportunity again. Even so, a great deal that was on our minds remained unspoken.

The conversation turned to film ...

I never had much luck with film. Not even with *The Dam*. I regarded the subject primarily in a symbolic way: a flooded village, where everything slowly disappears under the surface of the water—memories, history, traditions. But this approach ruled out any connection with concrete reality.

... and poetry.

In every nation, true literary creators are rare; they constitute a practically negligible layer of the population. A poet is a priest, even though he doesn't preach. He is a modern priest of the spirit. And his prestige lies in this poetic vocation, although he can use it —and abuse it—in areas in which he isn't quite competent. I have thought about this question in connection with *The Demon of Consent:* the poet as an official, a party secretary. These are two quite separate functions. The poet invokes his prestige as creator to prop up his position of social power. Too often, such a situation leads to abuse; how many times have we heard a poet-politician polemicizing and thereby compromising his deepest feelings!

Do writers wield political power in this country? An affirmative answer would imply that our writers are deeply involved in politics, that they possess the means for exerting power, possibilities for expression; in reality, Czech and Slovak writers are seriously circumscribed in these respects. And yet . . . poet and politician. In France, one man managed to combine these callings in a particularly happy way. I am speaking, of course, of André Malraux, a major author with a clear and definite concept of cultural politics which he was enabled by fortunate circumstances to put into practice. In my view, this significantly benefited not only France, but the whole world. One example of his influence is the recent world-wide surge of interest in the plastic arts, in which his concepts played a major part. It was Malraux who said that sculpture is divine creation, the creation of works which represent to the fullest our consciousness and our feelings. In the broader sense, culture is the sum total of works that deserve to be worshipped by mankind.

And literature . . .

All of this applies equally to literature. Whenever literature is degraded into the manufacture of slogans, creation is replaced by production. This process no longer expresses our fate and our situation in the world, but only abstract values. Certainly, there are periods which are extremely skeptical toward all impersonal values. But whenever I contemplate Kundera's conception of our national and cultural history, I can only wish that this viewpoint could be shared by the Ministry of Culture as well as by other influential agencies. Kundera reminded us of the basic meaning of our history. Ever since our cultural revival, the viewpoint expressed by Kundera has been in the forefront of our national consciousness, and this applies to Slovakia as well as Bohemia. If we agree on nothing else, we should agree on this. The poet on the throne . . .

Every conversation with Dominik Tatarka is a conversation that moves in circles, or rather in spirals; it always returns to its starting point, except that each time this point moves just a little bit higher; the answer never quite dovetails with the question. And whoever fails to understand and to respect this approach, whoever wants to stretch the spiral into a straight line, runs the risk of missing the point completely, of not grasping the method in Tatarka's madness.

The poet as politician. To what extent can he play his own part? How many things must he approve as a man of power which he disapproves of as a poet? That is one of the characteristic problems of the last two decades. Just consider our schools! Think of how carelessly we abandoned so many of our humanist traditions! We have turned literature into propaganda, and a kind of academic court sculpture has crept into our plastic arts. We built statues to foreign gods. Although this period was relatively brief, it almost made us forget the meaning of our national history. To make myself clear: when I speak of national humanist traditions, I am including the Christian tradition as well.

Personally, I find it most gratifying that Czech writers are once

again dealing with these questions, and they are finding excellent
formulations for bringing them to the center of our attention. In
one respect at least, Czech and Slovak authors should have an absolutely identical goal: the development of Czechoslovak socialist
democracy. That is the basic starting point and criterion. Whenever democracy is injured or suffers from insufficient development
in Slovakia, the results are felt in Bohemia, and vice versa. The
situation of the Slovak nation is basically the same as that of the
Czech nation and its culture. I am glad that Czech writers and other
intellectuals, when analyzing their own problems, are turning more
and more to consideration of Slovak questions as well. After all, it
is ultimately a matter of common gain or common loss.

*Of course, there are specific local, autonomous questions as well.
For example, the Slovak avant-garde, its character, traditions, influence...*

I suppose that's an indirect request for my biography. Very well.
By education, I am a professor of Czech. I studied in Prague, and so
the basic years in which a writer's mind is formed were in my case
spent in Prague. I was a direct participant in all the battles waged
by progressive youth of those days. My secondary schooling took
place in Nitra, and there were several professors there who had a
positive influence on me and who helped me to get rid of certain
unfortunate local tendencies. Nitra was a strongly clerical town,
and many of my fellow students were being prepared for service in
various foreign missions, such as the so-called Russicum in Rome.
Boys from Slovak villages were supposed to become missionaries
and to bring the Russian people back to the Catholic fold. And yet,
as I said, there were many excellent professors both in Nitra and in
Trencin who had a most wholesome influence on me.

*(At that moment, I thought again about the influence of teachers,
just as this question had occurred to me in my conversation with
Ludvik Vaculik and a number of others: How will the intellectual
generation which grew up in the 1950s and 1960s regard its teachers
and professors? How many educators will enter national cultural
history through the same little doors as their predecessors?)*

We felt equally at home in Czech and Slovak literature. We regarded writers such as Seifert, Halas, and Nezval as our own; these
were the poets closest to us and to this day I know their work by

heart. Vancura, too. Everything worthwhile stimulated the ferment which characterized cultural life in the First Republic. When I attended the university in Prague from 1934 to 1938, Vancura was regularly present at the discussions taking place in Masaryk College. I never felt any estrangement from my Czech colleagues; we had the same interests, the same tastes, the same political perspectives and hopes. And the same was true in 1938 and 1939 when I attended the Sorbonne. It was a truly international group of young people with similar outlooks—Poles, Americans, Frenchmen, Swedes. And suddenly the realization came that one belongs to no world and no country at all. The republic was crippled, and from Paris it was easy to see that final occupation of the land by the Germans was only a matter of days. Later, I tried to recapture this mood in *The Wicker Chairs.*

During those Paris years, I came to adopt a viewpoint which was later formulated as existentialist. (*It is often forgotten nowadays that existentialism didn't originate as a postwar phenomenon, but that it had its roots in the prewar atmosphere just described.*) The meaning and atmosphere of my first book, *Viewed with Alarm,* also comes from this period. Critics wrote of existentialist influences. Influences . . . Camus is a member of my generation; he was born in 1913. . . . In our literature, views and formulations which are actually quite original are often erroneously considered to be derived from foreign models, because of the prevailing belief that the literature of a small nation must necessarily assume the role of epigone and place itself under the tutelage of larger literatures. Yet the tensions and anxieties which gave rise to existentialism in France were the same as the tensions felt in Czechoslovakia, in spite of differences between a world power and a small country.

I returned from Paris via Prague. My birthday happens to fall on March 14th. In the morning, I left the inn where I was staying, crossed the river, and saw German troops marching down Wenceslaus Square while people on the sidewalks sang *"Kdoz jste bozi bojovnici"* ["You, the fighters for the Lord."]

These are, so to say, the archetypal experiences that molded a man, a writer, a generation—clenched fists and a Hussite hymn. Such generational bonds are not easily broken. That's why I find it hard to understand how Czechs can ignore matters that vitally affect their Slovak colleagues; it hurts to see such apathy.

But these aren't the only bonds, this isn't the only common background and atmosphere that shaped our sensibility. Take for example the activity of Slovak writers in 1950. It is paradoxical—as in a number of similar cases—that the attack of Stalinism first fell on a number of Slovak writers who were the least guilty of any kind of narrow nationalism. On the contrary, such people as [the literary critic Alexander] Matuska, [the essayist Michal] Chorvath, [the novelist Vladimir] Minac, and myself were the very embodiment of forces that bound the two nations and the two literatures together. Yet such absurd events occurred both then and later. The background of all this is a mystery to me to this day. Nobody has yet succeeded in explaining to me why we four were chosen rather than anyone else. Nobody even bothered to pretend that any of my books contained hostile ideology. Or Matuska—a man completely formed under the influence of Czech literature. Or Chorvath; or Minac, a young journalist, a partisan, author of the novel *Death Walks the Mountains*. Communists all. Fellow communists had gotten together and agreed to ostracize the four of us, to break off all friendship and contact. With few exceptions, the entire community of Slovak writers damned this small group of colleagues. That must never be forgotten. All sorts of intimacies were brought out into the open, a lot of dirty wash was dragged out. My attitude toward Soviet literature was considered suspicious: I was accused of liking Mayakovsky only because he committed suicide. A certain authoress asked me to confess to various misdeeds, after having read to me certain sections of my book *Man and Action,* which she had underlined. I was also accused of having had the wrong attitude toward the working class, since at one point in my novel a worker belched and at another he tried out a speech while standing before a mirror . . .

It would thus appear that my work begun in the late 1930s had been ripped apart. But I believe that the collection of my reviews and essays which is about to come out under the name *Highroads and Byroads* will demonstrate an organic continuity in my thought about literature and its mission.

What, then, were the actual consequences of my persecution? Nothing happened to me physically. But my books were suppressed, and in the few cases that my works were published they carried introductions that smeared as much of the contents as they could. It was evidently not a blow that was designed to destroy me, but only to frighten me. As always. Perhaps it didn't really matter who was chosen as target; it was important to frighten not any particular victim so much as a group of people associated with him. I am sure you are familiar with this situation.

How did you start writing?

My mentor was [the nineteenth-century Slovak novelist and short-story writer Martin] Kukucin. That was in Trencin, in my fourth year of gymnasium. A little later, I won a prize at the gymnasium for a prose piece that appeared in a student magazine. But in effect I come from the cultural periphery. I am a village boy, my father was killed in the war when I was two years old. As a child I had very little contact with books; I was more under the influence of folklore in the good sense of the term, folk creativity and imagination. The prize-winning piece I just mentioned was based on a story my mother told me—a tragic tale of unhappy love. In order to get a high mark in Slovak, I copied out excerpts from several volumes of Kukucin; his language, as well as his kindly humor, had a great impact on me. I was struck by a kind of primitive amazement that ideas could be so beautifully expressed with letters of the alphabet. This sense of wonder at the power of the written word hasn't left me to this day.

The other great cultural revelation was produced by the Prague theater. Until my arrival in Prague I had actually never seen a decent theater, although I had taken part in some amateur theatricals. And suddenly to come upon Burian's production of his own play, based on Pushkin's *Onegin!*

Then there were many other influences which would be incomprehensible to someone who had come from a conventional cultural background. For example, the itinerant tinkers from my region around Povazska Bystrica [a town in central Slovakia]. Eternal wanderers. One of them, old Rezak, used to herd goats with me when I was a boy. He had crisscrossed the world, and the only thing he had to show for his past was a silver chain with a Swiss franc. He told me about the wide world, and he recounted tales, too. Fantasy and reality mingled miraculously in his head. He told me of fabulous creatures, of beautiful mermaids, and these stories gave rise to longings that have stayed with me all my life. The longing to follow the sun, to follow it beyond the mountains where it joins its mother. How many great storytellers have I heard, at spinning-time or at various family gatherings, happy or sad . . . In the early days of the First Republic, folk creativity still flourished—embroidery, pottery, singing. One of my grandfathers was a composer of songs, both folk and religious, and he guided pilgrims all the way to Poland (my parents came from an area close to the Polish border).

When Sartre came to Czechoslovakia, he asked me why I wrote. *"Pour m'éterniser,"* I said. To make myself eternal. And at the same time I realized that memory is the most important thing of all. By means of analysis and creative formulation, the confused and vague impressions of life are etched into memory and given permanent form. Shortly after the war I was in Switzerland, in Lugano, in a country quite untouched by the fighting. And because I wrote about it, I know it here as if my trip had taken place only yesterday. Of course, in addition to memory and reformulation it is also a matter of moral, sensory, and intellectual consciousness . . .

When I came to Prague I wanted to study philosophy, but they told me that with my kind of background I'd never get a job in a hundred years. Czech and Latin was a better combination, they advised me. And so I simplified the whole problem by deciding on French, and I enrolled at the French Institute. There was a wonderful man there at the time, Joseph Pasquier; he sensed that I had talent for literary criticism, and my paper on André Chénier won me a fellowship for study in France.

In other respects, my sojourn in Prague did not prove conducive to my writing. I found it difficult to express myself properly in Czech, and my whole literary activity was limited to a single magazine contribution. The Czech language formed an insurmountable obstacle, not only for my writing but for my theatrical work as well. As a supernumerary in a production in Vinohrady, my part was limited to the shout: "Long live Rosmersholm!"

And there was another problem, too. I knew perfectly well that unless I got a scholarship I couldn't possibly afford to remain in college. And so literary activity had to be pushed aside, in spite of the fact that I continued to regard literature as the ultimate meaning of everything that I was doing. The same situation continued when I transferred to Zilina and to Martin [both in Slovakia].

We have almost forgotten that this expedition into the past was actually triggered by a question about the Slovak avant-garde.

I have already talked about what might be called the atmosphere of the First Republic. Our generation conceived of political prob-

lems from a broad, all-European point of view. Furthermore, nobody doubted the viability of the republic, not even the most
right wing Slovak elements. The impact of the Third Reich in
shattering this world view thus had tremendous psychological ramifications. In the midst of this ominous sense of Europe teetering on
the brink of disaster, doubts regarding civilized man's fate naturally
grew ever stronger. The question of the future of mankind somehow seemed to merge with the question of national survival. Consider, for example, the greatest figures of French literature: they
always thought as Frenchmen *par excellence.* The situation of
France was generalized by them into the situation of Man. This
way of looking at things, no matter how pessimistic, no matter how
tragic, is probably the most basic contribution of existentialism to
European culture. In the work of Camus—from *The Stranger* to
The Plague—this development can be clearly traced: from the
isolation of the individual to a new confirmation of human solidarity. To me, it all seems very clear and organically developed. In *The
Plague,* The Stranger becomes a man who recognizes larger ties and
bows to the community's demands, even though that community
may be infected with the plague or some other social evil. In spite
of the fact that we still have only a very short historical perspective
on Camus' work, we sense that his portrayal of historical reality is
essentially clear and correct.

Postwar Czech and Slovak writers apparently did not feel the
need for portraying a sense of isolation as keenly as did their French
colleagues. Our literary development was rooted in local conditions. The trends in our literature during the 1950s were not
simple parallels of currents in Soviet literature, but grew in our
own soil, in our own situation. Similarly, the existentialist wave
grew logically out of domestic conditions, out of changes in thought
and feeling, a sense of uncertainty, the necessity for rethinking the
basic situation of Man.

This fundamental uncertainty about Man's fate, expressed in
literature, film, or other forms of art, needn't imply inactivity, or
resignation as far as the solution of political questions is concerned.
On the contrary, I have recently come to recognize a new wave of
energy both in our literature and in our public life. From this viewpoint, the Fourth Writers' Congress was a historic occasion, which
marked the culmination of this tendency. The full statement is still
obscured by certain accents which some people like to call "hyster-

ical"; when these fade out, I believe that we will hear the important message emanating from the leaders of contemporary Czech culture. Unfortunately, it often happens in our country that the most positive statements are taken as provocations. That is a great error. I cannot imagine a writer worth his salt who hasn't wrestled with these questions and hasn't tried to formulate his own answers to them.

We kept circling back to the avant-garde . . .

In the 1930s, like every author who intensively experienced Czechoslovak surrealism as well as its French counterpart, I was a surrealist, too. However, my attitude toward this movement was rather independent. For instance, in my *Miraculous Virgin* there are numerous ironic elements that reflect a certain detachment. The work was written at a time when surrealism was receding as a force in poetry. To be sure, the situation that existed in Slovakia in the early 1940s called forth exactly the same kind of imaginative approach. Under these conditions, only highly indirect ways of projecting human sensibility made it possible for a poet to express himself. Slovak literature, somewhat underdeveloped by European standards, suffered from another difficulty as well, particularly as far as prose was concerned: namely, it labored under the burden of a rigid realism. By this I don't mean an over-all realistic canon, but rather a form of realistic verbalism. During the war years I became particularly painfully aware of the trite verbalism of Slovak literature, in connection with the development of a new generation of young prose writers. And so I conceived *Miraculous Virgin* as a weapon in the fight against this misuse of language. Certain aspects of the development of Slovak literature have not been sufficiently explored by literary historians and critics, and so we are still not clearly aware of the special circumstances under which our literary generation made its appearance. The call for imaginative expressions during the war was clearly sounded in such works as [Jan] Drda's *Town in the Palm of the Hand* or in his *Peter the Liar,* as well as in my *Miraculous Virgin.* As you know, this represented only a brief interlude, but nevertheless it resulted in new freedom and made many things easier.

A small literature such as the Slovak has the disadvantage of being represented during periods of crisis by only a small handful of names. That's why certain manifestations seem so sporadic and fragmented. There was a tiny group of us at the time; in addition to myself there was Cerven, [Frantisek] Svantner . . . but Cerven's collection was not published until after his death, and Svantner became silent after publishing two early books and he died quite young. This entire epoch of Slovak prose was thus only a thin layer, a few books.

When The Demon of Consent *came out, I was very eager to talk to you; I couldn't wait to interview you for the newspaper. But somehow it never worked out . . .*

The Demon of Consent? Its subtitle was "A tract from the end of an era." That's rather important. It was written to examine a certain theme and to get away from a mass of realistic detail. Theoretically speaking, it was a question of so-called fantastical prose, which is also represented in the genre of Utopian prose. Reality can be shifted either into a more abstract framework or into a framework further removed in time. Both of these approaches are motivated by the need to do away with troublesome realistic detail, to see a problem in its entirety, in its most general terms. During the Second Writers' Congress I talked metaphorically about odorless violets, and that idea actually gave me the impulse toward writing fantastical prose, which would not be vulnerable to attacks of censorship. *Double-entendre,* like metaphor, provides a dependable defense in such cases.

If I were to give a name to the general problem I was dealing with, it would be that seductive phenomenon known as collectivism: loss of the sense of personal responsibility in the name of a pretended social concern. Perhaps in its way my work represented our first political satire about people trying to hide their own cowardice behind a wall of general agreement with everything and everybody, people substituting a kind of collective mind for their own brains.

At the beginning, we touched upon questions of national cultural concepts as seen by the Slovaks and the Czechs. Somehow we got off the track . . .

I have long had the feeling that the conception of culture in Czechoslovakia is not sufficiently energetic, sufficiently activating. Until recently, our cultural perspective was limited to the establishment of harmony with certain models; we built statues to foreign gods; we unwittingly gave up our national individuality. When Julius Caesar described the lowliest tribes and nations that he had encountered in his campaigns, he always referred to them as *inculti;* in other words, tribes without cults, without gods. I am not advocating a revival of nationalism, nor cultivation of national exclusivity, but rather a determined effort at cultivating our own consciousness and sense of national existence.

The criteria of great sculpture can only be understood against the background of the art of sculpture as practiced by past epochs. The works of the past reflect the sensibility of those bygone eras, but at the same time such works serve to cultivate and to polish our own receptivity. In that sense they provide measures and criteria of contemporary creativity. Only a violent break in tradition could explain the tolerance that Czechoslovak citizens exhibited toward such things as the architecture of Nova Dubnica or of the main square of Ulan Bator or the gilded statuary exhibited at Moscow's agricultural exposition. Such works stem from a tradition completely foreign to our art. They belong to the tradition of court sculpture designed to serve *ad maiorem Caesaris gloriam.* Once we understand this we also understand why works of folk sculpture still remain far more lively than the products of monumental sculpture, whether dating from the First Republic or the last few decades. I am convinced that only on the basis of profound reflection regarding the direction and meaning of national development can we formulate a conception of culture which would help stimulate an artistic renaissance. I have already mentioned the French minister of culture (whose department is strangely enough also known as the *Ministry of Cults*), who cares not only about the preservation of the glorious products of the past, but who is equally concerned about assuring the immortality of contemporaries. Too many of our great men are still misunderstood, unreconciled to history; their work still awaits official recognition; after centuries they still haven't entered the Pantheon, the hallowed grounds of our forefathers. For example, after a hundred years the memory of J. M. Hurban [Slovak writer and patriot, 1817–1889] is still relegated to occasional local celebrations.

As I said before, culture means cultivation and honoring, and insofar as we are serious about fraternal co-existence between Czechs and Slovaks, we ought to think about a common Pantheon, in which the great figures from the past of both nations would find their place. It seems to me that in Prague, in the park on Petrin, next to the monument to K. H. Macha [nineteenth-century Czech poet, the founder of modern Czech poetry], there ought to be a stone with the name of Janko Kral [nineteenth-century Slovak romantic poet, associated with the Slovak national revival], and that similarly in Bratislava there should be a memorial to those cultural heroes whom both nations revere.

No nation can exist without pride, without the cultivation of pride. Even when a citizen is about to bare his head to the executioner's axe, he must feel with pride: *civis rei publicae sum.* I know that I am just throwing out fragments of ideas, but these are the kinds of fragmentary thoughts that are drifting in the current atmosphere of the country. Now it is a matter of putting them together into some sort of meaningful whole . . .

Recently, there has been a deterioration in the relations between the Czech and Slovak intelligentsia, between Czech and Slovak cultural workers. Each side has the feeling that the other has let it down, each sees only its own problems, and so contact is broken off; the Czechs occupy themselves only with their own problems and so do the Slovaks. This is bad, the worst thing that could have happened. What is the cause of this situation?

First of all, let me point to one positive aspect: whenever creative capability becomes concentrated and developed in any single place, this process strengthens the sense of cultural confidence in other places as well; there is faith in the continued growth of talent, capability, and courage. I believe that Slovaks should welcome the recent successes of Czech culture and I know that many Slovaks regard them as their own. Of course, deep in the heart of the Slovak people there is an indelible memory of the extensive flowering of Slovak culture during the First Republic, and of the similar flowering that took place in the last decade, errors and injustice notwithstanding. Certain paternalistic attitudes and statements on the part of the Czechs naturally irritate us, but they do not confuse us. For we know that we are continually producing more and more creative people in every area of culture, and that these people will sooner or later gain recognition in Bohemia [the western, Czech portion of Czechoslovakia] as well as throughout the rest of Europe. Let us never forget that just as the Czech intelligentsia cannot rely on the mediation of a greater, more advanced, or richer foreign culture, so

Slovak culture—if it wishes to be autonomous and original—cannot afford to accept Czech mediation. This is true in spite of the fact, which I readily admit, that Slovaks are still utilizing this mediation to a considerable degree. So far, mankind has found no better way of organizing culture than on a national basis.

If there is any unquestionably positive force in this republic, then it is our cultural life that has helped to forge the sense of nationality among our citizens. We may conclude that permanent bonds among citizens are not created by economic standards of life, but rather are forged by cultural endeavors. It was in the realm of culture that we developed values of which we can all be proud, and which not only bring us closer together but actually tie us into mutual bonds of fate.

But why the growing antagonism?

Try to name a single Czech critic, who in describing a particular area of literary activity during a particular period really tried to encompass the whole breadth of Czechoslovak creativity! Seen from a Slovak perspective, our cultural consciousness is not broad enough to include the entire republic. Slovaks in general feel a sense of injustice. The plans drawn up after the war, which envisioned equalization between the two parts of the country, remain largely on paper and it seems that in some respects the inequalities have become more glaring than ever. In Slovakia the impression is growing that the eastern part of the republic is being neglected at the expense of the western lands. I am not an expert in this field, but it seems to me that it is high time for Czech and Slovak economists and other professionals to get together and publicly clarify these matters, just as similar discussions have proven fruitful in the area of culture.

This is all the more important at this time because the current mood in Bohemia is shifting in the opposite direction. The Czechs have a tendency to blame their problems on others; they grumble about the industrialization of Slovakia . . .

As far as cultural progress is concerned, we have a right to be optimistic. In relation to economics, most of the facts are unavailable, and so we are facing a foggy mass of vague problems. This has unfortunate consequences, and sometimes these problems assume almost frightening proportions.

In addition, there are psychological forces to be taken into account. Large nations always give smaller nations the impression that they are guided by the motto "Foreign blood is cheap." Furthermore, large nations suffer from an almost total inability to empathize with the situation and mentality of a smaller one. It wasn't so long ago that we were asked to merge culturally with a larger entity—remember the Stalinist attitude toward linguistics, zones, hemispheres? By dialectical development, all such centralist attempts are inevitably countered by tendencies toward differentiation, or even tendencies which are totally centrifugal and aim toward regionalism.

We all know from our own experience what national egotism can be like, a nationalism totally turned in on itself. And yet I consider such a situation to be a fairly normal one; it is not necessarily harmful or dangerous, providing of course that it is coupled with a vigorous and steadily expanding democracy. If the two national egotisms —the Czech and the Slovak—were to discover democratic ways of airing each other out, then the two could develop as completely positive forces. This is not to say that an earthly paradise or idyllic harmony would ever be achieved; antagonisms will always remain. But it is certainly possible to make them more rational and to harness the tremendous tensions and energies generated by the two nations toward useful collaboration. The problem of nationality, like any other problem, can never be fully and finally resolved. This question must be approached anew, day by day.

But let us talk about the current situation, about the latest developments. Manifestations which appear on the surface of our national consciousness do not necessarily reveal anything about the reality which has already taken shape underneath. The awareness of the unavoidability of mutual co-existence of the two nations is a case in point. I can say that during the fifty years my generation has witnessed, Slovakia went through a tremendous and extremely important process of rebirth and *rapproachement*. And yet the Slovaks are not satisfied with the centralist conception of economics, especially in the light of their own cultural and economic development; in fact, it seems to me that dissatisfaction is even greater now than was the case before the war. Contemporary centralism seems more ominous than ever, and the sense of impotence in the face of the power apparatus, familiar to the Czechs, is many times more frightening to the Slovaks. And since there is a nation-wide lack of information with regard to the true state of affairs, people tend to accept the simplest explanation: the trouble is caused by the other side. I find such a situation very dangerous, and a similar psychological state has in the past served as fertile soil for the growth of fascist tendencies: I am not responsible, I don't know where my responsibility lies, so let us shift responsibility onto the other fellow. And the Czechs, suffering from their own sense of powerlessness, look for the scapegoat among the Slovaks. To use a historical parallel: slaves find it hard to understand one another. Only free people can communicate, people who are enlightened or at least informed. Our recriminations create a kind of fog which prevents us from orienting ourselves toward real goals and soluble problems. I am not talking about the way Czechs and Slovaks make fun of each other, brag about their respective successes, or engage in petty jostling. What is important is what lies beneath the surface, and the underlying reality is of course connected to economic and political problems. This helps to explain how it was possible that a man rooted neither in Czech nor in Slovak culture could for a long time act as a Slovak leader.* To this day there are regions of Slovakia, such as Kysuce, Orava, or eastern Slovakia, which bear little evidence that they belong to a socialist republic. In the early postwar years the Slovaks were exposed *ad nauseam* to slogans about the help provided to their land by the Czech working class. Nobody would use a slogan nowadays, for there is general mistrust of all statistical statements.

I have often thought of the scene in Sartre's *Roads of Freedom* in which the hero is carrying a sack containing two cats about to be drowned. In their panic, the two animals literally tear each other to pieces. Who is responsible for this terrible anxiety of two creatures tied up in one bag? One cat probably blames the other, without realizing that the main cause of their suffering is the man who plotted their fate. A somewhat similar thought was expressed by Tolstoy, when he compared Napoleon to an infant in a carriage. The infant tugs at the little straps that restrain him, in the belief that he is guiding the carriage.

If our two nations need any one thing, it is more light. Just as young Czech historians once played a tremendous role in defending the Slovak National Uprising against unjustified attacks, so Czech

---

* The reference is to Karol Bacilek, Minister of Security during the Prague trials, later Secretary of the Slovak Communist Party.—*Ed.*

economists could now perform an equally valuable service with regard to the economic problems that lie like a shadow across the relations between the two nations.

In Bohemia, we have a great deal of distrust toward so-called folk-creativity as a vital source of artistic creation, and in my opinion this skepticism is justified. We feel that this activity represents an artificially maintained folklore whose true sources dried up long ago. Apparently, the Slovak experience is different...

All contemporary creativity reflects something of the present and of the past. Take the revolutionary avant-garde. We now regard it as a miracle that Picasso and some other artists began to discover African art as far back as 1910 or even earlier. Today, African art has an honored place in Paris galleries. And precisely in this environment, surrounded by eccentric or commercial French sculpture, the African works give the impression that they are not mere statues but real gods, the gods of a continent. This has taught me an important lesson: It seems to me that the more intensive a national culture becomes, the more intensively it concentrates itself upon expressing the present, the more discoveries it makes of the nation's past as well. It discovers what we might call the nation's fate. It is in the highest manifestations of Czech prose that we feel this grasp of the history and myths of the Czech people. One can hardly imagine a major work of Czech literature which did not in some way make contact with a folk story; folk elements appear in ever new connections with ever new applicability. In Slovakia, there emerged an interesting sculptural phenomenon in the form of the sculptor Vladimir Kompanek, whose wooden pillars are reminiscent of the old Slovak culture in which wood played such a central part. We perceive these pillars as if they were divinities guarding our fate and our culture.

Similarly, I am convinced that there are no values in Czech culture which are entirely historical, entirely relevant only to the past. Through mysterious processes we are discovering, over and over again, the epochs of our national past, just as in examining bygone times we come upon buried layers of our consciousness and find new and often quite unexpected support in times of tragedy. It seems to me that in this respect Czech culture behaves just like any other living organism. For its own needs, as well as the needs of the people, it may find its way toward a romantic epoch, or out of the clear blue sky suddenly turn to folk art. After all the disappoint-

ment and skepticism of the past decades, after the shocks of the two
world wars, artists throughout the world are searching for values
which merit honor and deserve respect. All contemporary culture
searches for gods who can be worshipped, and the same is true of the
citizen, regardless of ideology or religious conviction. It's a matter
of finding universal hieroglyphs that can be read by people in both
hemispheres, east and west.

In this connection, the current wave of world-wide interest in the
plastic arts is highly significant. The same applies to architecture.
We are beginning to talk about the creation of a life environment.
When I was in Finland I was struck to see in small modern churches,
and in city buildings as well, that emphasis is still on a cult of nature,
a cult that long ago found expression in literature. I have the feeling that we are still bound hand and foot by old preconceptions and
discredited ideologies. I will try to express this thought in a somewhat unconventional way: the sculpture that we are beginning to
find here and there in playgrounds or public parks is an expression
of the worship of Relaxa—the goddess of a cult of psychological
relaxation. And if we ease the reins of phantasy a bit, we can pretend
that our cinemas are dark, underground temples devoted to the
celebration of the night cult of the goddess Cybele.

Sculpture and architecture involve public spaces and thus affect
the thinking of tremendous masses of people; they are capable of
arousing the emotions, stimulating the thoughts, and forming the
tastes of millions. In fortunate instances both sculpture and architecture are capable of establishing subtle connections with a
nation's cultural and political history. But how seldom this happens in practice! We talk a great deal about freedom, and yet when
we build a new movie theater or apartment house these structures
seldom express our ambitions, our freedom, the beauty and gen-
erosity of our people. Rather, our cinemas and dwellings too often
convey the idea of pressing utilitarianism and overcrowding. This
is bound to have an unfortunate effect.

In Slovakia, too, the sources of folk tradition have become eroded,
though not to the same extent as in Bohemia. I cannot believe that
Czech architects and sculptors—quite aside from poets and writers
—fail to feel the need for bringing out the latent sense of history
among their fellow citizens, thus creating a more meaningful and
more permanent symbolic language. I would consider it most
peculiar indeed if our sculptors produced works that could only be
interpreted in conjunction with foreign models, a Brancusi or a

Henry Moore. And even in the work of Brancusi there are symbols that have a local dimension; for example, a sign he created to represent eternity is, in one sense, related to a shepherd's staff stuck into the ground. It's hard for me to imagine that a Czech sculptor or architect, working on a monument to his native land, could fail to evoke some specific feature of the country in the memory of his audience, such as the characteristic wayside crucifix standing near a crossroad. In general, folk art like any other art is coated by several layers of ideology. Sometimes, an ancient statue, disfigured by a thick accretion of these layers, no longer affects us esthetically; it awaits the creative act of someone who will come along, remove the surface accretions, and allow us to view the work of art in a new way. Undoubtedly, the miracles of culture are born in the tension between past and present. But just how does this birth take place? Nobody has yet succeeded in explaining to me that miraculous phenomenon of nineteenth century Czech poetry, Karel Hynek Macha; or, to move to the present, the miraculous flowering of Czech cinema.

It seems to me, also, that the concept of "searching" has become rather devalued as a cultural tool. To search means to look everywhere. But I believe that it is more important now to concentrate and to focus on those things which a person honors in the face of all skepticism and despair. In a small but viable country such as ours, a minister of cultural affairs could perform a tremendous service by creating the proper conditions under which sculptors and architects might best express the current epoch. Such a minister would have to be a man with a great personal conception of culture, or at least serve as a zealous guardian of a great conception worked out by others.

In the meantime, unfortunately, our national cultural energies are totally devoted to the creation of pavilions for world fairs. It is high time that we build such a pavilion or cinema (I am not even talking of a Pantheon) for our own domestic needs.

You said earlier that a large nation finds it difficult to identify with the psychology of smaller nations. I have long been puzzled by the Czech blindness toward Slovak problems; after all, the Czechs themselves constitute a small nation that has been oppressed for centuries.

Yes, that's certainly an intriguing question. I hope that historians and psychologists can give us some answers. One historical circumstance which undoubtedly plays a role here is that the Czechs were thrown back for so many years on their own resources and their own existence. This has given rise to a parochial viewpoint, expressed by such slogans as "we Czechs," "Czech money," "Czech culture"— leaving the Slovaks out entirely. It is really surprising how difficult it is to integrate the contributions of others into one's consciousness; this is true even of persons relatively free of prejudice.

I have already pointed out how rare it is for a critic to examine some problem dealing with common questions of our two literatures in any given period. And yet it is quite evident that while the two literatures possess many specific characteristics, there are also numerous viewpoints and difficulties which they share in common. It is probably typical of smaller nations that, in spite of all assurances to the contrary, they are primarily interested in entities larger than themselves, either because they are fascinated by them or because they are afraid of them and look for ways of protecting themselves. I have attended a number of conferences and congresses where small nations enthusiastically expressed mutual interest and respect, but rarely were actual steps taken to study each other's cultural achievements. One would like to believe that this is largely an organizational and technical problem. After all, it takes relatively little effort to stay abreast of the cultural activity of a small country.

Oddly enough, the most significant response to my works came from Czech rather than Slovak readers. I don't know, however, whether the Czech reader regards Slovak literature as part of domestic cultural activity, or whether he is drawn to it by its exotic appeal. I must admit that in the last twenty years more was accomplished by the Czechs toward the encouragement of Slovak literature than ever before. However, I reiterate my doubt whether the Czechs have a concept of Slovak literature as something which is also their own, part of "our literature." I am not sure whether the day will ever come when the great monuments of Slovak culture will be accepted in the consciousness of the Czech mind as part of a shared cultural heritage.

To look at the other side for a moment—we Czechs often hear about the danger of Slovak provincialism . . .

Provincialism is not limited to the small. It's a danger that threatens the culture and literature of the greatest powers just as much as the small ones. Do you want examples? They probably aren't necessary. We know from experience that the surest way of changing literature into a nonentity is to isolate it from the contemporary world developments and force it into a narrow, parochial mold.

E. F. Burian, in defending the Czech avant-garde, once aptly remarked that the so-called traditional currents in Czech culture were actually Agrarian.* Similarly, it could probably be said that the traditional manifestations and currents in Slovakia were characteristic of reactionary political parties. The political right wing, at all times and places, holds on to this kind of traditionalism. It seems that in culture as in other areas of life the best way to defend traditional values is to strike out toward goals brought on by contemporary developments. During the past two decades we learned that a traditionalism out of touch with current reality involves slavish imitation of models and relies on means of expression that have long ago become shabby and exhausted.

Of course it is equally foolish to engage in a continual race, driven by the fear of being left behind. In this respect, the provincialism of the small is often different from the self-conscious and arrogant provincialism of the big. But in the end it comes to the same thing.

How do you stand in regard to the generations?

I would say that my generation has a sense of tremendous disappointment. All the great manifestations of the current epoch as reflected in literature express disappointment over the way socialism has been realized. And nobody has yet had the courage to say: you were right, your warnings were justified. I also believe that it is our duty to finally rehabilitate such figures as Gide, Malraux, Silone; this also applies to Hemingway, although in his case justice has already been done in a quiet and unobtrusive way. That is the human duty of all of us as contemporaries. This doesn't mean that we must agree with every word these writers ever wrote. But I ask you—how many of us are always right?

My generation feels not only disappointed, but cornered. It cannot find the means and the possibilities for realizing its opinions, its dreams. It is a tragic generation, but also a trusting one; it wants at least the right to examine the protocols and documents that have

---

* A Czechoslovak conservative trend before World War II.—*Ed.*

such an important bearing on its past existence. I wonder if I will ever learn the real truth about Trotsky's fate, the real truth about the Spanish Civil War.

My generation is also characterized by the fact that it is supremely aware of the destructive power of the state. The First Republic was a state which crushed us, and now this power has grown into an apocalyptic colossus and nobody knows how it moves, why it crushes, how and why the administrative apparatus is continually getting bigger.

The positive aspects of my generation lie primarily in cultural creativity. It is in this area that attempts at humanizing the impersonal state apparatus were carried out and are being continued. It is through cultural activity that my contemporaries are trying to secure breathing space for Man and to create the means for national and international understanding.

And our sons? Sadly, or bitterly, they turn away from their fathers. I think that they are right to do so. If they had the opportunity to take full part in all areas of our life, their judgment about us would be still more bitter and more radical.

And yet if we were to examine the last few decades more carefully, we would agree that there are certain key points where the generational gap vanishes and there is a meeting of minds. In the meantime, unfortunately, fathers and sons are still trying to communicate with each other only by means of hints and signs.

In your opinion, is all this a typical fate of a generation?

Why typical? I am not at all convinced that each generation is predestined to end up disappointed. In fact I believe that even my generation, in its last phase of creativity, could undergo a rebirth if it could only find an effective way of fighting for socialist democracy. But it is difficult, extremely difficult; there are so few opportunities beyond the peddling and hawking of personal opinion . . . The state apparatus has perfected itself to such an extent that it has grown over the heads of us all.

I should add that the members of my generation, insofar as they are concerned about the future, consider the international position of our country as one of the most basic problems to be resolved. It is the question of what role small nations are to play in the modern world. The young people will have to find an answer. Will they succeed where we have failed? Will they be able to re-establish those qualities which we used to call the virtues of citizenship and which have somehow disappeared? I sometimes have the impression that we are relying more on mechanical techniques in the defense of our country than on the convictions and strengths of its citizens. It used to be different, during the best moments of our history.

Finally, he emphasized one more time what he had repeated so many times in the course of this long, interrupted interview.

Always keep in mind that the Slovaks—those Slovaks worth their salt—will not shirk any struggle in which the Czechs are involved. Everything affects us all; only a fool can fail to see that.

Summer 1967

Eduard Goldstücker

Born 1913 in Podbiel, northern Slovakia. He was in England during World War II. After the war he held diplomatic posts in England and Israel and later taught German literature at Charles University, Prague. In the early 1950s he was arrested in connection with the Slansky trial, charged with treason and sentenced to life imprisonment. Released from jail in the late 1950s, he resumed his academic post at Charles University. As a leading Kafka expert he played an important role in the 1960s in the rehabilitation of Franz Kafka (until then an "unperson") at the Liblice international conference, which represented one of the first major clashes between the liberal and orthodox (mainly East German and Soviet) communist ideologists. After January, 1968 he was elected Chairman of the Czechoslovak Writers' Union and was its spokesman throughout the reform period, being fiercely denounced for his expressed opinions by the East German and Soviet press. After the Soviet invasion he accepted an invitation to teach at the University of Sussex in England.

Eduard Goldstücker

It was more than twenty years ago in the Luxembourg Palace that I first met this small, gentle person with the sad, kindly eyes. He was ready to advise and help me, a young man whose only real qualification for reporting on the Paris Peace Conference was arrogance—the arrogance of interviewing Molotov in the midst of a function which even emperors must perform for themselves. Later Goldstücker told me that this episode helped a great deal to establish rapport between us since it reminded him of his own adventures during another international conference, when he, too, was a youthful journalist without a penny to his name and when he, too, was wandering through a Europe devastated by war. But this he told me only many years later, when I had already become a few experiences richer while he was about to undergo his greatest period of trial. With his kindly smile he calmly assured me that everything would become clear in the end, that truth would prevail. There were many things happening at the time which puzzled him, but this belief in the ultimate triumph of truth was firm as a rock. It is difficult to imagine the terrible ordeals this rock was destined to undergo. Five years elapsed before I looked into those sad eyes again—five years that constitute a lifetime. Or rather a death-time. Now ten more years have passed. And I still have the feeling that he hasn't changed; that he still has that same look which is so boyish and yet, at the same time, so old; that he is still as I remember him from the Luxembourg Palace. Small, delicate, fragile—the type that supposedly can stand a great deal of punishment. He told me that he had never served in the army, neither here nor during the time he spent in exile in England, but that after being released from prison in the mid-1950s he had been called before the military draft board. At that time he was already over forty and God only knows what he had been through. The draft board members looked him over, then with typical military humor, said, "If we let a specimen like this get away, we'll never forgive ourselves." Knowing him as I do, I am sure he must have smiled at this joke himself.

In retrospect, his strange identification with Franz Kafka seems to have been fated from the first. More than anyone else, it was he who won an honored place for Kafka in contemporary Czech literary history. And it cannot be mere coincidence that no Kafka expert in the world has relived Kafka's life and suffered as much as he.

During those two days of the interview, it seemed that Kafka was once again living in Prague—a living presence, continually overwhelmed by real trials and castles, miraculously brought to life by people whose existence was unknown to him, people who lived in a world he yearned for but couldn't reach. We sat and talked, surrounded by the green hills of late summer; we wanted to forget this aspect of the story but were unable to because, after all, this was not merely literary history but our very life. Everything is paradoxical. Even Kafka's fate in this land . . .

It's not only a paradox—it's a very interesting phenomenon. Remember that the beginnings of Kafka's acceptance in our land are intimately bound up with the communist movement. The first Czech translations of Kafka, mainly by Milena Jesenska, appeared in Czech communist publications edited by S. K. Neumann, from 1920 to 1924. Why are you smiling?* If we were to smile like that all the time, the smile would probably remain frozen on our faces, like a tic. Well then, when Kafka died the *Communist Revue* printed a short eulogy that mentioned his hatred for unjust social orders and his sympathy for the oppressed.

---

* In the 1950s, when Kafka's works were officially banned in Czechoslovakia, Neumann, who died in 1945 after a controversial life as a committed anarcho-Communist poet, a reliable "realist," was the party-approved model of the Socialist writer.—*Ed.*

The second phase came in the late 1920s and early 1930s, when he was discovered by the Catholics. In Stara Rise [a Moravian town] a publisher named Florian brought out several short translations of Kafka, the most important of which was *Metamorphosis* translated by Father Vrana, who, incidentally, is still alive. Of course, it is necessary to point out that even though Kafka lived in Prague, very few Czech-speaking people actually knew him. The writer Jan Grmela, who was greatly interested in the German literature of Prague, wrote one of the Kafka obituaries. And yet, in spite of this interest and in spite of the fact that both men had lived in Prague for many years, Grmela mistakenly described Kafka as a physician.

In fact, interest in Kafka's work was so slight that when Pavel Eisner published his translation of *The Castle* in the mid-1930s, only a few copies were sold and so the Nazis were able to destroy the bulk of the edition in 1939. He became a significant European figure only during World War II and the immediate postwar years. In France, however, André Breton had called attention to him somewhat earlier, and French surrealists began to regard Kafka as one of their spiritual ancestors. The decisive turning-point, though, was World War II. The similarity between the Nazi world and the world of Kafka's works is only a superficial reason for this burst of interest. More basic was the growing realization on the part of writers that during a period in which Europe and the entire world were being ground up by the terrible mill of history in an unprecedented way, the significance of events could no longer be grasped by conventional literary means. Kafka demonstrated the tremendous possibilities of expressing the phenomena of modern life in a parabolic manner. Furthermore, all established ideologies had proven disappointing and had lost their credibility and this formed another bridge to Kafka, who was also unable to find a satisfactory solution to his problems in any system of ideas offered by his era.

Finally, there also occurred a certain discontinuity in human consciousness; humanity began to realize that the feverish expansion of technology was creating entirely new conditions for the life of Man. This was a moment in which alienation came to the fore, expressed most intensively by existential philosophy. And there was Kafka, who had expressed all this a generation before. Thus, the second phase of Kafka's penetration into European and world literary consciousness is connected with French existentialism; now it was the existentialists' turn to consider Kafka as a spiritual antecedent. Of course the existentialists made the error of regarding

Kafka as a philosopher, which he wasn't, rather than as the artist that he truly was. Kafka the artist—and that is the third phase—has only recently, in the past few years, begun to be accepted in France; the French are beginning to study exact translations, textual interpretations, artistic development, and so on.

He is great enough and contemporary enough so that there is room in his work for all the great movements of the last few decades —surrealism, existentialism, structuralism.

Things are complicated by the fact that after World War II—in the years of the cold war and the almost total isolation of the socialist part of the world—the official cultural position of the socialist countries was a sharp rejection of Kafka as a decadent antirealist, as a divisive force out of place in a society intent on building socialism. And because he had become so important in the rest of the world, battles began to swirl around him, and he became a weapon in the cold war. Those who used him in this way wished to see only one side of his work, which they interpreted as the depiction of Man in a totalitarian society, as a prophetic vision of the inhuman bureaucracy ruling the socialist world.

In our own country, interest in Kafka continued to be as high as in the rest of the world, even during the German occupation. It was particularly strong among graphic artists. Our graphic art inspired by Kafka, both from the viewpoint of quantity and quality, is probably unequaled in the world. How many times have I suggested an exhibit of Kafka art, an exhibition which would include the names of some of our most gifted artists!

From 1945 to 1948 nothing relating to Kafka was published here except for a collection of essays entitled *Kafka and Prague,* though the Petr publishing house was preparing to publish the complete works. The first volume, *Amerika,* had already been printed, but after February 1948 it had to be destroyed. And thus the stage was set for Kafka to become—as someone well put it—the spiritual Verdun of the time, a role that would doubtless have surprised Kafka no end. Both sides threw enormous forces at each other in this symbolic battle, and the losses on both sides were enormous. From 1948 to 1957 nothing written by or about Kafka was published, except for some indirect assaults in pamphlet form. It was only after the Twentieth Congress that sporadic articles started appearing, and even then there was the feeling that these represented something forbidden or at best barely tolerated. Sartre's statements at the Moscow Peace Congress of 1962, in which he called for the demilitarization of culture, had an important effect on further developments. Kafka was the very case in point he cited. He was simply asking that we should regard Kafka as an important phenomenon of world culture and that we should accept him as such and not approach him with ideological prejudice.

But it was only after the Twelfth Congress of the Czechoslovak Communist Party that conditions were created which permitted fundamental Kafka study and made it possible to carry out Sartre's request for complete "demilitarization" of Kafka. Since the Kafka conference, no belated cold war jingoist can use Kafka as a battering ram. On the other hand, we have made it forever impossible to dismiss Kafka in our country by means of such generalized, vague concepts as decadence. In short, Kafka had become a central point in the battle for breaking the isolation caused by years of Stalinism and the cold war. This history provided yet another example of the fact that every spiritual or intellectual current that is violently halted will—as soon as the violent opposition subsides or is removed —flow right on from where it was last stopped. Actually, this is the whole history of the intellectual and artistic avant-garde in socialist countries in a nutshell. No vital current of the mind can long be suppressed by force.

The suppression had only one result—and it was actually a good one—namely that Kafka penetrated into the consciousness of many people, especially the young, which might not have happened if he hadn't been turned into a symbol, into a kind of forbidden fruit. As soon as any new Kafka book or article appeared, people lined up to buy it. This certainly wouldn't have happened under normal circumstances, since Kafka is hardly a writer for the masses.

What about Kafka's predictions? Well, Kafka was not a prophet and never made any such pretensions. There is no question, however, that in his painstaking search for the truths of life under the conditions of the modern world he created in his work a certain atmosphere and certain images which later generations have identified with their own life-situations, their own powerlessness against the anonymous powers that rule their fate. It is a peculiar atmosphere, in which the greatest bestiality is combined with highest technology, the atmosphere of discrimination against a suppressed and relatively powerless minority.

Then, too, Kafka offers a great challenge with regard to the methodology of artistic creation. Kafka's work forces critics and literary historians, as well as everybody else concerned with modern literature, to take up the question of whether conventional literary means are capable of expressing the complex situation created by the history of our era. Realism, as we have inherited it, has shown its inability to capture the essense of reality by describing its superficial manifestations. This process began toward the end of the nineteenth century and is now fading. It has often been stated that existing methods of artistic expression are incapable of describing the Nazi experience. The German theoretician [Dr. Theodor] Adorno declared that, after Auschwitz, every poem was a crime. Of course, this question goes far beyond Naziism. The great problem is to find possibilities of expressing *any* situation poetically. Kafka created a literary method based on the principle of doubting the authenticity of reality as it is presented us, as it appears on its face value; or rather, he doubts the authenticity of this "face," suspecting that this may only be a façade, and that if we want the truth we must penetrate behind the façade. Thus we come to the two alternatives formulated by [the French Marxist philosopher Roger] Garaudy. To put them simply: Either we throw all modern art overboard, or we broaden the definition of realism until it can include it.

There's no other alternative?

That, of course, depends on the way the matter is formulated. We could just as well pose the problem as follows: The division of art into that which is "realistic" and thus acceptable, versus that which is "unrealistic" and thus unacceptable, has proven to be a sterile approach. To insist on old and clearly obsolete positions is a kind of conservatism which has been surpassed by the times and which has less and less to say. A literature that clings to obsolete methods necessarily degenerates into meaninglessness and provincialism.

It seems to me that the type of literature which is very complex and involves explorations beyond the limits of human and social reality is actually far more readily accepted today than more conventional literature which sticks to realistic expression. Isn't this one of the paradoxes of our time?

To what extent can our writers and artists portray the forms and conditions of contemporary life? The possibilities are greatly limited and perhaps it is time to come to some sort of agreement, to introduce new principles that would enable us to disassociate ourselves completely from the Stalinist legacy. I am thinking first of all of the principle that a writer, or for that matter any citizen in a socialist state, should have the right to disagree with particular developments in day-to-day political life without thereby casting doubt on his basic loyalty to socialism. In other words, the right of public disagreement. Secondly, we must not equate an artistic or journalistic expression of a writer with the pronouncements of his government. In brief, a citizen's opinion must not be taken as an official state act, as was unfortunately too often the case in the days of the so-called personality cult. Only in this way will we be able to create an environment in which our national diversity of opinion can be expressed; it has been repeatedly confirmed that such a diversity exists and that its free expression not only involves no harm to the state but, on the contrary, is an extremely important stimulus to thought and action in our society. Finally, it should be quite evident—though unfortunately this is far from the case— that opinions on political problems should be publicly aired not only by persons officially designated for this purpose, but by all citizens.

I am convinced that our society can safely permit itself a much greater degree of freedom. From the viewpoint of the recent past, we really are in a paradoxical situation; for while we have finally fully rehabilitated Kafka, and while all sorts of experimental works are now appearing without difficulty, works which describe the burning issues of the day or the historical and human experiences of contemporary life encounter serious obstacles. In practical terms, this means that the center of the current struggle has shifted from the problem of realism versus nonrealisim to the problem of the extent to which our artists can become engaged in the struggle for improving the conditions of daily life. This is what's really behind the current discussions about realism. Concepts such as realism and nonrealism simply obscure the real issue—namely, the issue of presenting reality as the writer sees it, a task which calls for a personal analysis of reality which may differ from the official picture. So long as this freedom is denied the artist, he is forced to resort to all sorts of cryptograms and other indirect methods of expression. Thus, a merely formal freedom can actually obscure and propagate a serious lack of real freedom. Or else the artist may scorn the cryptograms and turn his back on society and on the burning realities of his day.

These problems are particularly relevant to literature, because in

contrast to the materials available to graphic artists, the word itself
is a carrier of meaning and thus is placed immediately under the
ideological microscope. I am using "literature" in the broadest
sense to include all those forms of creativity that use language as a
means of expression; in other words, in addition to *belles-lettres* I
include such mass media as film, television, and journalism. At the
Fourth Congress of Writers I talked about the tension which has
organically developed in our society between our political leaders,
who for perfectly legitimate reasons wish to have a didactically
political literature, and our writers, who strive to establish the
broadest possible scope of literary creation. The crux of the struggle
is the question of the writer's freedom to differ from the official
position. In contrast to the past, we now have the freedom of non-
engagement. But this is far from sufficient. We have now reached
the critical point. Once more we find ourselves in a situation somewhat reminiscent of the 1950s; many writers thus have the unhappy
feeling that progress is taking the form of a spiral, that though we
may have reached a slightly higher plateau we are, in a sense, right
back where we started from. In addition, writers are aware that the
relative freedom that has been granted them is a freedom without
guarantees, a freedom that can be revoked at any time; this gives
rise to a kind of melancholy resignation. When I spoke of a critical
point I meant that the writers might well reach the conclusion that
the present method of dealing with intellectual questions has gone
about as far as it can, and that totally new approaches are needed.
There is much talk about the danger that hostile ideologies might
infiltrate our minds, but I think that the question should be examined from this other viewpoint also. It seems to me the time has
come when new and courageous thinking is needed. Our common
intellect has accumulated a tremendous amount of creative energy.
We need political approaches to culture capable of releasing this
energy, approaches with enough insight to realize that this energy
can produce more than a hundred atomic power stations. Today we
can still tap this energy; tomorrow may be too late.

Behind your opinion there is your life-experience . . .

Recently I gave a speech in the West. I was introduced as a man
who had undergone the typical fate of a Central European intellectual. These words puzzled me, and I have thought about them since.
What was the result of my experiences? At best, they have made me

into an honest witness of my time. This time is already quite long, and it is especially long on events, so that actually it could fill much more than the half-century span of a human life.

I was born a year before the outbreak of World War I. My first memory of my father was from his only visit home from the front. He was a minor clerk in a lumber firm; he returned from Albania sick with malaria. He tried to support a family, neglected his health, and died in 1924. The rest of my family perished in the gas chambers of Auschwitz during World War II.

Again and again, a man is amazed at the ever-changing pattern of his fate. A boy from a small, poor, Slovak village, who first saw the national flag flying over the village school as a symbol of mourning for the death of Emperor Franz Joseph . . . my first walk to the school in 1919 . . . the school had a single room in which the pupils of six grades sat together. That's where it all really started. I was one of the village boys, and yet I wasn't. The moment ordinary school hours ended and the compulsory religious instruction period began, I was marked out as different, separated from the others as a Jew. Actually, I was made aware of the religious question even earlier, at the end of the war, when some drunken youngsters decided to plunder our house. The village stood by us, our neighbors tried to protect us, but the family table at which we used to have our dinner bore the marks of a bayonet.

The difference between our family's standard of living and that of the rest of the village was slight, but I believe that we tried to compensate for the sense of insecurity typical of a minority by an illusion of our own superiority. This illusion has, I think, helped Jewish families survive for centuries in environments which could turn hostile at any moment. When I was a first-year gymnasium student my father died, without leaving any pension; my mother became a cook for his former colleagues and earned extra money by doing odd jobs as a seamstress. I traveled to school every day, often getting up at five in the morning to catch the train which took me to Trstena (which at that time had less than 3,000 inhabitants); the train arrived at seven and I used to wait for an hour in front of the gymnasium gate until it opened. If I missed the train it meant a four-mile walk.

The problem of being in a minority is that a person must continuously prove himself. He is never accepted completely, once and for all. Thus he is under constant pressure to exert himself, especially

in the intellectual sphere. In Trstena we had a teacher whose attitude to his Jewish and non-Jewish students was so radically different
that it was obvious even to us children. It is a fact—and let the
chips fall where they may—that it wasn't until I encountered Czech
teachers that I received any recognition of my abilities. When I was
fourteen years old we moved to Kosice, where my sister got a job
as a typist, and there in the fifth year of gymnasium I attracted the
attention of the outstanding Czech professor, Jaroslav Hnatek, who
for me belongs to that small circle of significant persons we remember all our lives. The good professor is still alive. I last met him just
before my arrest in 1951; he was a salesman in a bookshop that
specializes in Soviet literature.

Kosice, with its substantial Jewish population, became for me a
place of intensive intellectual growth. My development was typical
of the Jewish youth of the time. The first stage of this process was
admiration for the kibbutzim in Palestine, people who had left
everything behind in order to cultivate the earth in collective poverty and to prepare a base for the return of Jews to a normal national existence. But as soon as we got a glimpse at the problems of
life in a commune, we opened the window all the way: we began
to read Marx and Lenin; we studied the Russian Revolution, which
created such a fund of confidence throughout the world. Clementis'
magazine, DAV, and [Julius] Fucik's Tvorba [a Communist Party
cultural review] also exerted great influence. Our confidence was
even strengthened by the white areas of these works that had been
censored out. No doubt the censor didn't realize that he was defeating his own purposes. We have learned that lesson well. There are
no longer any white areas in our newspapers . . . The interest in
Zionism soon faded, since the great new ideas of equality and freedom, which applied to mankind as a whole, seemed to solve our own
particular problems as well, and seemed more attractive.

Then, in 1931, I came to Prague. After that I visited Slovakia
only during vacations, to see my mother. I did, however, spend a
prolonged sojourn in Leopoldov. This is a tremendous fortress, on
the Zilina–Kosice railway line, built by the Austrian monarchy for
defense against the Turks in 1667. But the usual thing happened:
by the time the fortress was finally finished the Turks had already
been soundly defeated. Since it had cost so much to build, however,
something had to be done with the fortress, and so around 1700
it was converted into a prison. The first major group of inmates

were the Protestants; they were the standard political prisoners of
the time; eventually they were sent to Italy.

Well then, Prague. For a long time I toyed with the idea of
studying medicine. Then for a while I was attracted to mathematics
and physics. In retrospect, I think that it was mathematics that kept
me from going insane during the 1950s. Following my arrest, I was
kept in custody for a year and a half while my case was being
"investigated." For the whole time of my stay in prison I was totally
isolated and saw no one except for members of the state security
force; I was also kept under intensive interrogation, which in the
first months was conducted day and night. Later, when I realized
that my mind was at stake, I decided that I must do something to fill
those endless hours. As I recall, we were waked at five and were allowed to lie down only after ten in the evening. That's seventeen
hours. If a person had nothing to do but ponder his fate for seventeen hours each day, he'd soon go to pieces. After a while I was given
some reading matter, on the average one book every ten days. I
generally finished the book in one day, the second day I reread, the
third day I would look at a few passages, and that was that. And so
I began to go over in my mind the mathematics I had learned as a
gymnasium student, and because after so many years I only remembered isolated fragments I had to derive all the equations and examples afresh. I had no writing implements, so I had to calculate mentally. I went through the basic axioms of geometry, then trigonom-
etry, but mainly I occupied myself with analytic geometry. It was
intensive mental work, requiring a great deal of concentration.
This kind of concentration is possible only in the isolation of solitary confinement. If I had to derive proofs for the ellipse today I
would find it difficult work. The process involved extremely long
equations that really taxed the mind, and only after lengthy and
complicated operations did I arrive at axioms that I had known as
a student but had since completely forgotten. As soon as I had the
formulas, I began to calculate examples. This helped to carry me
through the long, difficult time. Otherwise, I don't know what
would have happened . . .

*This reminds me of a Soviet woman whom [the Austrian Marxist
philosopher] Ernst Fischer told me about recently. She was an
expert on English literature and a member of an old literary family.
During the Stalinist period she was jailed for many years, and dur-*

ing her confinement she translated Byron's Don Juan, *memorizing her translation as she went. Thanks to the prison commander, she was later able to write down her translation, which she carried through all kinds of prison camps; finally, at the beginning of this decade, she succeeded in having it published. It is said to be a work of genius . . . But let's get back to the unhappy 1930s.*

The economic depression set in and I was discouraged from my planned study by reports of unemployment among mathematicians and physicists. A few months before I was to graduate from gymnasium, an old book dealer in Kosice put the collected works of Heinrich Heine in the window of his shop. I gathered all my savings, bought these seven volumes for fifty crowns, then decided to study German cultural history. I was accepted at the Slovak college of Charles University. After my arrival I found out that I was the only Jew among the eighty students enrolled in the college—the first Jew, in fact, in that college's history. People came to take a look at me as a curiosity. After two years I was expelled for subversive communist activity. In those years I wrote for various Slovak publications; I translated Heine, wrote on Spinoza, Turgenev . . .

My roommate in the college, Jozef Pucik, once brought back some notes and photographs made by leftist students on a sociological field trip into a poverty-stricken region of Slovakia. We worked the material up into an article and sent it under a pseudonym to *Tvorba,* where it was published. This opened up a new field of activity for me. The year 1933 was a crucial one for me in many ways. I was asked to join the communist student movement; I founded an organization at the philosophical faculty; there were international meetings, trips abroad, journalistic work, the intensive activity connected with the popular front, activity in the League for Human Rights—in short, politics became not only a need but a passion.

I keep coming back to the 1930s and thinking about them, and I wonder whether we—the communists of that time—do not deserve a great deal of blame for not seeing, or not wanting to see, the ominous developments that culminated in the Moscow purges of 1936–1938. In my opinion, the Moscow trials had a harmful effect on the international leftist public which went beyond mere divisiveness; they undermined the confidence of many party members and resulted in a serious narrowing of the base which the party had established among the intellectuals. It is a fact, and not just a nice sentiment for children or students to write in their notebooks, that the majority of those of real significance in our culture up till that point proclaimed its allegiance to the left. Everything seemed perfectly clear; the rise of Hitler in Germany was accompanied by the formation of the fascist right wing in our own country, which was the first political entity to use students in open warfare. In the notorious "battle of the insignias"* I was given a good thrashing; my friends searched for me in one Prague hospital after the other. The community of Czechoslovak writers served as a nucleus for the popular front among intellectuals; with the exception of [the conservative author Jaroslav] Durych, this was true of almost every significant writer. When philosophy students called an extraordinary meeting, writers from Nezval to Capek and Salda took part. The Moscow trials shattered this unity and reduced the chances for any combined effort. Gide's book *Return from the USSR* also created a sharp reaction. It was a very complex situation. As I said before, the Russian Revolution endowed us all with a tremendous fund of confidence, deep as the ocean, on which we sailed. This confidence was so deep that we were unwilling to acknowledge any hostile viewpoint, and all criticism was regarded *a priori* as enemy propaganda. That's why we were almost immune to doubt, and whatever small uneasiness managed to appear was zealously suppressed. What, then, was our guilt? In my opinion, our guilt lies in the fact that we let ourselves be changed from thinking and critically evaluating people into faithful, blindly obedient creatures. No criticism, regardless of its source or motive, can be automatically rejected but must be analyzed and evaluated. Doubts must be examined, not suppressed. When the 1930s are discussed, the point is often made that the main task was to support the Soviet Union as a bastion of socialism surrounded by a hostile capitalist world. On the other hand, documents made public after the discrediting of the so-called cult showed that if a significant number of old communists had objected to the unfortunate course Stalinism was taking, the terrible crimes and disasters could have been averted. Another of our errors, I think, was our failure to see the gradual changes that were taking place in the character of the party at

---

* The name given to a series of fierce clashes between Czech radical and right wing university students in the late thirties.—*Ed.*

various levels. Lenin created a certain party prototype which did involve iron discipline and which was based on the principles of democratic centralism, but which also took it for granted that the party's policies and decisions would be determined by the members —that is to say, by the membership community. This is where the basic changes started. The party began to grow increasingly rigid, the membership's influence steadily decreased; decision-making became the concern of a small circle of officials, and members were simply expected to carry out the decisions. In the end, democratic centralism became centralism, pure and simple.

It is also pointed out that many people, especially intellectuals, tend to stress the negative aspects of Soviet development and overlook the fact that, in these same years, the USSR succeeded in assuring the final victory of socialism and in changing a backward agricultural country into an industrial giant. This may be quite true, yet in the light of present experience we must question whether the type of socialism that finally emerged in the Soviet Union really corresponds to the ideals the founders of scientific socialism had in mind, and whether the methods used did not result in diverting socialist development from its proper course. That is the big question posed by such people as Sartre—the question of methods used to achieve a particular goal, when we know that the goal achieved is nothing more than the sum of the means used for its implementation. If you use methods incompatible with your goals you will not get where you want to go.

Furthermore, whenever the great successes of the Soviet Union are stressed, it should also be pointed out that the period between the two wars resulted in considerable degeneration in many aspects of the communist movement outside the Soviet Union. And it is an open question to what extent developments in Russia under Stalin were responsible for the failure of workers and other progressive forces to unite, and for the growing discord among these groups. As is well known, things reached such a state that at the very moment when the proletarian movement in Germany was under mortal danger from Nazism, the communists regarded the social democrats as their main enemies. I know, of course, that it is idle to speculate on what might have happened if things had developed differently; history knows no *ifs*. But we, the survivors, have the duty to exert ourselves to the utmost to learn from the experiences of our own lives.

Another argument: the danger to the republic. I happened to be in parliament when the presidential elections of 1934 were approaching. It was after Hitler had gained power; Masaryk was running once again, and delegate Dvorak coined the slogan: "Not Masaryk, but Lenin." This resulted in the arrest of communist deputies. The point is that even after the victory of Hitler, the party moved along lines that made any cooperation with democratic forces impossible.

To come back to the Moscow trials for a minute. Whatever else one may say about them, the fact is that they brought discord into the whole movement; they acted like a corrosive acid. Besides, no argument can justify a crime. The experience of those events clearly shows that, regardless of the outcome, the truth must be proclaimed —always and under any and all circumstances. Salda put it nicely in his polemic with Capek: Today's truth is tomorrow's reality. To which Capek replied that if truth were ever to prevail it would take one hell of a struggle. One more thing: the exposure of the so-called personality cult was, unfortunately, not carried through to the end. It failed to get to the heart of the matter. The party still has not returned to a genuine inner democracy in the sense we have been talking about.

Looking at things in retrospect, it is obvious that the disputes of the 1930s inflicted considerable damage on the communist movement. I'm not speaking only of the disputes connected with the trials, but also the dispute about surrealism and socialist realism, and similar disagreements. Within the party organization, people simply weren't given any opportunity to discuss such questions, and anybody who expressed doubts about the correctness of the party's approach was promptly branded as an enemy. Still, when it came to general cultural matters there was no break between those who held opinions contrary to those held by the rulers in the Soviet Union since the party did not insist on any particular standpoint as its official cultural position. There was considerable freedom in this area. Nezval used to say: "As far as cultural problems go, I'll use my own head; and I won't stand for any interference." The split came only when, in Teige's eyes, the trials went just too far, and then he publicly condemned them. Before that, he'd always sided with the party and I recall the public discussions in which he defended the Soviet Union against Gide.

The 1930s were, of course, also characterized by the victory of

Naziism in Germany and by a gradually intensifying campaign against Czechoslovakia, based on the claim that this nation had been artificially created to act as a kind of bolshevik base in the very center of the German sphere of interest. We young people were naturally apprehensive over the activity of the Henlein* movement within the country, toward which the government seemed to take a rather permissive attitude, as well as Goebbel's propaganda campaign, but we never doubted that the ground under our feet was solid and permanent. It never occurred to anyone that the Czechoslovak republic might some day vanish into thin air. In the fall of 1937 I met Bohumil Smeral [founder of the Communist Party of Czechoslovakia] in Paris and I told him that in view of the anti-Czechoslovak campaign being waged by the Nazis it might be a good idea to publish a book that would remind people of the parallel case of Austrian propaganda against Serbia in 1914. He smiled at my naïveté and said that it was too late to write books, that war might break out at any moment, and that the very existence of our country was at stake. I was shocked. I mention this episode to illustrate the fact that despite our passionate involvement in politics we thought and acted like average people everywhere—namely, we started from the self-evident assumption that the basic framework of our lives was stable and enduring. The shock was therefore all the greater when the ground suddenly caved in under our feet. I needn't discuss Munich, that story is well known. Another life-experience: precisely those foundations which should be the firmest are generally not quite as reliable as they seem.

On September 1, 1938, I started my first teaching job at the gymnasium. But after Munich many older teachers came to Prague from the border regions; we younger ones had to cede them our jobs; my gymnasium career ended that November. I managed to teach in a private commercial school for a few months, but then came the occupation. As a result of the Protectorate I automatically became a Slovak citizen and when a friend assured me that to remain in Prague meant certain death, I requested the party to give its consent for my emigration. I got out of the Protectorate rather easily, after having obtained a passport as a stateless person. In those

---

* Konrad Henlein, leader of the pro-Nazi, anti-Semitic Sudeten German Party, brought on the crisis between Germany and Czechoslovakia which resulted in the Munich Conference of 1938.—*Ed.*

days everyone helped as much as he could. The Slovak consulate actually offered to get me the famous *Gestaposchein,* or emigration permit. And so I arrived in Slovakia. From Slovakia I went illegally to Poland and, after a month and a half in Poland, managed to get on one of the last transports via Sweden to England. It was then just three weeks before the outbreak of the war. In Poland we were under the aegis of the Czech Refugee Trust Fund, and were helped by several people* who only a few years later found themselves in the same prisons.

In England, communist students enabled me to study at Oxford, where I remained for three years. I wrote my dissertation on early German history in German, because my English wasn't good enough at the time. (In 1951, after my arrest, they confiscated not only my dissertation but the birth certificates of my children as well, because these were written in German.) Then I worked in the education department of the Czechoslovak government-in-exile, in the department of foreign affairs; in 1944 I joined the staff of the Czechoslovak Embassy in Paris; at the end of 1945 I returned home. Shortly thereafter I took part in the Paris Peace Conference. In 1947 I was working at the embassy in London and in 1949 I was named ambassador to Israel. In 1951 I was recalled and transferred to the Swedish Embassy. My departure, however, was continually postponed, and since I had previously requested separation from the diplomatic service in order to work at the university, I was finally told that this request had been granted. In the meantime, though, I had to inform the Swedish Embassy that I was resigning my position because of poor health. I began to teach in the philosophy faculty. I lived in a hotel while my wife and children lived in Jicin. I had no inkling that the clouds then beginning to gather were about to burst over my head, too. On December 12, I was arrested. Once again, a sense of security had been shattered in a single instant.

I suppose we cannot ignore our own political trials . . .

No, we can't. I think about this period a great deal, I turn it over in my mind. It is such a crucial point in our lives that I'd like to be able to understand why all this took place, what purpose it served,

---

* The American Quakers Noel and Herman Field, the Czech Stalinist Vilem Novy, and others.

what its motives were. If I were to express my opinion very briefly, I'd say that the political trials aimed at old-guard communists were fashioned after the model of the French Revolution; the Jacobean dictatorship invented them, just as its authority began to disintegrate, as a means of retaining power. As soon as it began to solve the dispute within its own ranks by means of the guillotine, it signed its own death warrant. I see the transition from terror against the enemies of revolution to terror against the revolutionaries themselves as a manifestation of degeneration. The model of the French Revolution for our own trials can even be traced in certain details. For example, when they wanted to get rid of Danton they put him in a cell with some unimportant English spy and thus were able to implicate Danton as a foreign agent.

Trials of the kind we experienced were designed to serve a number of the government's purposes. Above all, this is what was involved: A party which has in its hands total and indivisible power cannot often come before the citizenry and explain failures simply by saying that it made a mistake. If that were to happen a few times, the citizens might eventually say they'd better let others handle the job. That's why mistakes and failures must be explained as the work of hostile forces. But since there no longer are any such forces within the country powerful enough to bring about major errors or disasters, it is necessary to create the impression that agents of an external enemy are at work. And since there is only one center of power, it is necessary to imply that the agents had penetrated to the very heart of government itself. In a word, public disappointment in government must be removed by that oldest method of primitive cults, namely, the scapegoat. Simple-minded people tend to calm down for a time when they can point their finger at a specific person as the perpetrator of their suffering. And so political trials are organized to serve as lightning rods for the anger of the masses.

Who should be picked as scapegoat? Those who for one reason or another make the government uncomfortable. First in line are those whose opinions regarding the solution of important questions differ from those of the group in power; there is always a chance that, in the event of a showdown, such people might become rivals in the struggle for power. Secondly, those people whose loyalty toward the ruling clique is not absolutely certain. To be specific: From 1951 to 1954, in the course of the trials of long-time communists, our government proceeded in precisely this fashion. As far as the first category of people is concerned, leading Slovak communists were brought to trial, because there actually were genuine differences of opinion as to Slovak politics. With regard to the second category, the thinking was more or less as follows: Stalin and his followers acted on the assumption that toward the end of the 1940s a new world war was imminent. This necessitated certain defensive preparations, including safeguarding the rear. I would like to point out that the process was similar to that used in ancient Rome when, at the conclusion of civil war, the victorious side would publish lists of persons who were placed outside the protection of the law and thus could be safely killed by anyone. These lists were not based on any concrete acts of the proscribed persons, but rather on their belonging to the enemy camp. Similarly, our political trials were not concerned with the acts or character of individual persons, but only with the question of whether these people came under a category which had been declared suspect and which had been chosen to collectively serve as scapegoat. For example, all people who had spent a significant amount of time in the West were summarily declared under suspicion, regardless of what they actually had or had not done. This applied to people who were émigrés in the West or who had fought in Spain, as well as to Jews in important party and state positions.

The decision to place Jews in this category was related to the emergence of the state of Israel. As you know, this state came into being in May 1948 as a result of a U.N. resolution, came under attack by seven Arab countries, and successfully defended its existence —thanks, in large part, to deliveries of Czechoslovak weapons. The first foreign diplomat to arrive in Israel was the Soviet ambassador. Soon, however, something happened which changed the attitude of the Soviet Union toward Israel. When the first Israeli ambassador, Golda Meir, arrived in Moscow, she was so warmly greeted by the Jewish public that Stalin began to suspect Soviet Jews of regarding Israel as their real homeland. After a few months Golda Meir was declared *persona non grata*. She had to be recalled and the first repressive measures against the institutions of Jewish cultural life in the Soviet Union went into effect. The Jewish press was eliminated, literature suppressed, the theater closed, and leading figures of Jewish cultural life were imprisoned or liquidated (for example, the great Jewish actor Michoels). Since the founding of Israel, the loyalty of Jews in leading positions in communist countries has been continually suspect. And in view of the more or less latent anti-Semitism that exists among the broad masses of the people it was quite easy to point to the Jewish leaders as agents of the enemy and as the perpetrators of errors and failures. The first of the trials, that of [Laszlo] Rajk in Hungary in 1949, was typical.

There is still a lot of confusion regarding the question of why the majority of defendants confessed to crimes they had never committed. I don't like to dwell on this subject, but the matter is so important that it deserves an answer.

It is necessary to talk about these things; even those of us who know so much about them must constantly remind ourselves of the truth. Well, then: people in certain selected categories were arrested and turned over to the appropriate agencies, whose purpose it was to use all available means in order to convert these people into criminals, who would then become in the eyes of the public the supposed perpetrators of past failures and debacles. What is called "investigation" is, under such circumstances, nothing but a technique for converting innocent people into criminals.

You ask why the accused persons so often confessed. Some time after my release I read a psychoanalytic study made in the West on this question, and the mystery of these confessions was explained as identification with the aggressor. I believe that this explanation comes close to the heart of the matter. Nobody who has not lived through the experience can fully understand the shattering shock that takes place the instant you learn that the highest authority in your life has turned you over to prosecution as a criminal. Up till that moment you have explicitly trusted this authority in everything, and even in those situations which you couldn't understand —such as the arrest of close friends—you assumed there were good reasons of which you were simply unaware. In the light of this attitude, at the moment of your own arrest you begin to examine yourself, you begin to question whether there isn't really something in your life which has made you guilty—even though, subjectively, you know there is no such thing. A long time before, however, you had already subordinated your reason to the higher reason of the party and you continue to do so even during this period of crushing shock. That is the logical consequence of substituting faith for reason. Your examiners are, of course, well aware of this phenomenon and they use it as a starting-point for a methodically planned procedure.

Incidentally, it's a sad comment on our society of that time that the security offices were the only places where psychology was consistently cultivated. The police and other security organs thus had a virtual monopoly on psychology.

In the course of further proceedings all means are employed to convince the prisoner that he is totally isolated, cast out, completely at the mercy of his examiners. And since his mind is split between the knowledge of his own innocence and his obedience to party authority, his defense is quite undermined.

This is combined with various degrees of physical and psychological violence, continual day–and–night interrogations, lasting for a series of weeks, months, and, if necessary, even years. As a result, the desire for peace, even if it must be paid for with one's life, transcends everything else. At the time of my rehabilitation after four years of imprisonment, one government official told me that if he had known as much about the methods of investigation as he did then, he would have immediately confessed to any crime he had been accused of.

There was no defense, because individuals were arrested not so that they could defend themselves but so that they could be transformed into enemies of the people. One of my examiners unwittingly confirmed this by repeating one phrase over and over again, whenever I declared that some outrageous accusation against me was not the truth. He used to say: "There is only one truth—the one we determine."

But the most important thing of all is this business of identifying with the aggressor. Our aggressors knew this, and counted on the fact that loyalty to the party would play an important role in their victim's behavior, during interrogation, during the trial, even on the gallows. This loyalty kept whispering to me, for example, that high party officials were certain to discover that those things of which I was accused, and to which I might even confess, were actually falsifications. Years later, one of the accused described to me how he had been forced to recount, for weeks on end, his conversations with Rudolph Slansky.* But since he had never conversed

---

* Slansky, General Secretary of the Communist Party of Czechoslovakia, was arrested in 1951 and accused of organizing an antiparty, antistate center. Executed in 1952, he was posthumously—and only partially—rehabilitated in 1963.—*Ed.*

with Slansky he finally decided, after undergoing numerous interrogations, to describe his conversation with Gottwald and pretend that Slansky had been present at this meeting, in the hope that Gottwald might read the confession and recognize the falsity of the whole business. This didn't happen, however; the accused was sentenced to life imprisonment and Slansky was executed for all sorts of trumped up crimes.

As far as the methods of interrogation are concerned, the fantasy of a decent person is insufficient to picture them. And anyone who hasn't encountered this experience can congratulate himself.

Perhaps it should be added that convicted communists, even after the sentence had been passed, had a much harder time of it than other prisoners, whether political or criminal. The charade continued even in prison. The unfortunate scapegoats were jailed together with their political enemies, including Nazis. In contrast to the judges, these prisoners regarded the scapegoats as true communists and thus blamed them for the current regime, as well as for their own fate behind bars. Thus, the scapegoats were always in danger of being lynched.

How was it possible—in the middle of the twentieth century, after all that the previous two centuries have accomplished for the emancipation of intellect—that we could regress so far as to substitute faith for intellect? Especially we Marxists, of all people . . .

First of all, I must remind you of that fund of faith based on the Russian Revolution and confirmed by the Soviet victory over Naziism. Socialism held out the great humanist promise: the hope of eradicating all forms of bondage and caste, as well as national, religious, and racial discrimination. The great longing for realization of such ideal human brotherhood strengthened faith and weakened the control of reason.

Every political movement that wants to achieve victory in its struggle depends on faith. But our experience should teach us that such faith is dangerous. Take the Nazis, for example. The danger is connected with the serious problem of our human propensity for being manipulated. As the trials themselves clearly demonstrate, the people in power proceeded in the clear conviction that the masses are fundamentally naïve, especially as far as the nature of power is concerned. Every generation learns anew that power is a very special category of existence and isn't measurable by the standards of the humanist ethical code. For example, my generation was convinced that the power that came into being in October 1917 was the first the world had ever known that would truly correspond to this humanist-ethical code. We were convinced that this was one more example of the way in which Lenin's revolution represented a milestone in human history. This wish was the father of the thought; faith was stronger than reason.

I am still not ready to give up the idea that socialism could give rise to a power that would act in harmony with the humanist legacy. Perhaps to some people this expression sounds like a cliché. For me, however, it has a very clear meaning. I am convinced that humanity has attained certain standards not only in the area of material existence, in matters such as hygiene and so forth, but also in the ethical sense, and that just as it would be extremely difficult nowadays to re-establish a twelve-hour day or child labor or to abolish smallpox vaccination or to advocate slavery or to use artistic approaches which are already obsolete, so, too, it would be equally difficult to abandon certain established ethical postulates, postulates of truth, freedom . . . As long as socialism fails to secure for its people a greater measure of freedom than any preceding system, its definitive victory cannot be assured. This is what I had in mind when I said at the beginning that our society can stand more freedom than it has been given up to now.

What about the practical aspects?

In the course of a recent symposium on the work of Karel Capek, some things became very clear to me. Every revolution, insofar as it managed to survive its initial stages, eventually went under because of its inability to find a transition from an extraordinary regime to normal government. An extraordinary period is inevitable during the course of a revolution, but it must not be allowed to last for years. That was the basis of the great controversy between Danton and Robespierre, which eventually destroyed both of them. And we stand before the same problems. Legal safeguards must not be permanently suspended.

In prison, while reading about the dialectic processes in nature and Engels' discussion of biological evolution, I hit upon a sentence which illumined a great deal for me: At every moment there is an infinite number of possible ways by which evolutionary development may proceed, but as soon as one of these possibilities becomes actualized all the others wither away. The same holds true of revolutions.

Recently, we have been greatly troubled by the question of Czech-German coexistence. We are painfully aware of the fact that this problem is becoming ever more pressing and requires a positive solution.

I want to emphasize at the outset that the relationship between Czechs and Germans is quite different from that existing between Slovaks and Germans. Throughout their history, the Czechs have had to cope with Germans, whereas for the Slovaks it was the Hungarians who posed a constant threat and Germans were regarded simply as foreigners.

As to the Czech-German problem, contemporary historians on both sides of the border now agree that during the nineteenth century the relationship was confused from both sides by the introduction of concepts from the arsenal of militant nationalism. Thus, the entire history of Czech-German relations was studied in the light of nineteenth-century chauvinism. Today it is useless to argue whether the Germans did or did not bring Western culture to our land, because it is now accepted as an objective historical fact that what we know as Western culture derives partly from Italy, partly from various nations bordering the Atlantic. Our German neighbors acted as an intermediary for this cultural flow, just as Germany in its turn was influenced by its neighbors to the south and to the west. This whole matter only took on a somber aspect when German nationalists attempted to use these facts to justify dominating Czech territories. In the same way, it is useless to debate whether Charles University, founded in Prague in 1348, was actually Czech or German. The fact of the matter is that the university was neither Czech nor German but Latin and was founded in the Czech capital to serve the needs of the large realm of which Charles was emperor.

Of course, there are many such questions. It is important to remember that the intellectual currents which came to us through German mediation were quickly integrated into our own culture and developed in their own specific way. Conversely, there were times when the Czech lands underwent a more intensive and rapid intellectual development than was the case elsewhere, and radiated significant influence abroad. The Hussite period is one example. It must also be pointed out that Germany always presented two different faces to the Czechs. One was the face of its culture, which was generally a positive influence—just consider how great an influence Goethe and Herder had on the Czech renaissance. The other face was that of political power, which often represented the desire to dominate. It is one of the unfortunate aspects of German historical development that German culture and German politics were commonly separated by a far wider gulf than was normally to be found in other countries. German culture and German power rarely, if ever, fused, and we see the tragic consequences of this to this day.

This mutual fondling and feuding could be discussed at great length. In the second half of the nineteenth century there arose a tendency—largely under Masaryk's initiative—to liberate the national culture from the prevailing strong German influence and to look toward broader horizons, to the English and, even more, to the French. This attitude was eminently sensible, but the fact remains that geographic proximity is the most enduring and determining factor when one is dealing with any relationship; geography is a crucial factor now, and it will continue to be so in the foreseeable future. Whoever is aware of this will not be surprised to learn that the overwhelming majority of Czech boys and girls entering gymnasium choose German as the language that opens up the world for them. As long as there is no new major migration of peoples—and such migrations are, I believe, no longer fashionable—we shall be surrounded by a region in which the major language is German, a language which today is spoken by over 80 million people in four countries.

Lately there has been a great deal of interest in Czech culture among the Germans. This is a heartening success, yet there is more to it than that, I believe.

This relates to the problem of the so-called universality of Czech culture, a problem that has been much discussed lately and, in my opinion, in a quite misleading manner. Whatever we do, only those works which have something of world importance to say will leave any mark on the world. Among Masaryk's fragments related to his book *The Czech Question* there are some paragraphs in which he says, in essence: We are rising from the dead, and the world expects us to say the saving word. If we don't give this word to the world, it will turn away from us and we will become the footstool of other nations. What is this saving word? It is, I think, the ability to tell the people of the world, in a contemporary manner, what we have learned from our extremely rich store of unique experience, and to explain how we visualize human fate on the basis of these experiences. There were instances in the past when we succeeded in accomplishing this; just think of Comenius. There are also instances closer to our own time. For example, when the Prague poet Rudolf Fuchs translated a selection of poems by [Petr] Bezruc into German and published them in the midst of World War I, they were greeted by many people in Germany as a revelation, because there was nothing in German poetry that corresponded to this powerful note of protest against national and social oppression. [Otakar] Brezina's *The Hands* created a similar reaction.

The demand of universality is important from still another point of view. We have reached a historic stage in which countries having an advanced industrial civilization have, in effect, transcended the national principle as the main organizational principle of human society. But there is still no new set of principles to replace the old. We are still using the old terminology, such as national economy, national defense, national culture, and yet, strictly speaking, it no longer makes sense in the modern world to talk of such things as national defense. And this is even more true in the realm of culture. To which national culture would you assign modern painting, for example? The same thing applies to verbal art. Literature is becoming more and more universal. Its fundamental problems are the same in America as they are, let us say, in Italy or here . . .

But to return to the Czech-German relationship. In certain respects, developments in this area were already anticipated long ago. German literature written by authors living in Prague is a case in point. Into which category would you place such works? German, Austrian, Czech, Jewish? It therefore follows that nowadays only those works have real significance which are part of the universal world-wide cultural activity. It is simply a matter of the extent to which we can communicate our specific contributions toward solving the existential problems of contemporary man. And it seems that, once again, Germany is acting as a kind of transfer station in the journey Czech and Slovak cultural work must make to reach the rest of the world. It is Germany's natural historical mission, which unfortunately has been too often cruelly neglected, to act as a cultural mediator between the eastern half of Europe and the West.

Do you really think that the nationalist principle has been transcended?

Look at it this way. The source of all light is universal, although the world is interested in our particular part of the spectrum, in our specific color.

On the one hand, the hard facts of modern existence have transcended nationalism, and yet on the other hand, as I tried to point out, no new principle has yet been found. Furthermore, and this may be an answer to your objection, this process has obviously not been equally rapid in every part of the world. That's why I talked only about advanced industrial societies. And although we ourselves are an advanced industrial country, we haven't really had an opportunity to live the nationalist phase to the full before this phase became obsolete. This contradiction has created a great deal of discord and tension. It goes without saying that before nationalism can be transcended it must first be fully realized, and this is an inevitable stage which cannot be skipped.

Teaching at the university as you do, you have an excellent view of our young people. How do they seem to you? What do you see in store for them?

Here every judgment is bound to be extremely subjective. I know that such generalizations are in vogue, but we still have insufficient sociological data on the basis of which we might form a correct picture of the young generation. All sorts of differing opinions were expressed with regard to student demonstrations, for example, and the degree to which teachers were responsible for student behavior. As a result, a commission of experts from all departments of the university was formed some time ago and given the task of conducting a survey of factors involved in the formation of young people's attitudes. It is my own subjective opinion that the most characteristic trait of the young intellectuals is the conviction that the ideologies that inspired their fathers have proven to be totally bankrupt. That's why they mistrust all ideologies. And because they grew up without any direct involvement in political life, they don't know how to think in political categories, to evaluate reality, and to plan alternatives. And because on the whole they are disappointed with our performance, they take great delight in whatever was most vilified by us, such as the pre-Munich type of democracy.

Every generation gets its character from an active minority. In today's student generation, this active minority has shown serious concern about important public questions. Even though these people oppose many present policies, I personally, if I myself were in a policy-making position, would try very hard to reach them.

As far as I know the young, I believe they suffer from the sense that the individual has no effect on public policy, neither here nor in the rest of the world. That personal decisions have no significance, and thus are unnecessary. This sort of attitude leads to escapism, or rather to the search for substitutes, which often take the form of romantic reactions. It would make an interesting study to examine the purely romantic elements in contemporary phenomena such as the passionate interest in jazz.

I also think that our young people are rather poorly informed, especially in comparison with their colleagues in the West. I am not thinking primarily of current political events in the world, but of intellectual currents. This is the unfortunate result of our prolonged isolation, especially during the years of the cold war. Young people in the West, particularly students, know a great deal and are effective debaters; they know how to refer to various thinkers and to cite their statements. On the other hand, I am not quite sure that their own views may not get lost in this plethora of information.

The incomplete education of our young people is also the result of a certain lack in our middle-level schooling, which provides the young with a great deal of knowledge but does not structure this knowledge into any meaningful over-all picture of the world and of life. Young people's knowledge is fragmentary, atomized; there is no connection between one thing and another. Our schools have not yet found a method of enabling a student to form a unified picture of anything—not even of our own national history, for example. As for world history, let us never even speak about it; there the situation is disastrous. It seems to me that the ever-expanding school curriculum should be limited to a certain basic minimum, but in such a way that the student would not leave with his head full of separate mental boxes, the content of which is not held down by any general framework and thus quickly evaporates.

With respect to the attitude of students to their studies, I think they are far more serious and diligent than we were. To some extent, I think this is due to the fact that, in comparison to my student years, higher education has become more and more like middle-level education; university students are expected to do homework assignments, and so on. But above all, the cream of the young generation—those people who give the generation its particular stamp—are passionately devoted to the truth and to justice. I suppose this is true of all young people, except that we found our truth in the ideology of socialism while things don't seem quite so simple today. And this creates anxiety and a sense of dissatisfaction. Young intellectuals in the West are more active, more engaged, because they have a greater scope for action, both organizationally and otherwise.

What is the relation of the young to literature, to art?

Above all, they are skeptical toward everything which they are told is capable of changing the world. This is because they've reached the conclusion that the world is, in essence, made up of two powers, neither of which cares very much about us and neither of which is susceptible to our influence. That's why the young tend to regard literature as a source of spiritual comfort rather than an instrument for changing the world.

If you were to sum up your own life-experience...

As I said before, a person is often amazed at the tricks life plays. Although I have now spent eleven continuous years at the university, I still get the old feeling of insecurity when I enter the building. Thirty-six years ago I came here as a student, now I am here as a teacher. In retrospect it seems like a very short time, and I suppose it really isn't so very long ago at that. Yet think of what a wealth of experience those years contained, of all we went through! I look at my students and I ask myself what they will probably be doing twenty or twenty-five years from now, when their own growing children will hold them responsible for the state of the world. And I ask myself what I as a teacher can do to make them aware of this responsibility even now and to prepare them for it. The only answer, the only experience I am sure of is that they must be told the truth. Always and everywhere. And it is our duty to interpret human culture for them, both past and present, to make them familiar with the humanist legacy of mankind—to make them feel that they are one link in the chain of generations. For a person who is conscious of his traditions cannot fall into barbarism—or at least is less likely to. Barbarism and bestiality, including all of its modern varieties, arise whenever people shrug off the demands of traditions created by the struggle, blood, and sweat of so many generations. If you wish, we could call it by the Latin word in its original meaning: *re-ligio*. Which means indebtedness to the past, to ancestors, and thus responsibility toward the future.

Summer 1967

Lumír Čivrný

Born 1915. His first book of poetry was published in 1938. After the war he held several party and higher governmental posts in the cultural field. Since the 1950s he has translated poetry, mainly by Latin Americans, and took part in various cultural and literary undertakings in South America. This experience led to his involvement with the general problems of cultural policy and he wrote many articles and also made a speech at the Fourth Writers' Congress on this subject. He headed the Czechoslovak Writers' Union's foreign relations committee.

Lumír Čivrný

It started a long time ago, so long ago that it seems like the very dawn of Czech history, though there are many people alive today for whom it still constitutes the only living present. It was during the early years of the German occupation. Kamil Bednar published an essay entitled A Word to the Young. *It provoked a lively controversy, and one of those who took part in the ensuing discussion was the young poet Lumir Civrny, whom we were just beginning to read.*

Bednar published my own response, too. But even before that, I had written an article entitled *Our Youth and Provisional Morality*. In it, I examined the question of the basic life-attitudes of a generation that was fated to encounter all experience in a provisional, tentative way. Let me offer a sociological reminder: In 1934, when I graduated from the gymnasium, there were more than 30,000 graduates with secondary-school diplomas or college degrees who were unemployed. And the closer the moment of German occupation approached—naturally, we couldn't predict this in advance, but it was obvious that the Nazi threat was becoming ever more menacing—the more every aspect of life came under a heavy cloud. It was a question of human existence, of the existence of humanity. If my article and Bednar's piece had been examined side by side, no basic difference in our view of the world would have emerged. The difference lay not in diagnosis but in therapy. Bednar tended to look to poetry for help while I relied more on politics. But this, while characteristic of us as individuals, had little to do with the problem we faced. It might be said that each of us had our own illusions, even though both of us opposed provisional morality in principle. This problem had, of course, occupied people for a long time and had stamped a characteristic attitude upon intellectual life for decades, but we responded to the problem in a different way from the previous generation. Milan Kundera had clarified this difference by analyzing the case of Vitezslav Nezval. Kundera noted that while some people blamed Nezval for an inability to see reality or even for succumbing to political pressure, Nezval was actually a believer in a naïve kind of Utopianism similar to that of Apollinaire (the two poets had other things in common, as well). Nezval believed that technical and social revolutions would radically alter all of reality—for the better, of course. This conception was shared by many great artists of the period between the world wars; among those familiar to me as a translator I can name Lorca, Alberti, Neruda. All of them also share a kind of sensual bond to the present moment, an ability to immerse themselves entirely in life.

Our sense of the provisional, undefined aspect of our lives was connected with anticipation of revolution. We felt the need for revolutionary change very strongly, though we didn't believe in Utopias. As a matter of fact, our most basic assumptions involved contradiction. During the early years after World War I, the question "where is your allegiance?" was largely rhetorical; the allegiance of almost all intellectuals was with the cause of socialism. The outbreak of the Spanish Civil War in 1936 marked the time when this sentiment reached its climax in the spontaneous worldwide movement of the cultural elite, which united itself not only in the negative sense of opposing fascism but also positively, for socialism. But the tide was soon to turn; the Moscow trials and other manifestations of the "cult" bred disillusionment. Gide was only one of many bitterly disappointed intellectuals. André Malraux still called his Spanish novel *Man's Hope,* but it already hints at all the negative forces that were to explode so destructively a number of years later.

Of course, we needed some perspective; we were all very young, in our early twenties. In poetry, the great hope of our generation

was Jiri Orten.* For me, he had become a symbol of the profound-
est anxiety as well as rock-bottom faith. I do not a wish to pin a
particular political label on Orten, or to claim him for the communist movement of the time. I simply consider him a representative
of a high level of humanism. As far as specific political orientation
is concerned, some of us, myself included, believed that our presence in the communist movement would give us a better opportunity to fight for its human face than would our withdrawal. Today,
this might be regarded as wishful thinking, but in those years when
we stood at the crossroads between life and carnage, freedom and
slavery, in those years between 1936 and 1938 it represented a certain hope; not Utopian hope, but the kind of hope which springs
from resistance and from a sense of self-preservation.

Even Camus had this hope. His work twice reached this point;
after the first tentative and interrupted attempts, he resumed where
he had left off twenty years earlier, in common with the theater of
the absurd. Because of this parallel development, the theater of the
absurd and Camus are often linked, but in my view the connection
is based only on a coincidence in time. Camus was the incarnation
of the generational attitude I have been describing. He was a man
who struggled for a revolutionary transcendence of the provisional,
who went beyond the resistance movement, beyond disillusion, beyond failure even; yet in spite of all he kept his hope alive, that
most difficult of hopes which leans on no support except a fragile
idea, a dream.

The contributions of this branch of French literature, represented by writers such as Malraux, Camus, and Sartre, were unique.
But in the poetry of my generation a somewhat similar note was
being struck, that combination of anxiety and hope, that return to
direct contact with basic values. The *Poetry Almanac* of the spring
of 1940 is characteristic. Unfortunately, this promise never materialized. Subsequent political developments . . . In those first years
after 1945 there was so much élan. But this period also contained
something else, a destructive spirit which obscured a lot that was
potentially useful. Those three great French names were thrown
into a bag, that bag which always seems to be at hand for getting rid

---

* Run over by a German ambulance in Prague during the war, Orten was left
to die because he was of Jewish origin. His poems—which show him to be a
precursor of existentialism—were proscribed reading during the 1950s.—*Ed.*

of uncomfortable ideas. And those narrow-minded individuals who always seem to be on hand to help tie the bag up never seem to feel the need for justifying their right to destroy. After all, such people are not interested in clarification, but in obscuring the truth. The bag is always ready for contemporaries. Twenty years ago it was Malraux, Silone, Hemingway, Teige, and Babel. Now there are others...

Once somebody is safely dead, he can be legitimized. In their own time, people like Stendhal, like Macha, refused to pretend that they didn't know. They didn't change the outer world much, of course, but at least they succeeded in one thing: in being hated. The more they displayed their moral idealism, the more they demonstrated their capacity for self-sacrifice, the more hated they became. And that can be taken as a sign of nobility.

Finally, one day, I met Civrny face to face. It was shortly after the liberation, when the Kultprop office on Prikopy served as a gathering place for so many wise, fine, intelligent people—one of whom was Civrny—and when I was still a dogmatic undereducated neophyte. With time we became friends. For the sake of coming to terms with the past, let us begin our interview with that era, though it won't be easy...

We are dealing with the problem of discontinuity and duration in life and in the material world. I often wonder about the way life seems to break apart into pieces which have no connection. One fragment, let us say, is the pre-Munich era. Another ends in May, 1945. And then we might generalize a bit and finish the next one in 1956. And then still another. The transitions between these fragments of life are far more abrupt than was the case in comparable experience of earlier generations. At least, so it seems to us; in any case, the changes we have witnessed are explosive enough to produce heart attacks. But there is another aspect, a more substantial one. Some people go through this process unaltered while others develop ever new faces. If you think back to people you know, you suddenly realize that you are seeing a particular person in his fourth, fifth, or even sixth incarnation. And then there are people who have a whole repertory of likenesses which they assume and discard like actors training themselves to remember past roles. Of course, a person has a right to change. But there is a question of credibility . . .

The occupation—that's a difficult subject to talk about. And the

generations? Character is not determined by birth certificate, although it is certainly significant whether a person had to postpone
certain aspects of life at the age of twenty or at forty.

Or death . . . Life always wants to be lived and a person wants to
"realize himself" even under the most unfavorable conditions. But
it was impossible to accept the occupation without paying a price.
I'm not talking about people who collaborated with the Germans
out of political conviction; those cases were quite rare. No, the people I have in mind are those who made their peace with the occupation, and they are far worse off. How shall I put it—"fellow-citizens
of evil"? It is said that in certain respects the occupation was a period
that made morality easy, since everything was either black or white.
All that was needed was to repudiate fascism. But this was achieved
even by outright fascists themselves, who negated the German
variety while supporting the Czech. Naturally, true antifascism was
identical with humanism, as Novomesky reminded us several years
ago. But how did this actually work? "I opposed German fascism,
ergo I was a humanist"—or "I was a humanist, *ergo* I couldn't help
but oppose German fascism"? As we have learned, there could be an
enormous difference between these two positions. And there still is.

Those various faces on a single faceless face! And that continuous,
unending confrontation with the past, with the period when "it was
so easy to choose." Actually, fronts are always easy to distinguish.
Evil does not parade around in any special uniform, even though
there are uniforms that are the incarnation of evil.

During the occupation, people who believed in man formed an
image of postwar society completely free of any kind of repression
or censorship. There was widespread belief that the new society
would put no restrictions in the way of human creativity and human
intelligence.

But as I said before, in real life evil is not limited to a particular
uniform. Truth and freedom are not replaced by lies and slavery
overnight. Rather, evil works slowly and subtly to penetrate regions
held by positive values. When you say "history," you are talking
about a constant process of camouflage and of stripping the camouflage off. When I first became aware of the conflicts between fathers
and sons, from the so-called position of the son, I believed that in
the course of my generation history would resolve this conflict.
Today I think otherwise. There are generations whose dreams,
fears, and hopes, as well as bravest deeds, are changed from a true

flame into false fire, a kind of artificial fireworks that serves to conceal other forces.

This is not intended as an alibi; I am merely wondering whether this feeling of fragmentation may not be an illusion, while life itself goes on, one and the same. When you think about it, what is really so new about our era? Stendhal—I am sure you are familiar with his diaries. Or with his portrait of Napoleon in the year 1837? Napoleon's defense against charges of treason? 1794? Look here...

He showed me the book, and we skimmed through it. True enough, there's little new under the sun. Some people still think that history began with this great event or that one ... How right that important party comrade was who came up to me once and asked in an irritated, reproachful, almost threatening tone: "What's all this history? Why are you people always carrying on about history, anyway?"
But let's see if we can still remember 1945.

You reminded me that we first met in the Kultprop office. To mention an irrelevant fact—I became a member of Kultprop in 1945 and left in 1947, both events having taken place without my initiative. But here is something more to the point: great evils may have their origins in periods of apparent prosperity and enthusiasm, and people of good will may unwittingly help to turn the course of historic events into unfortunate channels. The communists emerged from the occupation with great moral credit. Just remember the slogan—"the Party of the Martyrs." That was the time when Aragon wrote: "The party has given me back the French tri-color." From this sort of sentiment it was only a small step to the religious belief: "The party is always right."

To speak about myself—I have never written such political verse; in fact, in those days I wrote very little of anything. But I will always reproach myself for not having protested sufficiently against the writings of others. For example, when a certain article came out shamefully defaming Seifert, I did not remove my name from the editorial board of the magazine that published the attack. It would have been all the more easy to do so since we functioned as a board in name only; nobody ever called us to meetings or solicited our opinions; everything was done behind our backs. No, I shouldn't have said that. When evils are perpetrated in your name, you cannot justify yourself by claiming that you weren't consulted. Of course, there are eras when nobody can find out what viewpoint you actually expressed; there are even eras when not even a dead man can be sure that he died with a final, irrevocable, unchangeable point of view. And then, too, there are eras that produce a certain paralysis, when a man sees the evil which is perpetrated, but the very shamelessness with which it is disguised takes his breath away and prevents him from speaking or even from moving. This happens during historic phases that are still in a formative, unclear stage, when developments still have no name, or rather when they appear under the false, borrowed names of true values. When things at last appear under their true names, when the Mephistophelean fog evaporates, the battle becomes much easier. By that time, however, warnings and courageous reportage are somewhat belated and rather academic.

Again, I do not wish to offer alibis for anyone, least of all for myself. I only wanted to stress how difficult it was to have a face; everything must be paid for. I wanted to give myself further evidence that life does not consist in bits and pieces, but that it is always one and the same, and that paradise will always remain out of reach. Perhaps I haven't got hold of the right idea, but this idea seems to have a good hold on me. This notion about the limitations of life possesses me now just as it did in 1935, perhaps even more deeply now. Now that I've gotten rid of many former concepts, there is so much more room inside of me to be possessed.

I don't mean to imply that I am full of some kind of gloomy winter fog. I rejoice at the fact that creation goes on in spite of all sorts of obstacles, that we are producing wonderful works, works which offer us glimpses from within. For example, Tatarka's *The Demon of Consent*. That's one truly contemporary work behind which can be seen a real human face, not the cosmetically smooth mask of the uninvolved and disengaged. And yet this period . . .

You are probably thinking of the generational aspect.

I intended to say that this is one book which my generation was destined to write, spanning as it does five decades of this century starting with World War I. Our period has its unmistakable characteristics and one of the most striking of these is the predominant role politics plays in our lives. Many people, including myself, were, so to speak, "overwhelmed" by politics, in the same sense as one can be overwhelmed by love. Many of us still haven't been cured of

this disease, despite the fact that we have undergone drastic homeo-
pathic therapy. Politics constitutes our fate, even though we have
never become politicians. This phenomenon, too, has its roots in
the specific conditions of Czech history.

But let us return to literature. There, too, we find the basic concepts so typical of our time; for example, the idea that modern art
—the avant-garde—sprouts out of the ruins of abortive revolutions.
Doesn't this view imply that modern art is an illegitimate, unwel-
come child, which would never have seen the light of day if certain
revolutions had succeeded? If they *had* succeeded . . . It is one of the
ironic jokes of history, as we have learned from the fates of this century's avant-gardes, that after a revolution things turn out to be
different than expected. But perhaps this is too impatient an evaluation. In any case, how long does it take before one can judge
whether a particular revolution has succeeded? After all, revolutionary ideas affect artistic creation much earlier than they affect
political realities. To admit that a particular kind of art can only
be produced as a result of political frustration is to imply that artistic creation is somehow inferior to other manifestations of the
human spirit, such as politics. What I find most exciting about the
"modern" art of these last hundred years is precisely this tension
and polarity, this longing to change the world and at the same time
the desire to mine the depths of human subjectivity. Isn't this basically the same situation in which modern science finds itself? After
the social cataclysms we have experienced, the exploration of subjectivity seems to me to constitute a clear social duty.

Gramsci had some interesting things to say on this subject from
the point of view of revolutionary politics. He was intellectually
free, in his jail cell.

In your opinion, was there a real possibility of avoiding . . .

Of avoiding certain ways of distorting and oversimplifying life?
I suppose there was. But then some other "error" would have become manifest, and the attempt to avoid one error would have produced other negative consequences. Of course, one can explain anything this way. In any case, this kind of hindsight is useless: "It
could have been like this, if only it hadn't been like that."

Since we are reminiscing, permit met to recall one experience
from 1945. That May, I was launching the first public meeting of
cultural workers to be held since the occupation. Speaking for my-

self, as well as for a whole generation of people who had been silenced and isolated from the world, I listed the great names of artists from all over the world as proof that our will and our inner freedom have not been conquered during the period of enforced silence, as evidence that we have always regarded our land as an integral part of the large and indivisible world of human culture. But when, that very same evening, I began to encounter the mounting pressures of a new isolation, when I saw the Slavic world interpeted as being in opposition to other cultures, it was a terribly painful shock. Precisely because the Slavic nations emerged from the war with much moral credit, it seemed unthinkable to me that the supreme manifestation of human cultural and political solidarity—namely, the free flow of ideas—would once again be dammed up. I realized of course that certain political maneuvers were involved, too. For example, the political opponents of the Slavic East, of communism, wanted to exclude us from this planet; they wanted to banish from the human family anyone who thought differently from themselves. But still . . . This new isolationism hurt me for a long time; I kept blaming myself for my lack of courage in failing to speak out against it. Perhaps I didn't understand historical determinism? Hardly.

Rather, I believe that I simply failed to grasp how difficult it is for a man to come to terms with historical determinism while pursuing an active political goal; this applies to men in all parts of the world. In short, open-mindedness was difficult, and continues to be so.

At one time, it was fashionable to believe that today's youth had a harder life than we, their fathers, had to face. But if we return to that great word "hope"—since Malraux's novel, this word has become especially significant for me—I fail to see why it is supposed to be easier for us older people to *maintain* hope than it is for our sons to *conceive* hope. A cynic may feel relieved when he contemplates the disillusionment awaiting those sons of ours, but for those who dislike cynicism the problem remains, and it is the same problem today as it was yesterday or thirty years ago. It is a choice between indifference and feeling, between anesthesia and pain. But hope is born from pain. And this hope, again, is always one and the same: the hope that fate can be altered through human actions. Thus, the choice is always between true human life and vegetative existence. Vegetative existence can take place only when time is destroyed; only a person who lives fully in the present is capable of feeling the sense of time. When a life is frozen at a particular point, even weeping ceases to be real. If the last time I was hit by a policeman's club was thirty years ago, then my sense of pain is dead. I am alive only so long as I feel today's blows on today's backs, even if it is someone else's back.

Once again, the generations.

Yes, perhaps. I feel the generational bond as a commitment, a debt. Aphoristically speaking, I would say that our own generation has the duty to remain productive and young for as long as possible. As far as literature is concerned, it seems to me that a great deal of good work was spoiled by the "Messianic complex," and I say this without meaning to disparage any particular writer. Cultural politics are not the same thing as artistic creativity, and in our creative work of the last few decades there was far too much cultural politics. Admittedly, this didn't happen entirely of our own free will. But nothing exists as long as it is only a good intention; waiting for the right opportunity is deadly. A wait-and-see attitude may be appropriate for a military commander or a physician, but for most people the right moment to act is this very moment, now; no other moment will be any better. There are, of course, such mitigating circumstances as fatigue or suffering, but even these do not excuse inaction. Some victims of the "cult" belonged to the type of person who would willingly serve any cult at all, who enthusiastically adapt themselves to the production of new victims. They hoped to gain "face," but settled for secure jobs instead. This applies to many ambitious members of the new generation, too.

We have denounced the follies of the generations and the ills of our day. What else is left?

Only troubles. These never get smaller, they only change. If only we had learned that lesson in time!

At one time, when a Czech wanted to read something about himself, he had to reach either into his own past or into the literature of another nation. We talked so much about our own era that we completely lost sight of it. And then the authors from the distant past or distant lands spoke to us and invited us to come forward, and in this way we encountered ourselves. Was this preordained? Hardly, for even contemporary authors did not have us specifically in mind.

Rather, everything depended on our ability to open ourselves up to the world of ideas. Even in the realm of love there are certain key moments when a person stops caring about outward appearances and abandons himself completely; and it is at such moments that he receives the most in return. That's why those people who try to prescribe mental boundaries and permissible limits for ideas are always so ridiculous. As if they could know in advance where the next source of inspiration would appear!

Years ago, I became fascinated by Vercors' *The Guiding Star* (*Le Périple*). A tiny story, etched in acid, the author portrays a portrait of a home-grown French fascist with a hypertrophied ego, to whom nothing is too evil if it helps him impose his will on others. This man is pitted against his human opposite, and the lives of the protagonists are followed from childhood through the German occupation and finally the Algerian war. For me, the most interesting facet of the book is the way the fascist responds to the resistance movement; he is attracted to certain aspects of the antifascist cause; under different circumstances he might have adapted himself differently, but under the specific circumstances of that specific time he goes his own way . . . I still enjoy reading the book, but at one time the book was more than a matter of mere enjoyment—it was absolutely essential to me; I would have perished without it just as I would have perished without Arthur Miller's *The Crucible,* or without Stendhal, the author of a generation which scattered so many lost hopes all over Europe yet never lost not just its hopes but Hope. These books contain no easy solace, they are sad; but I keep on finding something in them which might be called the solidarity of man in facing his fate, an image of one's own search. A straight, fearless look—at oneself, at one's era, at everything.

History greets every generation with the centuries-old experience that evil cannot be contained within or behind any particular boundary—yet man always regards his own time as a period immune to the laws of history. Over and over, he deceives himself with the thought: yes, that's how it was, but this time it will be different. One day, when man will lie on his sickbed and lament over the destruction of the countryside, nature, the atmosphere, the oceans, he will leaf through old newspapers and with a wry smile recall the verses of his childish pride that celebrated factory chimneys, automobiles, space ships, and other feats in changing and subduing nature. Man is more interested in domination than in understanding. These are banal truths, but what is so sad is that even though made banal by thousandfold repetition these truths will not be heard. What good is it that everyone knows the seeds of decay sprout in the rich soil of prosperity? What good is it that everyone knows the consequences of the isolation of Spanish culture? At the peak of the golden age, Spanish rulers forbade study at foreign universities, broke off all contacts with the leaders of the Reformation, and thus helped to plunge Spain into centuries of stagnation. And Franco, himself spawned by stagnation and death, is repeating this process of isolation before our very eyes. But what good is such knowledge?

You were talking about the destruction of nature, about man being more interested in dominating than understanding . . .

Yes, we said that it is in reality one form of cynicism when people destroy nature without caring about the future. They received a certain heritage, the earth and the air and the water, but they don't care how they will pass on this inheritance to others. Some people think that the destructive side of technology and civilization is limited to such things as the hydrogen bomb. But the bomb is only a potential danger. The real and active destruction of the future lies elsewhere, in the devastation of the most fertile soil through reckless building, which in turn results in still further poisoning of the air and water. Man's destructiveness derives from his inability to relate to nature in any way other than as a conqueror, a disseminator of noise, a producer of waste, an irresponsible intruder. Vandalism will occasionally assume the guise of creation and expansion, but you can recognize such pseudoconstructive activity from the way it ravages a street, a village, or a countryside. The man responsible for this kind of "progress" often fails to realize that he acts like a twin brother of the vandal who, because of his unlimited ignorance of history, is capable of unlimited destruction. I don't know what literature can do in this struggle. Real art, by its very existence, is a call for reason, but it is a big question whether this call is being heard. All our lyric literature has fought the good fight, and so have many of our films. Take Otakar Vavra's film *Romance for a Bugle,* and note how every action takes place in a context of nature, with the outline of an age-old Czech horizon in the background. A similar attitude is prominent in the plays and poems of [Frantisek] Hrubin, and is also present in the films of the younger generation. They are rooted deep among the people, like Vaculik's *The Axe*.

Civilized barbarians seldom express themselves about art—there are, to be sure, some notable exceptions—but when they have something to say it is generally to the effect that art has little meaning as far as the progress of mankind is concerned. It has little meaning for *them;* but then what *does* have any meaning for them? Thoughtful and imaginative authors repeatedly challenge them to single combat, but they don't even hear the challenge. It is as if there were two races of men on this planet which have no contact with each other at all. This, it seems to me, is still another phenomenon that resists the neat schemes of Utopian theorists.

I don't really care to polemicize like this. But I have learned to resist the temptation of trying to find a solution for myself alone by taking refuge in a book of poems, by simply writing some poems myself, or by seeking a retreat in nature. No, I am still painfully clutching to the hope that man's destiny can be influenced by human involvement, and that the same is true of the fate of art and nature.

Do you see anything on the horizon to nourish this hope?

We are living in a world in which peace—though still not impossible to achieve—is only war that is postponed or localized; a world in which historical determinism appears in the form of two rival systems struggling for supremacy, war being the ultimate modality of the struggle. Under such conditions, one must be cautious about making optimistic pronouncements. Even the fact that there are "three worlds" is not much comfort.

I am living in one of those worlds. I know a little about the "rival" world, and I became introduced to the third through its poetry long before I ever set foot in it. That poetry seemed to me like a ship loaded not only with this third world's myths but with its reality as well. How ignorant I was of this reality! How ignorant we all were! At first, the big powers denied this third world its right to exist; they tried to keep it out of the human community. Then, when its will to live could no longer be denied, the big powers insisted that it transform itself in one or another of their own images. And this is more or less the situation today. I never cease to be amazed: this third world continues to act differently from the wishes of either of the big blocks, refusing to copy either model. It creates its own theory of historical determinism but, on occasion, ignores that as well. It cultivates a certain proud exclusivity of its suffering, its enthusiasm, its courage; this *mythos* has materialized into tangible form, like a blooming rose, in the recent death of its hero Ché Guevara. (Actually, I have only been talking about one part of the so-called uncommitted world.) This "uncommitted" segment of humanity accepts contact with the other parts of mankind only when its right to exclusivity is accepted—an understandable attitude but, at this particular stage of history, not very encouraging. The unity of mankind, a dream of countless generations, doesn't seem within easy reach, and fragmentation into exclusive groups doesn't help.

Yet there may be grounds for hope, after all. Perhaps we have talked about human unity when what we've really been thinking about is uniformity—uniformity in the name of the favorite concept of the moment. At one time we symbolized it by the sun, at another by the cross, at yet another by the crescent moon. That "other" symbol, the one used by the enemy, was invariably evil; unavoidably provoking war, it was unavoidably doomed to perish. When will we finally arrive at a point when we stop identifying unity with uniformity and start to conceive of human solidarity in terms of diversity? Unity in diversity, diversity as a precondition of unity.

Excuse this verbal outburst; perhaps, though, it can be forgiven a man as professionally involved with words as I am. Still, I should stick to reality. I should realize that mankind is only being offered a choice between a pair of unavoidable alternatives. But then again, history has often been offered two alternatives—and picked the third.

While we're on the subject of alternatives, I may mention that this year I had the opportunity of visiting five South American universities and of talking to young people who are extremely interested in this problem. I lectured on modern Czech poetry and some of the reflected light of this poetry seemed to have fallen on me, for the young people talked to me with great friendliness and frankness. They said, sometimes bluntly and sometimes more indirectly, that a country with our traditions should demonstrate more culture, more democracy, and more freedom if we wanted to serve as a model for an alternative social system. Of course, they praised our films and our art. I was there just as *Loves of a Blonde* by Milos Forman was being shown, and it certainly stood out brightly against the endless, monotonous stream of Westerns. I have also encountered students to whom neither Nezval, Wolker, Halas, nor Holan seemed sufficiently contemporary or radical.

After all, this is not a new experience for us. Not at all. The same thing happened many times before, for example, in Spanish poetry. In Spain, a courageous and honorable generation emerged in the 1950s which went so far as to abandon all esthetic values in poetry in order to use words solely as weapons against the Falangist dictatorship. That, in itself, was neither incomprehensible nor evil. The sad part of this experience was the fact that, out of the need to fit poetry out for action, a theory was developed which condemned most of the prewar avant-garde as unnecessary ballast. It is evidently extremely difficult to achieve a historic perspective; it seems that man must travel a long and twisting road before he is capable of gaining the kind of perspective essential if real values—so laboriously created—are to be preserved. It is ironic that at the very time when a nation is undergoing the most painful phase of its development, when it is suffering and needs to treasure every last cultural value it possesses, the wrong people assume power over culture and speak in the nation's name. So often, those who assume this power seem to be intellectual sado-masochists, gleefully hacking away at cultural roots and fruit-bearing branches, or what is even worse, at branches just beginning to blossom. This phenomenon is quite unlike the unavoidable drama that accompanies revolutionary change. It is, rather, a manifestation of immaturity, the immaturity of certain segments of the nation that temporarily succeed in gaining power.

A manifestation of immaturity—that's an expression we seem to encounter more and more frequently these days. To Milan Kundera, a major sign of Czech cultural immaturity is the hypertrophy of our lyric literature.

Yes. I can understand that. His critical attitude toward the glories of Czech lyricism is motivated by his concern for the richness and balance of our culture as a whole. And certainly there is something to be said for this view. Drama, for example, can flower only in a society which is clearly differentiated. Literary history describes the traditional centers of drama as urban focal-points of prospering civilizations, such as the Greek, Spanish, or English. A clearly differentiated society gives rise to dramatic conflict. The same is true of a society in motion. Drama cannot be created by inspiration alone; first it must be played by life itself. This doesn't mean that literature need not develop the ability to create dramatic works, but that once it *has* reached this level of proficiency, society must be generous enough to endow the dramatist with conflicts and types. Shakespeare's kings and noblemen were figures far from virtuous, yet feudal society permitted him to put them on the stage. Let us try to imagine a Shakespeare dealing with the producers of a provincial theater; he carefully measures his characters and conflicts to make sure they don't diminish the glory of the Elizabethan epoch and of its heroic representatives. When the conflict between the dramatist and society overshadows all else, it spells the end of drama. Sometimes this happens even before drama has fully arrived on the scene. (In modern times this applies to film also, as we all know.)

Yet, all the same, I believe that the dominance of the lyrical strain in literature doesn't necessarily imply a culture's immaturity or incompetence in other genres. The flourishing of a particular kind of art naturally involves certain definite conditions, but these are quite complex. For example, our contemporary Czech theater has unquestioned artistic potency, yet it isn't supported by the public; it suffers from the competition of television, auto-eroticism (a passion for automobiles), travel, and so on. It will not produce any Czech Shakespeare, but it is (for the above-mentioned reasons) a vital force in spite of it.

The Colombian poet Jorge Zalamea has written a book of essays entitled *Unknown and Forgotten Poetry*. The theme of the book is that there are no underdeveloped nations as far as poetry is concerned. He cites from all of human experience, from magic poetry, from the poetry of big nations and small tribes, the bible, living cultures and dead cultures, and all of it is excellent poetry. Of course, with a bit of demagogy one could use Zalamea's book to prove that poetry does not recognize underdeveloped nations, that in fact poetry is the strength of underdeveloped nations.

Naturally, it is dangerous to take a thesis like that of Zalamea and convert it into a dogmatic assertion; the problem of differentiation within poetry cannot be arbitrarily by-passed.

Furthermore, I am greatly pleased that strong lyricism is no longer the only outstanding feature of Czech literature. We now have good novels, as well as short stories. But I say this with a bad conscience. Our lyrical poetry is undoubtedly still swollen out of proportion, and I am only compounding the problem by translating foreign lyricism and adding it to our own. That should be cause for reflection.

Reflection on what? Yourself or our poetry?

Myself. But that's a private matter.

Before you run too far from private matters, at least tell us how you started out, what road you took and who were your guides and companions.

"I like it when somebody is from someplace," said the good soldier Schweik. In his usual tongue-in-cheek manner, Schweik meant to point out that to be "from someplace" implies no merit whatever. But to get to the point: I was born in Cerveny Kostelec—a reasonably well-delineated little town—but my actual birthplace was called Na Rybnicku and it was a tiny part of a tiny town. Of course, this little backwater carried on wars with the neighboring quarter, which was called Bedna—a rambling working class tenement house with enough people living in it to populate a small village. Both sides were armed with traditional Hussite weapons: flails, spiked clubs, and crossbows. But the commanders on both sides were so skilled in mobile warfare that only very rarely did hand-to-hand fighting take place. After a battle—when one did occur—we would generally forget the principles we had fought for and all join together to conduct an apple-stealing raid in the countryside. I completed my gymnasium study in Trutnov. There the warfare was elevated to an international plane; we engaged in extracurricular soccer matches with German students. After the game, the warriors on both sides shamelessly courted the admiration of female spectators, without regard for nationality. These experiences may have enriched my blood with a few drops of an ability to show interest and understanding for people who are different from myself, an ability that may become modern some day.

There are all kinds of ways of dealing with the world: you can stand still and wait until it comes closer, or else you can move closer yourself. Since I am more attracted to the latter method, I feel a great urge to come into closer contact with this countryside and everything that lives in it. The iron necessity of sitting behind the typewriter day in and day out, in line with the traditional meager existence of our intelligentsia, converts the world of paper into a landscape and relegates the longing for nature and for people into paper dreams. Under these conditions, childhood and the piece of earth where it was lived out looms constantly before men's eyes. This applies not just to myself: there is a particular feeling which persists throughout life—a sense for everything which is clearly fated and yet mysterious—and this feeling stems from one's childhood. Every person elaborates his own myth, and he who lives most intensely within his own is also most capable of understanding other myths. In other words, of understanding other people. That pseudorationalism so characteristic of our age, that cold intellectual calculus, that destructive and arrogant need of people estranged from everything to change everything according to their own will —this is causing terrible, inestimable damage to future life, because it is motivated by ignorance of the real present and lack of interest in the past.

But, once again, I am polemicizing. My own personal mythology originated in those foothills of our land that have produced a typical kind of visionary. On the wall of our house hung the framed portrait of two rather special saints. One was Jan Hus, and on the eve of his birthday my parents would place a lighted candle in the window. The other was the Spanish freethinking teacher Francisco Ferrer, executed in 1911. My father, when he was younger and before he had to struggle so hard against life's misery, occupied himself with all sorts of things which serious-minded people considered ridiculous: autosuggestion, telepathy, freethinking interpretation of the Bible, anarchism, Flammarion. He subscribed to a publication called *Havlicek,* ambitiously subtitled: *A Magazine Disseminating Truth Among the People.* Those words always come to my mind as an ironic commentary whenever I encounter some self-styled Havlicek,* who in the interests of the people and for the sake of the people disseminates lies. My father played the intellectual only in his spare time, out of naïveté and high spirits, for he worked almost all of his life as a dyer in a factory and a Jack-of-all-trades at home—he had also mastered the butcher's trade, but never practiced it.

My father's speech had never freed itself of expressions typical of

---

* Havlicek was the founder of Czech political journalism in the first half of the nineteenth century, but ironically also the name of the Communist Party official responsible for "cultural politics" in 1965–1967.

the southern Krkonose foothills, and he had a whole vocabulary of expressions which were quite individual. At certain times his speech assumed overtones of mysterious forces such as nature, time, and death, and there was always something in the way he spoke which transcended the common, everyday meaning of words.

Language fascinated me. The interplay between word and meaning was given a certain amount of form by my reading and by school, particularly the uncompromising insistence on linguistic purity practiced by my gymnasium professor of Czech, a man named Prochazka. If I ever accomplish anything important, it will probably grow out of these roots; and perhaps other roots, too, which I either don't know about or would prefer not to talk about since they touch on sensitive sides of my being. The myths of childhood and native land, that personal way of being a Czech, these were, of course, determined long ago. Though they do not provide a program for living, they do give strength. The ridiculous aspect of regionalism and the frightening ugliness of chauvinism both stem from a common origin—the need for false and artificial myths, a need which, in turn, arises from a sense of inferiority, of impotence.

As far as my present work is concerned . . . perhaps my long absence as a poet in my own right has been a bit of a ruse. Perhaps I insert a little bit of my own poetry here and there into other things I write and translate, in the hope that somebody will discover them. This isn't exactly stylistic purity, I admit. But I enjoy playing a practical joke now and then.

And so we apparently came to the opposite pole from where we had started . . .

Autumn 1967

Peter Karvaš

Born 1920. At present, one of the most important Slovak playwrights. He published his first book of experimental prose in 1946, then turned to the prevailing socialist realism of the time and wrote two novels dealing with the postwar social and political changes in Czechoslovakia, *This Generation* (1949) and *The Generation in Attack* (1952). After that, he wrote a book of satirical short stories and two plays, *Patient No. 113* (1955) and *The Diplomats* (1958), concerned with contemporary problems. His next play, *The Midnight Mass* (1959), in which he attempted to expose the social roots of Slovak fascism, was hailed as one of the best postwar plays in Czechoslovakia. A modern tragedy, *Antigone and the Others* (1962) was followed by a play about some of the psychological aspects of Stalinism, *The Scar* (1963).

Peter Karvaš

*Bratislava, in January of 1968. It was bitter, freezing cold, piles
of snow everywhere; the road to the Karvas house was like an Alpine
trail. He had told me in November that he had sufficiently recovered
from a personal tragedy to attempt the interview. The year he had
just gone through had been terrible, the worst that a human being
can experience; all the troubles and difficulties the rest of us carried
on our backs seemed like child's play in comparison. For a year, he
hadn't held a pen in his hand, hadn't appeared in print, hadn't conversed with anyone, had barely been alive. Barely, but alive. We
always wonder anew at the wonderful stuff a human being is made
of, to be able to withstand so much. His friends tiptoed around him;
after all Karvas was a high-strung, sensitive person; perhaps he might
even . . . But no; he was back on his feet, writing a letter: "Perhaps
the time has come to attempt the interview; perhaps it will mark
the beginning of my return . . ." And so we tried to settle down to
work; the heating was out of order, of course, and the room was as
cold as a warehouse. I was bundled up in my sweater while he paced
to and fro trailing a long wool scarf.*

I am sorry it took so long for us to get together; it's been more
than a year since I've tried to do anything like this. But I put it off
for another reason, too: I am afraid of improvisation, it terrifies me.

Improvisation seems to me to be one of the signs of our present culture, perhaps one of its central problems. Instead of a basic concept, instead of a point of view supported by thought and analysis, we see a continual stream of apish reactions to unforeseen complications. A vicious circle. We didn't realize, we don't know, we don't think—and so we reject, we improvise, we patch up. In creative work, improvisation is a very short-winded method; it may serve as a stimulus, an enchanting point of crystallization or an exciting magic process, but it can never serve as the artist's daily bread. In the realm of culture, improvisation is hell, or at least limbo. It is true that when a gifted writer and actor like Ivan Vyskocil improvises, some artistic progress may result, but improvisation on such subjects as cultural politics or problems of the generations—and I understand these are themes you are especially interested in—such speculation is bound to end in disaster. Then, too, I am a bit frightened. In the past, whenever I was involved in an interview it was based on questions submitted in advance, so that I had an opportunity to prepare answers which were in effect literary . . .

All the same . . .

The improvisation which has seized our cultural activity is simply the unavoidable result of the provisional nature of our times, and our inability to transcend it. Undemocratic and antidemocratic forces are still strong enough to prevent further development, while the democratic forces are not yet sufficiently powerful to tip the balance toward the future. This situation is therefore characterized by the preponderance of reaction rather than action. You can see this clearly in the case of young poets. New poetry is not only a reaction against old poetry—this is, of course, always the case—but it is also a reaction against the stupidity and vulgarity of the preceding epoch. Similarly, our cultural policy is still only a reaction to real and fictitious dangers, and is really only a somewhat more tolerable substitute for cultural pogroms. Improvisation is the opposite of conceptualization. Yesterday we improvised out of fear of conceptualization; today we are gaily improvising while conducting campaigns. Both of these attitudes have disastrous effects on politics as well as creativity. To cite one example: former esthetic tradition was closely bound by postulates and ideology, certain forms having been prescribed *a priori*. Contemporary esthetics represent a reaction against this rigidity, and this reaction has now brought about the disappearance of form altogether. Improvisation, no matter how useful it may be as a temporary tool, must never be raised to the status of an artistic principle. Otherwise, real art merges with dilettantism and a master who abandons himself to passion becomes indistinguishable from a dilettante who doesn't know his craft.

Of course, I have been talking about two different things which really should be kept distinct: the psychology of creativity and socio-political psychology. I am not insensitive to the charm and magic of improvisation, nor am I unaware that the movement of artistic creativity as a whole, as a stream in the nation's cultural life, is always to some extent predetermined and to some extent free; to the degree that it is free, it is lively, unpredictable, miraculous, and immeasurable, eluding the narrow conceptions of controllers and inspectors. Incidentally, I am sure that I don't have to explain that by the term "conceptualization" I don't mean something unchanged, permanent, nor simply an idea that pops out of somebody's head; rather, it is the final result of a long process that begins with the relationship between one human being and another. How can I say this concretely? The tree has a conception of growth and reproduction; a child has a conception of maturing; and the artist should have a conception of expressing himself, of addressing someone, of speaking to his contemporaries as truly and directly as he can. Of course, this is especially relevant and crucial in the case of writers . . . Tell me, am I gabbing too much?

No.

Here is something quite significant: people are always asking me only which writers are "difficult," whereas there are no problems with composers, graphic artists, or architects. I believe that one reason for this "difficulty" has to do with the nature of language. It is obvious that the word is a more fruitful carrier of meaning than a tone, a sentence more meaningful than a chord, the meaning of a poem a more concrete social force than color in painting or movement in dance. But there are other, apparently less elementary aspects of writings that are even more important in this respect. In music, landscape painting, or in portrait sculpture, ethical thought plays a much smaller role than it does in the novel or in drama. The necessity for concreteness and for a certain fullness of testimony leaves the writer no choice; he cannot simply run away from his testimony—from the problem of truth. He cannot withdraw from the battle into his private thoughts. Certainly, a piano concerto does not constitute direct testimony about the situation of the creator in his era to anywhere the same extent as literary works, such as drama. A play cannot exist except in the present; it cannot be yesterday's or tomorrow's in the same sense as a sonnet or a blues song. Or take the novel; "yesterday's novel" is equivalent to saying "bad novel." It is not my intention to denigrate the social role of other arts. The artist must be true to himself—this applies to all art; but the necessity of being true to himself "right now," at this very instant of social history, this necessity is probably more urgent in literature than in other arts. And in drama it is most urgent of all.

I feel like defending improvisation, but perhaps our difference is due to a misunderstanding. Just think of all the lectures and sermons we have been hearing recently, directed against improvisation in the name of so-called scientific rational approaches. There are many, many people whose ideal lies in the rule of computers which calculate the best political alternative and select correct responses for the most remote events. Perhaps I am old-fashioned, but I prefer my politics without electronics, even though I believe in information. I prefer democratic politics, even though this means that the optimal solution will not always be found, that shortcuts will occasionally be missed, that the majority generally decides badly and that the minority will have to exert itself over and over before it succeeds in convincing the mass of fellow citizens. All this means that I favor improvisation; after all, every serious situation in the life of the individual or of society, which is not totally manipulated in advance, requires a certain amount of improvisation.

I agree. Let us, then, make a distinction: on the one hand, operational flexibility, the culmination of certain learning processes; on the other, improvisation necessitated by formlessness, insufficient education, lack of underlying confidence. For that matter, I am improvising right now, aren't I? Certainly, even some of the greatest things in life are impossible without improvisation. There is no other heroism except an improvised one. Similarly, in art, too, improvisation often initiates great works. But in order for a person to improvise in Spanish, he must know Spanish, and if he is to improvise on a certain level, he must first achieve this level: humanly, philosophically, morally. None of us would oppose improvisation in so far as it succeeds in synthesizing laboriously gained experience and outlooks.

So what you actually oppose is dilettantism.

Yes. It's no coincidence that in order to improvise our cultural politics on the sorry level of recent years, we first had to vulgarize and deface Marxism and to arrest its development. Heroism or revolutionary political action is improvisation that derives from character and from a certain moral maturity, and it is characterized by the fact that it is in harmony with the meaning of history. Improvisation which is entirely based on a sense of personal danger and the desire to save one's skin and to remain in power—don't forget that this generally applies to people who would be absolute zeros without political power—such improvisation is generally a negation of historical development. There is a certain kind of freedom of action which Lenin called "the right to dream"; it manifested itself in Lenin's ability to bring his penetrating intelligence to bear upon a problem, to understand a historical moment and to act upon it. However, the kind of improvisation which we saw in our country in the area of cultural or economic policy stemmed from the desire to thwart historical development and to maintain the kind of *status quo* which people of limited stature and education were capable of handling.

Reaction and conservatism are always the viewpoint of people who are in some manner limited. This is also the reason why the idea of transcending a provisional situation creates so much fear. The provisional does not pose demands and challenges. The provisional is the paradise of the mediocre; *status quo* is the dream of fools. They don't understand that tomorrow will again be different from today, in spite of the fact that they themselves will perish— or perhaps because they will perish.

The mediocre and the provisional as a marriage made in heaven?

Let me tell you about an odd experience. Years ago, I was asked to prepare an analysis of the cultural-political situation. I did the best I could, not perfectly and not alone; I consulted as many intelligent people as I could get in touch with, but even so there were many errors and shortcomings in my report. After all, anger, disillusionment, and impatience could not help but color the work. But what shocked me about the fate of the report was not the way in which it was suppressed, although all sorts of means were arrayed for that purpose, ranging from pleas and exhortations to threats and censorship. Nor was I too upset that the report never saw the light of day,

not even after the entire Central Committee of the Czechoslovak
Writers' Union and many leading cultural and political figures gave
it their strong support. No, what I found so shattering about this
experience was the way in which the work was condemned out of
hand, quite independently of its content! I was asked again and
again to forego submitting my report, at a time when nobody could
possibly have had the slightest inkling of what this report actually
contained. The mere idea of a document which might conceivably
contain anything negative, anything that might actually prove
threatening to someone, or that might imply responsibility or guilt,
created panic. Finally, after the entire report was officially banned, I
ascertained that the people who had been most zealous in enforcing
the ban had never had any contact with the report in any form.
What does this mean? That there was no question of polemics or
thought, of a struggle between ideas, but only a battle for the right
to avoid thinking, the right to ignore what is objectively useful, the
right to remain uninvolved. In short, a total disregard for the question of what is socially useful and what is harmful.

*Situations arise from time to time when this kind of cultural
policy finds itself in hot water. How do bureaucrats deal with such
crises? By awarding titles and medals. In the fall of 1967 cartfuls of
medals were given out. But it didn't help one bit; all the dire warnings became dire realities. What then do we mean by cultural policy,
anyway?*

I dislike simple formulas, such as "cultural policy is the creation
of optimal conditions . . ." and so forth. Or the kind of formula
based on the idea that cultural policy differs from agricultural
policy only to the extent that culture is a different entity from agriculture, that it has its own inner structure and laws, and so on. This
is not the point. Agriculture may be prospering in one country, industry in another, commerce and finance in still another, but culture prospers only in those places where life itself prospers, or more
precisely, freedom. Cultural policy is not a branch of politics and
the condition of culture is not an index of cultural activity alone.
We can export wheat and import computers, or vice versa, and every
sector of the economy has its own operating laws, its own principles
and direction. In contrast, the condition of culture reflects the condition of the society as a whole, its relation to progress and freedom
in all its complexity and wholeness. And no matter from what stand-

point we look at it, the question of freedom is more important than the question of prosperity.

In the 1950s, when I began to travel abroad, Western Marxists asked me time and again about freedom. At that time, we didn't give much thought to this question. We dismissed it by defining freedom through some simple formula such as "consciously accepted necessity," or else we regarded freedom as a problem which would be solved automatically in due course, concurrently with such matters as urban development or the manufacture of screws. We acted as if we didn't realize that it was precisely this sensitive problem-area of socialist democracy that suffered the greatest deformation from the Stalinist cult of power and totalitarian terror. It was only later that we learned how complicated the question of freedom really was, especially as it applied to culture. We learned that the growth of freedom in this area, euphemistically described as "enlargement of the region of creativity," was a highly complex and delicate matter, that it would not simply fall in our laps as a by-product of industrial cybernetics, like leisure time, and that cultural freedom involved a lot more than just the right to criticize.

In recent years, our culture has rid itself of many reactionary influences. The need for political administration of culture is no longer regarded as a self-evident principle, but as a form of recidivism. Control of culture is no longer an occupational category, but only a waning activity for a few individuals.

If cultural criticism is one of the motive forces of society, then culture was one of the few areas in our society where criticism was genuine criticism—in other words, an area in which criteria and judgment were connected with the principle of personal responsibility. Thus, if it was shown that the right conditions for cultural development could not be created by the same methods as conditions for the optimal stimulation of egg production on poultry farms, this demonstration also indicated that the old "revolutionary" formulation of cultural policy was no longer adequate.

The proper conditions for cultural growth are not of a material nature, and have little to do with day-to-day directives addressed to censorship offices; rather, such growth is an integral part of the nation's spiritual, political, philosophical, moral, and economic climate—in short, of the entire atmosphere in which the nation lives during a concrete historical moment.

Cultural freedom does not mean "that which is permitted," nor "that which is *already* permitted." That type of question can be easily agreed upon, decreed, fought for. Real cultural freedom means much more; it refers to whatever is already ripe; it refers to those cultural forces which bear fruit only after nourishing themselves on the juices of courage, inspiration, talent, and erudition that flow from the life of the nation as a whole.

There is one problem: A political power which in the end bows to culture and grants it all the rights and privileges it demands must reckon with the possibility that this same culture will reciprocate by laughing in its face, and it must regard this as a normal development. I believe that has ramifications far beyond the area of culture alone.

When a particular class assumes power, it tries to promulgate laws that guide the development of society, not only for its own benefit but also in its own image. It puts pressure along these lines upon industry, politics, and also, of course, upon culture. If we forget for a moment all those dead ends and strange twists of the past twenty years, this approach seems rather logical. This is the starting-point that future cultural historians will have to take in trying to explain the surprisingly long persistence of dogmatic, didactic, and propagandistic art in the peoples' democracies or Communist China. In its own way, this is a lawful development and history records a number of similar deevlopments. Societal processes can be influenced in at least two ways (which also constitute the polar extremes): either a particular direction is imposed upon the process from the outside, or else an attempt is made to analyze and understand the underlying laws governing this process and to take advantage of them. (In our own country we praised the latter method and followed the former.)

The more specialized and refined a particular social process may be, the more specific must be the approach. The more complicated and differentiated a society becomes, the greater must be the quality, profundity, and intellectual subtlety of the undertakings designed to influence these processes. Otherwise, a spontaneous reaction will result.

Those are our experiences, simplified—or if you will, vulgarized into rules.

And now let's approach things from another end. Our criticism of the "cult" stopped at a certain level because our analysis stopped there, too. It stopped at the point where the question of general responsibility crossed over into the question of personal responsibility. By not pushing our criticism further, certain people were thus given the opportunity of carrying past attitudes over into the present with impunity. We never came to grips with the basic characteristics of Stalinism, such as the Stalinist principle that methods of wielding power may be interchangeably employed in influencing a variety of societal processes. For example, techniques of military command were carried over into the handling of civilian programs. This was especially typical of the early years. More recently, principles applicable to the era of the industrial revolution were transferred into the era of the scientific-technical revolution. Obviously, when principles are transferred in this simplistic way, they cannot possibly prove successful.

This brings us to still another way of approaching the subject: the doctrine of the interchangeability of method in coping with diverse processes became as popular and widely accepted as it did because it enabled people to make broad generalizations and radical oversimplifications of complicated phenomena. In the early days of the revolution and in relatively simple societies, this approach worked for a time. But in advanced stages of revolution and in complicated social situations it was doomed to failure. Pressure toward achieving higher standards of quality and higher levels of thought increased automatically and began to threaten the people in power. These people had generally assumed power at a time when sophisticated planning was not yet necessary, and they were unable to cope with the demands of the new situation. The so-called cult, which is really equivalent to the dictatorship of personal power, gradually became the only possible means of defending the old structures against the pressure of new demands. Airtight isolation, the absolutization of command from the top downward, the degeneration of discipline and thought, the liquidation of rival ideas and their propagators, acceptance of evil—these consequences were inevitable.

It seems to me that this dilemma of power is at the source of all the distortions in the status of the intelligentsia in socialist countries. In our part of the world, this dilemma has a specific character. As every schoolboy knows, the intelligentsia of the bourgeois regimes served primarily the interests of the ruling class. All the same, in the epoch of the scientific-technical revolution it is impossible to rule without the intelligentsia. On the contrary, it is becoming evident that under contemporary conditions the intelligentsia is being called upon to undertake ever new duties and assignments, tasks which were quite unknown in the days of the proletarian revolution. I am not concerned here with the well-known historical mechanism whereby the founder of proletarian ideology came from the bourgeois intelligentsia, the founder of Christianity was a Jew, the founder of Jewish religion and ethics an Egyptian, and so on. Rather, I am talking about a totally new situation—one which, it seems to me, concerns the very roots of revolutionary change. As we know, the classical Marxist thinkers believed that the vital sources of revolutionary inspiration included a certain revolutionary frame of mind which was related to collective labor and to direct personal contact with the most advanced methods of production. During the industrial revolution, these conditions were fully present in the proletariat. It appears, however, that increasing automation will result in a reduction of the collective nature of manufacture and that the growing use of electronics and cybernetics will create a situation in which contact with the most advanced methods of production will be reserved to a small, highly intelligent elite. This does not necessarily mean that the proletariat will cease to function as a decisive revolutionary force. It most certainly does mean, however, a radical alteration in the position of the intelligentsia and in its relationship to the working class. Low industrial qualifications will coincide with a conservative point of view, while a progressive viewpoint will necessarily go hand in hand with claims for the highest industrial competence. Stalinist mistrust and repression of the intelligentsia were thus quite logical. (I even have the impression that the anti-Semitic aspect of the "cult" was to some extent only a function of this anti-intellectualism, or at least that the two attitudes were intimately related.) No hatred is more terrible than a powerful but uneducated man's hatred of the intelligentsia. This is because intellect and education are the only limits to absolute power. Under numerous disguises, anti-intellectualism was a psychological as well as political underpinning of the "cult."

Another fundamental characteristic of Stalinism which proceeded quite logically from its basic nature was the dualism between theory and practice, a dualism totally foreign to true Marxism. It manifested itself as a purely utilitarian momentum of a practice belied by theory, and the dogmatic petrification of theory belied by practice. The situation in our country today: realization of the necessity for scientific direction, and spontaneous resistance to its employment; conception of revolution as an actualization of radical thought, and resistance to conclusions flowing from revolutionary practice. And further: panic growing out of the awareness that tomorrow's progress will go even further, and that the petrified revolutionaries of today will be the reactionaries of tomorrow unless they begin to grasp the true state of affairs. Monumental heads are always made of stone, and they never understand anything.

In this connection, there is one thing which I cannot quite understand and which frightens me. Take the United States of America, a country which has progressed further in the scientific-technical revolution than anyone else—and yet what role does culture really play in its life?

We must always bear in mind that, for us, the scientific-technical epoch is still rather theoretical; it isn't part of our daily routine. Our problems do not stem from the hypertrophy of civilization, but from malfunction of the most basic technical inventions. All the same, the social consequences of the scientific-technical revolution pose a more concrete problem for the present generation than the "cult" did for the generation of the 1940s. Thus, even yesterday was already too late to start relying on intelligence. One thing is absolutely clear: to ignore brain trusts and to depend on the unqualified single individual is, in today's world, a highly reactionary method.

If there was anything pure and beautiful in the beginnings of socialist humanism, then it was truly its closeness to the simple man. All of socialist literature and art turned toward him, all political campaigns were directed at him. But the vulgarization of socialist humanism, the schematization of our public life, resulted among other things in turning this simple man into a fetish. "Simple man" —suddenly, this slogan seemed to imply the license to sink below the level of the times. It seems to me that modern progressive man is not simple at all, but extremely complex. If we regard simplicity in terms of a limited number of moral and psychological traits, then simplicity can never act as a dynamic and positive social force unless it is coupled with great subtlety in understanding the world, a complex emotional life, and fully developed intellect.

We have witnessed the end of the era of "peasant intelligence" and at the same time a new generation has risen in our midst which was unscarred by class warfare and which is equipped with neither class experience nor "class intellect." Under these circumstances, it behooves us to undertake a penetrating study of the special laws governing various socio-historical periods. The delusion is still prevalent that such complex phenomena as cultural development can be guided without knowing their specific developmental laws, or even without admitting that such laws exist.

Conflict between power and cultural creativity is, of course, quite natural. If an artist shares a politician's world view, the politician expects that, in his own way, the artist will also share his behavior. (The higher the politician's level, the more emphasis he places on the words "in his own way." The lower the level on which the politician operates, the more naïve, primitive, and culturally unacceptable are his views about art's relation to society.)

Actually, the function of art is quite the opposite; it characteristically maintains a special tension with respect to society. And it is this very tension which gives a work of art its elemental ability to affect society. The "cult" solved the problem of the relation between power and culture by brutal simplification of the social demand. Liberal societies solve the problem—or rather fail to solve it—by abandoning culture to competition with anticulture, and by making culture harmlessly docile by ensuring commercial hegemony over artistic products of all kinds. (It is remarkable how quickly this particular feature of Western society was appropriated by our former vulgarizers and dogmatic cultural supervisors.)

What kind of cultural program should we promulgate? So far, we know mainly what we should *not* do; we have a wealth of negative experience. That's why the current stage still has the character of a reaction to the previous one, and this negative attitude is prolonged by every new error and clumsy tactic.

If socialist democracy is to prove superior to bourgeois democracy, it means nothing less than that the socialist state will have to provide a greater degree of freedom and that this freedom will be enjoyed by more people—in the realm of art and culture as in laundries and bakeries. The passionate campaign directed during the last two decades against formalism, decadent art, degenerate literature, and antiparty provocations has only served to convince large numbers of young people that these supposed dangers had as little reality as the famous "antistate center" or agents of imperialism in our midst. There are many things about current art and literature I don't like and—if you care to hear me say it—I would like to combat them. But in order to wage battle there must first be a battleground. I have no objection to ideological opponents, and I enjoy debating them. But our bureaucracy, with its endless supervising and officiating, rules out any such contest. My truth, or any other truth, is worth nothing until it has been tested in battle against its opponents.

Not so long ago, the slogan was that we foster an elitist culture . . .

There is no such thing as culture for an elite. You can only talk of a broader or narrower public for a particular kind of art. For that matter, the word "elite" can have a pejorative or positive meaning, depending on how it is used. The best surgeons constitute our surgical elite, the best soccer players our soccer elite, and in this sense the cultural public, too, has its elite. As an author, I wouldn't want to write for an elite, if this implies having fewer readers. It is, of course, a fact that fewer people listen to string quartets than to popular songs. If this makes the quartet lover a more elite listener, more power to chamber music.

There is a more important aspect to this question, though. The demand for art with a high standard of originality, complexity, and social relevance is often exploited by parasites who are simply incapable of addressing an audience in a meaningful way. Many artists react against the vulgar demand for easy comprehension and popular simplicity by acting as if inability to communicate were a guarantee of great profundity and the absence of a public a sign of high art. This predominance of reaction as compared to conception is also apparent within the works themselves, particularly in literature. The ideological—and thus also formal—predictability of many works of socialist realism has evoked a strong reaction manifested by a veritable deluge of amorphous works. Not only construction, but also composition, not only the stereotyped assertion but *any* assertion, not only cheap and superficial involvement but *any* involvement evokes suspicion. A few years back, all that was necessary for literary success was to agree with the preceding work, provided this agreement was expressed in grammatically correct form. In contrast, all that is necessary today is to prove that the present work has no reference whatever to anything produced in the past, and to do so in as vague a way as possible. (I hope that this remark will not give ammunition to the wrong people; such statements are frequently misconstrued.) In this connection, I am disturbed by a phenomenon which is especially typical of the most recent Slovak literature; namely, that even writers who have several years of experience under their belt still haven't transcended their earliest beginnings. Their first books still remain their best books, and their worth doesn't stem from organic growth but from the claim of having been the first to come up with a particular idea. Further development of their own voice was actually accompanied by decline. But this takes us far afield . . .

Perhaps not. On the contrary, we have come up against the generations and their shifts . . .

This is the story on the generations: I have often read that I belong to the generation of the National Uprising. That is a definition that leads to all sorts of interesting possibilities. You can narrow it down to include only the actual participants of the Uprising, and then you lose many writers of works thematically anchored in the Uprising. Or, to take the other extreme, you broaden the definition to include the entire literature concerned with the Uprising, and suddenly, you find that you have room for several generations of writers. It appears that this confusion has nothing to do with the chronological nature of literary development, but rather with the changing evaluation of the Uprising as a historical event and as a literary subject.

If we limit our discussion to the literary aspect, the matter is in essence rather simple. The Uprising as subject matter and inspiration has undoubtedly played a tremendous role in Slovak literature. Its thematic contributions are such that modern Slovak literature is unthinkable without it. The Uprising has provided a fund of material which has served to fortify Slovak literature during periods of waning vitality. It can even be said that attempts at discovering the truth of the Uprising compensated Slovak literature for its inability to penetrate to the reality of subsequent periods. It is significant that during a certain period it was as dangerous to publish truths about the Uprising as it was to objectively discuss current conflicts of contemporary society.

When it became necessary to impute guilt to the key figure of the Uprising, the entire movement had to be condemned as well. This period, during which interest in other people was limited to speculations about their guilt or innocence, was also marked by systematic distortion of the real nature of the Slovak National Uprising. Through a coincidence of circumstances literature was thus destined to stimulate the awareness of a historic phenomenon, which historiography itself—due to "objective reasons"—had to disregard until very much later. I don't want to go into historical details nor to gloss over the obvious fact that even literature was not entirely free from errors and distortions insofar as the true face of the Uprising was concerned. But if I were to define the generation of the Uprising in literary terms, I believe that the decisive criterion would be based on the extent to which a writer regarded the Uprising as a historical event rather than as a complex human problem. Many have gotten rid of the Uprising by relegating it to the area of history, glory, and, above all, official celebration. Others appropriate it as personal literary property on which it is possible to collect interest. When I speak of the generation of the Uprising, I am thinking of artists for whom the Uprising is not a literary crutch but a decisive life-experience, with all its complexities, errors, and guilt. I don't believe that my fellow citizens could ever perform anything purer, better, or more sincere than the Uprising. True art derived from the experience will live, whereas official Uprising literature will be solemnly and ceremoniously buried in monuments.

The cold drove us from the room where we had been sitting. We settled down in the next room, the walls of which were covered with paintings full of special magic. One portrayed a lady in a broad-rimmed hat and flowing skirt, posing before a painter's easel. She stood with her back to us, looking out into the garden.

That's my mother painting my aunt. And in the next picture, that's my grandfather, Dominik Skutecky; for some reason, I have been thinking of him a great deal lately. He was born near Bratislava, and when he was quite young he went out into the world. He studied painting in Munich, then lived for a while in Venice, and finally returned to Banska Bystrica; there, he painted boiler-makers in their copper workshops, as well as people from neighboring villages, peasants and ploughmen. He died in 1921, when I was one year old. Actually, nobody knew much about him for a long time. But twenty-five years after his death they decided that he was a great Slovak painter; there is a collection of his work in the National Gallery and from time to time monographs are published about him.

He pointed to a large painting, well-known from reproductions.

I am sure you are familiar with this one—the market in Banska Bystrica; that lady with the red umbrella is my grandmother, that's my aunt over there, and this little girl is my mother. As you see, I was born into a rather unlikely family. My uncle was an architect, another uncle a composer, my mother a painter, one of my aunts was a singer who married a Viennese Social Democratic journalist; in short . . . My father was a physician. He was no longer one of the long series of famous country practitioners, but on the other hand he did not yet belong to the new class of dehumanized professionals. He was an extremely practical man as well as a highly trained specialist, the author of theoretical books, and a tireless healer and consoler. When the fascists forbade him to practice, the neighboring villages protested and rebelled.

It was a rather cultivated environment. I cannot think of any exciting adventures from my childhood. My father never hunted nor felled giant trees, but he did travel over thirty kilometers in the middle of the night to help bring children into the world. My mother never baked homemade bread; she only painted pictures in the garden and in her studio. In short, things were quite different from the way country life is supposed to be; it was a family which is difficult to exploit for literary purposes.

My first great cultural experience? I remember the whole family going to see Ekk's film *The Road to Life*. In those days, Soviet films created great excitement in our family; my uncle was an official in the Czechoslovak-Russian Society. But it wasn't just the films that stimulated heated debates; we followed the whole political development of the 1930s, the political trials . . .

I actually made my cultural debut as a composer; in the sixth year of gymnasium I composed a song based on the words of a fellow schoolboy, and this was followed by other songs. But I imagined that I would become a doctor, and that from time to time I would toss off a story or two, just as my close school friend Karol Zachar [well-known Slovak actor and director] imagined that he would become a painter who'd occasionally dabble in amateur theatricals. When we get together nowadays, we both rather regret that things turned out differently.

During my final years at the gymnasium I began to publish in the Slovak magazine *Svojet,* as well as in one or two Prague publications. Then came 1939. I had to leave the university (though I did spend the 15th of March in Prague); I enrolled in technical studies for which I was eventually given credit after the war. But the man who had the greatest influence on preparing my mind for my future career was my gymnasium Latin professor, Jan Ulehla. He taught me the fundamentals of linguistic thinking, and he was the first to show me the importance of clear, logical thinking in general. After my return home I went through a number of occupations; I played in a jazz band, I designed neon advertisements, had a job in a construction firm, worked as a conscripted laborer in a camp, and had brief careers as a clerk in a shipping firm, photographer, and gardener. Then I moved to Martin, then to the newly founded theater in Matice; I took part in the Uprising, worked for the Free Slovak Radio, eventually moved to the mountains and from the mountains I crossed the front to Kosice, to the radio station of the Slovak National Council, then back to the theater—this time to the National Theater in Bratislava—combined with a playwriting stint for the Bratislava radio station. In the meantime, I had finished my studies and embarked on a new series of occupations—in diplomacy, in the government's cultural department. I became editor of *Kulturny Zivot* [the leading Slovac cultural weekly], secretary of the Union of Slovak Writers, and . . . for heaven's sake, that's enough. And all this time I have tried to keep on writing.

Why?

I don't know. Perhaps literature provides one of the few opportunities, one of the few methods or techniques whereby one can reach truth, even though this may be only a kind of *ad hoc* truth, a personal truth which one needs in order to live. I have a friend who is a hydroelectric engineer. He has dedicated his whole life to the project of building a great dam across the Danube. He and his colleagues have already worked out a number of plans, but none of them has yet been accepted. He is continually being thwarted, for reasons that have nothing to do with the merit of his ideas or national interest; but every time somebody turns down his project, a new set of variations is soon produced and step by step my friend seems to be getting closer to something important . . .

I wonder whether literature, in particular the drama and essay, doesn't represent this same sort of search, consisting of a series of approximations that are constantly being corrected. Like a miner who reaches the end of the shaft and keeps on going. He isn't down there in the mine just to reach the wall and turn back. And when a man sits down at the typewriter, behind him there may be a potential play or ruined scenario, and all he's got in front of him is a sheet of white paper. In short, literature is for me one of the methods of keeping going, of not capitulating. Every person must have his own means of declaring "no surrender," otherwise he's finished.

To make myself quite clear: this determination not to surrender must be linked in some way to another person, to all mankind. In this way, art is lifted to a religious plane, or at least an ethical one.

On the other hand, literary work never represented a solemn occasion for me; it never assumed the characer of a religious service. I have committed great blunders that have alternated with lesser ones. But this I know—the artist can never look for excuses, for alibis. His responsibility for his own work is the tax he pays for the great and exceptional privilege of self-realization in a world of serial mass production and widespread alienation. This responsibility extends to social duties as well.

By a roundabout way, we came back to the question of the generations. Perhaps it was the influence of the pictures on the wall, or perhaps it was the sociological turn in the discussion, Marshall McLuhan, Marcuse . . .

I believe that members of my generation—fellow artists as well as fellow citizens in general—are marked by a certain paradox. My contemporaries in Bohemia as well as in other European countries are generically characterized in their thought and in their work by a sense of anxiety, of collapsed certainties and disappointed ideals. The cause of all this was the enormously intense shock of World War II. In the Slovak consciousness, the turning point toward a more active and optimistic attitude was represented by the Uprising. As a result, the first works of Slovak literature that appeared after the war differed markedly from their Czech counterparts. A variety of influences was cited to explain this difference: the power of Slovak realistic traditions, the directness and elemental strength of the Slovak artist, intimate connection between Slovak drama and amateur theatrical enthusiasm, and so on. But the real reason for the character of postwar Slovak literature goes much deeper; it is rooted in specific life-experience, especially the Uprising. Naturally, I do not have in mind the Uprising as a military operation nor as an act with international political implications, but in the sense of a particular national attitude. Stalinist propaganda had a banalizing effect on all this; it reduced the Uprising to a historical cliché, and in the end the generation of the Uprising convinced itself that this view was somehow a more noble and correct one. Thus it is neither an accident nor an illusion that the rehabilitation of the Uprising coincided with a wave of reawakening sweeping across all the Slovak social and intellectual life.

The paradox I have mentioned lies in the fact that the fateful delays in converting the momentum of the Uprising into concrete political practice still fills the Uprising generation with a sense of missed opportunity and urgent need, while at the same time this generation is trapped in inaction and resignation. Furthermore, the new literary generation has learned to accept disengagement as a common gesture of protest, and the Uprising is no longer regarded as a unique phenomenon but as one of a series of pathetic encounters such as the battle of the Marne.

The new generation no longer has a direct relationship to the reality of the Uprising. Perhaps we had too great a tendency to idealize this epoch, to create myths and legends around it. But even though I know that the young always regard the experience of their fathers as limited and rather trivial, I am troubled by the apathy of the young writers toward the Uprising. It pains me that this new generation cannot grasp the Uprising as a universal impulse to action and as one of the basic models of engagement in the life of the nation. This apathy stems from the need for disengagement, the demand for noninvolvement as a means toward artistic freedom. This is a conception of freedom quite foreign to me.

What can we do about this attitude?

We may dislike it, but is by no means difficult to understand. Antagonism between fathers and sons is natural. And so is polarity between conventions and their active rejection, between tendencies toward petrification and tendencies toward originality. And everything becomes still more comprehensible when we recall the tremendous gap that existed between the plans, dreams, and illusions of the fathers and the social reality in which their sons grew up.

But understanding something doesn't mean that we must necessarily admire it. I must admit that I get quite concerned when distance and disenchantment become goals in themselves, when a tradition is destroyed without planting the seeds of a new one. Every truly creative act and work of art has a simultaneously destructive and constructive character; it doesn't cut itself off from tradition but transcends it; it converts it into a more vital one. If this isn't the case, we are dealing with empty gestures rather than with creation. This is true even when the work in question can point to total originality, and claim freedom from all forerunners and their mortal sins.

I agree. But I would add in defense of the young that their attitude represents a kind of defensive reflex. Most of them grew up on the periphery of the last regime. They are not communists, they are not Marxists and most of them probably never will be. As long as they don't feel that they have the same rights, the same oportunities, and the same responsibilities as their elders, they maintain this distance. Their problem is really the problem of us all, of our whole future ... A final question. Do you have any message for the Czechs?

Yesterday, when we started our interview, I was afraid that I was unprepared and would have nothing to say. Now I am terrified by the tremendous outpouring of my words. But to come back to your question—which puts us at the beginning of another interview—I believe that here in Slovakia you will not find a single person who doesn't have something to say to the Czechs. Anyone who denies it isn't telling the truth. It is truly fantastic when you consider how relatively minor things have grown into tremendous problems, only because people have found it polite, convenient, or even useful to remain silent. The reasons for silence are generally quite ephemeral, while the results of silence can be disastrous.

Thus, if I had to choose a single message I consider most important, it would be this: for heaven's sake, don't be silent about our burning problems and disagreements! Let us not pretend that they don't exist, because in this way we only succeed in making them more sensitive and more explosive. In this area, above all others, it is necessary to call a child by his right name as quickly as possible, before he grows up into an enemy or a parasite.

Shouldn't we perhaps rehabilitate improvisation, after all?

That's a question you will have to put to the others.

January 1968

Ivan Klíma

Born 1931 in Prague. He graduated from Charles University and after various editorial jobs on magazines and in a publishing house joined the staff of *Literarni Noviny*. His first book of short stories, *A Fine Day*, was published in 1960, followed by a book of reportage from the easternmost part of Slovakia, *Between Three Frontiers*, and in 1962 by a book-length essay on Karel Capek. Well received were both his novel *The Hour of Silence* and his play *The Castle*, in which he explored, as he did in most of his more recent work, the position and responsibility of the individual in an authoritarian, Kafkaesque society. Among his recent work are two books of short stories, *One Night Lovers* and *A Ship Named Hope* and several plays, like *The Jury* and others. He wrote articles published in *Literarni Noviny* and later in *Literarni Listy*. He was expelled from the party in 1967 for his speech at the Fourth Writers' Congress in which he strongly attacked censorship.

Ivan Klíma

It is a paradox typical of our time that the interview with Ivan Klíma almost didn't take place. We sat in the same office for many years, we saw each other almost daily, but for that very reason it proved difficult to find time for a quiet chat. At first this was my fault, later his. Finally, the matter was settled on the day when we were officially informed that the decision taken by the party in October 1967 had been reversed. This original decision meant closing Literarni Noviny *and strict sanctions against Klíma and myself, as well as Vaculik, [Pavel] Kohout and Kundera—in other words, the rather melancholy and unheroic heroes belonging to the first generation of the "builders of socialism." It was clear that we would begin where we left off, richer by one experience and poorer by one illusion.*

When I had settled him comfortably in an armchair, far away from telephones and other possible distractions, I asked him the first question: How are you doing?

I just finished a play called *The Jury.* It is based on a story that was published in *Orientace;* it will probably have its premiere in Germany. In the play, the court is in the midst of its deliberations when it is suddenly made clear that the sentence has already been carried out and the jurors must now decide what to do. Should they simply go away or debate the case? At this point, the mechanism of fear begins to make itself felt. Among other things, the play is concerned with the way fear deforms people.

How did you make the transition from prose to theater?

It was the other way around, actually—from theater to prose. I was born in 1931, and around 1956 I developed quite a mania for writing. I wrote a few novels but mainly plays. I never tried to have anything published, but [the author, playwright, director, and composer] E. F. Burian asked me to write a play for him after having read one of my stories in *Literarni Noviny*. Fired with enthusiasm, I finished the play in two weeks. He didn't throw it out, but only asked me to rewrite it. Fortunately, my initial spirit and courage had left me by then.

While we're talking about my graphomania as a new writer, I must tell you that I was terribly immature and undereducated. This was the toll taken by contemporary events and to this day the huge gaps in my reading give me an inferiority complex. I finished a few years of public school, then was shipped off to the Terezin concentration camp where, during the years in which the most avid reading normally takes place, I had only five books to choose from. The best one of the lot was *The Pickwick Papers*, which I read through at least ten times. For about three months I attended an underground school in the camp, then I got a few lessons from my aunt, and then a former professor of Czech took me under her wing after someone had shown her one of my poems. After I got out of the camp I jumped straight into the third year of gymnasium. I had to make up for lost time somehow or other, and because of all the catching up I had to do my studies were once again quite superficial. To make matters worse, I became very ill. I really started to read seriously only when I turned eighteen, and when I see how much young people know today I feel that I'll never catch up. You may say that in my profession the adventures and experiences of childhood are more important than formal reading. Perhaps that's true. But I'll never be able to shake off this sense of my background having been so deficient. I believe that my lack of education was responsible for the fact that I only started writing decently when I was approximately twenty-five.

I never really wanted to do anything else. It probably began in Terezin. With that poem I mentioned, called *Suicide*. I was eleven at the time.

Later, when I attended gymnasium, I used to write novels late into the night. Writing's never given me more delight than it did in those years. And I realized for the first time certain things which are much discussed these days: the importance of authenticity, for example; the courage to talk freely about oneself. My writing was authentic, all right. But as prose it was terrible.

I began to publish my work only toward the end of the 1950s. Stories, several novels, a monograph on Karel Capek,* a play called *The Castle*. That's how I started. The next play, *The Master*, was published, but never performed, and God only knows what will happen with *The Jury*. *A Ship Called Hope* will come out in book form . . . I am finding writing more and more difficult. You keep putting things away, saving them, getting ready. But perhaps I will write one more book, in which I'll say everything that's on my mind . . . I suppose every author has such an idea, and only one in a thousand succeeds in making it come true.

He talked on rather disjointedly. I steered the conversation toward his interest in Capek, an interest that had brought down upon his head the wrath of the high and mighty.

I had always admired Capek, though he wasn't my favorite author. Vladislav Vancura was actually more significant to me. I really can't say now why I picked Capek at that time. I suppose the fact that he, too, started as a journalist established a bond between us. (I joined the staff of the [weekly illustrated] magazine *Kvety* in 1956, then worked in a publishing house, and finally came to *Literarni Noviny*. The sojourn in the publishing house was an error which I'd like to warn others about; a young person doesn't belong in a job like that which requires taste, experience, maturity and, above all, freedom from personal literary ambitions.)

To get back to Capek, though. Another reason why I felt close to him was his philosophical manner of writing. He generally started with an idea, a philosophic design, and the story came later, if one

---

* The most important Czech writer of the pre-World War II period.—*Ed.*

can talk in this simplified manner. Then, too, I felt sympathy with the way he moved from genre to genre.

The Capek book caused me a lot of trouble. For that matter, I had trouble with censorship and with the publisher's precensorship in connection with practically all of my books. They returned my book of Utopian stories on the ground that it was too pessimistic, and it still hasn't been published. The manuscript of my novella *The Lepers* was made required reading for the entire Central Committee of the Writers' Union, and then it was returned to me. Their advice was beautifully touching: You're still a young man—why so pessimistic? It hasn't been published to this day. The most ironic aspect of the Capek episode was the fact that the main objections were raised against the first version; I am rather ashamed of this version myself now, because I criticized Capek for opinions and attitudes which were actually quite wise. I corrected this in the second edition, which came out four years later, and this version went through without a murmur of opposition despite the fact that from the point of view of the initial criticism it was far worse.

The biggest furor, however, was caused by my article in *Kvety,* entitled "The Personal Files of Karel Capek, Czech Author." I was fired from *Kvety*. They also instituted proceedings against me, but these were eventually dropped. Dismissal from the magazine was more of a relief than a punishment for me. The atmosphere of the publication, directed as it was by the central party apparatus, was by far the most depressing I have known since the end of the war. As a matter of fact, my novella *The Lepers* dealt with this very situation.

To come back to the first edition of my book on Capek. I had to fight hard just to be able to refer to Masaryk's *Conversations with Karel Capek* in the bibliography, whereas in the second edition I was freely permitted to devote an entire chapter to this subject. One might think that the personnel in the editorial office had changed in the meantime—but it hadn't. These were exactly the same people.

What about The Castle?

It was after some time limited to one performance a month, even though the theater was completely full each time; we were not permitted to distribute posters or to advertise the play in any way until it was removed from the repertory.

Of course, this was not due to any misunderstanding. The people responsible for this harassment had read the play and understood it perfectly. There was one misunderstanding, however, which I regretted very much. Some people took *The Castle* to be an attack on intellectuals. It isn't; it is only an attack on the treacherous segment of the intellectual community. A similar statement had already been made by Capek. He had pondered the circumstances that led to the triumph of Nazism and had shown that the worst treason was the failure of the intellectuals. At one time I disagreed with this statement, but I am beginning to share Capek's viewpoint more and more. The treason of people who are aware and lucid is worse than that of the confused and unconscious. Those educated and intelligent persons who shirk their true task, who are given high positions precisely because they are shirking their real mission—these are the people exposed in *The Castle*. Whoever felt himself insulted revealed his own bad faith. The inhabitants of *The Castle* have the sole occupation of pretending to be active, and their sole activity consists in justifying their own positions. Unfortunately, *The Castle* hasn't lost its topical relevance.

The Castle has another aspect, too. It shows that the treason implicit in this kind of attitude eventually leads people to commit all sorts of crimes. Also, the play tries to show that there is a tacit understanding between people in power and this sort of treacherous intelligence. Such a tacit understanding exists all over the world, in all sorts of guises and modifications. Every power needs its apologists, the rock on which it builds its church. That's probably the reason the play is so popular abroad.

Why are you so attracted to the theater?

I suppose one reason is the temptation to try my hand at all kinds of literary genres. I had already written stories, essays, reportage, part of a novel. So I decided to try writing something with dialogue —and it turned out to be *The Castle*.

Another reason: I always wanted to come in contact with people who are affected by what I write. And this is really possible only in the theater. The confrontation with the audience has its own particular excitement.

Opening night—it's like a great sports match. Nervous excitement. It's different with a book. First you look through a pile of proofs, then comes a carton full of copies; you don't quite know what to do with them, you leaf through them, admire the typography, then send a few copies to your friends; in three weeks the first review comes out, you don't even bother reading the next one, then a few friends tell you that they liked the book very much—after all that's what friends are for—and since you don't quite know how to answer them you just mumble: I'm very glad. Or else they suggest you change a few things here and there, and you say you'll have to think it over . . .

In the theater you experience a wonderful reaction. You feel the success or the failure in your very body. Of course there's always the danger that you'll succumb to your public or, in the end, even become its obedient servant.

And then there is another advantage of the theater—its timeliness. When something is going on in society, it is pleasant to write a play about it; people are waiting for the right words to appear, and it gives you a wonderful sense of accomplishment if you succeed, at least to some degree, in expressing the ideas which are in the air at the moment.

And finally there is that special magic which I still can't fully enjoy because I'm still a bit ashamed of it: theater as a game, as play. Many years ago I used to love puppet shows. When I was a boy I made everything myself. The theater, the puppets, the props, scenery, and of course the scripts for the plays. Theater is the objectification of your own illusions. You try all sorts of tricks. It is an image of life, and then again it isn't; you imagine all sorts of things that don't exist and suddenly they come to life. For example, the dance over the corpse in the Polish playwright Slawomir Mrozek's *Tango*. You can never get that kind of effect from the printed page; there are things which only the theater can accomplish.

When you were speaking of Capek, you mentioned the combination of journalism and literature. Do you think this is a good idea?

There is no doubt that the two activities are in many ways antithetical. But for that very reason they may complement each other. There is a dictum in sports that a tennis player should not take up ping-pong but something quite different, such as ice hockey. One activity can sharpen the other. A good journalist must be able to finish an article within a two-hour deadline, come what may. A writer has no such skill.

There is a certain system of signals that has been established between the newspaperman and his readers, though these signals may exist on different levels. The writer, on the other hand, continually disturbs and distorts these signals. But as I said before, I enjoy variety and whenever I was asked to contribute something to the newspapers the thought that I could do it successfully and that I had mastered this craft gave me great pleasure. And the journalist quickly finds out where he had succeeded and where he had failed; in this respect, the newspaper is similar to the theater.

I became a journalist mainly because I wanted to get acquainted with the atmosphere, which always had a special fascination for me. Whenever I am in a new environment, I am seized by a new enthusiasm. And a good newspaper, such as *Literarni Noviny,* keeps a person in close touch with a society, or at least with certain segments of society. When I left *Literarni Noviny,* or rather when the paper left me, I had the desperate feeling for a while of being cast out of society, out of the world.

What is your general opinion of the press at this moment?

When I spoke earlier of my sense of being half-educated and of the loss of many precious years, it occurred to me that the fault lay not only in poor schools but also in the general cultural level of our surroundings. After all, a person is educated by everything that goes on around him. The shutting down or muzzling of such publications as *Tvar, Kriticky Mesicnik,* or *Lidove Noviny* would have a catastrophic effect on the intellectual conditions of any country. Publications of that quality are an important means of communication. Without them it is impossible to orient oneself. When any group in power attempts to destroy such publications for the sake of making the job of government "easier," this constitutes an attempt to murder the nation and its culture. The reputation which our journals are now enjoying abroad is a tribute to the general cultural level of the country. I can remember the tremendous impression that Aragon's lecture at Charles University made on me. He didn't say anything really new, but the fact that his words were later read by a quarter of a million people had its own significance. In short: private thoughts, ideas expressed only to a small group of friends, have no chance to function.

Don't you think that literature has its own set of "signals," just as the press has?

Certainly, but in a different sense. All literature is based on signals, but these are continually changed and renewed.

For example, a major theme in American drama is that of the lyrical revolt, the revolt against conventions, against society. The entire system of signs and symbols derives from the fact that the American public feels itself being sucked into the dehumanized world of technology and thus has developed an almost sentimental attraction toward free nature. You find it in Steinbeck, Tennessee Williams, N. Richard Nash, Schisgal, even in Albee. Just think of the countless symbolic salamanders, birds, dogs, jaguars, and tigers. One of the main heroes of a play by Tennessee Williams explains that there are certain birds which have no legs, which can't alight anywhere, and must spend their entire lives flying in the sky. Nash's hero [in *The Rainmaker*] dreams of freeing caged birds.

The German playwright Wolfgang Hildesheimer transformed this theme into the area of the absurd and created the mysterious bird Guricho. Each character becomes defined through his relationship to symbolized nature, and the audience knows immediately that this character is our hero because he loves birds, while that other is a villain because he speaks ill of dogs. The audience is happy because it has now gotten its orientation. These are typical "signals" and one day, when people become too familiar with this set and start to laugh when they should be crying, they will be replaced by new ones.

Recently you devoted a lot of space in Literarni Noviny *to the problems of older people. Why?*

For this one reason: here is a group of people who are more defenseless than anyone else against the terrible pressure of our time, the pressure toward the dehumanization of society. Besides, we know too little about our ancestors; at best we know our own grandfathers. It is noteworthy that interest in those who came before us is waning in proportion to the growth of our knowledge regarding the age of the world. I personally consider it terribly important to know as much as possible about where we came from, since we know so little about where we are going. And we must start with those who are still alive, those still among us.

The Americanization of our life is so terrible precisely because it is affecting the area of human relationships much more than the area of technology—in fact, as a partial result of the failure of civilization and technology. The utilitarian attitude to life, to people who can no longer keep up with the others, is monstrous. Grandmothers are still more or less acceptable, because they help to take care of the children. But this, too, is more of a manifestation of in-humanity than of kindness. There is no reason why anyone should want to protect the rights of older people, everybody prefers to be on the side of youth. Young people can still be exploited. But an old man—what can he still do besides say "thank you"? And what is a "thank you" worth nowadays?

Why do you call it Americanization?

It has to do with the advance of technological and economic civilization. I really don't like to talk about this subject too much, since I've never been to America and can only base my opinions on what I hear and read . . . In any case, it isn't a matter of terminology but of phenomena. The chase after the American dollar isn't really any different from the chase after the Czech crown. The only basic difference lies in the fact that here the acquisitive drive is mani-fested mainly by cheating, stealing, and so on, whereas in America it is transformed into a value system. There is nothing wrong with the desire to better oneself materially; I'm not that strict a moralist. The moral question only enters when acquisitiveness is connected with hurting others. But of course that applies to socialism also, and I have rather peculiar and original ideas in this regard . . .

This is as far as we got, and we postponed the discussion to the following week. But events began to take on a tempo beyond the wildest imaginings of the optimists—or the pessimists. The merry-go-round that started to turn just before October began to spin wildly, and it wasn't until the end of February 1968 that we man-aged to sit down again in the same armchairs and resume our con-versation. You said you have some very original ideas on social-ism . . .

When I was in Israel a few years ago and visited the kibbutzim, it was my first encounter with an attempt to create a communist so-ciety along the lines envisioned by the socialist thinkers of the nine-teenth century. It is an attempt to organize manufacture on the basis of freedom and conviction, with all the moral consequences which that entails. It represents a community of people whose re-lationships are no longer governed by greed or envy, who do not wish to get rich at someone else's expense, or to insist on one's own comfort at the expense of the well-being of others. It is also an attempt to subordinate the interests of the individual to the in-terests of the collective in which he lives. (Naturally, this doesn't mean that the development of individuality is neglected; the goal is to harmonize the interests of the individual with those of the collective.) Finally, the kibbutz is an attempt to combine the system I have just described with principles of direct democracy.

This Israeli experiment was, of course, carried out by volunteers and succeeded in attracting only about four percent of the society—in other words, only those who really longed for such a manner of life. The kibbutzim were primarily drawn from the first generation of settlers, intellectuals who did manual work, and so there was an ideal combination of mental and physical activity.

Much as I was fascinated by this system, it seemed to me that it didn't have much of a future. The real problem came in the second generation, for here these principles began to encounter serious difficulties. The generation which grows up in this system—unless it is granted extraordinary freedom—no longer feels that it has exercised free choice in its life-situation. The system which is being offered to it, and in some respects almost forced upon it, seems too restrictive, too one-sided. That's the first problem, and there are others. As the collective gets bigger, direct democracy no longer works as well and it begins to take on some of the unfortunate aspects of our democracy of "meetings." Furthermore, as communism tries to ensure that all people work under equal opportunity it comes into conflict with technology, which threatens to undermine the very foundations of the system.

The kibbutz, nevertheless, represents the optimal realization of pure communism achieved so far. And it is limited to four percent of the population. From my point of view, if socialism is to be a real system capable of independent existence, it must be something much broader. It cannot be built according to any precise scheme calculated in advance, and it cannot be realized in one or two generations.

Consider just one problem essential for the functioning of society —work motivation.

A person may work voluntarily because he feels the need to work.

Or he may be forced to work.

Or he may work for money.

Once again, we were interrupted by events. People burst in with mimeographed sheets, the cameramen arrived, there was confusion, a new revolution, new illusions, hopes, dreams.

Six weeks later, in a different chair and a different era, we brought our interview to a close. The revolution had cooled off, so had the plans and illusions and what was left was just a glimmer of hope. We had spiraled to the same point where we had started talking a year before, except perhaps slightly higher. In a few months there will probably be another Writers' Congress. Some of our old adversaries have disappeared, others have risen, some of the rough edges have been smoothed over and the contours of a new front have begun to emerge—surprisingly similar to the old. History simply insisted on its rights and we became aware of its inevitability more than ever before. We were so much more experienced now, and somewhat embittered after the two springs of 1967 and 1968. And we knew perfectly well that we would begin everything from the very beginning, that the stone had rolled back to our feet, just as we had all thought we were nearing the top. And with this at the back of our minds, we resumed where we had left off.

Each of these three motives is characteristic of a particular social order; we have seen examples of all of them in the last twenty years and now we are back at the last one.

Each one of these motives has consequences for human relationships and for the human psyche. Thus, it isn't merely a matter of formal categories. For example, I cannot imagine a socialist society based on the ideal of working for money, even though at the moment I consider financial incentives a reasonable measure.

Israel convinced me of one thing: namely, that in the modern era, given the contemporary state of production and the current human psychological make-up, it is impossible to use ideological conviction as the sole motivating force. It simply would not work on a large scale. That's why the socialist system must depend on all three types of motivation; even some degree of coercion may be necessary. There are times and situations when it is unavoidable. Of course, I am not thinking of labor camps. There are people who work best when money is the incentive, in a socialist country as in any other. And there certainly are people who get their greatest satisfaction as a result of idealistic motivation. Socialism must simply create optimal conditions for the application of all three variants of motivation. It is a mystery to me, incidentally, why a society which calls itself socialist failed to give people the opportunity to form communes, which might have given a certain small but definite part of the population an ideal opportunity to live and work and to seek their satisfaction. Surely it would be a relatively simple matter to include such units in our system of social and economic life. But it isn't only a question of communes. In our socialist state we don't even have a real cooperative movement, that is, a system of collective economic undertaking.

I believe that each person must have the opportunity to realize his own ideals and concepts in all spheres of life, including the economic. Socialism cannot be regarded simply as socialization of means of production—in effect a bureaucratic nationalization—but rather as the creation of the greatest possible freedom for the realization of the plans and ideals of each individual.

We must remember that the form of socialism which we have realized in our country, and which was profaned by the Stalinist leadership, actually derives from a backward Russia of the nineteenth century. As a matter of fact, even classical socialism was marked by the ideas and philosophic attitudes of the mid-nineteenth century, including a certain worship of rationalism and scientific methodology. Think of the Utopian socialists who even planned the frequency of sexual intercourse per month, the prescribed themes for discussion during meals, and so on.

But is it really possible to create an optimal model, to calculate human happiness? I doubt it. In fact, I believe the very opposite; namely, that a completely calculated and rationalized life would bring about the death of society just as surely as total chaos would. People are not machines. The folly of this kind of thinking was particularly evident in the so-called scientific organization of culture.

How can culture be rationally directed? An environment conducive to culture cannot be calculated. Even if you surround an artist with wealth, which from a rational standpoint might be considered the best thing you could do for him, you are just as likely to destroy him as not. Forgive me, but if we are approaching the point in which man is totally predictable and calculable, I hope to die before this happy millennium is reached. Years ago, the slogan was: Away with religion! Religion is opium! Then came another slogan: The people must have an ideology! Very well then, an ideology. A scientific ideology. Culture, knowledge, education. It was all very rational. Too rational. It isn't surprising that scientific rationalism itself became a religion, for by trying to fill a need which was foreign to it the scientific basis was destroyed. I think that this transformation was imminent from the beginning, for scientific rational ideology shared the eschatological nature of religion. It offered salvation. And it worshipped a trinity: the Working Class, the Great Plan, Science. As soon as you proclaim a god before whom everybody is to bow down, you must begin to create a church with a multitude of priests and prophets. It is an eternally recurring process.

What can substitute for this new god?

Culture as an integrating force? That would be the same kind of nonsense. I think the solution is in *not* looking for a single integrating entity. Some people need culture, others religion, others nothing—or perhaps only a bed. Every attempt at integration must end in lack of freedom, not for a minority but for the majority. And in the creation of a new religion. A person may not even be aware that he has lost his freedom. He can be manipulated without knowing it; the emptiness can be filled in all kinds of ways—with the big beat, for example.

I said that socialism took over from religion the idea of building society in the image of a single god. In this respect it is a typically European development. My personal ideal of socialism is a polytheistic one; I believe that socialism is big enough to accommodate many gods. Socialism must give man the maximum freedom. In that sense it can truly become a higher step in the development of society. Of course, this also presupposes maximal development of productive capacity. Hungry people cannot build a free society.

We have just turned over a new leaf. In what ways do you think our current situation is really different?

We can now freely discuss almost all problems, many taboos have been lifted, and after a hiatus of twenty years we are now seeing signs of feverish activity. Such a period is extremely interesting, especially for a writer. In addition, we now have the hope that much of what we have stubbornly struggled for in the course of so many years may at last come to fruition. Perhaps we will even be able to associate with each other on the basis of what we want; up till now, the only common platform we had was agreement on what we *didn't* want.

This is quite new, that is true. But do we really have more freedom? Doesn't the new situation necessitate even greater internal limitations than before?

It is certainly a more demanding situation, and I have become very much aware how badly we are prepared to cope with it. Not just we, but the entire nation. The mountain of letters on the editor's desk clearly shows that, in this sense, society is still stuck in the morass of 1948, or even 1938.

But I certainly don't feel *less* free than before; I have been conscious of my inner responsibilities for a long time. Always, as a matter of fact. It is a good thing that a man can finally set his own limits, create his own sense of responsibility. I suppose this is the basis of human fate, of human freedom: self-definition. When somebody does it for you, you are a slave.

And culture?

It too will have the new experience of setting its own limits. Actually, though, every real creative artist had this sense before, too, and all those things I most respect in Czech and Slovak culture never recognized any other limits but their own.

But culture is the product of artists, and every nation has only a certain number of them—that number has neither increased nor decreased. We know that even under the conditions of the greatest tyranny there are people who succeed in expressing themselves, even though police terror naturally prevents broad dissemination of cultural products.

But what *has* changed, and drastically, is the role of all of us as citizens. We have all changed from passive observers to active participants. And this will certainly be reflected in art. By this I don't mean that it will have a positive effect on the peaks of artistic achievement; possibly quite the contrary. In revolutionary times all art slides back a bit. Society's demand for a certain type of art becomes more pressing and most artists tend to work extensively rather than intensively during such periods. I am almost certain, for example, that we are going to see a great deal of the so-called concentration camp literature from the 1950s. The critics will tend to favor it, there will be a reassessment of criteria, and so on. There are certain matters in the history of a nation which simply must find their way out into daylight.

I can't seem to get you to talk about the generations . . .

Recently a young lady submitted an article to me which tried to show that my generation had gone through so many changes, had become so skeptical and unenthusiastic that it would never wish to govern. I think this is true. Our generation has the feeling that whatever decisions it makes will turn out to be the wrong ones. We have learned through hard experience to consider all values as relative. The shift in values which we have watched with amazement through the years has created a certain amount of tolerance, skepticism, and lack of confidence in the correctness of any program. In addition, we are terribly deprived educationally, as I tried to demonstrate in my own case, and this may turn out to be a very dangerous failing. For every generation sometimes has power thrust upon it, and, if that generation happens to be undereducated, disaster looms ahead. On the other hand, in contrast to the so-called generation of the workers, which was very proud of its ignorance, the present one is quite aware of its handicap and many of its members try to catch up as best they can. Though most of us have passed the age when study is normally carried out.

Would you say something about the generation of our fathers? Nobody likes to talk about that.

Do you know why? What has happened in our country went far beyond problems of generations. International developments brought about violent upheavals and we cannot blame our fathers for having allowed these events to take place. What happened was a national tragedy. How can the problem of the generations be compared to it? The entire nation, all of us, were sacrificed at Munich, then again at Yalta, until I suppose there was no way to sacrifice us again. Perhaps our fathers might have resisted these catastrophes more directly and with greater moral courage, but there was nothing they could do to prevent them. I often feel sorry for them; life has given them a terrible beating.

And what about the young people?

I don't know too much about them, though lately I have had a little more contact with them. I like that passage in Kundera's *The Joke* in which he describes the teenager's need to assume a pose to conceal his lack of experience, his immaturity.

And then, too, it often seems to me—though this is perhaps all too obvious—that the young have neither strength nor a program. I am frightened by their political naïveté.

The past has maneuvered them into a pose of cynicism: "The

big beat is all that matters; we don't believe in anything." And yet
they have a tremendous longing for active ideas and positive values.
This worries me, for I think that they might be even more prone to
manipulation than we were, if someone comes along who knows
how to play on their fears. They grew up without any figures of
authority to emulate. There were no authorities within their reach
in our own country, and John Kennedy was too far away. If they
find somebody who gets up on the platform and knows how to deal
with them, they will hoist him up on their shoulders and march him
off all the way to the presidential palace, without asking who he is
or where he came from. Or whether he plans to chop off their little
heads the next day.

*I couldn't keep it back any longer, so finally I asked him the big
question: Now that they have taken us back into the party . . .*

Forgive me, but I can't talk about that. It is too complicated to
answer in a few sentences. I just want to note that, after a certain
age, a person's viewpoints are firm and hard to change, regardless of
whether he is inside a particular organized structure or not. And
perhaps a person who is determined to keep both his opinions and
his head may be better off outside an organization that insists on
conformity. Such an organization will always tend to have a simplistic attitude and to be influenced by tactical viewpoints and goals.
But as I said, the question is far too complex. I am sure that I will
return to it again. And probably more than once.

Spring 1968

Václav Havel

Born 1936 in Prague. Prevented because of his upper middle-class background from attending any institute of higher learning in the late 1950s and early 1960s, he worked at various jobs, including stage-hand in the theater whose house dramatist he later became. His plays *The Garden Party* and *The Memorandum* made him well known abroad. He also wrote some stories and experimental poetry as well as another play, *The Increased Difficulty of Concentration.* In 1968, Havel was the chief spokesman of a group of independent, nonparty writers within the Writers' Union. In his articles he presented the political views shared by many noncommunist socialists.

Václav Havel

He has a big picture-window facing Hradcany Castle, and a little alcove—I think that's what it's called—with a table and chairs. The windows of the Literarni Noviny *offices look out onto the same panorama, yet somehow I never pay much attention to the view, except when showing it off to a visitor from abroad. Then, too, ours is the most banal and picture-postcardlike in all Prague. Havel's isn't nearly as pretty but it's much more interesting, and whenever I visit his apartment I enjoy looking out of his window. Havel loves his apartment and wouldn't move anywhere else for anything in the world. And it seems to me that there is something about his alcove and his picture-window that is quite appropriate to the man, the blond, shy, boyish man I was interviewing in April 1968. I asked him what was currently on his mind.*

The main thing one thinks about these days is, of course, the current political situation. This is quite a new experience for me. I never bothered much with politics, I didn't think about political questions, but now I feel that it's impossible to stand on the sidelines; you're drawn in, whether you like it or not. I believe I have an advantage over the others you've interviewed so far; namely, that I can talk with absolute freedom. I am a little ashamed . . .

Is it really such an advantage?

I meant that we are talking at a time when we can say anything we please, whereas the others still felt the pressure—perhaps only subconsciously—to formulate their statements within certain permissible bounds.

I don't think that's true. None of the interviews was guided by the principle that what was said should necessarily be acceptable for publication.

I have always rejected compromise in this area, and if I can't say everything that I consider to be true I prefer to keep silent.

We started to talk about current freedom . . .

Of course, freedom is not so much a matter of the limits of possibility as it is a certain inner independence, which enables a person to surmount all such limits. Many people who talk quite freely today really aren't free at all. In other words, they are not expressing their own independent opinion, but merely repeating opinions that happen to be prevalent at the moment. Thus, they are as unfree as ever, though in another sense.

Principles that govern the cultural sphere are naturally different from political laws. Culture is concerned with truth; it tries to show reality as it is. Politics seeks to alter reality; it requires power and thus is generally a slave to it. Even when politics and culture exist in harmony, the two will always remain entirely different activities. The reason intellectuals make such poor politicians is that they are used to serving the interests of truth rather than using truth as a means of serving the needs of power. It is an open question whether intellectuals can ever play an active role in political life without becoming unfaithful to their main goal, which is truth. Politically engaged writers of previous generations frequently made the mistake of transgressing these boundaries, and in the end they failed to become either good writers or good politicians. It would be foolhardy to repeat their mistakes. Writers can play a political role insofar as they portray reality: they can sign petitions, but I cannot imagine myself joining a political party and working for it. It would put me into a schizophrenic situation. Of course, I am not referring to the internal politics that go on within artists' organizations; a writer should play his proper role in this area. However, even here the writer must keep a certain distance, a certain perspective.

I myself do not shirk this kind of "political" work in the Writers' Union, because I believe that I can manage to keep the kind of distance I've just mentioned. This, then, is the kind of politics a person can engage in without ceasing to be true to himself.

This was a very pressing problem of the day. Many people thought that writers unions and similar organizations should get directly involved in practical political life. After certain personal experiences, I had severe doubts on this score. I asked what his opinion was on this subject.

If these organizations help to ensure optimal conditions for the kind of creativity that is their members' real mission, then they will perform a valuable service for the nation. But as soon as they go beyond this point and engage in other kinds of activity, they lose all usefulness. I was involved within the Writers' Union in all sorts of projects designed to secure good conditions for literary development, such as the dissemination of a variety of literary publications, and so on. I considered such work highly important, and I often came in conflict with those who thought we should occupy ourselves with much broader matters, such as opposition to the government's cultural policy. In my opinion, this would have sapped our energy and diverted us from attainable goals to others hopelessly beyond our reach. Very often a small task successfully carried out can have far-reaching consequences, because it can serve as a model or catalyst for further action. I realized this quite clearly when *Tvar** was shut down. It was a small magazine with a circulation of only 3,500, virtually without influence. The battle for its survival seemed rather trivial to me, yet the very fact that such a battle was waged proved to have important ramifications. We demonstrated new ways of approaching problems of this sort, we held up a mirror to the customary way of doing things, we influenced many people. I am convinced that the solidarity of writers and other intellectuals that was demonstrated during the subsequent congress and the battle for *Literarni Noviny* had its origin in the *Tvar* affair. Many people who were rather slack at the start were encouraged to take a firmer stand. For many intellectuals, the story of *Tvar* caused a severe inner trauma and catalyzed the development of a new aware-

---

* Founded by the Czechoslovak Writers' Union in the early 1960s, *Tvar* was soon accused of spreading ideologically harmful ideas and was forced to stop publication.—*Ed.*

ness. Thus the struggle for relatively unimportant and "nonpoliti-
cal" goals can, under certain circumstances, have a very great—
and political—significance.

*Is there much difference in this regard between the situation as it
is now and as it was then? Don't you think that waging a struggle for
cultural policy in the broadest sense proved to be useful, after all?*

I think this is simply a matter of tactics. Personally, I am still
convinced that rather than tell the party how to conduct cultural
politics and rather than present abstract plans that have little
chance of being adopted, it is far better to present actual examples
of success. To show government leaders on a small scale what they
should be doing on a large scale; to stop making theoretical statements about health and administer a small dose of penicillin instead.

Let us return to *Tvar* for a moment. At the meeting of the Central Committee of the Czechoslovak Writers' Union in Bratislava,
where the matter came up for discussion, a number of people
wanted to save *Tvar* but only within the framework of a broader
criticism of our cultural policies. They came forward with certain
complex documents suggesting changes in the cultural orientation
of the party. What happened? They failed to save *Tvar,* and the
party rejected their proposals. If instead of making broad proposals
they had simply insisted on the continuation of *Tvar,* which would
have been a clearly defined and plausible objective, they might have
been more successful in influencing the party's orientation. A political act would have become a model. In cultural politics, actions
always speak louder than words and manifestos. Politics is not concerned with defining attitudes, but in changing reality.

I certainly don't think, on the other hand, that artistic organizations should not express themselves on broad political questions
affecting the entire society. But only on the appropriate level, on
the level of truth, whether the subject be Poland, Israel, or anything else. Emphasis on general principles, however, must never
stand in the way of concrete action. For example, the Fourth Congress brought up some very important matters; it was good that
they were discussed, but unfortunately this general criticism was
not followed up by those concrete steps that it was well within our
power to take: the creation of new journals, modernization of
statutes, election of officials, and execution of various other internal

tasks. I believe it is important to sweep one's own doorstep clean before doing anything else. It is absurd to attack dogmatism in general while it remains entrenched in our own committees.

All the same, the congress did play a societal role . . .

History has shown that everything that was said at the congress was essentially correct and that, eventually, it played a large role. But I was bothered by the fact that many of the broad principles that were presented found no application within the Writers' Union itself. And so it seemed to me that whatever progressive results came out of the meetings could be attributed not so much to the organization as to a few individuals, who utilized the congress to express themselves without censorship. But this isn't the real purpose of the organization. If it were, we might just as well disband it, now that censorship is no longer a problem.

What, then, should be the political purpose of the Writers' Union?

Insofar as we think of political activity in terms of sending our own representatives to parliament, attempting to promote someone from our own ranks as Minister of Culture, and so forth—I think that such efforts are mistaken. Of course, individual members have a perfect right to conduct such activity on their own, but I don't think the union should be involved. I don't believe that a society of artists should try to partake of state power. It is, of course, better if a director of a publishing house happens to be an enlightened writer rather than an appointed bureaucrat, but that is another matter.

A few years ago, Vaclav Havel and I sat perched on the marble-topped bar in the foyer of the Na Zabradli *theater, engaged in a discussion about absurdist drama with the theater audience. After a while, Havel asked me with his characteristic shy smile to excuse him because he had to go to a lecture at the drama institute. "What are you lecturing on?" I asked him. He smiled again. "I am not lecturing, I am a student." I stared at him in disbelief, for this was long after the opening of his play* The Garden Party; *he had completed the final version of* The Memorandum *and his name was beginning to be known throughout Europe. "Why, for heaven's sake?" I asked him. "Well, you know, I applied for admission many years ago, and*

they turned me down a few times. Last year they finally accepted me
and I didn't want them to think that success had gone to my
head . . ." I found this extremely funny, but later I realized that it
was quite characteristic of Havel. Now, when I reminded him of the
episode, we both laughed. He said:

Last year I finally graduated from that institute.

As you know, my father was an entrepreneur. He was a co-owner
of Lucerna [a large complex of buildings in Prague] and owned
various restaurants, and my uncle was a founder of the Barrandov
film studios. The family was thus quite bourgeois, perhaps upper
middle class. I mention this only in connection with my origins, for
such things undoubtedly have a bearing on the development of
one's mental outlook. I was born in 1936. The atmosphere at home
was more intellectual than is often the case, especially through the
influence of my mother's father who was an engineer, newspaperman, diplomat, even briefly a cabinet minister, and a bit of a writer
as well. This sort of background naturally exerted its influence
quite early; when I was nine years old I was set on becoming a scientist, politician, or journalist. This was in the crucial year of 1945.

But my so-called bourgeois origin had other consequences, as
well. During the war we were bombed out of our apartment. I left
with my parents for Moravia, where I went to school with village
children and, thanks to my family, had a privileged position among
them. I enjoyed various advantages; I was better dressed; I was a
kind of fat little model child from the city, somewhat spoiled, and
accompanied by a governess. I felt the gulf between the village kids
and myself. I was ashamed; I cried every time I was given some new
privilege. Why do I talk about this? Because apparently this was the
time during which I developed my sense of shame and my fear of
people. As a result of all these privileges I actually felt inferior. To
this day I feel this estrangement, this distance from the world
around me. Whenever I tried to create the opposite impression it
was always an attempt to compensate for my lack of confidence.
These traits also explain to some extent some aspects of my writing.
They also explain my life-long affinity for Kafka, for his sense of
isolation and alienation from the world. I understand the desire to
become accepted by the world, to gain the natural sense of belonging, and at the same time I am aware that this goal is forever beyond one's reach. The sense of absurdity, as it is called, stems from

the same source. The desperate striving to bridge the gulf between the world and oneself, to become part of the world, to attain a certain legitimacy—all this is nothing else but an attempt to find one's own meaning. One's own meaning, and consequently universal meaning as well. The constant inner tension between this desire on one hand and a certain inner conviction that the goal is destined never to be attained lead one to see the world as an absurdity deprived of meaning. Naturally, I am not sure whether this self-explanation on the basis of childhood experience may not be somewhat artificial, but I think that it is basically correct insofar as it is possible to see oneself with any objectivity at all.

After the February change-over, when I was twelve years old, a new situation emerged. The class struggle was directed against my family and, of course, against myself as well. That was a most valuable bit of education, for which I shall always be grateful both to my bourgeois ancestry as well as to the new regime. Continually rejected and ejected, I was continually forced to accept the worst among a set of alternatives; as a result, I was able to see everything from the very bottom. Reaction to reality became an automatic reflex for me. I was forced to come to grips with reality; in short, to use a cliché, I was forced to learn about life. If it hadn't been for February, I probably would have graduated from the English gymnasium, gone on to study philosophy at the university, attended Professor Cerny's lectures on comparative literature, and after graduation I would have ridden around in an imported sports car without having done the least thing to deserve it. In short, I would have been a cross between an educated man—far more educated than I am now—and a member of the *jeunesse doré*. I doubt, however, that I would have become a writer. In any case, my former alternatives were irrevocably closed to me. I went to school until the age of fourteen, then did manual work for a number of years. I thus learned no foreign languages and my education was quite sketchy, but on the other hand my segregated state continually forced me to transcend my own limitations. That's how I began to write. When I was about fifteen years old, a couple of friends and I founded the society known as the Thirty-sixers which was active for about three years. We organized seminars on politics, economics, and literature, put out a typewritten magazine, and in general tried to make up through our own initiative for outlets and stimulations of which we had been deprived. This proved to be quite

valuable for the formation of our minds and for finding our own
orientation.

(*It occurred to me that this situation was actually quite similar
to the one our generation faced at the beginning of the occupation.
We, too, formed similar groups and societies when we were in our
teens. The big difference was that we were searching for various
broad ideological solutions, whereas these young people naturally
took a different road . . .*)

I must say that I had more or less the same attitude toward the
contemporary situation—the period of the purges—as I do now;
I never saw the dictatorship of the early postwar years as a reasonable alternative to the former regime. I want to stress, however, that
this was not the result of any special moral exertion or clairvoyance
on my part, but a rather predictable result of my position, education, family background, and so on. Secondly—and this is very important—even though I was critical of the prevailing state of affairs
I hadn't the slightest desire to see a restitution of my father's former
property. I was always in favor of socialism in the sense of nationalization of major means of production. Perhaps it may seem like
opportunism for me to say this today, or then again perhaps not, I
don't know. But my socialist convictions never had their origin in
a desire to form a bridge between myself and contemporary developments. Such a bridge never existed, nor was there the slightest
possibility that it ever would. Rather, I believe that my socialist
leanings originated in my early childhood and in my sense of shame
for the privileges which I then enjoyed. This is certainly not a very
unique case. The most radical socialists often come from precisely
this type of background.

As a worker, I attended evening classes at a gymnasium for working people, which in itself was rather an absurd experience. These
evening courses were intended for foremen and proletarian leaders
rather than for the sons of the bourgeoisie. But in 1951 all of these
things were just in their beginnings, so that I escaped scrutiny;
before the directives that would have ended my further schooling
were issued, I already had a diploma in my pocket. After I graduated, in 1954, I wanted to study philosophy at the university; I
applied mainly as a matter of principle, however, knowing perfectly
well that I would not be accepted. I was refused admittance once
again the following year, and so in the end I enrolled in the only
field of study in which they were willing to accept me: a course on

the logistics of motor transport. After two years, convinced of the error of my move, I tried in vain to transfer to the cinema faculty, and shortly thereafter I was called up for military service. When I returned from the army I applied for admittance to the drama faculty, again in vain, and finally—as a favor to a friend—Jan Werich [actor, playwright, filmmaker, and outstanding satirist] got me a job as a stagehand at the ABC Theater. In 1960, I switched to the *Na Zabradli* theater, first as a stagehand, then doing a variety of other jobs until eventually I worked my way up to my present job as cultural adviser and reader of new plays. The drama school accepted me as a student at the very moment when I became a playwright. I graduated last year, along with children ten years younger than I am. I looked like a gentleman who attended the school in order to pick up young girls . . .

Around 1952 I started writing poetry. I played the role of a poet who refused to allow his work to be published. This pose was rather ridiculous, considering my age at the time. Today, of course, I am glad my poems weren't published; they were probably rather stupid. At that time my friends and I also systematically sought out certain writers who interested us. We visited Seifert. I met Holan, I became friendly with Zabrana, Kolar, Grossmann, Chalupecky, Hirsal, Hrabal, and others. These contacts, which I developed at such an early age, later proved to be extremely significant.

(Once again memories of the occupation came to mind—a certain villa in Dejvice, a garret in the Lucerna, people who meant so much to me. It was all so similar and yet so different. Some day, perhaps . . .)

These were mostly writers who were not publishing at the time . . .

(Just like during the occupation.)

. . . And for me as a young man all of this had the atmosphere of a secret adventure. For example, when I finally tracked down Jiri Kolar, whose books I loved, and found him "under the ice of the age," in Pasternak's words.

(That's just how we used to hunt for the novelist Ivan Olbracht or the poet Frantisek Halas, both eminent Communists!)

Kolar was writing some remarkable things at the time, which are still unpublished—a kind of anthology of the period, based on the confrontation of myths with the realities of contemporary life. Around 1957, when things started to change, we began to engage in a certain amount of public activity. We tried to arrange for group publication in [the short-lived Writers' Union monthly] *Kveten* (without any luck, since the editors didn't find us too interesting and since *Kveten* was about to be shut down anyway). We also arranged an evening of poetry; we collaborated with Kolar, and such writers as Hrabal, Skvorecky, Vera Linhartova, and Josef Topol were on the program.

My interest in theater began while I was still in the army. As a result of a kind of race discrimination based on class, I was serving with the army engineers, and the only opportunity for occasional escape was work in the theater. In a production we did of Pavel Kohout's *September Nights* I played the villainous role of Lieutenant Skovranek. As soon as my company commander saw my performance, he started persecuting me; he told me that in his mind I had become so identified with the role I was playing that he had been able to grasp my true nature at last. And he took away my honorary title as chairman of the youth organization in the company.

The second year we didn't know what to do, so we wrote the play *Life Before Us.* We deliberately wrote it so it would be the last word in socialist realism; we did it as a kind of gag and included a tremendous number of male roles in the play so as many of our pals as possible could be in it and goldbrick for a while. We won one contest after another; we got all the way up to the final round in the competition before a certain colonel—now the head of the national circus organization—finally unmasked us as the authors of an essentially antimilitary play that failed to bring out the importance of the party organization in the army. We were quite amused by the whole affair, because, as I said, the play was deliberately written to fulfill all the current criteria to the letter. But since these criteria constantly changed, we had set ourselves an impossible goal. The upshot of all this was that we returned to civilian life with quite unfavorable records.

I'll never understand how it happened that after this tragi-comic episode I didn't abandon theater forever but instead began to devote myself to it quite seriously. The fact is, though, that I promptly started to write *The Memorandum.* It took until 1965 for it to be performed, but the first version dates back to 1959. At that time there not only was no hope of its being performed, but friends even warned me against keeping a copy of the play in the house. What I am trying to point out is that, although my plays were eventually performed during a period when there was a great vogue for satire, they weren't conceived of as deliberate attempts to exploit a particular situation; instead, they represented a happy coincidence. Even when I was writing the military play as a gag, I knew and loved Ionesco and Beckett, and *The Memorandum* was deliberately written as a drama of the absurd. But as soon as the critics locked me into this category, I began to defend myself against such rigid attempts at pigeonholing. I write as I please, and it makes no difference to me whether my work is absurd, realistic, tragic, comic, or satirical; the less capable it is of being categorized, the happier I am.

In what way does your work differ from Western drama of the absurd?

I believe that domestic and foreign critics are correct when they point out that my work reflects a greater interest in social reality than is the case in the classical theater of the absurd. I suppose that people write about what most provokes them and I was always provoked by the problems of society.

At the same time, I think that my "socialness" belongs to quite a different category than the politically oriented plays of certain authors belonging to the older generation. The older playrights seem to have started with an *a priori* political viewpoint, a personal political history, interest, ideal. These *a priori* conceptions serve first of all as a filter through which reality is perceived, then as a principle on the basis of which reality is rearranged, and finally as part of the message which the artistic work is designed to transmit. In contrast to this type of political engagement (whose main representatives in Czech film are people like Jan Kadar and Elmar Klos), I consider the political content of my plays merely as part of a normal interest in the political side of contemporary reality. The world surrounds me and I witness it, report on it, and this report naturally includes testimony on the political side of things. That's why I have called the edition of my collected plays *Protocols*. In its own way my presentation of reality naturally involves a certain amount of interpretation, but it is based solely on contemporary life without any preconceived ideological framework. To return to examples from the cinema—the two poles are represented by Kadar–Klos [*Shop on Main Street*] on one side and Jan Nemec [*The Party and the Guests*] on the other.

The other point is this: even when I make use of concrete attitudes, events, and actions, I am not interested in them merely for their own sake, but they become a means for presenting certain societal or human mechanisms. When I use metaphors, similes, or codes, my purpose is not to fool the censor who might be more amenable to indirect expression. No, I use a metaphor because it enables me to suggest a much broader and multifaceted reality; it allows me to speak more forcefully and effectively.

In *The Memorandum* I worked a bit like a pop art painter who takes concrete segments of reality and arranges them in fantastic structures. The play not only includes direct quotes, such as the statement by Antonin Novotny that we mustn't be too subservient to the facts, but I also tried to incorporate certain key situations and attitudes of the past forty years. The method used was that of free-wheeling connections and associations; for example, there are references to the catastrophic end of Benes-type humanism, the analogy between Munich and the February change-over, and so on. And, of course, the incomplete and rather superficial renaissance we observed ten or twelve years ago. All this interests and inspires me, but it isn't the real meaning of the play. That meaning is perhaps something more generally valid and applicable.

The problem of alienation in contemporary society?

I think that's more closely connected with my last play. I agree with the critics, however, who have pointed out that this problem plays an important role in the first two plays as well. Those were concerned with alienation caused by societal mechanisms. The ultimate root of the alienation of modern man goes much deeper than that. It originates in the ever-increasing tension between the scientific and technical approaches to reality on one hand and the real needs and possibilities of human individuality on the other. We possess more and more data about man, about society, about ourselves, yet the picture of the world which this scientific knowledge gives us is becoming less and less applicable to our own lives. The question of the meaning of our lives puzzles us more and more; we face the task of self-realization with ever greater helplessness and hopelessness. This sense of alienation is universal throughout the

civilized world. In the West, technology represents a real and tremendously expanding power. Ours is not nearly as developed and
yet, paradoxically, technology is supposed to be the ultimate basis
on which our society rests and we are forever stressing the scientific
nature of all our undertakings and solutions. Thus, the emphasis
placed on science and technology is the same in both worlds, and so,
too, is the consequent alienation. The only difference is that our
alienation seems a bit more comical. That's why I don't believe the
theory that our alienation is not real and that the capitalists somehow suffer from "more alienated alienation." That's strictly an
ideological interpretation. I think that, just as there is only one kind
of freedom, democracy and justice, so, too, there is only one kind
of alienation.

To repeat, then: in my earlier plays I was concerned with the
superficial aspect of the problem, whereas in my last play I tried to
get to the root of alienation in terms of the universal conflicts I have
just described. This last play is probably less attractive to our audiences because it lacks the immediacy which the specific political
allusions gave to the older works.

During the last few months a number of foreign journalists have
asked me whether I thought my plays hadn't lost their timeliness,
in view of the fact that they were written for a specific purpose during a specific era. "What do you intend to do now?" they often asked.
I had to point out a very curious fact: *The Garden Party* and *The
Memorandum* are much more popular now than they were a year
or so ago. People are laughing at lines they hadn't laughed at before,
and in general it seems as though the two plays excite people more
than ever. I explain this phenomenon to myself as follows: in both
plays I tried to demonstrate the debacle that meets attempts to
regenerate a system by half-hearted methods that fail to get to the
root of the trouble. This necessarily leads to half-hearted attempts
which, in turn, only lead to a repetition of earlier failures; obsolete
methods are replaced by newer methods that are doomed to the
same ultimate breakdown since the basic approach has not been
altered. The situation in our country at this time is fluid and open.
The regenerative process in which we serve as witnesses and participants may collapse like its predecessors—or it may succeed. If
my plays show the first alternative, then the image they depict—
namely, an image of catastrophe—takes on a special timeliness at
present, for it acts as a challenge, a warning, an appeal to people to

do everything in their power to help realize the second alternative. It is an appeal to get to the very roots of our society and to make the basic changes that are essential if we are to avoid simply exchanging one set of clichés for another.

You said that you feel close to Ionesco and Beckett, and you also pointed out how you differ from them. Sometimes it seems to me that you are actually much more closely related to the authors of English theater of the absurd and to its long and ancient tradition.

I like the English theater of the absurd very much, and it is quite close to me. In fact, the entire tradition of English and Irish humor, with its emphasis on vitality and mystery—from Shakespeare to Sterne, Swift, Joyce, and now Stoppard—is much more exciting to me than the rather dry and rationalistic French tradition. This is probably a bit of overcompensation, too, since I myself have a strong sense of order along the French lines and thus am keenly aware of the dangers inherent in this attitude. It is certainly no accident that the mysterious Beckett is not a Frenchman but an Irishman. I consider Stoppard, Pinter, and Ann Jellicoe among the most influential playwrights in Europe. To a lesser extent, N. F. Simpson ...

You were among the first to introduce the themes of Czech and Slovak culture to contemporary European thought ...

I don't want to talk about the importance of our culture or the value of my own contribution. I really know too little about this subject. But I know some émigrés, especially in Munich. The basic situation in which they find themselves is quite odd. On the one hand, they feel a tremendous longing for their homeland. That cannot be disregarded. They read newspapers and magazines, listen to our broadcasts, and have an understandably strong desire to return for a visit. On the other hand, their personal political experience continually influences them against their homeland, and so they find themselves in conflict. (It is characteristic of every emigration that it tends to conserve those aspects of national life which existed at the time the emigration took place. For example, if we read anything written by the first postwar émigrés, we find that they still use the language of 1947, and we become aware of the changes that have since taken place in the language. This was always quite striking in the case of Czech-Americans; it is equally true of more recent émigrés. Their thinking and language are continually influenced by their new environment, and thus they cannot evolve in harmony with the changing conditions and attitudes at home.)

The basic situation under which the émigrés left—they either fled or were driven out by the communists—made such a deep impression on them that they are unable to summon the magnanimity needed to transcend their conflict with the new regime. As a result of the mutual suspicions which emigration tends to nourish, fellow émigrés are accused of collaborating with hostile forces—yet in a sense they are all collaborating, and sometimes to an even greater extent than the people at home. Their knowledge of what life is like now in this country is limited to what they read or hear on the radio. And whenever knowledge is received at second-hand—entirely from literature or information media—it is bound to be distorted. It leads to a certain way of "decoding" texts, a method which the émigré believes leads to discovery of reality. But since he is restricted to these texts and has no way of confronting them with material representing other viewpoints, he creates all sorts of artificial "keys" which have no relation to reality. Thus, I have known émigrés who have pored over piles of third-rate books and journals —publications I'd never even heard of before—in the hope of tracking down the truth about important developments at home. Ideas generated in this way are sure to be distorted. Yet even the émigrés must realize that a number of changes have taken place during the last twenty years and that the nation can no longer be neatly divided into evil party officials and good democrats. Naturally they support everything that promises to speed a restoration of democracy, and, hampered by their lack of information, they often mistake quite superficial or temporary phenomena as basic and significant. This is how that strange tension between affection for the homeland and resentment comes about; their own political history is continually being resurrected in its frozen, preserved form.

There is another important aspect to this matter. The habit of "decoding" texts, when applied to literature and art, necessarily leads to an overpoliticized and overideologized approach. For this reason, many émigrés no longer consider it important whether a work of art is good or bad, they no longer examine it with the criteria of art, but regard it solely from the viewpoint of how it affects our political life or what it has to say about political events.

This leads to a paradoxical situation. As a member of the younger generation and relatively unencumbered by immediate postwar history, I find myself facing the same difficulty in communicating with émigrés as I do in communicating with middle-aged people at home. Like the émigrés, members of the older generation at home look at art, culture, and everything else much too politically, and they continually filter reality through ideologic interpretations. Interpretations should follow reality...

A basic Marxist axiom, my generational imp whispered in my ear.

... whereas these people do the opposite. And I am not thinking of dogmatists or officials, but of creative people who are quite progressive, who are in the midst of things, support reasonable goals, have a positive influence on developments, and are, in fact, in many ways far more revolutionary than I am.

All the same, the similarity between the kind of dialogue I have with middle-aged communists here and with émigrés of the same age abroad is quite striking. Sometimes the similarity extends to surprising lengths. One of our communists, when he was twenty, worked on youth construction projects, while an émigré of the same age worked for Radio Free Europe. Each recalls his youthful experiences with a good deal of sentimentality, each knows that the philosophy represented by his particular project is no longer viable under today's conditions, yet neither is able to shake off the perspective of his early experience. And in this way a highly comical situation arises, in which these polemics are conducted on both sides of the barricade—and I'm not sure which of these barricades is bigger: the ideological or the generational.

Life-experience at the age of twenty leaves an indelible mark on a person's outlook, and I can't blame my discussion partners for being what they are. I know perfectly well that in a few years I will be in the same position with respect to my juniors. Whether we live here or abroad, whether we're young or old, it seems that all of us are subordinated to one law: the state of society at the time of our first awakening, at the time of our first attempts at political and personal self-realization, determines our basic outlook for the rest of our lives. And so whatever theme Skvorecky, for example, may choose, he always presents the atmosphere, mental attitudes, and problems characteristic of the period betwen the end of the war and the early 1950s. Or consider Hrabal, who always tends to suggest the atmosphere of the occupation. For my part—if I may include myself in such august company—I shall always be in some sense linked to the pseudodialectical tension between dictatorship and the thaw, between Stalinism and de-Stalinization, which was characteristic of the year 1956 when I was twenty years old.

It seems like a rather strange game: the spectators have left long ago, the bleachers are empty, and yet out on the field the two teams are still engaged in their eternal contest, or rather pseudocontest, in the belief that the outcome is of tremendous significance. Sentiment binds them to a time when it all started, and yet their intelligence tells them that what really matters now are other games in other arenas. Failure to come to grips with this situation results in eternal vacillation and half-heartedness.

The curse of the generation?

That is, of course, a very broad generalization, and too often a certain part of a generation tries to act as spokesman for the whole. All the same I believe that even though members of a particular generation may assume differing positions at different times, they have an essentially common outlook formed during the period of their youth. People who are now in their forties belong to many different camps. But the real marks of division of this generation are not quite clear. On the whole, people who reached their adulthood during the war years saw in the advent of communism the only sensible solution; they accepted communism as it then was and, by and large, enthusiastically joined in the task of building a new system. As time went on, discord among the members of this generation became more and more pronounced, and recently this disquiet took the form of opposition against the ruling political power. Nevertheless, in spite of all the disharmony and conflicts, the generation continued to be bound to the regime by a kind of umbilical cord; this cord may have been Marxism, ideology, party loyalty, or simply ingrained habits of political thinking. The conflict with the regime was expressed mainly in terms of disappointment over the professed aims of the government and its actual accomplishments.

Then there was the other part of the generation which refused from the very start to identify with the regime, or with which the regime refused to identify. Of course, we know very little about these people, because, through being deprived of education and the right of political expression, this part of the generation was completely atomized, so that now we can only deal with it in terms of isolated representatives. Despite the fact that the division between the two major segments of the "middle" generation is still a real and painful phenomenon, as I said earlier I believe that there are certain distinct common characteristics which characterize this generation as a whole.

In my own dialogue with the older generation, I naturally talk most often with members of its communist segment. I will therefore concentrate on these "old communists" to illustrate the major differences separating the generations today.

The basic conflict is not concerned with differences in political outlook or ideological explanation of the world. Such a conflict is more characteristic of the tensions within the older generation itself. No, it seems to me that I part company with my elders in quite a different sense, as if I had a different way of posing basic questions. They seem to approach reality by way of certain abstract categories, which seem to them to have great significance and to reflect concrete experience, though, in fact, the reality on which these categories are based has been undergoing constant flux. On the other hand, I believe that members of my generation tend to start from reality as it exists at the moment; they form general concepts on the basis of this reality and disregard categories which seem to have lost their relevance and which function more as incantations than as concepts. I personally don't care a bit about such questions as what is communism, how do you define Marxism or socialism, what constitutes a political party, what is the nature of politics, and so on. Instead, I am deeply concerned with the question of whether a particular concrete event or act is in itself, on the basis of my experience, good or bad. This is what I mean: I am surrounded by certain phenomena with which I completely identify and which I consider to be correct and useful, while there are others with which I shall never be able to identify and which I consider absurd. Naturally, this applies not only to external reality but also to specific ideas. To ponder such problems as to which of these phenomena is more communist and which is less communist, which is more socialist, which is more Marxist—this, it seems to me, is an absolutely useless activity that can only lead to the kind of mystical verbal juggling made notorious by the party bureaucracy. Insofar as I can, I try to distinguish justice from injustice, honesty from dishonesty, mental acuity from mental vacuity; and just as an idea is not made any better or worse by being labeled Marxist, so the moral aspect of the political trials of the 1950s was not altered one iota by the fact that they were carried out in the name of the party. I am simply trying to escape from the labyrinth of categories, headings, and pigeonholes and to look at things in their existential urgency. I suppose that's the basic difference between myself and my elders.

It is difficult to generalize about the new generation, too; it is difficult to describe it as a unit. It isn't organized or homogeneous, but I believe that the dislike of ideological interpretations and the desire to see reality in its raw essence is a characteristic trait. This direct attitude has its historical explanation in the destruction of class categories, the failure of ideologies. The contrast between the elimination of social injustice and the methods by which this was achieved also plays an important role. In short, we have witnessed both the completion of a social task as well as its profanation.

Among the members of my generation there are, of course, people of all kinds of political orientation, including both communists and noncommunists (though the number of communists has diminished), but the basic nonideological mode of seeing the world serves as a unifying trait. In the sphere of art this is reflected by the fact that members of my generation appear less political than their elders, less engaged, to have a greater tendency to accept art for its own sake.

In literature, the people who are closest to me and who seem to express this common generational affinity most clearly include Josef Topol and Vera Linhartova. (This approach is also characteristic of a number of other writers with whom I am less familiar, such as Vladimir Paral as well as members of the former staff of *Tvar*.)

What about people even younger than you?

In the circle I move in I am aware of differences between myself and people who are only five years younger than I am. (*This had been already mentioned by Kundera, who observed that in situations of great historical tension the interval between generations may be only five years or even less.*) The difference lies in the fact that they weren't directly involved in the events of the 1950s. Of course, there is a much more significant difference in the life-style of my generation and people ten years younger—today's students, for example. I am extremely interested in their way of thinking; I look for opportunities to come in contact with their attitudes and to get close to them, which often, of course, turns out to be a pretty futile enterprise. (A parenthetical remark: A member of the older generation can gain great respect among the young, not when he tries to emulate them but when he remains himself; of course, he must at the same time show an openness toward other attitudes and conduct a dialogue with them. Halas is an excellent example of someone with these abilities.) I am not yet able to formulate the difference in attitude between my contemporaries and this new generation. It seems to me that essentially they are in harmony with the ideas of my generation but try to carry them even further toward their logical conclusion. They have moved so far in this direction that, in the end, I myself stand accused of the same subservience to ideology, the same resentment toward the 1950s, the same tendency to compromise, and the same "politicalness" that repel me in my elders. I became aware of this when I came in contact with the concepts and thoughts of today's student movement. These people not only reject all *a priori* ideological filters, just as I do, but in contrast to myself they even refuse to confront people who use such filters to try to convict them of their dependence on ideology or mystification. In short, they refuse to have anything to do with them. Their attraction to concrete reality is far more radical than was the case before. Man is for them the sole measure of society, government, the world—and not just theoretically but in a very practical sense as well. The case of one of their unjustly treated colleagues mobilized them to an infinitely greater degree than all the action programs, theses, conventions, and whatever. And yet one cannot say that their sense of organization or their political engagement has suffered as a result. On the contrary. It seems to me that despite the apparent naïveté of their formulations they are far more sophisticated than we think. For example, when a certain leader declared that the students wanted their "own human program," the statement superficially seemed quite meaningless, yet in the context of today's situation it was simultaneously an extremely concrete demand and a tactical method of self-definition. And if this same student declared that "we are supporting Dubcek because he needs our help at the moment, but this isn't necessarily our final position," this rather strange way of putting things contained more political insight as well as a stronger distaste for compromise than many sophisticated debates that I carry on with my friends. Of course, it is possible that I put more meaning into this thing than is actually there; there is a kind of psychological complex that starts to operate when one first comes in contact with a newer and fresher generational attitude. So I will conclude with the words of the just-cited student leader: "This isn't necessarily my last word."

I hoped it wouldn't be as far as this talk was concerned. So I asked him a question that had long been on my mind: This interest in concrete, direct reality after so many years of ideological "filtering" —will it stimulate a great new wave of social literature, social art, of a naturalistic or at least highly realistic character?

It seems highly likely. For twenty years, man disappeared in the name of humanity. The natural reaction will be to see man as an individual, and in this way to examine the social structure in which he is placed, his private life, marriage, children, material conditions. Soon we may be able to write about things as they really are, which is a most attractive prospect. I believe that a new type of social realism will emerge, as well as a new psychological realism, sounding and exploring the unexplored. We shall define the reality that surrounds us in a more concrete way. Of course, this will take place in all spheres of life, not just within literature. In the area of politics, for example, the most concise and most concretely formulated program will have the greatest chance of success. In the end, we can succeed only on the basis of concrete reality, specific contexts. The de-ideologized attitude which I have mentioned will enable us to find solutions, even if only in limited ways.

They say that the wisest thing is to keep silent. But that's a very simple-minded point of view.

Now he was no longer polemicizing with me and my generation, but with someone else, known only to himself.

By expressing our opinions, we are constantly engaging in new adventures in the world and with the world. Whoever fails to do this fails to be alive.

We tried to live life to the full during that open-ended episode that started in 1968. And I thought of those people who had deluded themselves into believing that Havel was an exception, that he was an atypical and borderline phenomenon, and not a true representative of his generation. That is a mistake, a tremendous mistake and mystification. On the contrary, Havel expresses the feelings of his generation with absolute clarity across the lines of politics and other loyalties. And he speaks for the generation that follows him, too. Whoever fails to understand this will be played out and no more use to this country.

Spring 1968

Karel Kosík

Born 1926 in Prague. He is a philosopher and professor at Charles University, Prague. Since the late 1950s he has taken part in public discussions and magazine polemics concerning basic existential problems, in which he presented a modern and liberal concept of Marxism. Because of his views, he has been continuously under fire from orthodox ideologists. At the Fourth Writers' Congress he made a speech defining the role and responsibility of the intellectual. His most important work, translated into many languages, is *The Dialectic of the Concrete.*

Epilogue

Karel Kosík

Czechoslovak culture in general, and literature in particular, has a very intimate connection with the development of socialism in our country. During the past decade Czech and Slovak writers have played a truly extraordinary role. How would you explain this?

I am not sure whether a critical survey of the literature of the past decade can be expressed within the framework of that question. At this moment—early in the summer of 1968—we find ourselves in a rather unusual political situation. We lack the distance which we need if we are to orient ourselves. As yet, we don't have the perspective to distinguish between those aspects of our culture that represent only a superficial response to the immediate situation, and those that have real artistic merit which will enable them to live. I would rather leave this matter open. Only time will tell where the true, pure values really lie.

There is another question that intrigues me; namely, why our culture proved to be so effective, so vital. There was definite cross-fertilization between literature, art, and philosophy, so that we can truly speak of culture in the broadest sense of the word. I am not saying this because I am a philosopher, but because there was a particular cultural "common denominator" which emerged during the last few years and which manifested itself especially clearly in our cinema. During this period, Czechoslovak culture focused its attention on existential human problems, and the "common denominator" was the question: What is Man?

The causes of this phenomenon can be traced from a variety of viewpoints. For example: Why were philosophers so fascinated by Czechoslovak films, plays, novels, and poems, and why did they take such an active part in their interpretation? Apparently it was because they encountered in these works the very same problems they themselves had long been contemplating. By interpreting these works and commenting on them, they were thus actually answering their own questions by means of material supplied by others.

The fundamental reality of Czech culture hinged on the question: What is man? That is its political, critical, revolutionary essence. It did not consist of subtle political allusions nor explicit criticism of the political situation nor of veiled attacks on government leaders. Those were superficial, ephemeral things. The real, fundamental polemic of our culture lay in the fact that against the official—one might say "reigning"—concept of Man, it put forth an entirely different concept of its own. Thus, our culture attacked the ruling bureaucratic regime not in its secondary aspects, but in its very core and essence.

Perhaps I should clarify what I mean by the official concept of Man. I do not have in mind any theoretically and deliberately formulated portrait of Man. Rather, I am referring to a concept of Man implicit in the regime's political, economic, and moral functioning, one which was, at the same time, mass-produced by the regime because it required precisely this sort of human being. After all, people are not born as ambitious career-seekers, blind to the needs of others, unthinking, unfeeling, prone to demoralization; rather, a certain system requires such people for its smooth functioning, and so it creates them. Parenthetically, it may be worth remarking that the members of the ruling political group in Czechoslovakia, who were in a sense the archetypes for their own concept of Man, did not know how to laugh and considered laughter totally irreconcilable with their political position.

In dealing with the question "What is Man?" culture naturally formulated its answer quite differently. While the official view saw human characteristics in terms of Man's limits, emptiness, simplicity, and lack of dynamism, Czech culture emphasized Man as a complex creature, continually active, elastic, striving to overcome conflicts, a being irreducible to a single dimension. The fact that culture began to emphasize such basic aspects of human existence as the grotesque, the tragic, the absurd, death, laughter, conscience, and moral responsibility did not simply mean that these aspects suddenly reappeared in everyday life. Rather, the official ideology had simply refused to acknowledge their existence. Thus, official Marxist Man never died because ideology refused to acknowledge death; in fact, he didn't even have a body, since official ideology didn't recognize Man's physical nature. Furthermore, such an official man had no conscience, since this category likewise did not officially exist.

A man who has no conscience, who doesn't die, who cannot laugh, who is unaware of personal responsibility—such a man is of course the perfect unit needed in a manipulated, bureaucratically regimented system. In contrast, Man as portrayed by Czech culture of the last decade is a potential revolutionary, because he finds life in such a manipulated system unbearable.

This relationship between art and philosophy, whereby philosophy interprets art and looks to art for the solution of its own questions—this is, surely, a fairly general phenomenon. In what do you see its specifically Czechoslovak quality?

I suppose the way that our philosophy took part in contemporary political polemics was rather unusual, though this was certainly not an entirely specific characteristic. Perhaps one should say that those aspects that made the involvement specifically Czechoslovak resided not so much in the nature of our philosophy as in the situation to which it addressed itself. To be entirely honest, we mustn't overlook the fact that a large part of the publicity which our philosophy received was not in response to its own efforts, but resulted from the mediocrity of cultural supervisors like [Vladimir] Koucky or [Jiri] Hendrych and their clumsy attempts to expose philosophy as a dangerous, hostile force. In this connection, I am reminded of the remark made by the West German philosopher Jürgen Habermass when his Czech colleagues complained of official hostility and persecution. Habermass answered: "Your situation is much better than ours here in the *Bundesrepublik*. Here, we philosophers and sociologists are completely ignored both by the government and by the general public, and so we play no public or social role whatever."

But this brings me to the notorious weakness of Czech philosophy. The recent successes of our philosophers in the political area must not blind us to the fact that even during this past decade Czech philosophy has made only negligible progress of an intrinsically philosophical nature. We have made very little contribution to the clarification of such basic problems as the question of time, truth, existence, or nature; in short, questions on which *everything* depends, not just culture and politics but public life, interpersonal relationships, science, and so on. During the past decade, philosophy has succeeded in substituting a new image for the official portrait of Man, but this activity was limited and one-sided. The real problems of philosophy still await formulation and resolution.

Take, for example, the question "What is Nature?" This can be approached in several quite different ways. It can be approached from the viewpoint of the "dialectic of Nature," a concept used so often in recent years that it has even taken hold in our subconscious mind. It wasn't so long ago that there was a great debate going in France between Sartre and Garaudy on the question of whether this "dialectic of Nature" really exists or not. But what was so interesting about this dispute was not the differences of opinion separating the two men, but rather the ideas they tacitly shared. What they shared was an uncritical acceptance of a certain concept of Nature and a certain concept of dialectics. Both parties to the dispute conceived of Nature purely and simply as an object of scientific study —in other words, as a measurable and material object; they seemed to ignore the fact that Nature had a far richer and deeper meaning, as implied by the terms *physis* and *natura*.

If the term "dialectics of Nature" is to have a philosophical rather than merely ideological significance, the true *substantive* relationship between dialectics and Nature will have to be analyzed, which, under the given circumstances, means that layers of mystification and ideological accretion will first have to be removed. Dialectics understood in conjunction with *physis* or *natura* will then emerge as the dialectics of existence, of being and seeming, of originality and derivativeness, of the natural and the unnatural, of Nature and culture. This sort of inquiry will have nothing in common with that scholastic argument concerned with the question of whether the nature studied by physicists, chemists, and biologists is or is not dialectical; Nature understood in this sense is already the result of a reductionist process.

On the other hand, we often heard it said in recent years that Man "humanizes" Nature. Yet this claim ignores the fact that modern Man also devastates it, and that his relationship to Nature therefore consists in antithetical processes of humanization and destruction. It suffices to point to the polution of the air, the poisoning of the waters or to the ruthless exploitation of the soil— the destruction of those elementary things which make it possible for man to inhabit the earth. All these are such distressingly serious facts that modern Man will once again have to confront the question of his relationship to Nature in all seriousness, both theoretically and practically.

The situation of socialistic Czech culture is certainly ambiguous. We have talked about the last ten years, about the second decade after 1948. But there was also the first decade during which the essential part of Czech culture identified with official politics and somehow accommodated itself to the so-called deformations. In your view, was it particularly inclined to do so?

This is the over-all, global way of looking at things. But let us examine the question a little more closely. I must admit that I am somewhat confused. Let us return, for example, to film. It seems to me that the essential contributions made in this medium during the last decade were primarily made by new people, or at least people unburdened by membership in the ruling cinematic hierarchy. If some were involved in some way with positions of power within the world of the cinema, their connection was superficial and liberation from it was relatively easy. This is in sharp contrast to those of their colleagues who, in the 1950s, provided the ruling circles with a kind of cultural façade. These people of course found it more difficult to break with the "establishment"; some never succeeded in making a clean break and the majority still live in a state approaching permanent stagnation. I don't want to generalize too much—such questions can only be answered through examination of individual cases—but I cannot help feeling that the people who have formed the vanguard of the Czech cultural front since 1956 were newcomers on the scene.

And yet the fact remains that a great part of the Czech cultural representation—and, it seems, not its worst part—assumed positions of power in the late 1940s and early 1950s much more easily than would seem possible in retrospect, and certainly more easily than might have been the case in other Eastern European countries.

Again, I am not sure whether this "global," generalized view is really correct; perhaps our focus on the majority makes us overlook numerous significant exceptions. For example, our discussion of the period after 1945 is distorted if we don't include cases such as that of [the poet Vladimir] Holan. He was a man who reacted to the events of 1945 positively and conscientiously, but who soon found himself in conflict with forces representing an early form of Stalinism in our country. Similarly, we should also examine the development of the poets Seifert and Halas [both victims of severe party criticism], and only after we had succeeded in elucidating the fate of such individual artists could we arrive at a position that would justify generalizing. Only in this way would we have some basis for assertions about the extent to which our culture as a whole was capable of unmasking the antihumanist and antisocialist essence of Stalinism.

Another question which arises in this connection: By "paying their tax to the times," as the current expression goes, how many great artists have allowed their work to become barren or bastardized? How many extremely talented people have been seduced into producing propagandistic tracts rather than true works of art?

I trust you will understand that I am trying to clarify things for myself . . . There were certainly many who accepted the situation of those days with great enthusiasm—but if we range against them a few individuals such as those I have mentioned, and a few others such as Teige or Kalandra,* then the whole problem appears much more complex and multi-dimensional. I believe that we have been living under the illusion that Czech culture represented a unified, progressive, left wing current. In reality, soon after 1945 the initial burst of enthusiasm was replaced by sober reflection and disputes about our future course; naturally, these dissenting tendencies did not always have an opportunity to make themselves heard or felt.

---

* Karel Teige, poet, critic and artist, an older communist and the outstanding theoretician of the Czech avant-garde of the 1930s, was ousted from the party in 1937 when he refused to accept the Moscow trials and the banning of the surrealist group. He died in the late 1940s in Prague and later became the target of Stalinist attacks on modern art in the 1950s. His friend, the historian Zavis Kalandra, also ousted from the party during the Moscow Trials, was convicted and hanged in the late 1940s on trumped-up charges.—*Ed.*

Still other artists immersed themselves in official work to such an extent that they had no time for their own creativity, and now they are finding themselves in the midst of unfamiliar circumstances that make resumption of creative work extremely difficult. Of course, these are just random remarks; I intend to make a more concrete study of these questions at some later date.

But permit me one more remark. We are ready to explain past events entirely on the basis of Stalinism. We forget that quite independently of Stalinism, people always feel a need to progress and to develop, to correct past errors, to change their opinions, and this was true before Stalinism, as well as during and after. Thus, such phenomena as the rejection of dogmatism in favor of critical thought did not necessarily stem from a reaction to Stalinism, but might be explained on the grounds of generational development or other factors. A particular generation may start out with highly radical attitudes; it may be full of youthful revolutionary fervor, and then gradually grow more conformist as it "matures," and in the end it may adopt a totally uncritical attitude. That is one possible kind of generational development. It is also possible, however, for a generation to follow an entirely different course. For one reason or other, it may begin by adopting the ideas and criteria of its fathers, and only gradually come into conflict with these models so that it finally achieves its existence as an independent generation quite late—at the age of forty rather than twenty. Only belatedly do members of such a generation learn to stand on their own feet, crystallize their own view of the world, find their own unique method of thinking.

I only want to stress by all this that we shouldn't let Stalinism obscure certain general problems which actually derive from the passage of the generations.

In your view, what have been the basic experiences of this country during the past quarter of a century?

I believe that this question involves two different aspects—one theoretical, the other practical—involving socio-political realities.

As far as the theoretical side of things is concerned, the most basic common denominator of Czech intellectual activity was the desire to re-examine everything from the ground up, to question even the most "obvious" phenomena, to analyze matters which were apparently crystal-clear. Such questions as "What is socialism?" or "What is democracy?" or "What is the meaning of revolution?" were posed anew. The public discussion of such questions clearly indicated that we have discovered something quite important about our political experience; namely, that the "cult" did not really represent deformation and misuse of something that was originally undeformed and unambiguous, but that a much more fundamental phenomenon was involved. In other words, we learned that Stalinism was not a deformation of a particular conception of socialism, but a full realization of an entirely different conception of socialism, resting on principles and assumptions that weren't entirely clear even to its most loyal practitioners and ideological devotees.

Let us begin by looking at a typical banality of the Stalinist era; namely, its political dictionary. It is full of phrases such as "iron necessity of history," "iron discipline," "engineers of human souls," "gear levers," "the mechanism of society." This language reveals more than would appear at first glance. It betrays the hidden, unformulated basis on which the Stalinist conception of socialism rests—a particular view of history, Man, reality, Nature, truth, dialectics. The fact that this species of socialism established itself in our country in the special way it did was, of course, connected with definite historical causes which future historians will elucidate.

The conception of history as necessity unfolding with the inevitability of natural scientific law; the self-justification of socialism as both necessary and inevitable; the conception of Man as *homo economicus* or a manipulatable unit; the reduction of dialectics to a few elementary features; the perception of truth as a utilitarian tool—the sum of these ideological presuppositions shows us the source from which the well-known Stalinist period originated.

The results of the Czechoslovak experience can thus be briefly formulated as follows: It is necessary to examine everything anew, and it is especially necessary to rethink the basic assumptions of socialism. It seems to me that such notorius features of Stalinism as contempt for Man, destruction of freedom, collectivization, and concentration camps were not distortions but *consequences*. We will remain prisoners of the secondary and the superficial until we come to the realization that humanistic socialism stems from different roots than bureaucratic socialism, that each grows out of a different conception of history, Man, and truth. The Czechoslovak experience challenges socialism to a new critical self-examination, to philosophical analysis of its most basic and essential assumptions.

Secondly, the Czechoslovak experience urgently poses new questions regarding the social, political, and economic functioning of socialism; that is, of the socialist working model. So far I have tried to emphasize that it is impossible to create humanistic socialism without first clarifying certain basic philosophic questions. Now I want to point out that practical models of socialism cannot be planned nor adequately realized without understanding everything that has taken place in the theoretical and practical development of socialism during the last hundred years. We must fully exonerate and make widely available the work of Rosa Luxemburg, Bukharin, Trotsky, Lenin, Gramsci, and all the other pioneers who have thought about many of the problems occupying us to this day and who formulated practical solutions. We must be thoroughly familiar with the development of the socialist movement, its individual parties and factions, from an undistorted picture of the Paris Commune to the October Revolution of Lenin and Trotsky. For example, it is necessary to remember that the Paris Commune, described by Marx as an attempt at the dictatorship of the proletariat, actually had a two-party political system consisting of the anarchists and the Proudhonists. This does not support the ideological superstitions which have been uncritically repeated so often that they have assumed the status of self-evident truths. Similarly, we must remind ourselves that the Russian Revolution began with the existence of several political parties. It is necessary to emphasize such mundane facts in order to combat rigid, entrenched ideology.

Socialism as a historical phenomenon is undoubtedly so rich with concrete reality that it cannot be squeezed into ideological stereotypes. It is a living movement that will always be searching for the most suitable forms of realization and functioning. In other words, in analyzing the political, economic, and social problems of socialism we cannot allow ourselves to become bound and mystified by prejudices and rigid schemata. It is our duty to search in an objective and realistic way for the best methods of realizing socialism as a means of human liberation.

Does Czechoslovak philosophy or ideology have any specific contribution to make in this connection?

Philosophy, like culture, is an area within which nothing can be solved through violence or cheating. Philosophy develops by means of dialogue, the contest between one idea and another—or, if this

sounds too idealistic—in the encounter between idea and reality.
Thinking is of course always required, and it cannot be replaced by
slogans, boastful pronouncements, or ideology. The prohibition
against so-called anti-Marxist tendencies, accompanied by the
establishment of an absolute monopoly of thought, pronounced the
death sentence of Marxist philosophy. It ceased to be philosophy
and became ideology.

Today's intellectual situation in the world is characterized by the
co-existence of several basic philosophical currents, including
positivism, phenomenology, existentialism, as well as Christianity
and Marxism. The mutual confrontation of those currents proved
fruitful for each of them. And each becomes more meaningful the
more it can comprehend the legitimacy and contribution of the
others, the more truthfully and profoundly it can formulate the
problems posed by them. After 1948 this intellectual cross-fertilization was forcibly abolished in our country, and for this reason we
have automatically begun to sink below the level of world-wide
philosophical standards of thought and become a mere province.
Our current efforts to free ourselves from these provincial bonds
therefore necessarily involve re-establishment of contacts with the
basic intellectual currents prevalent in the world today.

As I said before, it is impossible to cheat in philosophy. In practice, this means that although certain philosophical currents can be
temporarily driven underground, they cannot be permanently
diverted in this manner. This explains the recent resurgence of
intellectual currents once stigmatized as positivism and Hegelianism; since 1956 these forces have succeeded in establishing a position for themselves within the larger framework of abstract Marxist
thought. A system of thought that was once contemptuously designated as positivist escapism in reality represented a serious attempt
at ideological critique, at formulating the scientific character of
philosophy and solving important questions connected with the
character and problems of modern science and logic. A system of
thought once dismissed as Hegelianism was in reality also an attempt at ideological critique as well as the formulation of philosophical problems connected with history and human existence.

During the Middle Ages, philosophy developed within a theolog-
ical system and in conflict with theology; it had to go through a
certain stage before it could free itself from theology and stand in
open conflict against it. In a strikingly similar manner, twentieth-

century philosophy developed within an ideological system, and it took a certain time before the pressure of inner conflicts resulted in an emancipation of philosophy from ideology, and eventually philosophy began to adopt a clear anti-ideological position.

The person of T. G. Masaryk* surely must have special significance as far as the Czechoslovak experience is concerned.

The return to Masaryk is conditioned by two circumstances. First of all, our current process of democratization is finding in Masaryk the democrat many suggestions and vital ideas. This is quite a normal historical development; various generations in various historical situations tend to return to key figures of the past.

But the return to Masaryk is accompanied by other circumstances as well. People are turning to him not merely as a thinker, not merely as a democrat, but also as a personality. Masaryk became relevant for the very reason that Czechoslovak socialism failed to produce a personality of a stature comparable to that of Masaryk. And this failure is closely connected with the nature of the particular type of socialism we have known in our country.

In the early 1950s, I wrote an article about Masaryk which I now consider superficial and one-sided. I don't mean to imply that today's approach to Masaryk and his work should be uncritical. I cannot help feeling that Masaryk was greater as a philosopher of practical politics and practical life than as a thinker dealing with basic philosophical questions. He is highly stimulating in areas related to morality and individual responsibility, politics, and power, but he is less original and profound where basically philosophical matters are concerned. This may help to explain the resurgence of a Masaryk cult, a Masaryk ideology. People celebrated and praised him without really knowing his work. For that matter, we have known since 1945 that Masaryk was studied more carefully by his opponents than by his followers.

How is this related to the experiences of Czechoslovak socialism?

There is undoubtedly some connection between the disregard into which Masaryk had been cast and the attitude of our former leaders who seemed to begrudge Masaryk even his success in win-

---

* Masaryk, founder of the modern Czechoslovak nation, became an "un-person" in 1948, when his statues were removed from public places, his books from libraries, his name from history books.—*Ed.*

ning independence for our country in 1918. They acted as if the liquidation of democracy and the falsification of the history of the First Republic and its leaders were prerequisites for the development of socialism in Czechoslovakia. This nihilism even went so far that our official leaders expressed shame over the twenty-year existence of Czechoslovakia as a democratic state—a bourgeois democratic state, to be sure. This attitude may have some similarity to that of the Comintern in the 1930s, when the Social Democrats, and not the Nazis, were considered to be the main enemies of socialism.

This nihilism finally culminated in the absolute leveling of all differences, all peculiarities and special characteristics of this country's development, and antihumanist, antidemocratic forms of government were violently imposed. It is one thing to criticize bourgeois democracy, to transcend it as well as such leaders as Masaryk; it is quite another thing to destroy everything valuable which that period produced. A socialism that grows out of democratic traditions in a democratic country naturally confronts different problems and wears a different countenance than does a socialism that grows up in countries lacking such traditions. Perhaps the foregoing could be summarized in this way: In 1948, everything democratic was destroyed in the name of socialism, while in 1968 we are in a sense returning to democracy, again in the name of socialism. Were these developments determined by historic necessity? Or was it a matter of an unnecessary historic detour, which other nations with similar traditions will be able to avoid?

Nations . . . We have our experiences with this side of things, too.

As soon as you mentioned the word "nation," I was reminded of two significant Czech publications from the years 1929 and 1930. I have in mind S. K. Neumann's *The Nation's Crisis* and Josef Hora's *Culture and Politics*. Both of these works already contained criticism of a phenomenon that would later come to be called Stalinism. They confirm my view that Stalinism is not merely a system of repression, violence, and terror, but that this combination of administrative, bureaucratic and technocratic measures comes into being under certain specific conditions. These conditions involve the destruction of morality and conscience of the human being as a responsible individual; critical thought is replaced by false slogans and responsibility by mass irresponsibility. I have the impression that Stalinism cannot be fully explained by Russian conditions nor by the conditions of socialism. Rather, I see Stalinism as one polar complement of the crisis that gripped mankind in the twentieth century, and that manifested itself both in the East and West in forms which, though different in their specifics, still shared certain features in common. Stalinism is both the product and the producer of a certain historical form of mass society; that is to say, a society in which an anonymous and irresponsible mass has replaced thoughtful and responsible individuals. In such a society, inter-subjective relations between people, based on the possibility of dialogue, understanding, conflict, and play, are replaced by univer-sal manipulation of people and things. In this sense Stalinism ap-pears to me as a system of brutal leveling that affects not only the individual but the entire nation as well.

Perhaps someone will object that far from leveling the nation and nations, Stalinism continually stressed patriotism, national unique-ness and pride, and so on. But all this talk of national uniqueness and the Stalinist ideology of nationhood were in themselves indica-tive of the way that Stalinism reduced such complex concepts as the nation to the level of clichés and stereotypes.

If we examine the matter more closely, we may find that the Stalinist lexicon was really just an up-dated version of the old Imperial Austro-Hungarian jargon.

It would be a useful undertaking to examine the lexicon of the Stalinist era, the language that was used for conversation, writing, oratory, and to study its role in maintaining ideologic mystification. For the function of language during this period was to conceal, to distract, to level. The contemporary official theory of language would also be worth attention. What was meant by "language" in those days? Language was characterized as a means of communica-tion, as an instrument, and thus as something which Man uses like a hammer or a saw. An instrumental, technical conception of lan-guage. Again, it isn't accidental that the Marxist aestheticians of the period—and this applies even to such outstanding people as [the Hungarian Marxist philosopher and literary theoretician György] Lukacs—were incapable of comprehending the purpose and meaning of language in the composition of an artistic work. They were incapable of recognizing language as the most funda-mental element in literature. The apathy of official Marxist literary criticism in respect to language was, of course, a direct result of its erroneous conception of language as an instrument. If we regard language not as a mere tool but as an entity fundamentally connected with human existence, with the life of Man, then we gain not only the possibility of understanding its literary significance, but from the way language is used—from jargon, slang, contemporary expressions—we learn a great deal about particular strata of society, as well as about society as a whole. Understood in this way, language has a tremendous revelatory and demystifying power. Of course, this presupposes that we know how to grasp what language tells us.

What is your impression of the radical, socialist left wing in the nonsocialist world, of its youth?

In this connection, the responsibility of the intellectual seems to me to be an extremely important concept. Every person is to some extent responsible for his behavior and its consequences. And because in the case of the intellectual the main field of action is thought and the relationship between ideas and reality, the intellectual must give careful consideration to the responsibility of his thinking. First of all, the intellectual acts responsibly to the extent that he refuses to become an ideologue, a person who systematizes false doctrines and lends them a veneer of truth and justification. The existence of a true intellectual involves daily struggle between thought and ideology.

But the responsibility doesn't stop there. The intellectual must be consistent in his thinking, his thought must find fruition in conclusions and consequences. The intellectual becomes irresponsible as soon as he fails to think an idea through and submits it to the public in an incomplete and unthought-through form. Every idea that is only partially thought through and whose full consequences have not been explored either degenerates beyond recognition or else requires unforeseen and uncontrollable means for its concrete realization. Let me give you an example: the problem of power and violence. There are two typical, one-sided viewpoints in this regard. One is the attitude of noble souls who shrink from violence and reject all violence on principle. Such an attitude, in effect, constitutes passive observance of the evil that occurs in this world, and may in the end become a form of hypocrisy and apathy. The other is the attitude of the commissar who wants to change the world at any cost and who doesn't hesitate to use violence in order to achieve his ends. The danger of this attitude is that violence easily becomes the end rather than the means, and goals of reformation eventually become realized as deformation. In this connection, two serious questions present themselves. The first may be expressed this way: Everyone who wants to change the world must be perfectly clear in his own mind under what conditions violence is justified, and what consequences result from the use of all violence, including revolution, both in its victims as well as its perpetrators. A true revolutionary is thus only that person who is clearly aware of the limits and dangers connected with violence; this includes the danger that he himself will become deformed through the use of violent methods.

The other is the well-known question of human transformation. As in the first case, I consider an intellectual to live up to his responsibility only when he fully examines the justification and alternatives of revolutionary violence. In considering the question of human transformation, it is first of all necessary to precisely formulate just what such a transformation signifies, and to set the boundaries between human education and human derangement.

Here is a question which has been the subject of so much mystification: the intellectual and the worker . . .

When contemplating this relationship we are often in the thrall of the well-known fable which likens segments of society to parts of the human organism. For example, we speak metaphorically about the relationship of workers and intellectuals as the union of hands and brains or as the union of practice and theory, without realizing how false and misleading such concepts may be. The hands-brain analogy implies that workers have no brains and intellectuals have no hands, and that the union is thus based on mutual insufficiency. Furthermore, such a union implies that henceforth the intelligentsia will think for the workers while the workers will labor for the intelligentsia. In this way, the proletariat is in principle assumed to be incapable of thought, and the intelligentsia is in principle believed to be incapable of work. The remnants of this reactionary conception still exist in various guises, so that the proletariat still believes that intellectual people don't "really" work, while the intelligentsia see workers "merely" as a labor force.

Another barrier to the revolutionary political union of workers and intellectuals is posed by class prejudice, which exists on both sides. The intellectual approaches workers as a preacher, or else he behaves in a servile manner. Either he is under the impression that he has come to instruct an uneducated, inert mass, in which case he sees his relationship to the workers in terms of teacher–pupils, preacher–congregation—in short, as active individual facing a passive mass. Or else he tries to "adapt" himself to the workers; he grins and grimaces, plays at being the workers' "pal," slaps them on the back, tells anecdotes, calls them by their nicknames and, in general, behaves with the utmost servility, which also includes denigrating intellectuals.

A revolutionary political union between workers and the intelligentsia should be founded on mutual dialogue and mutual give-and-take. The intelligentsia and the workers, as two modern social entities, have a number of natural traits in common; both groups have a great capacity for seeing things in their entirety, a way of transcending everything partial and one-sided. Furthermore, both have an outstanding critical ability, including the capacity for self-criticism. Abnormal circumstances have driven the intelligentsia into a position of needing to convince others of their own usefulness and importance; in this way, they have been unable to perform their normal role of criticizing society as well as themselves. The revolutionary union of the workers and the intelligentsia proceeds from the assumption that both groups have brains as well as hands, that both think and work.

This union is designed to create something new in the history of politics, and it is the result of mutual contact and dialogue. The union in no way implies that one group will adapt itself to the other, that one will take over from the other; that would be no union but mere leveling. If I were to characterize the meaning of this union in a few words, I would say: *revolutionary wisdom* and *wisdom of revolution*. Mutual and two-sided political contact and dialogue between workers and intellectuals should give rise to an important value of public and social life—political wisdom. Wisdom in politics rules out opportunism and slickness, as well as cowardice and superficiality. Revolutionary wisdom and wise radicalism should, at the same time, serve as guarantees against hysteria and demagogy, against the ambitions and vanity of individuals, against cowardice, exaggerated caution, and proverbial Czech narrow-mindedness.

May 1968

H2 _